Esprit Basic Research Series

Edited in cooperation with
the European Commission, DG III

Springer
Berlin
Heidelberg
New York
Barcelona
Budapest
Hong Kong
London
Milan
Paris
Santa Clara
Singapore
Tokyo

F. Baccelli A. Jean-Marie I. Mitrani (Eds.)

Quantitative Methods in Parallel Systems

With 64 Figures

Springer

Volume Editors

François Baccelli
Alain Jean-Marie

INRIA
Institut National de Recherche
en Informatique et en Automatique
2004, route des Lucioles
F-06561 Valbonne Cedex, France

Isi Mitrani

Department of Computing Science
University of Newcastle
Newcastle upon Tyne NE1 7RU, UK

Cataloging-in-Publication Data applied for

Die Deutsche Bibliothek - CIP-Einheitsaufnahme

Quantitative methods in parallel systems / F. Baccelli ... (ed.). - Berlin ; Heidelberg ; New York ; Barcelona ; Budapest ; Hong Kong ; London ; Milan ; Paris ; Tokyo : Springer, 1995
(ESPRIT basic research series)
ISBN 3-540-60125-2
NE: Baccelli, François [Hrsg.]

CR Subject Classification (1991): D.1.3, I.6, F.3, G.3

ISBN 3-540-60125-2 Springer-Verlag Berlin Heidelberg New York

Publication No. EUR16614 EN of the European Commission, Dissemination of Scientific and Technical Knowledge Unit, Directorate-General Information Technologies and Industries, and Telecommunications, Luxembourg.
Neither the European Commission nor any person acting on behalf of the Commission is responsible for the use which might be made of the following information.

Typesetting: Camera-ready by authors/editors
SPIN 10084551 45/3142 - 5 4 3 2 1 0 - Printed on acid-free paper

Preface

It is widely recognized that the complexity of parallel and distributed systems is such that proper tools must be employed during their design stage in order to achieve the quantitative goals for which they are intended.

This volume collects recent research results obtained within the Basic Research Action Qmips, which bears on the quantitative analysis of parallel and distributed architectures.

Part 1 is devoted to research on the usage of general formalisms stemming from theoretical computer science in quantitative performance modeling of parallel systems. It contains research papers on process algebras, on Petri nets, and on queueing networks.

The contributions in Part 2 are concerned with solution techniques. This part is expected to allow the reader to identify among the general formalisms of Part 1, those that are amenable to an efficient mathematical treatment in the perspective of quantitative information.

The common theme of Part 3 is the application of the analytical results of Part 2 to the performance evaluation and optimization of parallel and distributed systems.

Part 1. Stochastic Process Algebras are used by N. Götz, H. Hermanns, U. Herzog, V. Mertsiotakis and M. Rettelbach as a novel approach for the structured design and analysis of both the functional behaviour and performability (i.e performance and dependability) characteristics of parallel and distributed systems. This is achieved by integrating stochastic modeling and analysis into the powerful and well investigated formal description techniques of process algebras.

A stochastic, timed process algebra is developed by P.G. Harrison and B. Strulo to describe formally discrete event simulation. It is able to describe the passing of time and probabilistic choice, either discrete, between a countable number of processes, or continuous, to choose a random amount of time to wait. An operational semantics and equivalences are defined over it, that imply equations which can be used to compare and transform processes representing simulations.

S. Donatelli, H. Hermanns, J. Hillston and M. Ribaudo show how Generalized Stochastic Petri Nets (GSPN) and Stochastic Process Algebras (SPA) can both be used to study functionality as well as performance of parallel and distributed systems. The comparison of these modeling facilities highlights points where ideas and techniques have been, or can be, exchanged between the two paradigms.

The last contribution of this part focuses on results by E. Teruel, M. Silva, J.M. Colom and J. Campos concerning the structural analysis of sequential processes cooperating via message passing through a set of buffers. Both functional — boundedness, deadlock-freeness, liveness, existence of home states — and performance — marking ergodicity, computation of visit ratios and insensitive throughput bounds — properties are considered.

Part 2. A rather general class of such models is encompassed by the *QMIPS example*, which covers various multiprocessor systems executing groups of tasks subject to precedence constraints. In the paper by F. Baccelli, B. Gaujal, A. Jean-Marie and J. Mairesse, the analysis of these models is carried out by means of linear recurrence relations in the (max, +) algebra. This approach enables new analytical approaches and the efficient implementation of massively parallel simulations.

The formalism of process algebras is combined with the spectral expansion solution method in the paper by I. Mitrani, A. Ost and M. Rettelbach. This approach allows models with infinite number of states to be specified in simple process algebra terms, and then solved in a manner transparent to the user. The applicability of the solution to the model is determined automatically.

The introduction and use of networks with positive and negative customers (G-networks) in modeling and optimization is a relatively recent development which has generated considerable interest. S. Chabridon, E. Gelenbe, M. Hernandez and A. Labed review a number of results in that area. A graphical tool for solving G-network models is also presented, as well as an application to a non-trivial problem involving load balancing in distributed systems.

The next two papers deal with the solution of two-dimensional Markov processes. O.J. Boxma, G.M. Koole and I. Mitrani study a polling system with two queues; one of them is served exhaustively, and having lost the server, claims it back when its size reaches a certain threshold. The model is solved both analytically and by the power series expansion method. W.J. Cohen considers a large class of two-dimensional random walks where the only allowable transitions out of a state are to the nearest neighbors. By way of an illustration, he gives an explicit solution for a difficult two-server shortest-queue problem.

Another model involving negative customers is studied by P.G. Harrison and E. Pitel. They analyze the equilibrium distribution of an M/G/1 queue where a negative arrival causes the removal of the most recent job. The problem is reduced to a Fredholm integral equation of the first type, but since the latter does not have a reliable numerical solution, an alternative iterative algorithm is presented.

The remaining two papers in this part are devoted to the solution of models formulated in terms of Petri Nets. G. Chiola, C. Anglano, J. Campos,

J.M. Colom and M. Silva derive operational inequalities which can be used for obtaining performance bounds that are insensitive to probability distributions. These results are likely to extend to Well-Formed Coloured nets. J. Campos, J.M. Colom, H. Jungnitz and M. Silva develop an approximate iterative technique for calculating the throughput of stochastic strongly connected marked graphs. State space reduction enables the solution of models that would otherwise be intractable.

Part 3. An interesting and rather difficult scheduling problem is examined by S. Borst. This concerns the allocation of jobs of different types to several parallel servers. A characterization of the optimal policy (which depends on both the first and second moments of the service time distributions), is achieved.

The problem of the scheduling of task graphs is considered by Z. Liu. The particularity of this study is that task running times are assumed to be random variables, instead of known constants as in the literature of deterministic scheduling. The goal here is to illustrate the approach based on sample path analysis and stochastic comparison techniques.

The execution of sets of tasks with precedence constraints on MIMD multiprocessors is studied by S. Chabridon and E. Gelenbe. They devise algorithms which ensure that jobs run correctly even when processing units fail. The effect of these algorithms on the performance of the system is evaluated by means of analytical approximations and and by simulation.

When a number of processors share distributed data, the problem of maintaining consistency among different copies has to be addressed. The Standard Coherent Interface (SCI) protocol is evaluated by A.J. Field and P.G. Harrison. The approximate analysis is based on determining a fixed point describing the stationary distribution of the cache line states.

A system where jobs from a common source can be routed through a number of different and unreliable nodes is modeled by N. Thomas and I. Mitrani. Breakdowns leave queued jobs in place but affect the subsequent routing. Several types of routing strategies are compared and a near-optimal heuristic is proposed.

The last two contributions concern applications of Stochastic Petri Nets. G. Chiola, G. Franceschinis and R. Gaeta use Well-Formed nets to model several parallel computer architectures with high degrees of symmetry. It is shown that the models are adequate for this class of applications. The different types of symmetries are easily mapped onto the allowed specification formalism.

G. Balbo, S.C.Bruell and M. Sereno consider a class of nets whose stationary probabilities have product form. They show that the network state distribution seen by a token about to enter a place is related to the corresponding time-average distribution in a net with a lower load. These results can be used to determine the expected sojourn time of a token at a place.

The editors would like to thank warmly Ephie Deriche for her very efficient handling of the LaTeX *structuring of this volume.*

F. Baccelli, A. Jean-Marie and I. Mitrani

June 1995

Table of Contents

Part II. Techniques

[1] Game played by two players who use a basket strapped to their wrists or a wooden racket to propel a ball against a specially marked wall, called *fronton*.

List of Contributors

C. Anglano
Dipartimento di Informatica
Università di Torino
Corso Svizzera 185
10149 Torino
Italy

F. Baccelli
INRIA Sophia Antipolis
2004 Route des Lucioles
BP 93
F-06902 Sophia Antipolis Cedex
France

G. Balbo
Dipartimento di Informatica
Università di Torino
Corso Svizzera 185
10149 Torino
Italy

S.C. Borst
CWI
P.O. Box 94079
1090 GB Amsterdam
The Netherlands

O.J. Boxma
CWI
P.O. Box 94079
1090 GB Amsterdam
The Netherlands

S.C. Bruell
Computer Science Department
University of Iowa
Iowa City
USA

J. Campos
Dept. de Informática e
Ingeniería de Sistemas
Centro Politécnico Superior
Universidad de Zaragoza
María de Luna 3
E-50015 Zaragoza
Spain

S. Chabridon
EHEI
Université René Descartes
45, rue des Saints-Pères
75270 Paris Cedex 06
France

G. Chiola
DISI
Università di Genova
3 Viale Benedetto XV
16132 Genova
Italy

J.W. Cohen
CWI
P.O. Box 94079
1090 GB Amsterdam
The Netherlands

J.M. Colom
Dept. de Informática e
Ingeniería de Sistemas
Centro Politécnico Superior
Universidad de Zaragoza
María de Luna 3
E-50015 Zaragoza
Spain

S. Donatelli
Dipartimento di Informatica
Università di Torino
Corso Svizzera 185
10149 Torino
Italy

A.J. Field
Department of Computing
Imperial College
180 Queen's Gate
London SW7 2BZ
U.K.

G. Franceschinis
Dipartimento di Informatica
Università di Torino
Corso Svizzera 185
10149 Torino
Italy

R. Gaeta
Dipartimento di Informatica
Università di Torino
Corso Svizzera 185
10149 Torino
Italy

B. Gaujal
INRIA Sophia Antipolis
2004 Route des Lucioles
BP 93
F-06902 Sophia Antipolis Cedex
France

E. Gelenbe
Dept. of Electrical Engineering
Duke University
Durham, N.C. 27708-0291
USA

N. Götz
IBM
European Networking Center
Broadband Multimedia Communication
Vangerowstr. 18
D-69115 Heidelberg
Germany

P.G. Harrison
Department of Computing
Imperial College
London SW7 2BZ
U.K.

H. Hermanns
University of Erlangen-Nürnberg
Informatik VII
Martensstr. 3
D-91058 Erlangen
Germany

M. Hernández
LAMIFA
Université d'Amiens
33, Rue St.Leu
80039 Amiens
France

U. Herzog
University of Erlangen-Nürnberg
Informatik VII
Martensstr. 3
D-91058 Erlangen
Germany

J. Hillston
University of Edinburgh
Kings Buildings
Mayfield Road
Edinburgh, EH390F
U.K.

A. Jean-Marie
INRIA Sophia Antipolis
2004 Route des Lucioles
BP 93
F-06902 Sophia Antipolis Cedex
France

H. Jungnitz
Dept. de Informática e
Ingeniería de Sistemas
Centro Politécnico Superior
Universidad de Zaragoza
María de Luna 3
E-50015 Zaragoza
Spain

G.M. Koole
INRIA Sophia Antipolis
2004 Route des Lucioles
BP 93
F-06902 Sophia Antipolis Cedex
France

A. Labed
EHEI
Université René Descartes
45, rue des Saints-Pères
75270 Paris Cedex 06
France

Z. Liu
INRIA Sophia Antipolis
2004 Route des Lucioles
BP 93
F-06902 Sophia Antipolis Cedex
France

J. Mairesse
INRIA Sophia Antipolis
2004 Route des Lucioles
BP 93
F-06902 Sophia Antipolis Cedex
France

V. Mertsiotakis
University of Erlangen-Nürnberg
Informatik VII
Martensstr. 3
D-91058 Erlangen
Germany

I. Mitrani
Computing Science Department
University of Newcastle
Newcastle upon Tyne NE1 7RU
U.K.

A. Ost
University of Erlangen-Nürnberg
Informatik VII
Martensstr. 3
D-91058 Erlangen
Germany

E. Pitel
Department of Computing
Imperial College
London SW7 2BZ
United Kingdom

M. Rettelbach
University of Erlangen-Nürnberg
Informatik VII
Martensstr. 3
D-91058 Erlangen
Germany

M. Ribaudo
University of Edinburgh
Edinburgh, EH390
Scotland

M. Sereno
Dipartimento di Informatica
Università di Torino
Corso Svizzera 185
10149 Torino
Italy

M. Silva
Dept. de Informática e
Ingeniería de Sistemas
Centro Politécnico Superior
Universidad de Zaragoza
María de Luna 3
E-50015 Zaragoza
Spain

B. Strulo
Department of Computing
Imperial College
London SW7 2BZ
U.K.

E. Teruel
Dept. de Informática e
Ingeniería de Sistemas
Centro Politécnico Superior
Universidad de Zaragoza
María de Luna 3
E-50015 Zaragoza
Spain

N. Thomas
Computing Science Department
University of Newcastle
Newcastle upon Tyne NE1 7RU
U.K.

Part I

Formalisms

Stochastic Process Algebras

Constructive Specification Techniques Integrating Functional, Performance and Dependability Aspects

N. Götz[1], H. Hermanns[2], U. Herzog[2], V. Mertsiotakis[2] and M. Rettelbach[2]

[1] IBM ENC Heidelberg, Germany
[2] University of Erlangen-Nürnberg, Germany

Summary. We introduce *Stochastic Process Algebras* as a novel approach for the structured design and analysis of both the functional behaviour and performability (i.e performance and dependability) characteristics of parallel and distributed systems. This is achieved by integrating stochastic modelling and analysis into the powerful and well investigated formal description techniques of process algebras.

After advocating the use of Stochastic Process Algebras as a modelling technique we recapitulate the foundations of classical process algebras and – using our Stochastic Process Algebra TIPP – present extensions taking into account the requirements of performability analysis. We briefly survey the state-of-the-art by summarizing various applications, existing tool support and recent advances.

1. Introduction. The Indivisibility of Functional and Temporal Behaviour

Designing parallel and distributed systems we have to consider both functional specification and temporal aspects (Performance, Dependability). Usually these aspects are separated from each other. System designers use distinct hardware and software specification techniques while performance and dependability assurance is the task of modelling specialists. Such a separation was reasonable for uniprocessors and classical communication systems because it offers several advantages, mainly simplicity and understandability. Unfortunately, however, performance evaluation is often ignored and considered only when a complete misdesign is obvious. The same is true and even worse when regarding dependability aspects.

The situation is changing since distributed and parallel systems became the focus of general attention and a clear trend is observable: specification techniques have been extended by time attributes and performability evaluation techniques have been enhanced in order to capture the impact of functional dependencies. Such a combination of qualitative and quantitative modelling aspects is needed in many situations. Three typical examples may illustrate this:

- Specifying communication protocols often requires timeout mechanisms. Dependent on the selected time value the protocol may deadlock or not.

- Analysing the performance of parallel processors and distributed systems, we definitely have to consider functional dependencies and synchronisation of communicating subtasks. Program execution times, resource utilisation and speedup values significantly depend on these functional properties.
- Investigating systems, which are prone to hardware or software failures, has to deal with a strong correlation between the functionality, failure rates and performability measures.

The need for combined specification methods was already recognised in the seventies. The most successful examples are Stochastic Petri Nets (SPN) [1], Stochastic Graph Models [42, 43] and Stochastic Automata Networks [35]. We propose and recommend Stochastic Process Algebras [24, 12, 11, 27, 28, 25] mainly because of four important reasons:

1. Languages are the principal means for the design of hardware and software components: process algebras are abstract languages tailored to the description of parallel and distributed systems.[1]
2. Design automation and mechanisation are only possible, if we use formal techniques with a solid theoretical basis: process algebras are well founded, permit a detailed formal specification and support the process of implementation and verification.
3. Structuring is the only way to deal with complex systems: process algebras offer a design methodology, called constructivity, that allows to systematically build complex systems from smaller ones: there are operators available for composition as well as mechanisms for abstraction. And very important, process algebras offer an algebraic characterisation of equivalent system behaviour.
4. Combining stochastic modelling and analysis with the well investigated formal description technique of process algebras provides a rich source of further developments. The comprehensive theories of process algebras, which have been developed mainly during the last decade, bear an enormous potential also for performance and dependability modelling in general, for the modelling of distributed and parallel systems including high speed networks, mobile communication systems, for the modelling of manufacturing lines, etc.

This paper is organised as follows: in Section 2 we will give an overview on how everything began. We will introduce TIPP as an example of a Stochastic Process Algebra in Section 3, where we especially highlight the nice and important algebraic features of the approach. Section 4 illuminates the concept by means of a small example. Section 5 gives references to various case studies and Section 6 discusses tool support that is actually available. In Section 7

[1] To be specific: we do not expect process algebras to be the specification languages of the future. However, we do expect such languages to overtake their exciting features.

we will give an overview on recently obtained results. Section 8 concludes with a brief summary indicating also further challenges.

2. The Roots of Stochastic Process Algebra

Classical process algebras such as CCS [31], CSP [29] or ACP [3] are purely functional, i.e. the relative ordering of events is modelled, and alternative behaviour is expressed by non-determinism. From the very beginning their basic intention was to systematically build complex systems from smaller ones. The foundation is comprehensive and solid, excellent introductions may be found in the above mentioned books of Hoare [29] and Milner [31].

In the late eighties deterministic time descriptions were integrated in order to attack the "time-out" problem common to most communication protocols. Reed and Roscoe [37] may have initiated these research activities; a good overview on various approaches can be found in [33]. At about the same time, the first publications appeared dealing with both the functional and probabilistic behaviour of systems. The next step followed immediately and all the aspects - functional, probabilistic and deterministic temporal behaviour - were unified in one approach. To our knowledge, the dissertation of H. Hansson [14] treated all fundamental aspects for the first time extensively.

It is quite astonishing that Nounou and Yemini [34] have presented already in 1984 an approach containing most ideas of Stochastic Process Algebras. They began with a functional description and then mapped probabilistic and stochastic temporal features onto this basic process. They also show some performance results under exponential assumptions. We do not know why they did not continue research in this direction.

Attracted by lectures on classical process algebras and thrilled by the idea of systematic hierarchical modelling techniques, we started with a framework on Stochastic Process Algebras [24, 23] in the late eighties. We steadily extended our knowledge and got more and more involved in this exiting research area [38, 13, 12, 15, 11, 21]. Being sure that Stochastic Process Algebras offer some fundamental advantages, we have shown their basic ideas and concepts at many occasions, and have tried to demonstrate that this is an attractive alternative approach and a promising research area for many research groups.

Today there is a lively cooperation and interchange of ideas between the different research groups [27, 25] and several Stochastic Process Algebras have recently been published: Hillston's PEPA [28], Buchholz's MPA [6], Gorrieri et al's MPA [4]; our own language TIPP together with a tutorial introduction of its fundamental ideas has been published in [12]. Prototype tools are available for both PEPA [8] and TIPP [19]. The theoretical basis of TIPP is summarized in [11, 21].

3. The Stochastic Process Algebra TIPP

In this section we will present the main features of our Stochastic Process Algebra TIPP. The reader is expected to be familiar with the basic concepts of performance evaluation, reliability theory, and process algebras. A summary of the fundamental ideas and applicability of Stochastic Process Algebras can be found in [12].

The claim of Stochastic Process Algebras is to support the systematic description and construction of complex systems. Important features are therefore:

- the composition of components,
- the abstraction of details,
- the possibility to exchange subsystems, and
- the verification of functional and temporal properties.

In order to achieve these objectives one has to provide all elements of a complete process theory (cf. Fig. 3.1). The syntax of the language allows a modular and compact description of components and their interrelations. The semantic model (usually a labelled transition system) describes precisely and unambiguously the meaning of each language expression. The definition of equivalent behaviour allows to compare the behaviour of different components and systems with each other. Most important, the axiomatisation allows to provide algebraic laws permitting the comparison of systems (and components) already on the syntactic level. Last not least the semantic model, containing all information, can be analysed in order to obtain functional properties (e.g. deadlock, liveness), temporal properties (performance and dependability measures) as well as mixed properties (e.g. probability of deadlock, probability distribution functions of tagged event sequences).

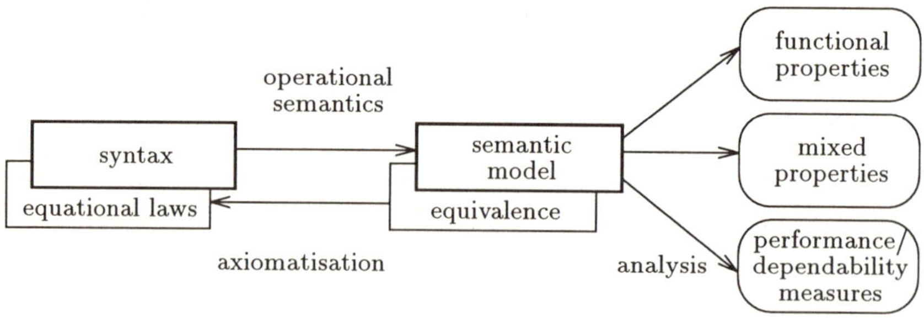

Fig. 3.1. Overview on the Stochastic Process Algebra approach

It is important to note that usually the modelleris only concerned with the syntactic description and the resulting characteristics, while all other elements and transformations can be hidden by automatic tool support.

3.1 Syntax

The process algebra TIPP – *ti*med *p*rocesses and *p*erformability evaluation – is an extension of the classical abstract languages CSP [29] and CCS [31] including random time variables. The basic elements to describe processes are actions and operators. Actions describe relevant activities of the system; they are considered to be atomic. By means of the operators, process descriptions can be composed from smaller ones in order to yield descriptions of more complex systems. Formally, the ways how descriptions can be built are defined by a grammar.

We assume a fixed set of action names $Act := Vis \cup \{\tau\}$, where we use τ as a distinguished symbol for internal, invisible actions and Vis as the set of regular, visible activities. An action named a can either be exponentially distributed or passive. Exponentially distributed actions – denoted by pairs of action name and rate (a, λ) – happen instantaneously after a duration that is exponentially distributed with rate λ. Passivity is indicated using the rate[2] 1.

Definition 3.1. *The set $\mathcal{L}$ of valid system descriptions of TIPP is given by the following grammar, where $a \in Act$, $\lambda \in \mathbb{R}^+$; $S \subseteq Vis$, $X \in Var$, Var is a set of process variables.*

$$P \ ::= \ Stop \ | \ (a,\lambda).P \ | \ P+P \ | \ P \,\|_S\, P \ | \ P\backslash a \ | \, rec\ X : P \ | \ X$$

To summarise the intuitive meaning of these basic elements: *Stop* denotes the halting process, the *prefix*ed process $(a, \lambda).P$ behaves as P after the action a has happened. The *choice* operator '+' allows to model alternative behaviour. By means of the *parallel* operator '$\|_S$' two processes are modelled to proceed independently, but they have to synchronise on actions within the set of synchronizing actions S. If no synchronisation is forced, we may omit the empty set index $\emptyset$. The *hiding* operator '\' provides an abstraction mechanism for actions that are internal at a certain level of specification. Infinite behaviour is formally expressed by means of the *recursion* operator '*rec*'. This can be regarded as a compact notation for the recursive equation $X := P$, where X may appear in P. In the remainder of this paper we will frequently use the latter notation, instead of using the *rec*-operator.

3.2 Semantics

The behaviour of a process of this language is formalized in a structural operational style (cf. [36]). The deduction rules in Figure 3.2 define a labelled transition system (LTS) as a domain for the semantic model, consisting of nodes representing states or process behaviours and arcs representing transitions between them. These arcs are labelled with pairs of actions and rates[3].

---

[2] We investigated several ideas to represent passive actions. The above presented way leads to correct rates and posseses nice algebraic properties.

[3] An additional third label is used for reasons of semantic consistency, cf. [12]. For the purpose of this paper we can neglect this label.

Each of these arcs ($P \xrightarrow{a,\lambda} Q$) symbolises that P can evolve to Q by performing the action a with rate λ.

Definition 3.2. *The transition relation* $\longrightarrow \subseteq \mathcal{L} \times (Act \times I\!R^{+} \times Lab) \times \mathcal{L}$ *is defined as the least relation satisfying the rules in Figure 3.2, where* $Lab := \{\epsilon, +_l, +_r, \|_l, \|_r, (,)\}$.

$$\frac{}{(a,\lambda).P \xrightarrow{a,\lambda,\epsilon} P} \qquad \frac{P \xrightarrow{a,\lambda,w} P'}{P + Q \xrightarrow{a,\lambda,+_l w} P'} \qquad \frac{Q \xrightarrow{a,\lambda,w} Q'}{P + Q \xrightarrow{a,\lambda,+_r w} Q'}$$

$$\frac{P \xrightarrow{a,\lambda,w} P'}{P \|_S Q \xrightarrow{a,\lambda,\|_l w} P' \|_S Q} \; (a \notin S) \qquad \frac{Q \xrightarrow{a,\lambda,w} Q'}{P \|_S Q \xrightarrow{a,\lambda,\|_r w} P \|_S Q'} \; (a \notin S)$$

$$\frac{P \xrightarrow{a,\lambda,v} P' \quad Q \xrightarrow{a,\mu,w} Q'}{P \|_S Q \xrightarrow{a,\lambda\mu,(v,w)} P' \|_S Q'} \; (a \in S) \qquad \frac{P\{(recX : P)/X\} \xrightarrow{a,\lambda,w} P'}{recX : P \xrightarrow{a,\lambda,w} P'}$$

$$\frac{P \xrightarrow{a,\lambda,w} P'}{P\backslash a \xrightarrow{\tau,\lambda,w} P'\backslash a} \qquad \frac{P \xrightarrow{b,\lambda,w} P'}{P\backslash a \xrightarrow{b,\lambda,w} P'\backslash a} \; (a \neq b)$$

Fig. 3.2. Semantic rules of TIPP

3.3 Equivalences

Due to the strict formal semantics of TIPP it is possible to reason about the behaviour of a system in an algebraic setting. For example it is possible to characterise systems with the same functionality, but potentially different temporal characteristics. This is formally captured by an equivalence relation called *functional bisimulation* defined in [21], based on the definition of strong bisimulation in [31]. The idea is that the two systems can simulate each other in any of the states they are going through.

From the performance point of view it is more interesting to classify systems by means of their functional and temporal behaviour, as well. This classification is formally carried out by *Markovian bisimulation* ($\sim_M$) [21], an equivalence relation that abstracts away from different syntactic possibilities to describe the same behaviour. Hillston has pointed out that an equivalence of this kind can be exploited for state space reduction based on lumpability [28].

Functional and Markovian bisimulation are congruences, i.e. they allow the exchange of equivalent components that may be specified fairly different *without* changing the overall behaviour of the complex system. This embodies one of the main advantages of the SPA approach, *constructivity*: a complex system can be constructed step by step of smaller components. These components may be subject of some optimisation or manipulation effort – as long as the optimal candidate exhibits equivalent behaviour, the behaviour of the whole system is *not* affected.

Strictly speaking, these equivalences are defined on TIPP's *semantic* model. They interrelate transition systems rather than syntactic descriptions. Every equivalence class consists of equivalent, but not necessarily identical transition systems. Some of them are smaller, others are larger. This is due to additional information that is irrelevant under the behavioural view of the equivalence.

3.4 Axiomatisation

As the states of our transition systems are labelled with the corresponding process descriptions of $\mathcal{L}$, the bisimulations mentioned above also induce equalities on the *syntactic* level. For Markovian bisimulation this equality can be completely characterised by a set of equational laws (cf. Fig. 3.3). All these laws, together with four additional laws dealing with recursion, form a sound and complete axiomatisation of $\sim_M$, as long as no recursion over hiding and parallel composition occurs. The proof is carried out in [21].

$$
\begin{array}{rclrcl}
P + Stop & = & P & Stop \backslash a & = & Stop \\
P + Q & = & Q + P & (P+Q)\backslash a & = & P\backslash a + Q\backslash a \\
(P+Q)+R & = & P + (Q+R) & ((b\,,\,\lambda).P)\backslash a & = & (b\,,\,\lambda).(P\backslash a) \quad a \neq b \\
(a\,,\,\lambda).P + (a\,,\,\mu).P & = & (a\,,\,\lambda+\mu).P & ((a\,,\,\lambda).P)\backslash a & = & (\tau\,,\,\lambda).(P\backslash a)
\end{array}
$$

$$
\begin{array}{rclrcl}
P \parallel_{\{\}} Stop & = & P & (P \parallel_S Q) \parallel_S R & = & P \parallel_S (Q \parallel_S R) \\
P \parallel_S Q & = & Q \parallel_S P & & &
\end{array}
$$

$$
\begin{aligned}
P \parallel_S Q = {} & \sum_{a_i \notin S} (a_i\,,\,\lambda_i).(P_i \parallel_S Q) + \sum_{b_j \notin S} (b_j\,,\,\mu_j).(P \parallel_S Q_j) + \\
& \sum_{a_i \in S} \sum_{b_j = a_i} (a_i\,,\,\lambda_i \mu_j).(P_i \parallel_S Q_j)
\end{aligned}
$$

$$
\text{where } P \equiv \sum_i (a_i\,,\,\lambda_i).P_i \text{ and } Q \equiv \sum_j (b_j\,,\,\mu_j).Q_j
$$

Fig. 3.3. Axiomatisation of Markovian bisimulation

4. Example. A Multiprocessor with $MMPP$ Arrival Stream

In order to demonstrate the expressiveness of Stochastic Process Algebras and to show how some basic but frequently used modules like arrival streams, processors or queueing and scheduling mechanisms can be described and analyzed with TIPP, we present as a simple example a $MMPP^2|M|4$ queueing system with two types of customers and non-preemptive priorities.

One of the main advantages of process algebras is that they allow the creation of highly modular model descriptions. In our case, we can consider our system as the parallel composition of two components or processes:

$$System := Load \parallel_A Machine \qquad \text{with} \qquad A := \{hp\_job, lp\_job\}$$

The process *Load* represents the *MMPP*-arrival stream, the server is modelled by the process *Machine* and A contains the interfacing actions.

4.1 Load modelling

The arrival stream is supposed to be a Markov Modulated Poisson Process with two phases. During a normal phase jobs arrive with the rates λ_1 and μ_1, while in a busy phase arrivals occur with the rates λ_2 and μ_2. The process LP_i models the low priority job stream and HP_i represents the high priority job stream. The action c that is performed with rate ϕ leads to a change in the phase of the arrival processes and is performed synchronously by the two arrival processes.

$$\begin{array}{lcl}
Load & := & HP_1 \parallel_{\{c\}} LP_1 \\
HP_1 & := & (hp_job, \mu_1).HP_1 \\
 & + & (c, \phi).HP_2 \\
HP_2 & := & (hp_job, \mu_2).HP_2 \\
 & + & (c, \phi).HP_1
\end{array}
\qquad
\begin{array}{lcl}
LP_1 & := & (lp_job, \lambda_1).LP_1 \\
 & + & (c, \phi).LP_2 \\
LP_2 & := & (lp_job, \lambda_2).LP_2 \\
 & + & (c, \phi).LP_1
\end{array}$$

4.2 The machine model

The server consists of six processes that are composed in parallel. Two of them represent the queueing component and four model the service unit

$$Machine := (Q_0 \parallel_{\{get\_lp\_job\}} R_0) \parallel_B (P \parallel P \parallel P \parallel P)$$

where $B = \{get\_hp\_job, get\_lp\_job\}$.

Jobs are processed according to a FIFO strategy with priorities. To realize this scheduling mechanism we introduce for each class of jobs a separate queue process with maximum capacity l. The queue Q_0 stores the low priority jobs while the queue R_0 accepts the high priority jobs.

$$\begin{array}{lcl}
Q_0 & := & (lp_job, 1).Q_1 \\
Q_i & := & (lp_job, 1).Q_{i+1} \\
 & + & (get_lp_job, \alpha).Q_{i-1} \\
Q_l & := & (get_lp_job, \alpha).Q_{l-1} \\
 & + & (lp_job, 1).Q_l
\end{array}
\qquad
\begin{array}{lcl}
R_0 & := & (hp_job, 1).R_1 \\
 & + & (get_lp_job, 1).R_0 \\
R_i & := & (hp_job, 1).R_{i+1} \\
 & + & (get_hp_job, \alpha).R_{i-1} \\
R_l & := & (get_hp_job, \alpha).R_{l-1} \\
 & + & (hp_job, 1).R_l
\end{array}$$

The priority mechanism is realized by appropriate synchronization of the two queue processes. The process Q_i for instance is only able to deliver a job to a processor, if the other queue is in state R_0, i.e. if no high priority job is waiting to be processed. Otherwise, the action *get_lp_job* is not enabled.

Each processor waits until it can carry out a *get_hp_job*-action or a *get_lp_job*-action. The service time of high priority jobs and low priority jobs is exponentially distributed with rate ν and ξ, respectively.

$$P \;:=\; (get\_hp\_job, 1).P_0 \;+\; (get\_lp\_job, 1).P_1$$

$$P_0 \;:=\; (hp\_job\_ready, \nu).P \qquad\qquad P_1 \;:=\; (lp\_job\_ready, \xi).P$$

4.3 Model simplification

To evaluate the above specification, we derive the semantic model based on the semantic rules of TIPP first (see Figure 3.2). By doing so we may observe that the transition system contains much too detailed information. This is due to the modular representation of the processing component where each processor is modelled individually. The number of states of the model would be clearly smaller if we do not distinguish the individuals and represent the whole processing component by a single process. However, to do this by hand makes model creation more difficult and error prone. With process algebras like TIPP this simplification can be done systematically using the equational laws of Markovian bisimulation. Moreover, an automation of this reduction step appears to be feasible and is currently under investigation.

In the above case, a simplified version of the server can be obtained as follows. Using the defining equation for each processor P the description expands to

$$\begin{aligned}
&P \,\|\, P \,\|\, P \,\|\, P \;=\\
&\quad (get_hp_job, 1).(P_0 \,\|\, P \,\|\, P \,\|\, P) \;+\; (get_lp_job, 1).(P_1 \,\|\, P \,\|\, P \,\|\, P) +\\
&\quad (get_hp_job, 1).(P \,\|\, P_0 \,\|\, P \,\|\, P) \;+\; (get_lp_job, 1).(P \,\|\, P_1 \,\|\, P \,\|\, P) +\\
&\quad (get_hp_job, 1).(P \,\|\, P \,\|\, P_0 \,\|\, P) \;+\; (get_lp_job, 1).(P \,\|\, P \,\|\, P_1 \,\|\, P) +\\
&\quad (get_hp_job, 1).(P \,\|\, P \,\|\, P \,\|\, P_0) \;+\; (get_lp_job, 1).(P \,\|\, P \,\|\, P \,\|\, P_1)
\end{aligned}$$

We may notice that the various subprocesses differ only by the position of the active processor. This information is redundant if we do not want to distinguish the individual processors. Markovian bisimulation takes this into account by comparing the behaviour of processes instead of their internal state. Clearly, the behaviour of $(P_1 \,\|\, P \,\|\, P \,\|\, P)$ and $(P \,\|\, P \,\|\, P \,\|\, P_1)$ is not distinguishable for an external observer. Consequently, applying the axioms we can reduce the expression above and obtain

$$P \| P \| P \| P \;=\; (get\_hp\_job, 4).(P_0 \| P \| P \| P) + (get\_lp\_job, 4).(P_1 \| P \| P \| P).$$

The same reduction is repeated for the processes $(P_0 \,\|\, P \,\|\, P \,\|\, P)$ and $(P_1 \,\|\, P \,\|\, P \,\|\, P)$. Again, some subprocesses appear that are amenable for subsequent reduction. This iterative procedure terminates, because the whole number of subprocesses of our description is limited. Finally, we substitute the parallel components by arbitrary process variables and replace the original server $(P \,||\, P \,||\, P \,||\, P)$ by the simplified version, named (for example) $P_{simple0}$, where

$$\begin{array}{lcl} P_{simple0} & := & (get\_hp\_job, 4).P_{simple1} + (get\_lp\_job, 4).P_{simple2} \\ P_{simple1} & := & \dots \\ & \vdots & \end{array}$$

The decrease of the state space size is immense. Instead of $O(e^p)$ states the simplified model complexity is of order $O(p^2)$, where p is the number of processors.

4.4 Numerical results

To investigate the performance of this model we analysed numerically the underlying Markov chain using the Gauß-Seidel method. We derived some performance measures that are presented in Figure 4.1. In these graphs the mean queue length as well as the throughput for high priority jobs and low priority jobs are shown dependent on the arrival rate for low priority jobs during the busy phase (λ_2).

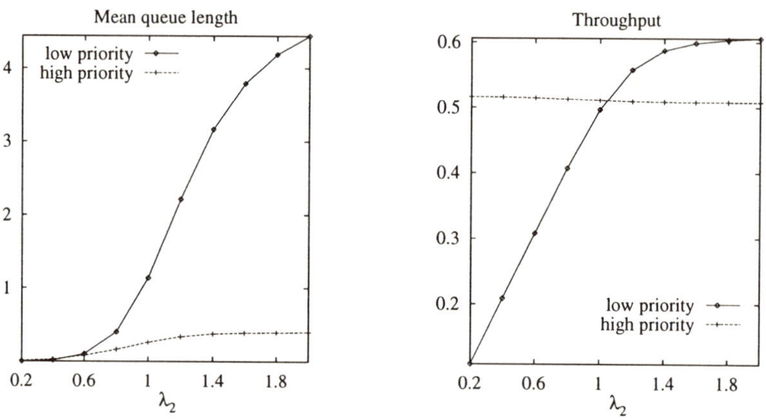

Fig. 4.1. Performance measures

5. Case Studies

During the last years we have applied TIPP to construct and analyze systems of various types. These practical experiences demonstrate that this approach is a suitable way to construct large system in an elegant way, under integral consideration of performance and dependability aspects. The case studies include

- data transfer with multiple send-and-wait communications [13]
- multiprocessor and task graph modelling [12]
- electronic mail system (with J. Hillston) [12]
- alternating bit protocol [20]
- robot control system (with S. Gilmore, J. Hillston and R. Holton) [10]
- multiprocessor mainframe with software failures [18]

All these models were built up out of small modules that were composed to obtain the entire system. The application of the semantic rules (generation of the state space) was done automatically in most cases. Restrictions to the complexitiy (number of states) of the models are only due to the numerical solution methods. Reduction of the state space by means of our notion of equivalence was partially performed. The multiprocessor mainframe example additionally contains concepts for the decomposition of the generated state space along the structure given by the modular process description.

There were various types of performability measures derived such as response time, availability of components, failure probabilities, mean execution times and many more.

6. Tool Support

At the moment there are two tools available, the *PEPA Workbench* [8] and our *TIPP-tool* [19]. TIPP-Tool is a prototype modelling tool for creating and evaluating stochastic process algebra models of parallel and distributed systems. It supports a LOTOS-oriented input language ([5]) and apart from facilities to apply functional analysis based on reachability analysis, it comes up with numerical solution modules for the stationary as well as transient analysis of the Continuous Time Markov Chain (CTMC), underlying a TIPP-specification. The input language and the emphasis on efficient numerical evaluation techniques represent the main difference to the *PEPA Workbench*, another modelling tool for SPAs relying on symbolic evaluation of the underlying Markov chain [8].

The derived labelled transition system serves as a base for further reduction into a CTMC. For the steady state analysis of the underlying CTMC the TIPP-tool uses a variety of numerical algorithms: LU-factorization, power method, and Gauss-Seidel iteration scheme. It supports also transient analysis by providing methods to compute the mean time to absorption of an absorbing Markov chain or the transient state probabilities. For the latter, a refined randomization scheme is provided, similar to the method adopted by Lindemann in [30].

The result of numerical analysis is usually a vector with state probabilities. In order to obtain more sophisticated and expressive results the user can specify measures. This is done via rewards beeing assigned to states that match a certain regular expression the user has to specify. Experiment series are also supported by allowing rates to be symbolic variables. The specification of the model as well as the measures and experiments is supported through a graphical user interface.

7. Recent Extensions

With respect to the elements of a complete theory (cf. Fig. 3.1) extensions of the approach are possible on each described level, i.e. the syntax of the language, the semantic concepts and the evaluation strategies. Recent research has lead to extensions of the language expressiveness that have been shown to fit into the concept of SPA sketched above.

The introduction of immediate and probabilistic actions to achieve the expressiveness and the modelling power comparable with Generalised SPN is described in [13, 19]. Apart from adapting the semantic rules, we achieved new notions of equivalent behaviour that are conservative extensions of classical notions. They allow to eliminate immediate actions inside of arbitrary components of a complex system as soon as these actions do not have an observable impact on the environment. This feature, known as *congruence property* can also be carried out on the specification level, because an extension of the set of equational laws has been established.

The application of these laws on the syntactic level can avoid state space explosion. For this purpose, an on the fly reduction algorithm based on term rewriting has been proposed in [13]. Its efficient implementation is currently under development. Starting from a highly modular syntactic system description this algorithm will automatically produce a syntactic representation for a compact semantic model *before* the state space is generated.

The structural operational style of the semantics described in Section 3 is the usual approach to define the behaviour of process algebraic system descriptions. A completely different semantic concept has been published in [40]. In this paper a denotational semantics is presented for a restricted set of operators directly mapping syntactic descriptions onto transition matrices. The benefit of this concept is that it is paid attention to get a minimal semantic model in each step of model creation. Another denotational semantics has been established in [21]. The semantic domain of this approach is a class of Stochastic Petri Nets. This link between SPN and SPA has lead to fruitfull cooperation within the QMIPS project, cf. [7, 17] and provides interesting insight into properties of different SPAs.

Another positive outcome of the QMIPS project concerns the performance analysis of certain classes of systems. In [32] the evaluation of an infinite number of states is made possible by connecting the process description language to the Spectral Expansion solution method by means of an appropriate semantic concept.

The solution of large models for performability analysis usually suffers from the stiffness problem. This difficulty has been tackled by developing a *time scale decomposition* technique for SPA that uses structural properties of the system description [26]. Currently considerable work is going on aiming at characterizing classes of SPA descriptions that are amenable to product form solutions, cf. proceedings of the 3rd PAPM-Workshop [4].

8. Summary and Outlook

Stochastic Process Algebras have been proven to provide a valuable concept to systematically construct complex systems including both functional and temporal aspects.

A complete theory is available for Stochastic Process Algebras with Markovian, i.e. exponentially distributed durations of actions. Only recently immediate actions have been included allowing elegant modelling and analysis of management functions (e.g. scheduling) and dependable systems (stiffness).

Ongoing and future research will cover mainly three different directions:

- extension of the theoretical basis,
- efficient and structured evaluation techniques (including tool support), and
- widespread application to complex system modelling and analysis.

The Workshop on *Process Algebras and Performance Modelling* has been established as an annual forum to exchange ideas and research results, where the scientific community dealing with SPA meets regularly. The participation in this workshop as well as valuable discussions with various external research groups indicate that the general interest in SPA is steadily increasing.

References

1. M. Ajmone Marsan, G. Balbo, and G. Conte, *Performance Models of Multiprocessor Systems.* MIT Press, 1986.
2. F. Baccelli, A. Jean-Marie and I. Mitrani, editors, *Quantitative Modelling in Parallel Systems.* Springer, 1995.
3. J. A. Bergrstra and J.W.Klop, "Algebra of Communicating Processes with Abstractions", *TCS*, **37**(1), pp. 77–121, 1985.
4. M. Bernardo, L. Donatiello, and R. Gorrieri, "MPA: A Stochastic Process Algebra", Technical report tr94-10, University of Bologna, 1994.
5. T. Bolognesi and E. Brinksma, "Introduction to the ISO Specification Language LOTOS", *In* P.H.J. van Eijk, C.A. Vissers, and M. Diaz, editors, *The Formal Description Technique LOTOS*, pp. 23–73, Amsterdam, 1989. North-Holland.
6. P. Buchholz. "Markovian Process Algebra: Composition and Equivalence", In U. Herzog and M. Rettelbach, editors, *Proc. 2nd Workshop on Process Algebras and Performance Modelling*, pp. 11–30, Regensberg/Erlangen, July 1994. Arbeitsberichte des IMMD, Universität Erlangen-Nürnberg.
7. S. Donatelli, H. Hermanns, J. Hillston, and M. Ribaudo, "GSPN and SPA Compared in Practice: Modelling a Distributed Mail System", In Baccelli, Jean-Marie and Mitrani [2].

8. S. Gilmore and J. Hillston. "The PEPA Workbench: A Tool to Support a Process Algebra-Based Approach to Performance Modelling", In G. Haring and G. Kotsis, editors, *7th Int. Conference on Modelling Techniques and Tools for Computer Performance Evaluation*, pp. 353–368, Wien, May 1994.
9. S. Gilmore and J. Hillston, editors, *Proc. 3rd Workshop on Process Algebra and Performance Modelling.* Springer, 1995.
10. S. Gilmore, J. Hillston, R. Holton, and M. Rettelbach. "Specifications in Stochastic Process Algebra for a Robot Control Problem", CSG Report Series ESG-CSG-7-94, Computer Systems Group, Dept. of Computer Science, University of Edinburgh, December 1994.
11. N. Götz. *Stochastische Prozeßalgebren – Integration von funktionalem Entwurf und Leistungsbewertung Verteilter Systeme.* PhD thesis, Universität Erlangen–Nürnberg, Martensstraße 3, 91058 Erlangen, April 1994.
12. N. Götz, U. Herzog, and M. Rettelbach, "Multiprocessor and Distributed System Design: The Integration of Functional Specification and Performance Analysis Using Stochastic Process Algebras", In *Proc. 16th Int. Symposium on Computer Performance Modelling, Measurement and Evaluation, PERFORMANCE 1993, Tutorial.* Springer LNCS **729**, 1993.
13. N. Götz, U. Herzog, and M. Rettelbach. "TIPP – Introduction and Application to Protocol Performance Analysis", In H. König, editor, *Formale Beschreibungstechniken für verteilte Systeme.* Saur Verlag, Reihe: FOKUS, 1993.
14. Hans A. Hansson. *Time and Probability in Formal Design of Distributed Systems.* PhD thesis, University of Uppsala, 1991.
15. H. Hermanns. "Semantik für Prozeßsprachen zur Leistungsbewertung", Master's thesis, Universität Erlangen–Nürnberg, IMMD VII, November 1993.
16. H. Hermanns, U. Herzog, J. Hillston, V. Mertsiotakis, and M. Rettelbach. "Stochastic Process Algebras: Integrating Qualitative and Quantitative Modelling", Technical Report 11/94, Universität Erlangen–Nürnberg, IMMD VII, Martensstr. 3, 91058 Erlangen, May 1994.
17. S. Donatelli, H. Hermanns, U. Herzog, J. Hillston, V. Mertsiotakis, M. Rettelbach and M. Ribaudo. "Process Algebras and/or Petri Nets for Integrated Performance Modelling?", Tutorial at the SIGMETRICS/PERFORMANCE'95, 1995.
18. H. Hermanns, U. Herzog, and V. Mertsiotakis. "Stochastic Process Algebras as a Tool for Performance and Dependability Modelling", In *Proc. of IEEE Int. Computer Performance and Dependability Symposium*, pp. 102–111, Erlangen, April 1995. IEEE Computer Society Press.
19. H. Hermanns and V. Mertsiotakis. "A Stochastic Process Algebra Based Modelling Tool", submitted to 11th U.K. Performance Engineering Workshop for Computer and Telecommunication Systems, 1995.
20. H. Hermanns, V. Mertsiotakis, and M. Rettelbach. "Performance Analysis of Distributed Systems Using TIPP – a Case Study", In J. Hillston and R. Pooley, editors, *Proc. 10th U.K. Performance Engineering Workshop for Computer and Telecommunication Systems*, pp. 131–144. Department of Computer Science, University of Edinburgh, 1994.
21. H. Hermanns and M. Rettelbach. "Syntax, Semantics, Equivalences, and Axioms for MTIPP", In U. Herzog and M. Rettelbach, editors, *Proc. 2nd Workshop on Process Algebras and Performance Modelling*, pp. 71–88, Erlangen-Regensberg, July 1994. IMMD, Universität Erlangen-Nürnberg.
22. H. Hermanns, M. Rettelbach, and T. Weiß. "Formal Characterisation of Immediate Actions in SPA with Nondeterministic Branching", In Hillston [4].
23. U. Herzog. "EXL — Syntax, Semantics and Examples", Technical Report 16/90, Friedrich-Alexander University Erlangen-Nürnberg, IMMD VII, 1990.

24. U. Herzog, "Formal Description, Time and Performance Analysis. A Framework", In T. Härder, H. Wedekind, and G. Zimmermann, editors, *Entwurf und Betrieb Verteilter Systeme*, pp. 172–190. Springer Verlag, Berlin, IFB 264, 1990.
25. U. Herzog and M. Rettelbach, editors, *Proc. 2nd Workshop on Process Algebras and Performance Modelling*, Arbeitsberichte des IMMD (Informatik), **27-4**, Universität Erlangen–Nürnberg, 1994.
26. J. Hillston and V. Mertsiotakis, "A simple Time Scale Decomposition Technique for SPA", In Hillston [4].
27. J. Hillston and F. Moller, editors, *Proc. 1st Workshop on Process Algebras and Performance Modelling.* Department of Computer Science, University of Edinburgh, 1993.
28. Jane Hillston, *A Compositional Approach to Performance Modelling.* PhD thesis, University of Edinburgh, 1994.
29. C.A.R. Hoare, *Communicating Sequential Processes.* Prentice-Hall, Englewood Cliffs, NJ, 1985.
30. C. Lindemann, "DSPNexpress: A Software Package for the Efficient Solution of Deterministic and Stochastic Petri Nets", In *Proc. 6th Int. Conference on Modelling Techniques and Tools for Computer Performance Evaluation*, pp. 15–29, Edinburgh, September 1992.
31. R. Milner, *A Calculus of Communicating Systems.* Prentice Hall, London, 1989.
32. I. Mitrani, A. Ost, and M. Rettelbach. "TIPP and the Spectral Expansion Method", In Baccelli, Jean-Marie and Mitrani [2].
33. X. Nicollin and J. Sifakis, "An Overview and Synthesis on Timed Process Algebras", In Springer LNCS **600**, editor, *Real-Time: Theory in Practice*, 1991.
34. N. Nounou and Y. Yemini, "Algebraic Specification-Based Performance Analysis of Communication Protocols", In *Proc. Int. Workshop on Protocol Specification, Testing and Verification, 4th*, pp. 541–560, 1985.
35. B. Plateau and K. Atif, "Stochastic Automata Network for Modeling Parallel Systems", *IEEE Trans. on Software Engineering*, **17**(10), pp. 1093–1108, 1991.
36. G. Plotkin, "A Structural Approach to Operational Semantics", Report DAIMI FN-19, Computer Science Department, Aarhus University, September 1981.
37. G.M. Reed and A.W. Roscoe, "A Timed Model for Communication Sequential Processes", *Theoretical Computer Science*, **58**, pp. 249–261, 1988.
38. M. Rettelbach, "Leistungsbewertung mit Prozeßalgebren", Master's thesis, Universität Erlangen–Nürnberg, IMMD VII, Februar 1991.
39. M. Rettelbach, "Towards a Theory of Generalised SPA", In Hillston [4].
40. M. Rettelbach and M. Siegle. "Compositional Minimal Semantics for the Stochastic Process Algebra TIPP", In U. Herzog and M. Rettelbach, editors, *Proc. 2nd Workshop on Process Algebra and Performance Modelling.* University of Erlangen-Nürnberg, IMMD, 1994.
41. M. Ribaudo. "On the Relationship between Stochastic Process Algebras and Stochastic Petri Nets", PhD thesis, University of Torino, 1995.
42. R. Sahner and K. Trivedi, "Performance Analysis and Reliability Analysis Using Directed Acyclic Graphs", *IEEE Trans. on Software Engineering*, **SE-13**(10), October 1987.
43. F. Sötz, "A Method for Performance Prediction of Parallel Programs", In H. Burkhart, editor, *CONPAR 90–VAPP IV, Joint Int. Conference on Vector and Parallel Processing. Proceedings*, pp. 98–107, Zürich, Switzerland, September 1990. Springer–Verlag, Berlin, LNCS **457**.

Stochastic Process Algebra for Discrete Event Simulation

P.G. Harrison and B. Strulo*

Department of Computing, Imperial College, U.K.

Summary. A stochastic, timed process algebra is developed to describe formally discrete event simulation. It is able to describe the passing of time and probabilistic choice, either discrete, between a countable number of processes, or continuous, to choose a random amount of time to wait. We define an operational semantics and derive equivalences over it that imply equations which can be used to compare and transform processes representing simulations. We discuss notions of equivalence of simulations and illustrate with examples that include queues.

1. Introduction

We consider the process of constructing models of the performance of systems comprising a workload and a collection of processing resources. We require a formalism that is both high level and has a formal semantics to make the behaviour of the language explicit and rigorous. Then we can perform mechanical simplification and abstraction or at least prove the validity of manually derived results. This parallels the use of formal semantics in conventional programming languages, as discussed in say [11].

We derive a process algebra which may be used to describe discrete event simulations by taking a relatively high level language that has a formal semantics of parallelism, *viz.* CCS, and adding constructs to represent a real-number time and various probabilistic features. In this way we can derive semantically sound axioms relating sub-expressions of a program. Such axioms can form the basis of mechanisable program transformations which, for example, may allow simpler or more efficient or more mathematically tractable simulations to be derived from another with a clearer specification. Again this compares to program transformation in declarative languages [4].

Our language is based on the timed CCS of [22]. It takes its impatient actions from Moller and Toft's temporal CCS in [13] though their calculus does not generalise directly to real number time. Our language has a similar purpose to TIPP proposed in [5]. The major difference is in our treatment of non-determinism. The models of TIPP execute non-deterministic choices with uniform probability while in ours such choices must be explicitly resolved. A further difference is that our language is not restricted to *Markovian* systems, *i.e.* its time delays need not be exponential random variables. This provides greater generality at the expense of mathematical tractability, in contrast to

* Now at British Telecom Research Laboratory, Martlesham Heath

Hillston's work on the Markovian process algebra PEPA [8] which can solve relatively large models analytically.

In the next section we discuss the language informally and present its syntax. In section 3 we present the operational semantics formally and show it has the properties we expect. We next introduce bisimulation equivalences over this operational semantics, strong in section 4 and weak, abstracting from internal behaviour, in section 5. Finally we show the power of the language by a series of examples. Proofs of the technical results are omitted due to lack of space, but they may be found in [20].

2. Language

Our language is defined so that CCS is a sub-calculus in the sense that the operational semantics of the pure CCS terms in our language is the same as in CCS itself. As in CCS, communication and synchronisation are represented *via* an alphabet of atomic actions or labels which we will write Λ. Each action has a conjugate action represented by an overline and the conjugate to the conjugate is the original action. There is also a distinguished self-conjugate, invisible (or silent) action which represents internal activity of a process invisible to the outside. Thus we have visible actions in $\Delta = \Lambda \cup \overline{\Lambda}$ and a complete alphabet $Act = \Delta \cup \{\tau\}$ including the names, the co-names and the invisible action.

Our language is presented as an algebra over two sorts. We use two sets of variables, $PVar$ of sort *Process expression*, and $TVar$ of sort *Time*. We use an algebra of time expressions giving a set of expressions $TExp$. This has the operator $+$ indicating addition and $\dot{-}$ indicating non-negative subtraction *i.e.*

$$x \dot{-} y = \begin{cases} x - y & x \geq y \\ 0 & \text{otherwise} \end{cases}$$

The other symbols are the non-negative real numbers $\mathbb{R}^+$. We define the process expressions as

Definition 2.1. *The set of process expressions, $PExp$, is the least set including*

$$X \qquad nil \qquad (t).P \qquad \alpha.P \qquad \alpha[s \leftarrow t].P \qquad \mathcal{R}[s \leftarrow f].P$$

$$\sum_{i \in I} [q_i]P_i \qquad P + Q \qquad P \mid Q \qquad P[S] \qquad P \backslash A \qquad rec(X = P)$$

where $X \in PVar$, $P, Q \in PExp$, $s \in TVar$, $t \in TExp$, $\alpha \in Act$, I is a finite indexing set with the $P_i \in PExp$, S is a relabelling function $S : Act \to Act$, $A \subset Act$ is a set of actions with $\tau \notin A$, q_i are probabilities in $[0, 1]$ with $\sum q_i = 1$, and f is a probability density function over the $\mathbb{R}^+$.

We identify the set of *processes*, *Proc* to be the closed process expressions *i.e.* those with no free variables of either sort. We require a recursive expression to have its free variable "guarded" by some action so that each recursive unwinding requires at least one labelled transition before it can be repeated.

We will use $P \triangleq E$ to assign the process expression E a name P. We will use the convention that processes (and process variables) are represented by names with an initial capital and will represent actions by names with an initial small letter. We now go through the syntactic constructs giving their informal meaning.

First, *nil* is a process constant representing a deadlocked or terminated process which can perform no action and must simply delay or idle from now on. $(t).P$ represents a process which must delay for t time units and then becomes process P while $\alpha.P$ represents a process which can perform an α action and then become P.

Next we have an action prefixing $\alpha[s \leftarrow t].P$ which also represents a process which can immediately perform an α action. If the α is performed the process becomes P but here the free variable s is replaced by the value t and so the process becomes $P\{t/s\}$. The essential difference is that in $\alpha.P$ the prefixing cannot delay (we say it is *impatient*). The process $\alpha[s \leftarrow t].P$ can delay for any time t' but records this delay and so becomes $\alpha[s \leftarrow t + t'].P$. This *patient* prefixing binds the variable s in P. Of course if s is not free in P then we need not concern ourselves with s or t, and for convenience we may write $\alpha[].P$ in this case (the brackets distinguishing patient from impatient prefixing).

We view this delaying behaviour as analogous to that of the value-passing part of CCS. We imagine a global clock, broadcasting the passage of time, to which all processes waiting for a synchronisation listen. Then the execution of the action causes the time value variable to become instantiated to the passing of time it has heard from that clock. The process may act on that value later, perhaps by then delaying less if it has already been delayed.

$P + Q$ represents a process which waits until P or Q are ready to participate in some action. Then it will choose non-deterministically between them. Once we have shown that no ambiguity arises we will use $\sum_{i \in I} P_i$ to represent finite sums. Thus consider $short.P_1 + long.P_2$. This process offers a choice between two alternatives, controlled by its initial action.

$\dot{\sum}_{i \in I}[q_i]P_i$ represents a process which will immediately and randomly become one of the P_i on the basis of the q_i probabilities. This is a straightforward finite probabilistic choice not subject to any control. We will write this as $[p]P \dotplus [q]Q$ in the binary case.

$\mathcal{R}[s \leftarrow f].P$ represents a process which can immediately sample a random variable with the specified density f and become $P\{t/s\}$ for some t. Although this is a form of uncountable probabilistic branching, the resulting processes are highly restricted in that they are identical except in the values of certain time expressions and hence certain delays.

The parallel construct $P \mid Q$ represents two processes placed in parallel and allowed to communicate and synchronise. We use the usual CCS rules for this. Similarly relabelling $P[S]$ and restriction $P \setminus A$ come directly from CCS. $P[S]$ behaves like P but with all its actions renamed by the function S. $P \setminus A$ behaves like P but is not allowed to perform any action in A.

As a simple example to explain these constructs, we consider a situation where a sequence of tasks arrive randomly, forming a workload. Then some (we choose two) processors service the queue, first come first served. The Workload chooses a random time (density function f_1) and then waits for that time. Then it restarts itself in parallel with a new Task.

$$Workload \triangleq \mathcal{R}[s \leftarrow f_1].(s).\,(Workload \mid Task)$$

The Task requests a processor, executes for a random time, and then releases the processor and terminates.

$$Task \triangleq \overline{procreq}[].\,\mathcal{R}[s \leftarrow f_2].(s).procrel.nil$$

The Processor accepts a request, accepts a release and restarts.

$$Proc \triangleq procreq[].\overline{procrel}[].Proc$$

Then our system is

$$System \triangleq Workload \mid Proc \mid Proc$$

3. Semantics

The operational semantics of these processes are described in terms of three types of transitions between processes. We first define probabilistic transitions which we assume to be resolved first. The idea is that any probabilistic part may be assumed under any circumstances to have already been resolved before any other actions are considered.

Then we have the standard CCS type of *labelled* transitions which are labelled from *Act* and happen non-deterministically following the usual behaviour of a CCS-type language. Transitions labelled with τ must happen immediately, *i.e.* before any evolution can take place, and the impatient actions must also happen before any evolution. We call impatient actions and τ actions *immediate.*

When no more immediate transitions are possible the system becomes *stable.* Then, all parts of the process synchronously undergo a timed *evolution* transition via their (t) actions. This represents the passing of time and continues until further probabilistic or immediate transitions are possible. It is shown in [20] that a process cannot evolve past the potential of performing a sampling or immediate transition.

The possible transitions are described via inference systems. We say the transitions are the least relation between processes that satisfies the given inference rules. We define the labelled transitions first as they are the simplest and most familiar.

Labelled transitions are defined in Figure 3.1 and are very similar to the standard CCS rules. In the Sum and Parallel rules we use preconditions

$$\frac{}{\alpha.P \xrightarrow{\alpha} P} \qquad \text{Prefix1}$$

$$\frac{}{\alpha[s \leftarrow t].P \xrightarrow{\alpha} P\{t/s\}} \qquad \text{Prefix2}$$

$$\frac{P \xrightarrow{\alpha} P'}{(0).P \xrightarrow{\alpha} P'} \qquad \text{No-Delay}$$

$$\frac{P \xrightarrow{\alpha} P' \quad \neg Q \hookrightarrow}{P + Q \xrightarrow{\alpha} P'} \quad \frac{Q \xrightarrow{\alpha} Q' \quad \neg P \hookrightarrow}{P + Q \xrightarrow{\alpha} Q'} \qquad \text{Sum}$$

$$\frac{P \xrightarrow{\alpha} P' \quad \neg Q \hookrightarrow}{P \mid Q \xrightarrow{\alpha} P' \mid Q} \quad \frac{Q \xrightarrow{\alpha} Q' \quad \neg P \hookrightarrow}{P \mid Q \xrightarrow{\alpha} P \mid Q'} \qquad \text{Parallel}$$

$$\frac{P \xrightarrow{\alpha} P' \quad Q \xrightarrow{\overline{\alpha}} Q'}{P \mid Q \xrightarrow{\tau} P' \mid Q'} \qquad \text{Communicate}$$

$$\frac{P \xrightarrow{\alpha} P'}{P[S] \xrightarrow{S(\alpha)} P'[S]} \qquad \text{Relabel}$$

$$\frac{P \xrightarrow{\alpha} P'}{P \backslash A \xrightarrow{\alpha} P' \backslash A} \quad \alpha \notin A \text{ and } \overline{\alpha} \notin A \qquad \text{Restrict}$$

$$\frac{P\{rec(X = P)/X\} \xrightarrow{\alpha} P'}{rec(X = P) \xrightarrow{\alpha} P'} \qquad \text{Rec}$$

Fig. 3.1. Labelled transitions

like $\neg P \hookrightarrow$. This means P cannot perform a probabilistic transition and is formally defined by our probabilistic transitions in the next section. These preconditions force all probabilistic choices to be resolved before any labelled transitions. The Prefix2 rule shows the way in which time variables are bound by the execution of an action. The No-Delay rule allows zero delays to be disregarded when any transition is to be inferred. We will thus be able to deduce that $(0).P = P$.

We would like to define our probabilistic transitions in a similar way and deduce a probability distribution over transitions. But consider the process $[\frac{1}{2}]P + [\frac{1}{2}]P$. A natural transition inference system will infer a transition with probability half to P for this process but by two possible inferences. We need to keep these two transitions separate so that each has probability a half but the total probability of a transition to P is 1. So we distinguish our transitions by a special index shown as a subscript. This index essentially represents the probability space over which our distribution is defined. Choosing an index chooses the particular transition (and inference) from all the possible probabilistic transitions (and inferences) for the process.

We define the probabilistic transitions in Figure 3.2. Each transition has an associated probability measure, shown above it, and its associated index, shown as a subscript. Indices come from the set $Index_0$ which we define:

Definition 3.1. *The set of index atoms is defined by*

$$Atom = \{[i] : i \in \mathbb{N}\} \cup \{(t) : t \in \mathbb{R}^+\}$$

The set of general indices, Index, is the least set including

$$\langle\rangle \qquad a.l \qquad l \mid l' \qquad l + l'$$

where $l, l' \in Index$, $a \in Atom$. *The set of single step indices,* $Index_0$, *is the subset of indices containing exactly one atom.*

Thus the transitions are a relation from $Proc \times [0,1] \times Index_0 \times Proc$.

The index carries the part of some complex process that has given rise to this probabilistic transition. The atom, a, indicates how the probabilistic choice has been resolved while the rest of the index skeleton mirrors the rest of the process which has not resolved any probabilistic choices it may hold.

This relation captures our fundamental idea of how we wish *single* probabilistic transitions to operate. We combine multiple transitions into a relation from $Proc \times [0,1] \times Index \times Proc$ with another inference system, figure 3.3. The indices now represent all the probabilistic choices that go to make up the complete transition. Here we use the function $lf : Index_0 \times Index \rightarrow Index$ defined by

$$\begin{aligned} lf(\langle\rangle, m) &= m \\ lf(a.\langle\rangle, m) &= a.m \\ lf(l + l', m + m') &= lf(l, m) + lf(l', m') \\ lf(l \mid l', m \mid m') &= lf(l, m) \mid lf(l', m') \end{aligned}$$

Indices are trees of real and natural numbers and so it is straightforward to define measurable sets. We call *Borel* the σ-field of measurable sets from *Index*. Then it is straightforward to define integration and the probability associated with any such set of indices:

$$\frac{}{\sum_{i\in I}[q_i]P_i \overset{q_i}{\underset{0}{\hookrightarrow}}_{[i].\langle\rangle} P_i} \quad \text{Resolve}$$

$$\frac{}{\mathcal{R}[s\leftarrow f].P \overset{f(t)}{\underset{0}{\hookrightarrow}}_{(t).\langle\rangle} P\{t/s\}} \quad \text{Sample}$$

$$\frac{P \overset{q}{\underset{0}{\hookrightarrow}}_l P'}{(t).P \overset{q}{\underset{0}{\hookrightarrow}}_l (t).P'} \quad \text{Delay}$$

$$\frac{P \overset{q}{\underset{0}{\hookrightarrow}}_l P'}{P+Q \overset{q}{\underset{0}{\hookrightarrow}}_{l+\langle\rangle} P'+Q} \quad \text{Sum1}$$

$$\frac{Q \overset{q}{\underset{0}{\hookrightarrow}}_l Q'}{P+Q \overset{q}{\underset{0}{\hookrightarrow}}_{\langle\rangle+l} P+Q'} \quad \text{Sum2}$$

$$\frac{P \overset{q}{\underset{0}{\hookrightarrow}}_l P'}{P \mid Q \overset{q}{\underset{0}{\hookrightarrow}}_{l|\langle\rangle} P' \mid Q} \quad \text{Parallel1}$$

$$\frac{Q \overset{q}{\underset{0}{\hookrightarrow}}_l Q'}{P \mid Q \overset{q}{\underset{0}{\hookrightarrow}}_{\langle\rangle|l} P \mid Q'} \quad \text{Parallel2}$$

$$\frac{P \overset{q}{\underset{0}{\hookrightarrow}}_l P'}{P[S] \overset{q}{\underset{0}{\hookrightarrow}}_l P'[S]} \quad \text{Relabel}$$

$$\frac{P \overset{q}{\underset{0}{\hookrightarrow}}_l P'}{P\backslash A \overset{q}{\underset{0}{\hookrightarrow}}_l P'\backslash A} \quad \text{Restrict}$$

$$\frac{P\{rec(X=P)/X\} \overset{q}{\underset{0}{\hookrightarrow}}_l P'}{rec(X=P) \overset{q}{\underset{0}{\hookrightarrow}}_l P'} \quad \text{Rec}$$

Fig. 3.2. Single step probabilistic transitions

$$\frac{P \overset{p}{\underset{0}{\hookrightarrow}}_l P'}{P \overset{p}{\hookrightarrow}_l P'} \quad \text{Any-Samples}$$

$$\frac{P \overset{p}{\underset{0}{\hookrightarrow}}_l P' \quad P' \overset{q}{\hookrightarrow}_m P''}{P \overset{p\cdot q}{\hookrightarrow}_{lf(l,m)} P''} \quad \text{Mult-Samples}$$

Fig. 3.3. Probabilistic transitions

Definition 3.2. *The* index probability measure, $\mu^* : Proc \times Borel \to [0,1]$ *is the Lebesgue integral*

$$\mu^*(P, I) = \int_{l \in I} p_P(l)$$

We now wish to move this structure over to *Proc*. Using the usual definition of $q_P^{-1}(S) = \{l \in Index_P : q_P(l) \in S\}$, we define:

Definition 3.3. *The measurable sets w.r.t. P are*

$$\overline{B}_P = q_P(Borel) = \{S \subseteq Proc : q_P^{-1}(S) \in Borel\}$$

The σ-field of measurable sets is $\overline{B} = \bigcap_{P \in Proc} \overline{B}_P$ and the process probability measure, $\mu : Proc \times \overline{B} \to [0,1]$ *is*

$$\mu(P, S) = \mu^*(P, q_P^{-1}(S))$$

We take μ to be undefined if $\neg P \hookrightarrow$.

Thus $\mu(P, S)$ is the total probability that P may become a member of S by a probabilistic sampling transition. Finally, to prove that $\mu(P, .)$ is a probability measure we have

Lemma 3.1. *If $P \hookrightarrow$ then $\mu(P, Proc) = 1$*

Eventually no more immediate or probabilistic transitions will be possible. The only thing the process can then do is to evolve in time.

First we define a single step evolution relation $\overset{t}{\leadsto}_\circ$ in Figure 3.4. These rules do not allow the inference of a zero time evolution (trivial induction). Also we have no rules to allow $\alpha.P$ to evolve; it is this that makes it "impatient".

These rules capture our essential ideas about evolution. However they only allow evolutions between the simplest changes of syntactic form of processes. Thus for example we do have $(1).(1).P \overset{1}{\leadsto}_\circ (1).P \overset{1}{\leadsto}_\circ P$ but not $(1).(1).P \overset{2}{\leadsto}_\circ P$. This is necessary to ensure that parallel constructs are checked for immediate transitions at every stage at which they are possible. But we do wish to combine allowable transitions so we add a new level of transition. Our evolution transitions are thus defined in Figure 3.5. Thus we now have $(1).(1).P \overset{2}{\leadsto} P$ as required.

4. Strong bisimulation

We now wish to define notions of equivalence over process expressions. We can follow Milner [12] and look at the standard ideas of bisimulation for the immediate and evolution transitions but it is not immediately clear how such a notion generalises to the probabilistic transitions.

$$\frac{\neg P \hookrightarrow}{(t+u).P \overset{t}{\rightsquigarrow}_{\circ} (u).P} \quad t > 0 \qquad \text{Reduce-Delay}$$

$$\frac{P \overset{t}{\rightsquigarrow}_{\circ} P'}{(0).P \overset{t}{\rightsquigarrow}_{\circ} P'} \qquad \text{No-Delay}$$

$$\frac{\neg P \hookrightarrow}{(t).P \overset{t}{\rightsquigarrow}_{\circ} P} \quad t > 0 \qquad \text{End-Delay}$$

$$\frac{}{nil \overset{t}{\rightsquigarrow}_{\circ} nil} \quad t > 0 \qquad \text{Nil}$$

$$\frac{}{\alpha[s \leftarrow t].P \overset{t'}{\rightsquigarrow}_{\circ} \alpha[s \leftarrow t+t'].P} \quad \alpha \neq \tau \text{ and } t' > 0 \qquad \text{Idle}$$

$$\frac{P \overset{t}{\rightsquigarrow}_{\circ} P' \quad Q \overset{t}{\rightsquigarrow}_{\circ} Q'}{P + Q \overset{t}{\rightsquigarrow}_{\circ} P' + Q'} \qquad \text{Sum}$$

$$\frac{\neg P \mid Q \overset{\tau}{\rightarrow} \quad P \overset{t}{\rightsquigarrow}_{\circ} P' \quad Q \overset{t}{\rightsquigarrow}_{\circ} Q'}{P \mid Q \overset{t}{\rightsquigarrow}_{\circ} P' \mid Q'} \qquad \text{Parallel}$$

$$\frac{P \overset{t}{\rightsquigarrow}_{\circ} P'}{P[S] \overset{t}{\rightsquigarrow}_{\circ} P'[S]} \qquad \text{Relabel}$$

$$\frac{P \overset{t}{\rightsquigarrow}_{\circ} P'}{P \backslash A \overset{t}{\rightsquigarrow}_{\circ} P' \backslash A} \qquad \text{Restrict}$$

$$\frac{P\{rec(X=P)/X\} \overset{t}{\rightsquigarrow}_{\circ} P'}{rec(X=P) \overset{t}{\rightsquigarrow}_{\circ} P'} \qquad \text{Rec}$$

Fig. 3.4. Single Step Evolution transitions

$$\frac{P \overset{t}{\rightsquigarrow}_{\circ} P'}{P \overset{t}{\rightsquigarrow} P'} \qquad \text{Any-Delay}$$

$$\frac{P \overset{t}{\rightsquigarrow} P' \quad P' \overset{t'}{\rightsquigarrow}_{\circ} P''}{P \overset{t+t'}{\rightsquigarrow} P''} \qquad \text{Add-Delay}$$

Fig. 3.5. Evolution transitions

We wish to make processes equivalent only if they define equal probability measures over sets of their descendants. We would like to say $P = Q$ iff $\mu(P, S) = \mu(Q, S)$ for all sets of processes S, but we do not wish to distinguish processes if their measures differ only on sets which separate equivalent descendants. Thus we define:

Definition 4.1. *For an equivalence relation $\mathcal{R} \subset Proc \times Proc$ we define $\overline{B}(\mathcal{R}) \subset \overline{B}$ as*

$$\{S \in \overline{B} : S \text{ is a union of } \mathcal{R}\text{-equivalence classes}\}$$

In other words $\overline{B}(\mathcal{R})$ are all the measurable sets which don't separate $\mathcal{R}$-equivalent processes.

We proceed to define our fundamental equivalence following Milner.

Definition 4.2. *An equivalence relation $\mathcal{R} \subset Proc \times Proc$ is a* strong bisimulation *iff*

$P \mathcal{R} Q$ implies for all $\alpha \in Act$, $t \in \mathbb{R}^+$, $S \in \overline{B}(\mathcal{R})$:

1. *if $P \xrightarrow{\alpha} P'$, then $\exists Q'$ such that $Q \xrightarrow{\alpha} Q'$ and $P' \mathcal{R} Q'$.*
2. *if $Q \xrightarrow{\alpha} Q'$, then $\exists P'$ such that $P \xrightarrow{\alpha} P'$ and $P' \mathcal{R} Q'$.*
3. *if $P \overset{t}{\rightsquigarrow} P'$, then $\exists Q'$ such that $Q \overset{t}{\rightsquigarrow} Q'$ and $P' \mathcal{R} Q'$.*
4. *if $Q \overset{t}{\rightsquigarrow} Q'$, then $\exists P'$ such that $P \overset{t}{\rightsquigarrow} P'$ and $P' \mathcal{R} Q'$.*
5. *if $P \hookrightarrow$ then $Q \hookrightarrow$ and $\mu(P, S) = \mu(Q, S)$.*
6. *if $Q \hookrightarrow$ then $P \hookrightarrow$ and $\mu(P, S) = \mu(Q, S)$.*

Many equivalence relations (including both the empty and identity relations) are strong bisimulations. But say P and Q are related by some strong bisimulation relation. Then they have the equivalence property we require since their descendants are still related by that same equivalence relation. So we define strong bisimulation between processes by:

Definition 4.3. *Two processes P and Q are in strong bisimulation, denoted $P \sim Q$, iff there is any strong bisimulation with $P \mathcal{R} Q$.*

Thus $\sim \; = \cup\{\mathcal{R} : \mathcal{R} \text{ is a bisimulation}\}$ and in fact $\sim$ is the largest strong bisimulation

We have defined an equivalence over processes which preserves the transition behaviour of those processes. We now look at the algebraic behaviour of this equivalence by finding various sound axioms for $\sim$. The most obvious ones are given in the theorem that follows.

Theorem 4.1.

1. $P + nil \sim P$
2. $P + Q \sim Q + P$
3. $P + (Q + R) \sim (P + Q) + R$
4. $P \mid nil \sim P$
5. $P \mid Q \sim Q \mid P$

6. $P \mid (Q \mid R) \sim (P \mid Q) \mid R$
7. $nil \backslash A \sim nil$
8. $(\alpha.P)\backslash A \sim \alpha.(P\backslash A)$ *if* $\alpha \notin A$ *and* $\overline{\alpha} \notin A$
9. $(\alpha.P)\backslash A \sim 0$ *if* $\alpha \in A$ *or* $\overline{\alpha} \in A$
10. $(\alpha[s \leftarrow t].P)\backslash A \sim \alpha[s \leftarrow t].(P\backslash A)$ *if* $\alpha \notin A$ *and* $\overline{\alpha} \notin A$
11. $(\alpha[s \leftarrow t].P)\backslash A \sim nil$ *if* $\alpha \in A$ *or* $\overline{\alpha} \in A$
12. $P + Q\backslash A \sim (P\backslash A) + (Q\backslash A)$
13. $(t).P\backslash A \sim (t).(P\backslash A)$
14. $\mathcal{R}[s \leftarrow f].P\backslash A \sim \mathcal{R}[s \leftarrow f].(P\backslash A)$
15. $(\sum[p_i]P_i)\backslash A \sim \sum[p_i](P_i\backslash A)$
16. $nil[S] \sim nil$
17. $(\alpha.P)[S] \sim S(\alpha).(P[S])$
18. $(\alpha[s \leftarrow t].P)[S] \sim S(\alpha)[s \leftarrow t].(P[S])$
19. $(P + Q)[S] \sim P[S] + Q[S])$
20. $(t).P[S] \sim (t).(P[S])$
21. $\mathcal{R}[s \leftarrow f].P[S] \sim \mathcal{R}[s \leftarrow f].(P[S])$
22. $(\sum[p_i]P_i)[S] \sim \sum[p_i](P_i[S])$
23. $rec(X = P) \sim P\{rec(X = P)/X\}$

We thus have associativity (and commutativity) for + and |, and henceforth omit brackets and abbreviate multiple sums by $\sum_{i \in I} P_i$ and multiple parallels by $\prod_{i \in I} P_i$ (for I finite). We will similarly drop the brackets from indices in *Index*.

We might have expected $P + P \sim P$ but this is not true for probabilistic P where the two P on the LHS can choose independently (without resolving the +) and become different. It is of course true for P with $\neg P \hookrightarrow$.

More interesting laws are the following:

Theorem 4.2.

1. $P + P \sim P$ *if* $\neg P \hookrightarrow$
2. $(t).nil \sim nil$
3. $(0).P \sim P$
4. $(t)(t').P \sim (t + t').P$
5. $(t).(P + Q) \sim (t).P + (t).Q$
6. $(t).(P \mid Q) \sim (t).P \mid (t).Q$
7. $\tau[s \leftarrow t].P \sim \tau.P\{t/s\}$
8. $\alpha[s \leftarrow t].P \sim \alpha[s \leftarrow 0].P\{s + t/s\}$
9. $\tau[s \leftarrow 0].P + (t).Q \sim \tau[s \leftarrow 0].P$ *if* $t > 0$
10. $\alpha.P + (t).P' \sim \alpha.P$ *if* $t > 0$ *and* $\neg P' \hookrightarrow$
11. $P + \sum_{i \in I}[q_i]P_i \sim \sum_{i \in I}[q_i](P + P_i)$
12. $P \mid \sum_{i \in I}[q_i]P_i \sim \sum_{i \in I}[q_i](P \mid P_i)$
13. $\sum_{i \in I}[p_i]P_i + \sum_{j \in J}[q_j]Q_j \sim \sum_{i \in I, j \in J}[p_i.q_j](P_i + Q_j)$
14. $\mathcal{R}[s \leftarrow f].(t).P \sim (t).\mathcal{R}[s \leftarrow f].P$
15. $P + \mathcal{R}[s \leftarrow f].Q \sim \mathcal{R}[s \leftarrow f].(P + Q)$
16. $P \mid \mathcal{R}[s \leftarrow f].Q \sim \mathcal{R}[s \leftarrow f].(P \mid Q)$

17. $\alpha[s \leftarrow 0].P + (t).\,\alpha[s \leftarrow t].P \sim \alpha[s \leftarrow 0].P$

The most important result however is the expansion theorem. In CCS it is well known that $\alpha.nil \mid \beta.nil \sim \alpha.\beta.nil + \beta.\alpha.nil$. This is true in our language also but we must also consider the other forms of prefixing. We do not have that

$$\alpha[].nil \mid (2).\beta.nil \sim \alpha[].(2).\beta.nil + (2).\beta.\alpha[].nil$$

The problem here is that the initial α may be delayed, say by one time unit. Then the delay between its execution and the subsequent β needs to be reduced by that one time unit. In fact we have

$$\alpha[].nil \mid (2).\beta.nil \sim \alpha[s \leftarrow 0].(2 \dot{-} s).\beta.nil + (2).\beta.\alpha[].nil$$

We state the expansion theorem in its full generality as:

Theorem 4.3. *If* $P = \left(\sum_{i \in I}(t_i).\,\alpha_i[s \leftarrow 0].P_i\right)$, $Q = \left(\sum_{j \in J}(t'_j).\,\beta_j[s \leftarrow 0].Q_j\right)$ *then*

$$\begin{aligned} P \mid Q \quad \sim \quad & \sum_{i \in I}(t_i).\,\alpha_i[s \leftarrow 0].\left(P_i \mid \sum_{j \in J}(t'_j \dot{-} t_i \dot{-} s).\,\beta_j[s \leftarrow (t_i + s) \dot{-} t'_j].Q_j\right) \\ + \quad & \sum_{j \in J}(t'_j).\,\beta_j[s \leftarrow 0].\left(Q_j \mid \sum_{i \in I}(t_i \dot{-} t'_j \dot{-} s).\,\alpha_i[s \leftarrow (t'_j + s) \dot{-} t_i].P_i\right) \\ + \quad & \sum_{\alpha_k = \overline{\beta_l}} ((t_k \dot{-} t'_l) + t'_l).\tau.\,(P_k\{t'_l \dot{-} t_k/s\} \mid Q_l\{t_k \dot{-} t'_l/s\}) \end{aligned}$$

If $P = \left(\sum_{i \in I}(t_i).\,\alpha_i[s \leftarrow 0].P_i\right)$, $Q = \left(\sum_{j \in J}(t'_j).\beta_j.Q_j\right)$ *then*

$$\begin{aligned} P \mid Q \quad \sim \quad & \sum_{i \in I}(t_i).\,\alpha_i[s \leftarrow 0].\left(P_i \mid \sum_{j \in J}(t'_j \dot{-} t_i \dot{-} s).\beta_j.Q_j\right) \\ + \quad & \sum_{j \in J}(t'_j).\beta_j.\left(Q_j \mid \sum_{i \in I}(t_i \dot{-} t'_j).\,\alpha_i[s \leftarrow (t'_j + s) \dot{-} t_i].P_i\right) \\ + \quad & \sum_{\alpha_k = \overline{\beta_l}} (t'_l).\tau.\,(P_k\{t'_l \dot{-} t_k/s\} \mid Q_l) \end{aligned}$$

If $P = \left(\sum_{i \in I}(t_i).\alpha_i.P_i\right)$, $Q = \left(\sum_{j \in J}(t'_j).\beta_j.Q_j\right)$ *then*

$$
\begin{aligned}
P \mid Q \quad \sim \quad & \sum_{i\in I}(t_i).\alpha_i.\left(P_i \mid \sum_{j\in J}(t'_j \dot{-} t_i).\beta_j.Q_j\right)\\
+ \quad & \sum_{j\in J}(t'_j).\beta_j.\left(Q_j \mid \sum_{i\in I}(t_i \dot{-} t'_j).\alpha_i.P_i\right)\\
+ \quad & \sum_{\alpha_k=\overline{\beta_l}, t_k=t'_l} (t_k).\tau.(P_k \mid Q_l)
\end{aligned}
$$

We can also show that the $\sim$ relation is a congruence, *i.e.* that $P \sim Q$ implies $C[P] \sim C[Q]$ for any context $C[-]$. This is essential because we wish to use the algebraic laws to reason about complex processes.

5. Weak bisimulation

As for standard CCS we wish to abstract from the τ action by moving to a weak version of bisimulation. We would certainly like $\alpha.\tau.nil$ to be considered equal to $\alpha.nil$ since their only observable behaviour is to perform α and terminate. The former has an internal state change before it terminates but we wish to consider that invisible.

We also wish to make arbitrary τ actions in the midst of a long evolution transition invisible. So we define a new evolution relation.

Definition 5.1.

$$
\begin{aligned}
&P \overset{t}{\rightrightarrows} Q \quad \textit{iff}\\
&\qquad \exists n > 0, m_i \geq 0, \textit{ and times } t_i > 0 \quad \textit{with } P \overset{\tau^{m_0}}{\longrightarrow}\overset{t_1}{\rightsquigarrow}\overset{\tau^{m_1}}{\longrightarrow} \ldots \overset{t_n}{\rightsquigarrow}\overset{\tau^{m_n}}{\longrightarrow} Q\\
&\qquad \qquad \qquad \qquad \qquad \qquad \qquad \qquad \textit{and } t = t_0 + t_1 + \cdots + t_n
\end{aligned}
$$

We define our fundamental equivalence as in the strong case using these modified relations and obtain $\approx$ as the largest weak bisimulation It may be shown that $\sim$ is a refinement of $\approx$, *i.e.* $\sim \subseteq \approx$. We would certainly expect this since we wish to consider $\sim$ processes as identical and hence not distinguishable by any other meaningful equivalence.

Thus all the algebraic laws we established for $\sim$ are sound for $\approx$. We also have the important new law that $\tau.P \approx P$. Unfortunately this law makes $\approx$ fail to be a congruence. In particular the initial τ on the LHS can resolve a $+$ context in a way which the RHS cannot match. Thus we have for example

$$\tau.\alpha.nil \approx \alpha.nil \quad \text{but} \quad \tau.\alpha.nil + \beta.nil \not\approx \alpha.nil + \beta.nil$$

since in the latter equation the left hand side may become (silently) $\alpha.nil$ and thus unable to perform a β while the right hand side may not move internally (*i.e. via* τ actions) to any bisimilar term and will thus will always be able to perform a β. This is the usual example of the problem caused by initial τ actions but we also have an interesting new problem. We know

$$\tau.\mathcal{R}[s \leftarrow f].P(s) \approx \mathcal{R}[s \leftarrow f].P(s)$$

but if we write

$$P \triangleq [\tfrac{1}{2}]\tau.\mathcal{R}[s \leftarrow f].P(s) \dot{+} [\tfrac{1}{2}]\,\mathcal{R}[s \leftarrow f].P(s)$$

$$Q \triangleq [\tfrac{1}{2}]\,\mathcal{R}[s \leftarrow f].P(s) \dot{+} [\tfrac{1}{2}]\,\mathcal{R}[s \leftarrow f].P(s)$$

we have $P \not\approx Q$ since writing $S = \{P(t) : t \in \mathbb{R}^+\}$ we have $\mu(P, S) = \frac{1}{2}$ while $\mu(Q, S) = 1$.

This means we cannot use $\approx$ for algebraic reasoning. We require a congruence defined by $P = Q$ iff $\forall$ contexts $C[-]\quad C[P] \approx C[Q]$.

It is difficult to immediately prove properties of this $=$ relation and so we start with an alternative three stage characterization of equality. We define $P =_1 Q$ if any single action makes them weakly bisimilar, $P =_2 Q$ if any evolution makes them $=_1$, and $P =_3 Q$ if their probabilistic transitions respect $=_2$.

It can be shown that $=_3$ is in fact the congruence associated with $\approx$, the relation we have chosen as $=$. The proof is straightforward but long.

We are now in the position of standard CCS with $\sim\, \subset\, =\, \subset\, \approx$ and $\sim$ and $=$ congruences. In particular, we have the following rules analogous to those of CCS.

Theorem 5.1.

1. $\alpha.(t).\tau.P = \alpha.(t).P$.
2. $\tau.P + P = \tau.P$.
3. $\alpha.(P + \tau.Q) = \alpha.(P + \tau.Q) + \alpha.Q$.

We also have the rules from elementary probability theory for amalgamating nested probabilistic sums. For example

$$[\tfrac{1}{2}]P \dot{+} [\tfrac{1}{2}]\left([\tfrac{1}{2}]Q \dot{+} [\tfrac{1}{2}]R\right) = [\tfrac{1}{2}]P \dot{+} [\tfrac{1}{4}]Q \dot{+} [\tfrac{1}{4}]R$$

Similarly we can combine probabilistic sums with a final $\mathcal{R}[s \leftarrow f].P$ for example

$$\sum [q_i]\,\mathcal{R}[s \leftarrow f_i].P = \mathcal{R}[s \leftarrow f].P$$

for the appropriate density function f. Taking these together with the axioms listed in theorems 4.1,4.2,4.3,5.1 we have moved from operational semantics and a formal semantic definition of equality to a set of purely syntactic algebraic equations. These include the expansion theorem and (as shown in section 6) enable us to move from simulations written in a specificational style to other equivalent simulations. The transformation may be mechanisable or at least mechanically verifiable and the resulting simulation may be simpler, more efficient, or at least in some standard form such as a GSMP.

6. Examples and speculations

6.1 Generalised Semi-Markov Processes (GSMP)

The GSMP as discussed in Whitt [21] is one of the most general yet tractable stochastic processes for modelling discrete event simulations (see *e.g.* the detailed exposition in Shedler [19] or Iglehart and Shedler [9]). We show we can represent systems modelled by a GSMP in our formalism.

Heuristically a GSMP has some countable set of states A through which it moves at times determined by a finite set of clocks C. Each state has associated with it some subset of the clocks, $E(a)$, specified by the function $E : A \to 2^C$. These are the clocks which will race to trigger a transition from that state. Once a state has been entered the clocks run down synchronously until one, say $c \in C$, has reached zero. Then a state transition occurs. The new state is chosen randomly by the probability function $p : A \times C \to (A \to [0,1])$ which assigns a probability to each possible choice of next state based on the current state and whichever clock ran down first. The new state has a new set of associated clocks. Where these include clocks already set for the previous state their settings remain unchanged. Where the clocks were not associated to the previous state they need to be set. This is done by choosing a time with a probability density function depending on both the previous and current states and events $f : A \times C \times A \times C \to (\mathbb{R}^+ \to [0,1])$ (we write $f(a, c, a', c')$).

Finally we need to specify an initial distribution $q : A \to [0,1]$ to choose our initial state and an initial clock setting probability $f_0 : A \times C \to (\mathbb{R}^+ \to [0,1])$ (*i.e.* for each state $a \in A$ and clock $c \in E(a)$ we have a distribution $f_0(a, c)$).

Our representation of the GSMP selects an initial state *via* the distribution q.

$$GSMP \triangleq \sum_{a \in A} [q(a)] St0_a$$

In parallel with this state it starts all clocks associated with the events in $E(a)$.

$$St0_a \triangleq St_a \mid \prod_{c \in E(a)} Clock0_{ac}$$

These initial clocks have a special distribution f_0. Here the to_c action says clock c has timed out, while the can_c action is used to cancel the clock.

$$Clock0_{ac} \triangleq \mathcal{R}[s \leftarrow f_0(a, c)].(s).to_c + \overline{can_c}[]$$

Each state waits for any clock from $E(a)$ to time out and cause its state to change:

$$St_a \triangleq \sum_{c \in E(a)} \overline{to_c}.StCl_{ac}$$

Note that this behaviour is potentially non-deterministic. However a condition on the distributions of our clock settings can ensure that the probability of two clocks timing out at the same instant, and hence a non-deterministic choice having to be made, is zero.

The state having received a time out chooses its succeeding state a' *via*,

$$StCl_{ac} \triangleq \sum_{a' \in A} [p(a,c)(a')] StClSt_{aca'}$$

then it cancels any outstanding and no longer required clocks.

$$StClSt_{aca'} \triangleq (\bigodot_{c' \in E(a) \setminus \{c\} \setminus E(a')} can_{c'}).StClSt1_{aca'}$$

where $\bigodot$ abbreviates finite indexed multiple prefixing (where the order does not matter). Finally it starts the new state and any new clocks required.

$$StClSt1_{aca'} \triangleq St_{a'} \mid \prod_{c' \in E(a') \setminus (E(a) \setminus \{c\})} Clock_{aca'c'}$$

These new clocks use their standard distribution.

$$Clock_{aca'c'} \triangleq \mathcal{R}[s \leftarrow f(a,c,a',c')].(s).to_{c'} + \overline{can_{c'}}$$

6.2 Two processor queue

We return to the simple example presented in the informal description of our language. We consider a situation where a sequence of tasks arrive randomly, forming a workload. Then two processors service the queue, first come first served. The Workload waits a random time and then restarts itself along with a new Task.

$$Workload \triangleq \mathcal{R}[s \leftarrow f_1].(s).(Workload \mid Task)$$

The Task requests a processor, executes for a random time, and then releases the processor and terminates.

$$Task \triangleq \overline{procreq}[].\mathcal{R}[s \leftarrow f_2].(s).procrel$$

The Processor accepts a request, accepts a release and restarts.

$$Proc_1 \triangleq procreq[].\overline{procrel}[].Proc_1$$

Then our initial presentation of the system will be

$$System_1 \triangleq (Workload \mid Proc_1 \mid Proc_1) \setminus \{procreq, procrel\}$$

However if we examine the behaviour of $System_1$ we find it can do nothing (except $\overset{t}{\rightrightarrows}$) and hence it is $=$ to *nil*. This is because we have made all its internal behaviour invisible. We need to decide what part of that behaviour we wish to monitor. So we add probe actions to the processor which amounts to a decision to evaluate processor utilisation.

$$Proc = procreq[].probe_1.\overline{procrel}[].probe_2.Proc$$

Here $probe_1$ indicates to the observer the acquisition of a processor while $probe_2$ indicates its release. So our new system is

$$System \triangleq (Workload \mid Proc \mid Proc) \setminus \{procreq, procrel\}$$

We can rewrite *System*, using the expansion theorem repeatedly, as:

$$System = \mathcal{R}[s \leftarrow f_1].Pr0(s)$$

where

$$\begin{array}{rcl}
Pr0(s) & \triangleq & (s).\mathcal{R}[s' \leftarrow f_1].\mathcal{R}[s'' \leftarrow f_2].probe_1.Pr1(s', s'') \\
Pr1(s, s') & \triangleq & (s).\tau.\mathcal{R}[s'' \leftarrow f_1].\mathcal{R}[s''' \leftarrow f_2].probe_1.Pr2(s'', s' - s, s''') \\
 & & +(s').probe_2.Pr0(s - s') \\
Pr2(s, s', s'') & \triangleq & (s).\tau.\mathcal{R}[s''' \leftarrow f_1].Prq(s''', s' - s, s'' - s, 1) \\
 & & +(s').probe_2.Pr1(s - s', s'' - s') \\
 & & +(s'').probe_2.Pr1(s - s'', s' - s'') \\
Prq(s, s', s'', 1) & \triangleq & (s).\tau.\mathcal{R}[s''' \leftarrow f_1].Prq(s''', s' - s, s'' - s, 2) \\
 & & +(s').probe_2.\mathcal{R}[s''' \leftarrow f_2].probe_1.Pr2(s - s', s'' - s', s''') \\
 & & +(s'').probe_2.\mathcal{R}[s''' \leftarrow f_2].probe_1.Pr2(s - s'', s' - s'', s''') \\
Prq(s, s', s'', n) & \triangleq & (s).\tau.\mathcal{R}[s''' \leftarrow f_1].Prq(s''', s' - s, s'' - s, n + 1) \\
 & & +(s').probe_2.\mathcal{R}[s''' \leftarrow f_2].probe_1 \\
 & & \qquad .Prq(s - s', s'' - s', s''', n - 1) \\
 & & +(s'').probe_2.\mathcal{R}[s''' \leftarrow f_2].probe_1 \\
 & & \qquad .Prq(s - s'', s' - s'', s''', n - 1)
\end{array}$$

for $n > 1$.

The relationship between this version and a Generalized Semi-Markov Process representation should be clear (see section 6.1). Each named process represents a state and its parameters represent clocks. At each state transition either a clock is passed on after having run down or is reset by a random choice. Thus we have taken a high-level description of a simulation and rewritten it using formal rules into a low-level GSMP style description.

6.3 Equivalence

Consider now a random walk on the integers which is stochastically equivalent to a single server queue with exponential distributions. We represent exponential distributions by their rates r_1, r_2, r_3. The equations for a simple random walk are:

$$\begin{aligned} W_0 &\triangleq \mathcal{R}[s \leftarrow r_1].\epsilon_0.(s).\,([p]W_0 \dot{+} [q]W_1) \\ W_n &\triangleq \mathcal{R}[s \leftarrow r_1].\epsilon_n.(s).\,([p]W_{n-1} \dot{+} [q]W_{n+1}) \qquad n > 0 \end{aligned}$$

The ϵ_n actions here are probes showing us by an impatient action when we reach a state in which the system is just starting a wait at position n.

A single server, single class queue is described by:

$$\begin{aligned} B_0 &\triangleq \epsilon_0.\overline{\alpha}[].B_1 \\ B_n &\triangleq \epsilon_n.\,(\overline{\alpha}[].B_{n+1} + \gamma[].B_{n+1}) \qquad n > 0 \\ S &\triangleq \mathcal{R}[s \leftarrow r_2].(s).\overline{\gamma}[].S \\ P &\triangleq \mathcal{R}[s \leftarrow r_3].(s).\,(\alpha[] \mid P) \end{aligned}$$

Here α represents an arrival while γ represents a departure or service. The ϵ_n actions this time show when the queue has just obtained n items. We then define

$$Q_n \triangleq (B_n \mid S \mid P)\backslash\{\alpha, \beta, \gamma\}$$

and wish to show $W_n = Q_n$. Using axiom 16, theorems 4.1 and 4.2, the expansion theorem (twice) and theorem 5.1 (axiom 1), together with properties of the exponential distribution, we derive:

$$\begin{aligned} Q_n =& \mathcal{R}[s \leftarrow r_2 + r_3].\Big([\tfrac{r_2}{r_2+r_3}]\,\mathcal{R}[s' \leftarrow r_3].\epsilon_n.(s)\,(B_{n-1} \mid S \mid (s').\,(\alpha[] \mid P)) \\ & \dot{+}[\tfrac{r_3}{r_2+r_3}]\,\mathcal{R}[s' \leftarrow r_2].\epsilon_n.(s)\,(B_{n+1} \mid (s').\overline{\gamma}[].S \mid P)\backslash\{\alpha, \beta, \gamma\}\Big) \end{aligned}$$

To complete the transformation we introduce the further axiom

$$\alpha.\sum[q_i]Q_i = \sum[q_i]\alpha.Q_i$$

This axiom is intuitively obvious but it is not sound under bisimulation. This is because the LHS has a state in which it has performed α but not yet made the choice while the RHS has no such state.

7. Conclusions

We have formally presented a language powerful enough to write both arbitrary parallel programs (since it includes CCS) and arbitrary discrete event simulations. We do not rule out non-determinism, indeed we adopt the CCS approach of explaining parallelism via non-determinism. Our approach is to say that a process which exhibits non-determinism is not a valid simulation in the sense that our chosen performance measures still have some dependence on the resolution of this non-determinism. In other words we have not adequately specified the behaviour of some parts of the system to derive its performance.

We have presented a formal semantics for the language and this allows us to prove properties of programs written in the language at a semantic level. We have also derived algebraic tools which allow us to transform programs at a syntactic level and, for example, find out if they do exhibit non-determinism. We can use these tools to transform a program written in a clear high-level style into one that is closer to well understood models of simulation such as GSMPs or is perhaps more efficient or simpler to understand.

References

1. J.C.M. Baeten and J.A. Bergstra, "Real time process algebra", Technical Report CS-R9053, Centrum voor Wiskunde en Informatica, October 1990.
2. L. Chen, "An interleaving model for real-time systems", Technical Report ECS-LFCS-91-184, LFCS, University of Edinburgh, November 1991.
3. L. Chen, S. Anderson and F. Moller, "A Timed Calculus of Communicating Systems", Technical report, University of Edinburgh, 1990.
4. A.J. Field and P.G. Harrison, "Functional Programming", Addison Wesley, 1988.
5. N. Götz, U. Herzog and M. Rettelbach, "TIPP — a language for timed processes and performance evaluation", Technical Report 4/92 IMMD7, University of Erlangen-Nürnberg, November 1992.
6. H.A. Hansson, "Time and Probability in Formal Design of Distributed Systems", PhD thesis, Uppsala University, P.O. Box 520, S-751 20 Uppsala, Sweden, 1991.
7. M. Hennessy and T. Regan, "A process algebra for timed systems", Technical report, Sussex University, April 1991.
8. J. Hillston, "A Compositional Approach to Performance Modelling", PhD thesis, Edinburgh University, 1994.
9. D.L. Iglehart and G.S. Shedler, "Simulation of non-markovian systems", *IBM Journal of Research and Development*, **27** (5), pp. 472–479, September 1983.
10. M. Loève, "Probability Theory", Van Nostrand, 1963.
11. R.E. Milne and C. Strachey, "A Theory of Programming Language Semantics", Chapman and Hall, 1976.
12. R. Milner, "Communication and Concurrency", Prentice Hall, 1989.
13. F. Moller and C. Tofts, "A Temporal Calculus of Communicating Systems", In Concur '90, number 458 in LNCS, 1990.
14. F. Moller and C. Tofts, "Behavioural abstraction in TCCS", In Proceedings of the 19th Colloquium on Automata Languages and Programming, **623** in LNCS, pp. 579–570, 1992.
15. X. Nicollin and J. Sifakis, "An overview and synthesis on timed process algebras", In Kim G. Larsen and Arne Skou, editors, Proc. CAV 91, **575** in LNCS, pp. 376–398, 1991.
16. I. Phillips, "Refusal testing", *TCS*, **50**, pp. 241–284, 1987.

17. A. Pnueli, "Linear and branching structures in the semantics and logics of reactive systems", In Proceedings of the Twelfth Colloquium on Automata Languages and Programming, **194** of *LNCS*, 1985.
18. S. Schneider, "An operational semantics for timed CSP", Technical report, Programming Research Group, Oxford University, February 1991.
19. G.S. Shedler, "Regenerative Stochastic Simulation", Academic Press, 1993.
20. B. Strulo, "Process Algebra for Discrete Event Simulation", PhD Thesis, Imperial College, University of London, 1994.
21. W.Whitt, "Continuity of Generalized Semi-Markov Processes", *Mathematics of Operations Research*, **5**, pp. 14–23, 1980.
22. W. Yi, "A Calculus of Real Time Systems", PhD thesis, Chalmers University of Technology, S-412 96 Göteborg Sweden, 1991.
23. W. Yi, "CCS + Time = an interleaving model for real time systems", In Proceedings of the Eighteenth Colloquium on Automata Languages and Programming, **510** in LNCS, pp. 217–228, 1991.

GSPN and SPA Compared in Practice

Modelling A Distributed Mail System

S. Donatelli[1], H. Hermanns[2], J. Hillston[3], and M. Ribaudo[1]

[1] University of Torino, Italy
[2] University of Erlangen-Nürnberg, Germany
[3] University of Edinburgh, UK

Summary. Generalized Stochastic Petri Nets (GSPN) and Stochastic Process Algebras (SPA) can both be used to study functionality as well as performance of parallel and distributed systems. In order to provide insight into the similarities and differences between the formalisms, we study the model construction process in both by means of a large example, a distributed electronic mail system. This comparison of the modelling facilities highlights points where ideas and techniques have been, or can be, exchanged between the two paradigms.

1. Introduction

Generalized Stochastic Petri Nets (GSPN) is a well-established high level modelling paradigm which has been widely applied in performance analysis. In contrast, Stochastic Process Algebras (SPA), such as PEPA [14], TIPP [9], and MPA [2, 4] have recently emerged and are yet to gain general acceptance. Inspired by process algebras such as CCS and CSP, SPA are algebraically based paradigms which provide a model construction methodology allowing models of large systems to be built out of smaller building blocks.

This paper relates GSPN and SPA to each other by means of a case study taken from the field of communication systems. The reader is assumed to be familiar with the main concepts of GSPN as well as SPA, since introductions to both topics are readily available [1, 9].

The paper is organised as follows. Section 2 briefly compares GSPN and SPA from different perspectives. This comparison will subsequently be illustrated by means of the example. The system under investigation is sketched in Section 3 and modelled in both formalisms in Section 4. The similarities and differences between the two models, illustrating the points discussed in Section 2, are presented in Section 5. Section 6 illustrates the use of a recently developed SPN semantics of SPA to translate a model from one formalism into the other, and the differences which arise when the SPN model is formed in this way. Finally, Section 7 presents a brief summary and indicates some challenging areas for future work.

2. Comparison between GSPN and SPA

In this section we briefly recapitulate the comparison of [7] from the general perspective of Stochastic Process Algebras.

2.1 Notational level

The first and most obvious difference is on the notational level. GSPN offer a *graphical* representation of a system, that is attractive for visualisation purposes. Many additional concepts like inhibitor arcs or colours have been developed to address specific problems (e.g. blocking, large systems, etc.). On the other hand, SPA provide a *textual* specification language, close to programming languages (e.g. LOTOS).
This notational difference appears to be immense. However, the formal translation from SPA to GSPN, due to [21], shows that the expressiveness of the two formalisms is similar.

2.2 State versus Action

The notion of *state* differs in the two formalisms. For GSPN, the marking defines a (distributed) state in which the firing of transitions evolves the model from state to state. SPA, in contrast, are behaviour-oriented descriptions where the system is described by the sequences of *actions* its components can engage in.

2.3 Compositionality and Equivalences

One of the central features of model construction with SPA is the ability to build complex systems out of smaller ones by composition. Therefore the specification reflects the modular structure of the system. On the contrary, the corresponding GSPN is a *flat* representation of the system.
There is no well-established notion of equivalence for GSPN which admits formal reasoning about different descriptions. In SPA the existence of sophisticated equivalence notions which respect the language operators is the key to constructive system design. Notions like Markovian Bisimulation allow the exchange of components within a system specification with equivalent ones, without affecting the system's behaviour (functional and temporal).

2.4 Abstraction Mechanism

When specifying large systems it is useful to have suitable means to hide internal aspects of components (timing as well as functionality). GSPN do not support a clear notion of functional abstraction whereas temporal abstraction is provided by immediate transitions.

In contrast, SPA include a hiding operator dedicated to functional abstraction. Temporal abstraction is currently under development. At the moment the use of immediate actions is allowed in TIPP; their formal treatment is founded [13, 19], but *not* yet automated.

2.5 Analysis Techniques

Functional as well as performance analysis is supported by both formalisms. Analysis may take place at the description level or on the underlying representation of the full state space. This lower level description corresponds to the Markov chain used for performance evaluation. It is clearly preferable, especially for large systems, to analyse systems at the high level.
For GSPN, there is a rich family of structural analysis techniques working on the high level which is the net itself. These techniques provide a deep insight into the properties of the model.
High level analysis of SPA specifications can reveal certain *basic* properties like finite state space or (necessary conditions) for ergodicity. Current work focusses on characterising SPA models which generate Markov chains susceptible to efficient solution techniques, such as product form and time scale decomposition [22, 11, 16].
On the Markov chain level the situation is similar. Many efficient solution methods are known and implemented for GSPN, for example:

- Direct & iterative solution methods;
- Techniques using model information, e.g.
  - Detection of product form models [8];
  - Detection of symmetries based on lumpability [5];
  - Superposed GSPN using tensor algebra [6];
- Randomization [17];

For SPA the class of implemented algorithms is mostly restricted to standard techniques. Sophisticated techniques exploiting model information are nevertheless known:

- State space reduction based on lumpability [15];
- Regularities e.g. spectral expansion [18], near complete decomposability [16];
- Hierarchies, e.g. decomposition/aggregation, tensor algebra [4, 20];

The definition of performance measures is another interesting difference. The natural way for GSPN is to define measures via *token distribution* in certain places of interest. Due to their inherent behaviour orientation this is not straightforward for SPA. Approaches to define state oriented measures have been proposed, e.g. by associating rewards with certain activities [14]. This approach in turn is natural for transition based measures such as throughput, that need a more detailed knowledge in the GSPN context.

2.6 Tool Support

Because of the long tradition of research and application of GSPN for model construction there is a large (and still increasing) number of tools available that support the design process as well as the subsequent analysis. The tools range from commercial software products up to public domain tools for special purposes. The opposite is true for SPA — there are only two prototype tools that support the model construction and evaluation: TIPP-Tool, partly developed within the QMIPS-project focussing on numerical evaluation and PEPA-Workbench, allowing symbolic analysis of medium size systems.

2.7 Translation from SPA to GSPN

It is evident that currently there is much more support, both in terms of developed theory and tools, for GSPN. Therefore it could be beneficial to establish a translation from SPA to GSPN which would allow SPA to take advantage of this greater level of support.
Any SPA model can be represented as a GSPN and details of the translation can be found in [21] where, following the approach introduced by Goltz [10], a compositional net semantics for SPA has been defined. Starting from the net representations of two components P_1 and P_2 it is possible to derive the net representation of the system $Q := P_1 \ op\ P_2$ (where *op* is a syntactic operator of the language) by defining appropriate operations at the net level. Due to lack of space we cannot describe here the entire procedure and we simply show, in Figure 2.1, the mapping of each syntactic operator of the language into the corresponding GSPN model.

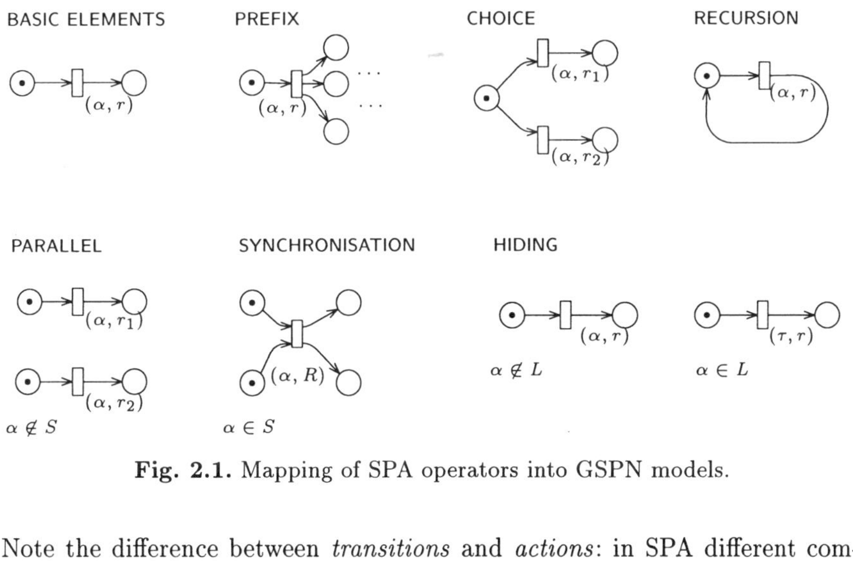

Fig. 2.1. Mapping of SPA operators into GSPN models.

Note the difference between *transitions* and *actions*: in SPA different components can perform actions with the same name resulting in several transitions representing the same action; in GSPN, by definition, transitions must have distinct names. Therefore, the translation includes a labelling function $l : T \rightarrow Act \times \mathbb{R}^+$ which maps transition names into (*action name, rate*) pairs.

3. A Distributed Electronic Mail System

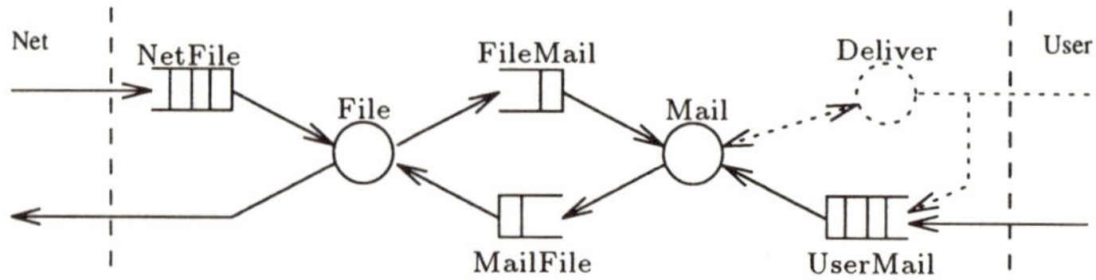

Fig. 3.1. The e-mail system under consideration.

In this section we illustrate the comparison between GSPN and SPA by means of an example taken from the field of communication systems: a distributed electronic mail system. The original system was first studied in [3], where CCS is used to investigate its functionality. Practical experience showed that the system contained a deadlock[1] and this was confirmed by the CCS model. In [12] this model was extensively analysed with respect to its performance and reliability, using SPA. Here we consider the system represented in the different modelling styles of GSPN and SPA. The system consists of three entities and four buffers (cf. Fig. 3.1) which interact as follows:

- `File` is responsible for the 'blue book' file transfer protocol, in particular:
  - passes files from the `MailFile` buffer to the network,
  - passes incoming files to the `FileMail` buffer,
- `Mail` is responsible for the 'grey book' electronic mail protocol; thus it
  - passes messages from the user (buffer `UserMail`) to the buffer `MailFile`,
  - reads mail out of buffer `FileMail`, creates a process `Deliver`, and waits until this process has finished,
  - afterwards it handles all files contained in `UserMail` (prevents delay for posting messages),
- `Deliver` sends the message to the user, or forwards it to (one or more) other domains, dependent on the users advice.

[1] The system was running on DEC VAX/VMS at the University of Edinburgh in the 1980s. After a long period of continuous working the system deadlocked.

4. Modelling the system

The dynamic creation of a process `Deliver`, whenever incoming mail leaves the `Mail` entity, is modelled statically as a single component that is responsible for delivering and forwarding, which is invoked from the `Mail` entity.
For performance evaluation, all execution times are assumed to be exponential and our basic unit is one second. The time for copying pointers is assumed to be negligible compared with delivering a whole file anywhere which has the longer mean time, $10^{-3}s$. The internal buffers are modelled with only one position, whilst the external buffers, which collect mail from users and from the network, have 5 positions. These buffer sizes are unrealistic but the intention of the example is to illustrate both approaches with a modest sized system which is easy to understand. This restriction does not reflect a limitation of either modelling technique.

4.1 GSPN model

The GSPN model shown in Fig. 4.1 is a *flat* graphical representation of the e-mail system. Several activities (removing of a message from a buffer, synchronisation between `Mail` and `Deliver`) take a negligible amount of time compared with the (decisive) arrival rates of incoming and outgoing mail and they have been modelled using immediate transitions.
The main disadvantage of this model is that it does not reflect the structure of the system and therefore it is difficult to identify at the net level the entities (processes and buffers) within the system.
Performing the structural analysis techniques we found that all the places are covered by some P-semiflow and all the transitions are covered by some T-semiflow. The first property ensures that the net is bounded, i.e. its state space is finite while the second property is a necessary, but not sufficient, condition for the initial marking to be a home state.
Among all the P-semiflows those listed in the table below are particularly interesting since they allow us to identify the places that belong to each process.

$p_1 + p_2 = 5$	`NetFile`
$p_3 + p_4 = 1$	`FileMail`
$p_5 + p_6 = 1$	`MailFile`
$p_7 + p_8 = 5$	`UserMail`
$f_1 + f_2 + f_3 = 1$	`File`
$m_1 + m_2 + m_3 + m_4 + m_5 = 1$	`Mail`
$d_1 + d_2 + d_3 + d_4 = 1$	`Deliver`

Once established that the net is bounded we can compute the underlying state space. The reachability graph of this model has 2880 states, but most of them are vanishing: only 903 states are tangible and only these need to be

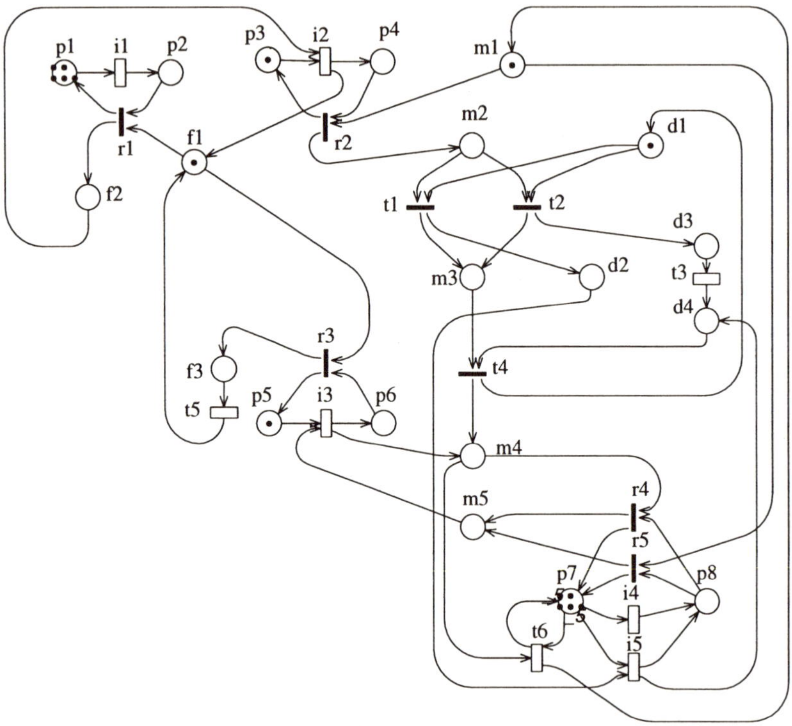

Fig. 4.1. GSPN model of the e-mail system.

considered for performance evaluation. Furthermore, the reachability graph contains the following dead markings[2]

M_{d_1} :	$5 * p_2 + p_4 + p_6 + 5 * p_8 + d_2 + m_3 + f_2$
M_{d_2} :	$5 * p_2 + p_4 + p_5 + 5 * p_8 + d_2 + m_3 + f_2$
M_{d_3} :	$5 * p_2 + p_4 + p_6 + 5 * p_8 + d_1 + m_5 + f_2$

M_{d_3} represents a situation in which the four buffers are full, the `Deliver` is waiting for the `Mail` process, the `Mail` wants to insert a message into the buffer `MailFile`, and the `File` wants to insert a message into the buffer `FileMail` (circular waiting). The other two deadlock situations are more interesting. They differ only in the status of the `MailFile` buffer which does not contribute to the deadlock. The situation occurs when the buffer `UserMail` is full, but `Deliver` wants to post a message into it. The buffer cannot be emptied because the process `Mail` is waiting for `Deliver` to finish.

[2] A marking is described as a list of non empty places: $n * p$ means that place p contains n tokens (if n is omitted p contains one token).

A manual reset can be introduced performing recovery actions modelled by timed transitions with high firing rates. These transitions are enabled in the dead markings and their firings move back the net into the initial state. This leads to an irreducible Markov chain suited to steady state analysis. An approximation of the MTTF of a given deadlock can be computed by considering the inverse of the throughput of the corresponding timed transition. As we said previously, the natural way of defining performance measures in GSPN is via the distribution of the tokens in certain places. In this case for instance, we can compute the mean number of tokens in place p_2 which gives the mean number of messages waiting to be delivered to the `File` process. For the sake of the comparison with the SPA specification we can replace the immediate transitions of the GSPN model of Figure 4.1 with timed ones, so that all transitions take some time (mean $10^{-4}s$) to be completed. With this transformation the reachability graph has 2880 tangible states and three deadlocks.

4.2 SPA Specification

The components of the SPA specification correspond directly to the system entities described in Section 3. The process *File* manages the file transfer, it collects incoming mail from the net, and delivers it to the *Mail* process, or takes outgoing mail from an internal buffer to deliver it to the net.

$$\begin{array}{rcl} File & := & (nf\_remove, 10^4).(fm\_insert, 10^4).File \\ & + & (mf\_remove, 10^4).(file\_send, 10^3).File \end{array}$$

The *Mail* process forwards outgoing mail to the *File* process or passes incoming mail to the process *Deliver* and waits until the mail is delivered. It will process all user mail, until the *UserMail* buffer is empty, before handling incoming mail.

$$\begin{array}{rcl} Mail & := & (fm\_remove, 10^4).(md\_start, 10^4).(md\_stop, 10^4).Mail1 \\ & + & (um\_remove, 10^4).(mf\_insert, 10^4).Mail1 \\ Mail1 & := & (um\_empty, 10^4).Mail \\ & + & (um\_remove, 10^4).(mf\_insert, 10^4).Mail1 \end{array}$$

The process *Deliver* delivers the mail to the user with probability p; with probability $1-p$ the mail is forwarded to another site, i.e. it is copied into the buffer responsible for outgoing mail.

$$\begin{array}{rcl} Deliver & := & (md\_start, p).(letter\_deliver, 10^3).(md\_stop, -).Deliver \\ & + & (md\_start, 1-p).(um\_insert, 10^4).(md\_stop, -).Deliver \end{array}$$

In order to allow a structured description, we assume that the buffers, *NetFile*, *FileMail*, *MailFile* and *UserMail* are passive—their temporal behaviour is determined by the active processes using them. We modelled them in the usual way, sketched here in terms of a standard buffer:

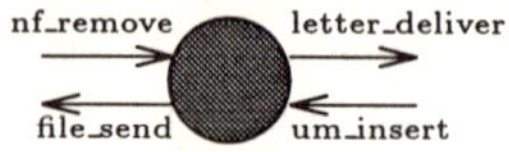

Fig. 4.2. Abstract view of the system's functionality.

$$\begin{aligned}
Buffer_0 &:= (insert, -).Buffer_1 \ + \ (empty, -).Buffer_0 \\
Buffer_i &:= (insert, -).Buffer_{i+1} \ + \ (remove, -).Buffer_{i-1} \\
Buffer_{max} &:= (remove, -).Buffer_{\max -1}
\end{aligned}$$

The overall system is modelled by the parallel composition of all processes. Functional abstraction ensures that only those activities which interact with the environment are visible (cf. Figure 4.2). Note that this abstraction does not affect the temporal behaviour of the system. An external observer will easily witness the internal delay due to the message processing mechanism.

$$\begin{aligned}
System \;&:=\; (NetFile\|_\emptyset FileMail\|_\emptyset MailFile\|_\emptyset UserMail)\,\|_{S_2} \\
&\qquad\qquad (File\|_\emptyset(Mail\|_{S_1}Deliver))\,\backslash(S_1 \cup S_2)
\end{aligned}$$

where

$$\begin{aligned}
S_1 &:= \{md_start, md_stop\} \\
S_2 &:= \{um_insert, um_remove, nf_remove, fm_insert, fm_remove, \\
&\qquad mf_insert, mf_remove, um_empty\}
\end{aligned}$$

This specification can be analysed syntactically. Its structure[3] ensures that the state space will be finite. Applying the operational semantic rules leads to a transition system and Markov chain with exactly the same number of states and deadlocks as in the case of the GSPN model with all timed transitions. This model is susceptible to the performance analysis on the Markov chain. Using the moment method, the mean time to failure (MTTF) of the system dependent on the rate of incoming and outgoing mail λ $(= \lambda_{in} = \lambda_{out})$ has been computed [12].

Here the manual reset is represented by adding appropriate actions with high activity rates which are enabled when the system becomes deadlocked. Unlike in the GSPN model, it is not easy to compute the mean number of messages waiting to be delivered by associating a reward with activities. However the throughput of outgoing messages is readily computed by associating a reward of 10^3 with the activity *file_send.*

It would also be possible to abstract away some timing information in the SPA specification, as in the GSPN model, but currently there is no tool support for such an extension.

[3] This syntactic property is known as *rs-freeness*: No static combinator like $\|_S$ or $\backslash$ occurs in the scope of a recursive defining equation

5. Comparing the developed models

As usual, the most striking difference between the GSPN model and the SPA model is notational. The textual representation of SPA makes the components of the system immediately apparent. Although we showed how this information can be derived in the GSPN, it is not readily available. In contrast, quantitative information such as the number of places in the buffer is perhaps more accessible as a number of tokens in the GSPN than as a subscript to the process name in the SPA model.

The distributed state is clear in the GSPN models where several transitions may be enabled at the same time. An analogous situation can occur in the SPA if several of the top level processes in the specification enable individual activities at the same time. However, recognising the currently active parts of the model is more difficult in the SPA model.

The benefits of the temporal abstraction in the GSPN as a means to reduce the state space has been demonstrated. The benefits of the functional abstraction provided by the SPA model are not so immediately apparent. However the hiding of all the interactions between the processes and the internal buffers ensures that if this system were embedded into a larger one no direct interference with the existing processes could occur. No similar mechanism is available in the GSPN: this is to be expected since no constructive methodology for model building is available in GSPN.

Performance evaluation proceeds in the same way for both models via the underlying Markov chain. However, we have shown how the formalisms take different approaches to the definition of performance measures as rewards over the steady state probability distribution. State based measures are much more easily defined in GSPN whereas transition based measures are more easily defined in SPA.

6. Transforming SPA to GSPN

In this section we investigate an alternative approach to developing a GSPN[4] model of the system—applying the translation rules introduced in Section 2. directly to the SPA specification.

Applying the formal transformation of [21] leads to a labelled GSPN which reflects the modular structure of the mailing system. Figure 6.1 shows the translation of the system's entities in isolation. For readability we do not present here the complex net which is obtained modelling the vast number of synchronisations between buffers and processes. Its reachability graph is larger than the original one, it has 4506 states and 5 deadlocks. This phenomenon is caused by the *denotational* transformation style: if two identical

[4] In fact the model developed is an SPN model since immediate activities do not appear in the above SPA specification.

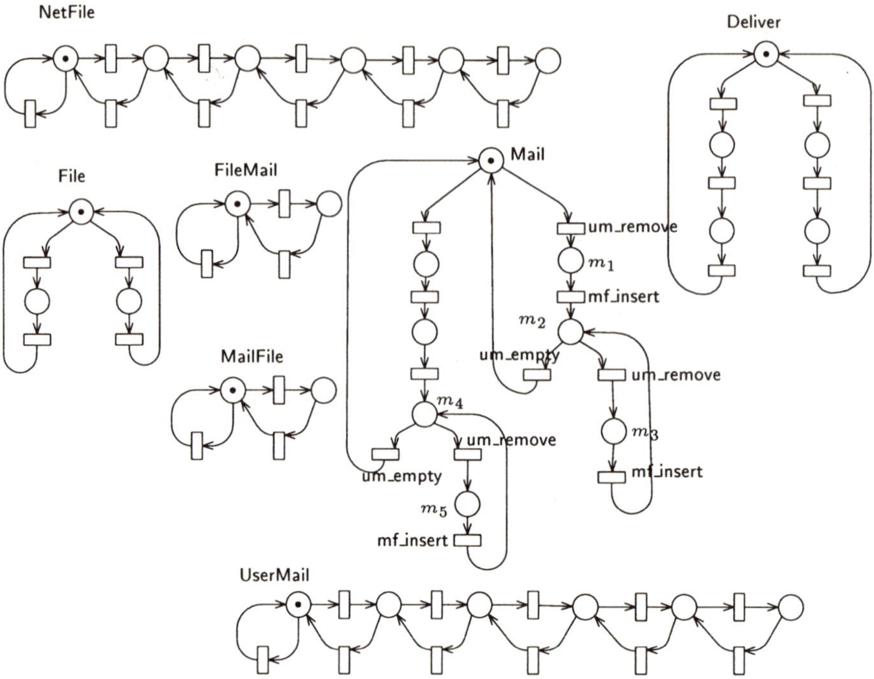

Fig. 6.1. "Modular" GSPN model without synchronisations.

submodels are combined via another operator like the choice operator, these submodels are repeatedly represented in the net.

A closer look at the `Mail` specification illustrates this point. There the process `Mail1` is active after a successful mail delivery (i.e. after *md_stop*) or after forwarding a mail towards process `File` with *mf_insert*, whereas in the operational semantics used to evolve the SPA model this process (and all its subsequent behaviour) only appears once.

On the other hand, two distinct places (m_2 and m_4) represent `Mail1` in the GSPN model of Figure 6.1, leading to two different markings in the underlying reachability graph.

Using this additional insight we can reduce the GSPN representation of the `Mail` process and obtain the smaller net shown in Figure 6.2: `Mail1` is represented only once by folding the pairs of places (m_2, m_4) and (m_3, m_5) and the corresponding transitions with the same label. Moreover only one of two repeated patterns of behaviour (transition sequences *um_remove*, mf_insert) is explicitly modelled in the reduced GSPN model of Figure 6.2.

Another reduction can be performed when modelling a buffer. In the upper part of Figure 6.1 is shown the net corresponding to the `NetFile` buffer. In this case the net can be folded to a more compact representation, using only

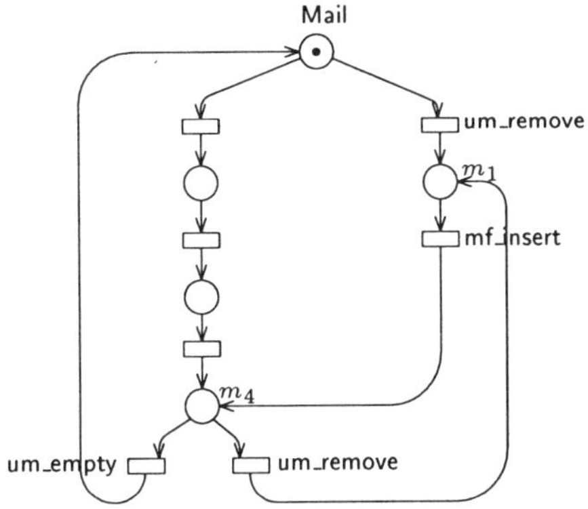

Fig. 6.2. Reduced GSPN model for the `Mail` process.

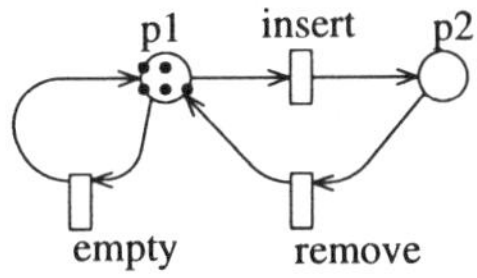

Fig. 6.3. Reduced GSPN model of the buffer.

two places and three transitions as sketched in Figure 6.3. Notice that place p_1 contains initially five tokens to model the free positions in the buffer.
The GSPN model obtained by applying these simplifications is isomorphic to the original net of in Figure 4.1.
These results suggest that it may be feasible to provide a richer set of analysis procedures for SPA models by taking advantage of the translation rules, and transforming them into GSPN models. In the example above, although the net produced has a larger state space it is just a different net level representation of the same system. Moreover, the manipulations applied to demonstrate this are standard techniques and could possibly be automated.

7. Conclusion

To conclude, we have used a sizeable case study to illustrate a comparison of two formalisms which support both functional and performance analysis of parallel and distributed systems. The example, a distributed electronic mail system, highlights some of the respective strengths and weaknesses of GSPN and SPA.
Structural analysis of the GSPN model provided valuable insight into the structure and behaviour of the system. No analogous techniques are currently available in SPA but it should be pointed out that the information gained in the GSPN model was readily available by inspection in the SPA model.

The GSPN model has a much more explicit notion of state and was more amenable to the definition of performance indices. However the SPA model had an explicit compositional structure which made the model particularly easy to understand. This is just part of the constructive methodology for modelling which also includes functional abstraction, equivalence relations and formal reasoning.

GSPN is a much more mature paradigm and this is apparent in the number and scope of GSPN results, and the efficiency of the analysis algorithms. However, the authors are confident that many of these techniques may be imported into SPA. Indeed, the inclusion of immediate actions into SPA is strongly influenced by experience with GSPN [19]. On the analysis level work is also progressing in this area [16]. Meanwhile we have demonstrated that there is the possibility of translating SPA models into an equivalent GSPN which can exploit existing techniques. This ongoing cross-fertilisation between SPA and GSPN is one of the successful outcomes of the QMIPS-project.

The translation rules summarised and illustrated in this paper suggest that it may be possible to develop a *hybrid* modelling methodology which would allow one part of a system to be modelled using one formalism while another part is modelled using the other. Of particular interest is the idea of combining the visualisation of small components by means of GSPN with the powerful composition mechanisms of SPA, as indicated in Fig. 6.1. This is an area for future work.

References

1. M. Ajmone Marsan, G. Balbo, G. Conte, S. Donatelli, and G. Franceschinis. *Modelling with Generalized Stochastic Petri Nets.* John Wiley & Sons, 1994.
2. M. Bernardo, L. Donatiello, and R. Gorrieri. Modelling and Analyzing Concurrent Systems with MPA. In U. Herzog and M. Rettelbach, editors, *Proc. of 2nd Process Algebra and Performance Modelling Workshop*, 1994.
3. G. Brebner. A CCS-based Investigation of Deadlock in a Multi-process Electronic Mail System. *Formal Aspects of Computing*, 5(5):467–479, 1993.
4. P. Buchholz. Compositional Analysis of a Markovian Process Algebra. In U. Herzog and M. Rettelbach, editors, *Proc. of 2nd Process Algebra and Performance Modelling Workshop*, 1994.
5. G. Chiola, C. Dutheillet, G. Franceschinis, and S. Haddad. Stochastic Well-Formed coloured nets for symmetric modelling applications. *IEEE Transactions on Computers*, 42(11), November 1993.
6. S. Donatelli. Superposed generalized stochastic Petri nets: Definition and efficient solution. In *Proc. of 15th Int. Conference on Application and Theory of Petri Nets*, Zaragoza, Spain, 1994.
7. S. Donatelli, J. Hillston, and M. Ribaudo. A Comparison of Performance Evaluation Process Algebra and Generalized StochasticPetri Net. to appear in PNPM '95, 1995.

8. S. Donatelli and M. Sereno. On the Product Form Solution for Stochastic Petri Nets. In *Application and Theory of Petri Nets*, pages 154–172. Springer Verlag, 1992.
9. N. Goetz, H. Hermanns, U. Herzog, V. Mertsiotakis, and M. Rettelbach. *QMIPS book*, chapter Stochastic Process Algebras: Constructive Specification Techniques Integrating Functional, Performance and Dependability Aspects. Springer, 1995. to appear.
10. U. Goltz. CCS and Petri nets. Technical Report 467, GMD, July 1990.
11. P. Harrison and J. Hillston. Exploiting Quasi-reversible Structures to find Product Form Solutions in MPA Models. In S. Gilmore and J. Hillston, editors, *Proc. of 3nd Process Algebra and Performance Modelling Workshop*. Springer-Verlag, 1995.
12. H. Hermanns, U. Herzog, J. Hillston, V. Mertsiotakis, and M. Rettelbach. Stochastic Process Algebras: Integrating Qualitative and Quantitative Modelling. Technical Report 11/94, Universität Erlangen–Nürnberg, IMMD VII, Martensstr. 3, 91058 Erlangen, May 1994.
13. H. Hermanns, M. Rettelbach, and T. Weiß. Formal characterisation of immediate actions in spa with nondeterministic branching. In *Proc. of 3rd Process Algebra and Performance Modelling Workshop*, 1995. to appear.
14. J. Hillston. *A Compositional Approach to Performance Modelling.* PhD thesis, University of Edinburgh, 1994.
15. J. Hillston. Compositional Markovian Modelling Using a Process Algebra. In W.J. Stewart, editor, *Numerical Solution of Markov Chains.* Kluwer, 1995.
16. J. Hillston and V. Mertsiotakis. A Simple Time Scale Decomposition Technique for SPA. In S. Gilmore and J. Hillston, editors, *Proc. of 3nd Process Algebra and Performance Modelling Workshop.* Springer-Verlag, 1995.
17. C. Lindemann. DSPNexpress: A Software Package for the Efficient Solution of Deterministic and Stochastic Petri Nets. In *Proceedings of the 6th International Conference on Modelling Techniques and Tools for Computer Performance Evaluation*, pages 15–29, Edinburgh, September 1992.
18. I. Mitrani, A. Ost, and M. Rettelbach. *QMIPS book*, chapter TIPP and the Spectral Expansion Method. Springer, 1995. to appear.
19. M. Rettelbach. Towards a Theory of Generalised SPA. In S. Gilmore and J. Hillston, editors, *Proc. of 3rd Process Algebra and Performance Modelling Workshop*, 1995. to appear.
20. M. Rettelbach and M. Siegle. Compositional Minimal Semantics for the Stochastic Process Algebra TIPP. In U. Herzog and M. Rettelbach, editors, *Proc. of the 2nd Workshop on Process Algebras and Performance Modelling*, pages 89–106, Regensberg/Erlangen, July 1994. Arbeitsberichte des IMMD, Universität Erlangen-Nürnberg.
21. M. Ribaudo. *On the Relationship between Stochastic Process Algebras and Stochastic Petri Nets.* PhD thesis, University of Torino, 1995.
22. M. Sereno. Towards a Product Form Solution for Stochastic Process Algebras. In S. Gilmore and J. Hillston, editors, *Proc. of 3nd Process Algebra and Performance Modelling Workshop.* Springer-Verlag, 1995.

Functional and Performance Analysis of Cooperating Sequential Processes *

E. Teruel, M. Silva, J.M. Colom and J. Campos

Depto. de Informática e Ing. de Sistemas, Universidad de Zaragoza, Spain

Summary. This paper presents some results concerning the structural analysis of sequential proceses cooperating via message passing through a set of buffers. Both functional — boundedness, deadlock-freeness, liveness, existence of home states — and performance — marking ergodicity, computation of visit ratios and insensitive throughput bounds — properties are considered.

1. Introduction

The design of distributed systems is usually a complex task, compelling the use of formal methods. A major trend in the modelling of concurrent and distributed systems is the use of a single formalism during the entire design and analysis process [9, 16]. Such formalism should provide:

- Basic modelling features like: simple primitives for the modelling of *sequence*, *choice*, and *synchronisation*; hierarchical and modular modelling methodologies; the possibility of parametrisation of models...
- A well founded logical theory providing the definition of functional properties like deadlock-freeness or the absence of (buffer) overflows, and validation algorithms for them.
- A natural representation of time and the possibility of qualitative and quantitative analysis of performance properties.

At present, two modelling paradigms satisfying these requirements are that based on *programming language constructs*, like CCS [11] or CSP [10], and that based on *graphical constructs*, like Petri nets [22], both extended with the corresponding time representations. In this paper we consider the latter and, in particular, we concentrate on systems obtained by the application of a simple modular design principle: several *sequential processes* execute concurrently and *cooperate using asynchronous communication by message passing through a set of buffers.* The restrictions imposed to the connectivity of buffers aim at preventing *competition.* The possible information contained in messages can be disregarded, paying attention to the control flow only. In other words, messages can be considered as *authorisations.* Application domains where this class of systems appear are computer networks, information systems, operating systems, real-time systems, nonsequential programming languages, and discrete part manufacturing systems, among others.

* This work was partially supported by the European ESPRIT BRA Project 7269 QMIPS and the Spanish PRONTIC 242/94.

Several works exist concerning functional and performance analysis of systems of sequential processes communicating through buffers modelled with Petri nets. Various aspects of modelling and functional analysis can be found in [15, 17]. A first approach to efficient (with polynomial time complexity on the net size) performance analysis was presented in [6], stressing both functional and performance aspects. In this paper we bridge qualitative and quantitative aspects of *Deterministic Systems of Sequential Processes*, with the goal of obtaining benefits in both the validation of functional properties and the evaluation of performance indices of such net systems. The present paper is an updated version of [5]; some conjectures from [5] were proven in [14], from which we incorporated also some denotations.

The paper is organised as follows: in Section 2. the class of Deterministic Systems of Sequential Processes is defined. Section 3. deals with functional analysis, and Section 4. considers performance properties.

2. Deterministic Systems of Sequential Processes

The class that we consider in this paper is an extension of that introduced in [17], although we keep the same name. In that work, sequential processes are modelled with *safe State Machines* while the communication among them is described by their connection through particular places called *buffers.* Their buffers are private in the sense that each of them has only one input and only one output sequential process. Our extension allows that several sequential processes deposit messages (tokens) in a buffer.

2.1 Basic Definitions and Notations of Petri Nets

Let us recall some definitions and notations about Petri nets (see [22] for a more comprehensive presentation).

A *P/T net* is a 4–tuple $\mathcal{N} = (P, T, Pre, Post)$, where P and T are disjoint sets of *places* and *transitions* ($|P| = n$, $|T| = m$), and Pre and $Post$ are the *incidence functions* representing the input and output arcs: $Pre, Post\colon P \times T \rightarrow I\!N = \{0, 1, 2, \ldots\}$, which are usually represented in matrix form. The *incidence matrix* of the net is defined as $C = Post - Pre$. The incidence function of a given arc is called *weight* or *multiplicity.* When all weights are 0 or 1 the net is called *oridinary.* A net can be seen as a bipartite directed graph in which places and transitions are the two kinds of nodes. The conventional dot-notation is used for *pre-* and *post-sets* of (a set of) nodes. *Flows* are integer annullers of C. *Semiflows* are semipositive flows. Right and left annullers are called T- and P-(semi)flows respectively. Flows are important because they induce certain invariant relations which are useful for reasoning on the behaviour. Several structural properties are based on them. For instance, a net is *consistent* when it has a positive T-semiflow, and *conservative* when it has a positive P-semiflow.

A function $M: P \to IN$, usually represented in vector form, is called *marking*. A *P/T system*, or *marked Petri net*, $(\mathcal{N}, M_0)$, is a P/T net $\mathcal{N}$ with an *initial marking* M_0. A transition $t \in T$ is *enabled* at marking M iff $\forall p \in P$: $M(p) \geq Pre(p,t)$. A transition t enabled at M can *fire* yielding a new marking M' (*reached* marking) defined by $M'(p) = M(p) - Pre(p,t) + Post(p,t)$ (it is denoted by $M \xrightarrow{t} M'$). A sequence of transitions $\sigma = t_1 t_2 \dots t_n$ is a *firing sequence* in $(\mathcal{N}, M_0)$ iff there exists a sequence of markings such that $M_0 \xrightarrow{t_1} M_1 \xrightarrow{t_2} M_2 \dots \xrightarrow{t_n} M_n$. In this case, marking M_n is said to be *reachable* from M_0 by firing σ, and this is denoted by $M_0 \xrightarrow{\sigma} M_n$. The *reachability set* $R(\mathcal{N}, M_0)$ is the set of all markings reachable from the initial marking. The function $\vec{\sigma}: T \to IN$, usually represented in vector form, is the *firing count vector* of σ. If $M_0 \xrightarrow{\sigma} M$, then $M = M_0 + C \cdot \vec{\sigma}$, which is referred to as the *linear state equation* of the net. A marking M is said to be *potentially reachable* iff $\exists \vec{\sigma} \in IN^m$ such that $M = M_0 + C \cdot \vec{\sigma} \geq 0$. Denoting by $PR(\mathcal{N}, M_0)$ the set of all potentially reachable markings, $PR(\mathcal{N}, M_0) \supseteq R(\mathcal{N}, M_0)$.

A place $p \in P$ is said to be *k-bounded* iff $\forall M \in R(\mathcal{N}, M_0)$, $M(p) \leq k$. A P/T system is said to be (marking) k–bounded iff every place is k–bounded, and bounded iff there exists some k for which it is k–bounded. A P/T system is *live* when every transition can ultimately occur from every reachable marking, and it is *deadlock-free* when at least one transition is enabled at every reachable marking. M is a *home state* in $(\mathcal{N}, M_0)$ iff it is reachable from every reachable marking, and $(\mathcal{N}, M_0)$ is *reversible* iff M_0 is a home state. Boundedness is necessary whenever the system is to be implemented, while liveness is often required, specially in reactive systems. A net $\mathcal{N}$ is *structurally bounded* when $(\mathcal{N}, M_0)$ is bounded for *every* M_0, and it is *structurally live* when *there exists* an M_0 such that $(\mathcal{N}, M_0)$ is live. Consequently, if a net $\mathcal{N}$ is structurally bounded and structurally live there exists some marking M_0 such that $(\mathcal{N}, M_0)$ is bounded and live, and we say it is *well-formed*.

Let $\mathcal{E}$ be the set of Equal Conflict sets of a net $\mathcal{N}$, i.e., the quotient set of the Equal Conflict relation, which is "being the same transition or having the same non-null pre-incidence function". A general necessary condition for well-formedness of polynomial time complexity is:

Theorem 2.1 ([21]). *Let $\mathcal{N}$ be a P/T net.*
If $\mathcal{N}$ is well-formed, then it is conservative, consistent, and rank$(C) < |\mathcal{E}|$.

2.2 Deterministic Systems of Sequential Processes, and Other Subclasses

State Machines are ordinary Petri nets such that every transition has only one input and only one output place ($\forall t \in T$: $|{}^\bullet t| = |t^\bullet| = 1$). State Machines allow the modelling of sequences, decisions (or conflicts), and re-entrancy (when they are marked with more than one token) but not synchronisation. Some trivial properties of State Machines are:

- The rank of their incidence matrix equals their number of places minus one.
- They are conservative (thus, structurally bounded).
- Structural liveness is equivalent to strong connectedness, which is equivalent to consistency.
- Liveness is equivalent to strong connecteness and being marked.
- Provided liveness, k–boundedness is equivalent to containing k tokens.

Regarding the timing, it is assumed that every cycle in a State Machine contains at least one timed transition. Topologically speaking, strongly connected State Machines are the Petri net counterpart of classical closed monoclass queueing networks. In *closed* networks, no customer leaves the system or arrives from the outside, hence the population is preserved. The corresponding property in Petri nets terminology is *conservativeness*, which leads to global token conservation laws for any initial marking.

Deterministic Systems of Sequential Processes are used for the modelling and analysis of distributed systems composed by sequential processes communicating through output-private buffers. Each sequential process (SP) is modelled by a safe (1–bounded) State Machine. The communication among them is described by *buffers* (places) which contain *products/messages* (tokens), which are produced by some processes and consumed by others. Each buffer is *output-private* in the sense that it is an input place of only one SP (see Figure 2.1, where shaded places are the buffers).

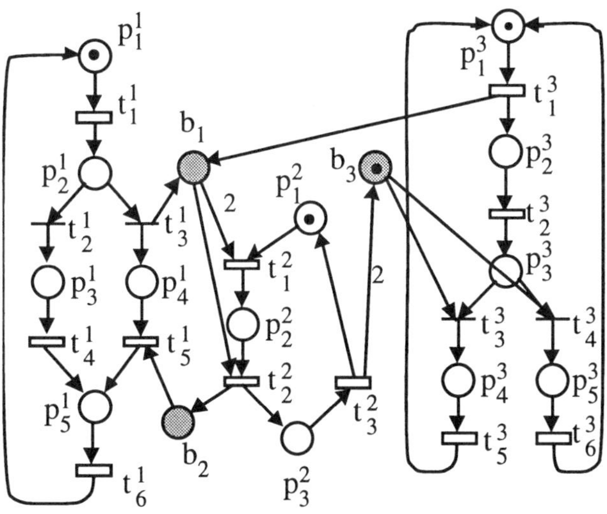

Fig. 2.1. A bounded and live Deterministic System of Sequential Processes.

Definition 2.1. *A P/T system* $(\mathcal{N}, M_0)$ *is a* Deterministic System of Sequential Processes (DSSP) *iff* $P = P_1 \cup \ldots \cup P_q \cup B$ *and* $T = T_1 \cup \ldots \cup T_q$ *are such that:*

1. $\forall i,j \in \{1,\ldots,q\}, i \neq j$: $P_i \cap P_j = \emptyset$, $T_i \cap T_j = \emptyset$, $P_i \cap B = \emptyset$.
2. $\forall i \in \{1,\ldots,q\}$: $(\mathcal{S}P_i, M_{0i}) = (P_i, T_i, Pre_i, Post_i, M_{0i})$ *is a safe strongly connected State Machine (where* Pre_i,$Post_i$, *and* M_{0i} *are the restrictions of Pre, Post, and* M_0 *to* P_i *and* T_i*).*
3. $\forall b \in B$:
   a) $|^\bullet b| \geq 1$ *and* $|b^\bullet| \geq 1$.
   b) $\exists i \in \{1,\ldots,q\}$, *such that* $b^\bullet \subseteq T_i$.
   c) $\forall p \in P_1 \cup \ldots \cup P_q$: $t, t' \in p^\bullet \Rightarrow Pre(b,t) = Pre(b,t')$.

The first two items of the previous definition state that a DSSP is composed by a set of SP's ($\mathcal{S}P_i, i = 1,\ldots,q$) and a set of buffers ($B$). By item *3.a*, buffers are neither source nor sink places. The output-private condition is expressed by condition *3.b*. This, together with *3.c* which forbids that a buffer affects the resolution of conflicts in an SP, prevents competition. This definition generalises the class of DSSP's defined in [17], where buffers are required to have not only a single output SP (output-private) but also a single input one (input-private). From a queueing network perspective, DSSP's are a mild generalisation of *Fork-Join Queuing Networks with Blocking* where servers are complex (safe State Machines with a rich connectivity to buffers).

Another interesting subclass of P/T nets are *Equal Conflict* nets [20]:

Definition 2.2. *A P/T net* $\mathcal{N}$ *is an* Equal Conflict (EC) *net iff* $\forall t, t' \in T$: $^\bullet t \cap {}^\bullet t' \neq \emptyset \Rightarrow \forall p \in P$: $Pre(p,t) = Pre(p,t')$.

EC nets generalise the ordinary subclass of Extended Free Choice nets. Many nice results from the Free Choice theory have been recently extended to EC net systems:

- [20] The potential reachability graph of a live EC system is *directed.* Thus, live EC systems do not have *killing spurious solutions* (spurious solutions that do not enable any transition), and live and bounded EC systems have home states. Since a bounded strongly connected EC system is live iff it is deadlock-free, liveness of a bounded system can be determined by checking absence of integer solution to some linear equation system [19].
- [21] The possibility of marking boundedly and lively a given EC net can be determined in polynomial time: $\mathcal{N}$ is well-formed iff it is consistent, conservative, and rank(C) $= |\mathcal{E}| - 1$. Moreover, if $\mathcal{N}$ is well-formed, it can be decomposed in a meaningful way, similarly to the decomposition of a Free Choice net into State Machines and/or Marked Graphs. Liveness of the whole system can be compositionally characterised in terms of the liveness of the analogues to State Machine components.

Observe that, in a DSSP, all the private conflicts of the SP's are Equal Conflict sets, by the assumption that buffers do not disturb choices. All the remaining transitions are elementary Equal Conflict sets. Neither DSSP's are a subclass of EC nets nor the converse. Nevertheless, if it happens that all buffers of a DSSP have exactly one output Equal Conflict set ($\forall b \in B: b^\bullet \in \mathcal{E}$), that is, if they are *strictly* output-private, then obviously they are EC, and they are called *Equal Conflict DSSP (DSSP/EC)*. Naturally, DSSP/EC's inherit all the nice properties of EC net systems. In fact, by means of several transformations preserving, among other properties, boundedness, liveness and the existence of home states (see [5]), the results that are valid for the DSSP/EC subclass can be extended to many non EC nets, although *not* all DSSP's can be transformed into EC. As an example, we can transform the net of Figure 2.1 into a DSSP/EC by pre-fusion of t_1^2 and t_2^2 into t_{12}^2 [3]. The new transition has b_1 with weight 3 and p_1^2 as inputs and b_2 and p_3^2 as outputs. Place p_2^2 has been removed.

2.3 Time Representation

One of the advantages of Petri net models for the design and analysis of concurrent and distributed systems is that they can be naturally extended by time attributes in order to evaluate the system performance. We consider net systems with timed transitions. Marking and time independent Coxian random variables associated to the firing of transitions define their *service time.* The mean values of these variables are denoted s_i for each transition t_i of the net.

For the modelling of conflicts we use *immediate transitions* with the addition of (marking and time independent) *routing rates* [1]. In other words, for the subset of immediate transitions $\{t_1, \ldots, t_k\} \subset T$ being in conflict at each reachable marking, we assume that the constants $r_1, \ldots, r_k \in \mathbb{Q}^+$ are explicitly defined in the system interpretation in such a way that when $t_1, \ldots, t_k$ are simultaneously enabled, transition t_i, $i = 1, \ldots, k$, fires with relative rate $r_i/(\sum_{j=1}^{k} r_j)$. Consequently, routing is completely decoupled from duration of activities. The only restriction that this decoupling imposes to the system is that *preemption* cannot be modelled with two timed transitions (in conflict) competing for the tokens. (In other words, a *race policy* cannot be modelled. Our constraint is equivalent to the use of a *preselection policy* for the resolution of conflicts among timed transitions.)

Assuming the above described time interpretation, the timed model has almost surely the *fair progress* property, that is, no transition can be permanently enabled without firing. Additionally, it has the *local fairness* property, that is, all output transitions of a shared place simultaneously enabled at infinitely many markings will fire infinitely often. (In other words, all possible outcomes of any conflict have a non-null probability of firing.)

The *visit ratio* of transition t_i with respect to t_j, $v_i^{(j)}$, is the average number of times t_i is visited (fired) for each visit to (firing of) the reference transition t_j. The computation of visit ratios is interesting for the performance analysis of formal models. For example, it is well-known that the steady-state probability of a state in a product-form queueing network with single-server semantics [8] depends on the *average service demands* of customers from station i, defined as:

$$D_i^{(j)} \stackrel{def}{=} v_i^{(j)} \cdot s_i \qquad i = 1, \ldots, m \tag{2.1}$$

The computation of average service demands is also very important in the performance analysis of stochastic Petri net models. In Section 4., applying the theory presented in [7], we use these values to compute upper and lower bounds for the *throughput* of transitions, i.e. the average number of service completions (firings) per time unit, in a bounded and live DSSP.

3. Functional Analysis of DSSP's

One of the benefits of using restricted subclasses of nets is the availability of results that facilitate the analysis. In the case of DSSP's, we have a polynomial time characterisation of well-formedness, and a simple algebraic sufficient condition for liveness, based on the equivalence of liveness and deadlock-freeness, which is also proven to be necessary for DSSP/EC.

3.1 The Coarse net of a DSSP

In order to concentrate on the *interconnection level* of the net, we want to obviate the details regarding the inner structure of the SP's, while keeping relevant information concerning the effect on the buffers. A first approach could be substituting a (coarse) transition for each SP, keeping the interconnection with buffers. This is the *coarse structure* proposed in [15], which is not enough for analytical purposes (see [14]). To keep more information on the effect of buffer interconnections, we give symbolic relative rates to conflicting transitions (e.g., r_2^1, r_3^1 to t_2^1, t_3^1 in the example net of Figure 2.1), which are assumed to be *normalised* (e.g., $r_2^1 + r_3^1 = 1$), and take them into account when computing the coarse model. The idea is to replace each SP by a transition whose effect on the buffers is the same as that of the original SP in the long term when respecting the given rates. This is done using the unique minimal T-semiflow of each SP respecting those rates (see [14]). We call the obtained coarse model *coarse net*, even if it is not a net in a strict sense, because arc weights may not be natural numbers. We even speak of strong connectedness, conservativeness, or consistency: we would say, for instance, that the "net" in Figure 3.1, which is the coarse net of the DSSP of Figure 2.1, is strongly connected, conservative ($Y \cdot C = 0$ for $Y = [1\ 1\ 1]$), and consistent ($C \cdot X = 0$ for $X = [1\ r_3^1\ 2r_3^1]$).

With the aid of the structure theory of Choice-free nets [18], and using the fact that the coarse net is obtained by linear combinations of the transitions of the DSSP, the following properties of the coarse net are proven in [14]:

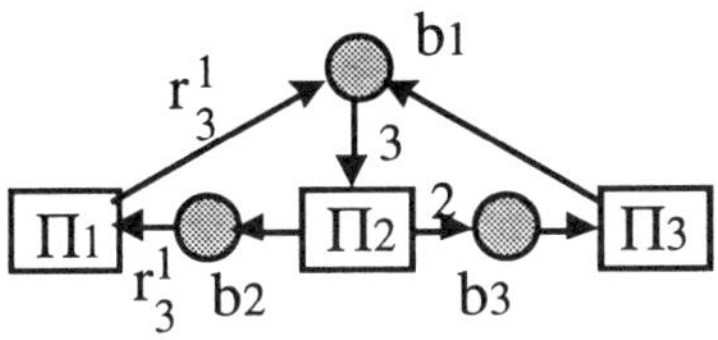

Fig. 3.1. The coarse net of the DSSP of Fig. 2.1.

Proposition 3.1 ([14]). *Let $\mathcal{N}$ be the net of a DSSP.*
If $\mathcal{N}$ is conservative and consistent, then:

1. *The coarse net of $\mathcal{N}$ is strongly connected, conservative and Choice-free. If $\mathcal{N}$ is well-formed, then its coarse net is also consistent.*
2. *rank*$(C) < |\mathcal{E}|$.

Observe that, in the example, the coarse net is a conservative and consistent Choice-free net *for all* (positive) rates. It is also interesting to observe that the complete T-semiflow structure of $\mathcal{N}$ is somehow represented in the coarse net thanks to the parametric weighting.

3.2 Well-Formedness and Liveness

The first important fact concerning liveness analysis of DSSP's is that liveness and deadlock-freeness are equivalent, assuming boundedness and strong connectedness.

Theorem 3.1 ([5]). *Let $(\mathcal{N}, M_0)$ be a bounded strongly connected DSSP. $(\mathcal{N}, M_0)$ is live iff it is deadlock-free.*

Combining Proposition 3.1.2 with Theorem 2.1, and also making extensive use of the T-semiflow structure of DSSP's and of Theorem 3.1, the following characterisation of well-formedness is obtained in [14]:

Theorem 3.2 ([14]). *Let $\mathcal{N}$ be the net of a DSSP.*
$\mathcal{N}$ is well-formed iff it is conservative, consistent, and rank$(C) = |\mathcal{E}| - 1$. Moreover, there exists M_0 such that $(\mathcal{N}, M_0)$ is a bounded and live DSSP.

If $\mathcal{N}$ is not well-formed, for which we have given a polynomial time characterisation, then for every bounded initial marking the system deadlocks. In performance terms, the system presents null throughput for any initial configuration of resources/customers due to a problem that is rooted on the net structure, so this should be checked prior to any other — more complex — analysis.

In case $\mathcal{N}$ is well-formed, the problem is determining whether the initial marking makes the system live or not. To achieve this, Theorem 3.1 can be used, so only deadlock-freeness needs to be proven, instead of liveness. In [19] a general sufficient condition for deadlock-freeness in terms of the solvability over the naturals of a set of linear equation systems is given. The basic idea is to ask for absence of potentially reachable deadlock markings. In the particular case of DSSP's, among other subclasses, such algebraic condition can be expressed as a single linear equation system (use the rules presented in [19] plus the particular transformation shown in Figure 3.2, that preserves deadlock-freeness — actually it preserves the language modulo a projection — thanks to the output-private and the State Machines' safeness hypothesis).

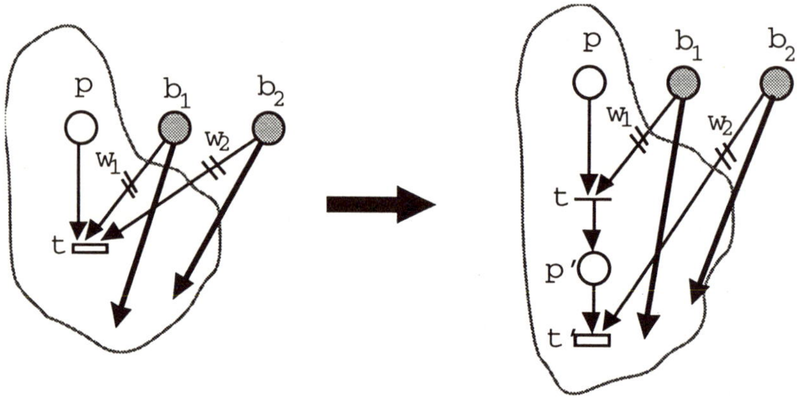

Fig. 3.2. A transformation preserving deadlock-freeness. (Place p must *not* be a choice place.)

As an example, the sufficient condition for liveness of the net of Figure 2.1 — which is well-formed — is absence of *natural* solutions to the linear equation system below. The first line defines the set of potentially reachable markings (i.e., it is the state equation). The following three lines express disabledness of "private" transitions of the three State Machines (i.e. transitions whose only input is a State Machine place), and the last four express disabledness of the transitions having some buffer as input ($SB(b)$ denotes the *structural (marking) bound* of buffer b, that is defined as $\max\{M(b) \mid M \in PR(\mathcal{N}, M_0)\}$; the structural bound of State Machine places is obviously one).

$$
\begin{aligned}
&M = M_0 + C \cdot \vec{\sigma} \\
&M(p_1^1) = M(p_2^1) = M(p_3^1) = M(p_5^1) = 0 \\
&M(p_3^2) = 0 \\
&M(p_1^3) = M(p_2^3) = M(p_4^3) = M(p_5^3) = M(p_6^3) = 0 \\
&SB(b_1) \cdot M(p_1^2) + M(b_1) \leq SB(b_1) + 1 \\
&SB(b_1) \cdot M(p_2^2) + M(b_1) \leq SB(b_1) \\
&SB(b_2) \cdot M(p_4^1) + M(b_2) \leq SB(b_2) \\
&SB(b_3) \cdot M(p_3^3) + M(b_3) \leq SB(b_3)
\end{aligned}
$$

This general sufficient condition is also necessary in the case of EC systems [20]. (We conjecture that it is so also for DSSP's; safeness of the SP's is necessary here, because there are examples of DSSP nets with a 2–bounded SP having killing spurious solutions.) In the example net, if we pre-fuse t_1^2 and t_2^2, as described above, to get a DSSP/EC, we have to replace the two conditions involving b_1 by:

$$SB(b_1) \cdot M(p_1^2) + M(b_1) \leq SB(b_1) + 2$$

and now absence of natural solutions is equivalent to liveness.

4. Performance Analysis of DSSP's

4.1 Home States and Ergodicity

It is well-known that under (possibly marking-dependent) exponentially distributed random variables associated to the firing of transitions and Bernouilli trials for the succesive resolutions of each conflict, the underlying *Continuous Time Markov Chain* (CTMC) is isomorphous to the reachability graph of the untimed net model [2]. Thus, the existence of home states leads to ergodicity of the marking process for bounded net systems with exponential firing times.

Theorem 4.1 ([5]). *Let $(\mathcal{N}, M_0)$ be a live and bounded DSSP/EC with Coxian random variables associated to the firing of transitions and Bernouilli trials for the succesive resolutions of each conflict.*
The underlying CTMC of $(\mathcal{N}, M_0)$ is ergodic.

Although the property is stated for DSSP/EC, again the result can be extended to many non EC nets by the corresponding net transformations preserving the existence of home states. We conjecture that DSSP's have home states too, that is, that the ergodicity result holds for the entire DSSP class.

4.2 Computation of Visit Ratios

The computation of the average service demands of tokens from transitions, Equation (2.1), is useful for the performance analysis of timed systems. Assuming that the average service times of transitions, s_i, are known, then it is necessary to compute the vector of visit ratios to transitions, $\vec{v}^{(j)}$.

If $\mathcal{N}$ is consistent, the visit ratio vector normalised for t_j, $\vec{v}^{(j)}$, should be a T-semiflow of $\mathcal{N}$. Otherwise stated (observe that $v_i^{(j)} \geq 0$ by definition):

$$C \cdot \vec{v}^{(j)} = 0 \tag{4.1}$$

The conflicts in the SP's of a DSSP are free, because the buffers do not condition the conflict resolution. Structurally speaking, these conflicts correspond to Equal Conflicts at the net level. On the sequel, for easy presentation, Equal Conflict sets will be supposed to have at most two transitions; otherwise serialise choices into binary ones. Let t_a and t_b be in Equal Conflict relation. The corresponding visit ratios should verify the following equation:

$$r_b \cdot v_a^{(j)} - r_a \cdot v_b^{(j)} = 0 \tag{4.2}$$

An equation like (4.2) holds for every (binary) Equal Conflict. Rewritten in vector form: $r_{ab} \cdot \vec{v}^{(j)} = 0$, which for the set of all Equal Conflicts leads to:

$$R \cdot \vec{v}^{(j)} = 0 \tag{4.3}$$

where R is a matrix with $m - |\mathcal{E}|$ (number of binary Equal Conflicts) rows and m columns. In other words, $m - |\mathcal{E}|$ is the number of independent linear relations fixed by the routing rates at (binary) Equal Conflicts, so rank$(R) = m - |\mathcal{E}|$. Using this together with Theorem 3.2, it follows that:

Theorem 4.2 ([5]). *Let $\mathcal{N}$ be a well-formed DSSP net.*
The system of equations:

$$\begin{pmatrix} C \\ R \end{pmatrix} \cdot \vec{v}^{(j)} = 0, \; v_j^{(j)} = 1 \tag{4.4}$$

has only one solution (i.e., the vector of visit ratios depends neither on the marking, provided it allows infinite behaviours, nor on the service times).

4.3 Performance Bounds

This section is devoted to present some *insensitive* (i.e., holding for any probability distribution function for the firing times) performance bounds. Basically, throughput upper bounds are computed by finding the slowest isolated subnet among those generated by P-semiflows of the net, and are presented in the next theorem.

Theorem 4.3 ([7]). *For a DSSP, $(\mathcal{N}, M_0)$, a lower bound for the mean interfiring time $\Gamma^{(j)}$ of transition t_j (or its inverse an upper bound for the throughput σ_j^*) can be computed by solving the following linear programming problem:*

$$\begin{array}{rll} \Gamma^{(j)} \geq & \textit{maximise} & Y \cdot Pre \cdot \vec{D}^{(j)} \\ & \textit{subject to} & Y \cdot C = 0 \\ & & Y \cdot M_0 = 1 \\ & & Y \geq 0 \end{array} \qquad (LPP1)$$

where $\vec{D}^{(j)}$ is the vector of average service demands for transitions.

We remark that the computation of the above bound has polynomial time complexity on the net size. This is because the computation of vector $\vec{D}^{(j)}$ is polynomial and because linear programming problems can also be solved in polynomial time.

If the solution of (LPP1) is unbounded and since it is a lower bound for the mean interfiring time of transition t_j, the non-liveness can be assured (infinite interfiring time). If the visit ratios of all transitions are non-null, the unboundedness of the problem (LPP1) implies that a total deadlock is reached by the net. This result has the following interpretation: if (LPP1) is unbounded then there exists an unmarked P-semiflow, and the system is non-live.

Concerning throughput lower bounds, provided the net system is live, they can be derived by summing up the service time of all transitions, weighted by the visit ratios. This computation implies a complete sequentialisation of all the activities represented in the model.

Theorem 4.4 ([7]). *For a bounded and live DSSP, $(\mathcal{N}, M_0)$, an upper bound for the mean interfiring time $\Gamma^{(j)}$ of transition t_j (or its inverse a lower bound for the throughput) is:*

$$\Gamma^{(j)} \leq \sum_{i=1}^{m} s_i \; v_i^{(j)} = \sum_{i=1}^{m} D_i^{(j)} \tag{4.5}$$

where s_i, $v_i^{(j)}$, and $D_i^{(j)}$ are the mean service time, visit ratio, and average service demand, respectively, for transition t_i, $i = 1, \ldots, m$.

We remark that the above bound, provided the system is bounded and live, can also be computed in polynomial time, since the vector of visit ratios can be computed with such complexity.

Bounds for other performance indices can be computed using classical formulas in Queuing Networks theory such as Little's formula.

The number of tokens in a place defines the lenght of the represented queue (including the customers in service!). Thus it may be important to known bounds on average marking of places.

As an example, in [4] it has been shown that the following are lower and upper bounds for the average marking, $\overline{M}$:

$$\overline{M}^{lb} = Pre \cdot \mathcal{S} \cdot \vec{\sigma^*}^{lb} \tag{4.6}$$

$$\overline{M}^{ub}(p) \quad = \quad \max \{ \; M(p) \mid B \cdot M = B \cdot M_0 \; , \; M \geq \overline{M}^{lb} \; \} \qquad (LPP2)$$

where $\mathcal{S} = \text{diag}\,(s_i)$, $\vec{\sigma^*}^{lb}$ is the vector of throughput lower bounds, and the rows of B are the basis of left annullers of the incidence matrix of the net.

As an interesting remark, the reader may check that a structural absolute bound for the marking of a place is given for conservative nets (i.e., $\exists Y > 0$, $Y \cdot C = 0$) by the following expression:

$$SB(p) \quad = \quad \max \{ \; M(p) \mid B \cdot M = B \cdot M_0 \; , \; M \geq 0 \; \} \qquad (LPP3)$$

The constraint in (LPP3) being weaker than that in (LPP2) ($M \geq \overline{M}^{lb}$ is transformed into $M \geq 0$), it is obvious that $\overline{M}^{ub} \leq SB(p)$.

In [13], additional results on the approximate throughput computation for DSSP's have been derived, based on iterative response time approximation algorithms.

References

1. M. Ajmone-Marsan, G. Balbo, and G. Conte, "A class of generalized stochastic Petri nets for the performance evaluation of multiprocessor systems", *ACM Transactions on Computer Systems*, **2** (2), pp. 93-122, 1984.
2. M. Ajmone-Marsan, G. Balbo, and G. Conte, *Performance Models of Multiprocessor Systems.* MIT Press, 1986.
3. G. Berthelot, "Checking properties of nets using transformations", in G. Rozenberg (ed.), *Advances in Petri Nets 1985*, **222** of *Lecture Notes in Computer Science*, pp. 19-40. Springer Verlag, 1986.
4. J. Campos, G. Chiola, and M. Silva, "Properties and performance bounds for closed Free Choice synchronized monoclass queuing networks", *IEEE Trans. Automatic Control*, **36** (12), pp. 1368-1382, 1991.
5. J. Campos, J. M. Colom, M. Silva, and E. Teruel, "Functional and performance analysis of cooperating sequential processes", In O. J. Boxma and G. M. Koole (ed.) *Performance Evaluation of Parallel and Distributed Systems. Solution Methods*, **106** of *CWI Tracts*, pp. 233-251. CWI, 1994.
6. J. Campos and M. Silva, "Steady-state performance evaluation of totally open systems of Markovian sequential processes", In M. Cosnard and C. Girault (ed.) *Decentralized Systems*, pp. 427-438. North-Holland, 1990.
7. J. Campos and M. Silva, "Structural Techniques and Performance Bounds of Stochastic Petri Net Models", In G. Rozenberg (ed.) *Advances in Petri Nets 1992*, **609** of *LNCS*, pp. 352-391. Springer-Verlag, 1992.
8. E. Gelenbe and G. Pujolle, *Introduction to Queuing Networks.* Wiley, 1987.
9. U. Herzog, "Performance evaluation and formal description", In *Procs. of the IEEE Conference CompEuro 91*, pp. 750-756, Bologna, Italy, May 1991.
10. C.A.R. Hoare, *Communicating Sequential Processes.* Prentice Hall, Englewood Cliffs, NJ, 1985.
11. R. Milner, *A Calculus of Communicating Systems.* Prentice Hall, London, 1989.
12. T. Murata, "Petri nets: Properties, analysis, and applications", *Proceedings of the IEEE*, **77** (4), pp. 541-580, 1989.
13. C.J. Perez, J. Campos, M. Silva, "On approximate throughput computation of DSSP" Submitted paper. March, 1995.

14. L. Recalde, E. Teruel, M. Silva, "On Well-formedness Analysis: The Case of DSSP", To appear in J. Desel (ed.) *Proc. of Int. Workshop on Structures in Concurrency Theory*. Springer-Verlag, 1995.
15. W. Reisig, "Deterministic buffer synchronization of sequential processes", *Acta Informatica*, **18**, pp. 117-134, 1982
16. M. Silva, "Interleaving functional and performance structural analysis of net models", In M. Ajmone Marsan (ed.) *Application and Theory of Petri Nets 1993*, **691** of *LNCS*, pp. 17-23, Springer-Verlag, 1993.
17. Y. Souissi and N. Beldiceanu, "Deterministic Systems of Sequential Processes: Theory and tools", In F.H. Vogt (ed.) *Concurrency 88*, **335** of *LNCS*, pp. 380-400, Springer-Verlag, 1988.
18. E. Teruel, *Structure Theory of Weighted Place/Transition Net Systems: The Equal Conflict Hiatus.* PhD thesis, DIEI. Univ. Zaragoza, June 1994.
19. E. Teruel, J.M. Colom and M. Silva, "Linear analysis of deadlock-freeness of Petri net models", In J.W. Nieuwenhuis et al. (ed.) *Second European Control Conference*, **2**, pp. 513-518, North-Holland, 1993.
20. E. Teruel and M. Silva, "Liveness and home states in Equal Conflict systems", In M. Ajmone Marsan (ed.) *Application and Theory of Petri Nets 1993*, **691** of *LNCS*, pp. 415-432, Springer-Verlag, 1993.
21. E. Teruel and M. Silva, "Well-formedness of Equal Conflict systems", In R. Valette (ed.) *Application and Theory of Petri Nets 1994*, **815** of *Lecture Notes in Computer Science*, pp. 491-510, Springer Verlag, 1994.

Part II
Techniques

Analysis of Parallel Processing Systems via the (max,+) Algebra

F. Baccelli, B. Gaujal, A. Jean-Marie, and J. Mairesse

INRIA Sophia-Antipolis, France

Summary. A basic model of parallel processing is revisited. Recent results on computation and simulation of this model are reviewed. These results rely on the linearity of the model with respect to the so called $(\max, +)$ algebra.

1. Introduction

A simple queueing theoretic model of parallel processing systems proposed in [7], and which was used as a testbed within the Qmips project [18], is revisited. In [7], this model was shown to be amenable to a representation via max and + operations, which lead in particular to a characterization of the stability region.

The aim of the paper is to review these results to the light of their linearity within the $(\max, +)$ algebra, together with recent computational and structural results on $(\max, +)$ linear systems [4], which bring a new insight into this model. These new results pertain to the stability of the model ([87, 86, 88]), to the analytical characterization of its stationary or periodic regimes ([26, 9, 78, 80]) and to new simulation techniques which are not based on the event list ([3, 55, 58, 11]).

2. The Basic Problem

The basic model under consideration in this paper is the so called Qmips model (see [18] and [7]). A practical instance for such a model is that of a signal processing system which acquires data produced by sensors and has to process these data in parallel on a multiprocessor architecture. More precisely, the following queueing theoretic description of the system can be made:

Workload Model : (arrival and required service) The workload of the system consists of a sequence of *tasks*, where each task is represented by a *task graph.*
Let $0 = T_1 \leq T_2 \leq \cdots \leq T_n \leq \cdots$ denote the arrival times of the tasks, (i.e. the n-th set of data is produced by the sensors at time T_n) and $\tau_n = T_{n+1} - T_n$ the corresponding interarrival times.
Task n, which corresponds to the set of actions to be performed on the data acquired at time T_n is characterized by a directed acyclic graph $G_n = (V_n, E_n)$, referred to as the n-th task graph, where the nodes in

V_n represent the subtasks of task n (i.e. sequential computations to be performed on these data), and the arcs in E_n represent the precedence constraints between these subtasks. The processing times of subtasks can be deterministic or random variables. Figure 2.1 shows three tasks with different structures.

The semantics of task graphs are the following:

- nodes are sequential subtasks;
- arcs represent precedence constraints (and possibly communications); predecessors and successors refer to the "and" logic.

Thus, the precedence graph is such that if $(i, j) \in E_n$, then subtask j can start its execution only after subtask i has completed its execution. In particular, if several subtasks are predecessors of subtask j, then this last one has to wait for the completion of all of them before starting its own execution.

We will consider the particular case when all external data are available from time 0 on. In this case, the execution of the successive task graphs amount to the parallel execution of loops. This case will be referred to as the *saturated* case.

Multiprocessor Type : (servers)

Denote by $\mathcal{K} = \{1, \cdots, K\}$ the set of $K \geq 1$ (possibly heterogeneous) processors in the system. The processors have infinite local memories.

Operating Mode : (service discipline)

The assumptions are the following: mapping of subtasks on processors is static, scheduling is FIFO (at task level) and execution is non-idling and nonpreemptive.

There is a static mapping which assigns subtasks in V_n to processors. Let V_n^k be the set of subtasks assigned to processor $k \in \mathcal{K}$. It is assumed that G_n defines a total order on the subtasks of V_n^k, for each $k \in \mathcal{K}$. If this is not true, then a total ordering is chosen by adding extra precedence constraints to the initial ones.

Let b_n^k, e_n^k be the first and the last subtasks of V_n^k, respectively. According to the FIFO rule, subtask b_{n+1}^k is executed only after subtask e_n^k is completed. This set of additional dependencies is represented with larger arcs on Figure 2.1. Due to the non-idleness assumption, subtasks are executed as soon as possible.

Note that the FIFO scheduling is only enforced locally (i.e. for all k, one only starts processing subtasks belonging to V_{n+1}^k after the completion of e_n^k. This does not rule out the possibility of multiprogramming at task level: at a given instant, it is quite possible to have subtasks belonging to V_n and V_m, $n \neq m$, being processed on different processors. Our model will allow us to cover the case when the multiprogramming degree is limited by a constant N (i.e. if subtasks belonging to V_n and V_m, $n \neq m$, are processed on different processors at the same time, then necessarily $|m - n| \leq N - 1$).

Communication Network :

Communication overhead is assumed to be independent of the state of the system. Without loss of generality, we can then assume that the communication overhead between subtasks i and j, $(i, j) \in E_n$, is instantaneous. If this is not the case, we can insert a communication subtask between i and j. The communication subtask will be executed by a communication processor or channel. The resulting task graph fulfills the above assumption.

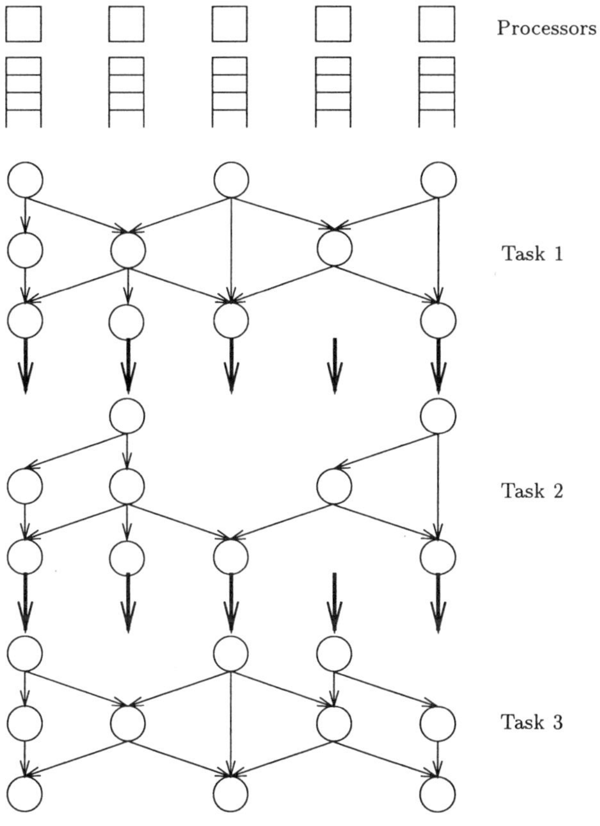

Fig. 2.1. Basic problem under consideration

A task is said to be complete if all its subtasks have completed their execution. One of the key questions for this model is the computation of the statistical properties of the response time $R_n = C_n - T_n$ of task G_n, where C_n is the completion time of task G_n.

Under what conditions is the system stable? Given that the system is stable, what are the statistics of R_n asymptotically?

The aim of the present paper is to show how these problems can be formalized and addressed via the so-called (max, +) algebra.

3. Modeling via (max, +)-Linear Recurrence Equations

3.1 Algebraic Framework

The basic reference algebra throughout this paper is the so-called (max, +)-algebra on the real line $\mathbb{R}$. The set $\mathbb{R}$ completed with $\varepsilon = -\infty$ (which we will denote $\mathbb{R}_{max}$) is a commutative semi-field when endowed with the two operations $(\oplus, \otimes)$, where $\oplus$ is max and $\otimes$ is $+$. The neutral element of $\oplus$ is ε and that of $\otimes$ is $e = 0$. As in the conventional algebra, $\otimes$ has priority over $\oplus$ in all arithmetic expressions.

From this basic semi-field, one defines vectors and matrices with entries in $\mathbb{R}_{max}$. The space of K dimensional vectors will be denoted $\mathbb{R}^K_{max}$, that of square matrices $\mathbb{R}^{K\times K}_{max}$ etc. The sum and the product of two matrices are defined through the following natural formula: if A and B are matrices of adequate sizes,

$$(A \oplus B)_{ij} = A_{ij} \oplus B_{ij}, \tag{3.1}$$

$$(A \otimes B)_{ij} = \bigoplus_k A_{ik} \otimes B_{kj}. \tag{3.2}$$

For square matrices, the neutral element of $\oplus$ is the matrix $\mathcal{E}$ with all its entries equal to ε. That of $\otimes$ is the identity matrix E with $E_{ii} = e$ for all i and $E_{ij} = \varepsilon$ for all $i \neq j$. We will denote $A^p = A^{p-1} \otimes A$.

For more on this formalism, the reader could refer to [4].

3.2 Recurrence Equations

Task Graphs. Consider task graph G_n; the precedence constraints which are necessary to obtain a total ordering on the subtasks of V_n^k are assumed to have already been taken into accoun).

Since G_n is assumed to be acyclic, there exists a numbering of the subtasks by layers, where the number of layers varies from 1 to L [1], and such that:

- there is at most one subtask of level l allocated to processor k. It may be that there is no such subtask; if it exists, this subtask will be denoted (l, k).
- subtasks $(1, k)$ exist for all $k = 1, \ldots, K$.
- the precedence constraints of G_n with (l, k) as end subtask only involve subtasks of the form (p, j) with either $p < l$, or $p = l$, but $\sigma_l(j) < \sigma_l(k)$, where $\sigma_l(.)$ is some permutation of $\{1, \ldots, K\}$.

[1] in general, L, and the data defined below depend on n

Assume that the epochs at which processor k starts working on subtask $(1,k)$ is given and equal to $X(0)^k$, and denote $X(l)^k$ the time at which all subtasks (p,k) with $p \leq l$, complete on processor k. Let l be a fixed integer and (l,k) be an existing subtask. We denote

- $S^k_{l,p}$ the set of processors j such that there exists a subtask (p,j) which is a predecessor of (l,k).
- σ^k_l its execution time on processor k.

Then we have:

$$X(l)^k = \left\{ \max_{i \in S^k_{l,l}} X(l)^i \vee \max_{i \in S^k_{l,l-1}} X(l-1)^i \vee \ldots \vee \max_{i \in S^k_{l,0}} X(0)^i \right\} + \sigma^k_l . \quad (3.3)$$

If subtask (l,k) does not exist, the above equation is still valid if we take

- $S^k_{l,p} = \emptyset$ for all $p \neq l-1$ and $S^k_{l,l-1} = \{k\}$;
- $\sigma^l_l = 0$.

Let $X(l)$ be the column vector $(X(l)^1, \ldots, X(l)^K)^t$. Using the $(\max,+)$ formalism, we can rewrite this equation as the vectorial relation

$$X(l) = A(l,l) \otimes X(l) \oplus \ldots \oplus A(l,0) \otimes X(0), \quad (3.4)$$

where the square matrix $A(l,p)$ is defined by:

- whenever (l,k) exists, $A(l,p)_{ki} = \sigma^k_l$ if $i \in S^k_{l,p}$ and ε otherwise;
- otherwise, $A(l,l-1)_{kk} = e$, $A(l,l-1)_{kj} = \varepsilon$ for $j \neq k$, and all other entries of the type $A(l,p)_{ki}$ are equal to ε.

Note that, up to a change of basis associated with the permutation σ_l, the matrix $A(l,l)$ is strictly lower triangular (this is equivalent to the acyclicity assumption on V_n).

The rest of the computation is inspired by the type of manipulations that would be performed in the conventional algebra case. Let $A(l,l)^\star$ denote the series

$$A(l,l)^\star = E \oplus A(l,l) \oplus A(l,l)^2 \oplus \ldots . \quad (3.5)$$

It is easy to check that this series converges (essentially because $A(l,l)$ is strictly lower triangular) and that for all $l \leq L$,

$$X(l) = A(l,l)^\star \otimes A(l,l-1) \otimes X(l-1) \oplus \ldots \oplus A(l,l)^\star \otimes A(l,0) \otimes X(0). \quad (3.6)$$

Finally, when denoting $\overline{A}(l,p)$ the matrix $A(l,l)^\star \otimes A(l,p)$, a direct induction argument gives the formula

$$X(l) = A(l) \otimes X(0), \quad (3.7)$$

with

$$
\begin{aligned}
A(l) = {} & \overline{A}(l,0) \\
\oplus & \bigoplus_{0<m_1<l} \overline{A}(l,m_1) \otimes \overline{A}(m_1,0) \\
\oplus & \bigoplus_{0<m_1<m_2<l} \overline{A}(l,m_2) \otimes \overline{A}(m_2,m_1) \otimes \overline{A}(m_1,0) \\
\ldots & \\
\oplus & \bigoplus_{0<m_1<\ldots<m_p<l} \overline{A}(l,m_p) \otimes \ldots \otimes \overline{A}(m_{n+1},m_n) \otimes \ldots \otimes \overline{A}(m_1,0) \\
\ldots & \\
\oplus & \overline{A}(l,l-1) \otimes \overline{A}(l-1,l-2) \otimes \overline{A}(l-2,l-3) \otimes \ldots \otimes \overline{A}(1,0). \quad (3.8)
\end{aligned}
$$

Note that the matrices $A(l)$ are obtained from the data associated with G_n only. As already mentioned this matrices depend on n in general.

Example. Consider the example of Figure 3.1, where all graphs G_n have the same topology and the same execution times denoted σ_i for subtask i. The numbering of the subtasks by layers is easy to derive from the figure. It is easily checked that $A(l,l) = \mathcal{E}$ for all l, and that

$$
\begin{aligned}
A = A(7) &= \begin{pmatrix} \sigma_6 & \sigma_6 & \varepsilon \\ \varepsilon & e & \varepsilon \\ \varepsilon & \sigma_7 & \sigma_7 \end{pmatrix} \otimes \begin{pmatrix} e & \varepsilon & \varepsilon \\ \sigma_4 & \sigma_4 & \sigma_4 \\ \varepsilon & \varepsilon & \sigma_5 \end{pmatrix} \otimes \begin{pmatrix} \sigma_1 & \varepsilon & \varepsilon \\ \varepsilon & \sigma_2 & \varepsilon \\ \varepsilon & \varepsilon & \sigma_3 \end{pmatrix} \\
&= \begin{pmatrix} \sigma_1\sigma_6 \oplus \sigma_1\sigma_4\sigma_6 & \sigma_2\sigma_4\sigma_6 & \sigma_3\sigma_4\sigma_6 \\ \sigma_1\sigma_4 & \sigma_2\sigma_4 & \sigma_3\sigma_4 \\ \sigma_1\sigma_4\sigma_7 & \sigma_2\sigma_4\sigma_7 & \sigma_3\sigma_4\sigma_7 \oplus \sigma_3\sigma_5\sigma_7 \end{pmatrix}. \quad (3.9)
\end{aligned}
$$

Whole System - Absolute Times. Let

- X_n^k be the time at which the last subtask of V_n^k is completed on processor k and X_n be the associated vector;
- Y_n^k be the time when the first subtask of V_n^k starts its execution on processor k and Y_n be the associated vector.

We have $Y_{n+1}^k = \max(X_n^k, T_{n+1})$. Thus, Equation (3.8) shows how to construct a matrix A_n (this is actually the matrix $A(L)$ which is associated with graph G_{n+1}) such that $X_{n+1} = A_n \otimes Y_{n+1}$.

So we obtain the following (max, +)-linear recurrence for the state vectors X_n:

$$X_{n+1} = A_n \otimes X_n \oplus B_{n+1} \otimes T_{n+1} \quad (3.10)$$

where $B_{n+1} = A_n \otimes H$, and H is the $K \times 1$ matrix with all its entries equal to e.

Other variables of interest can be represented in a similar way. For instance, the vector Y_n satisfies a similar recurrence equation with

$$Y_{n+1} = A_{n-1} \otimes Y_n \oplus H \otimes T_{n+1}. \quad (3.11)$$

3.3 Variations

Saturated Case. We can also consider the cases when the infinite sequence of data is available from time from time 0 on, or what will be equivalent for us, the case when there are no external data at all, so that the epoch when processor k can start working on G_{n+1} coincides with the epoch when it completes the last subtask of V_n^k; in both cases, $X_n = Y_{n+1}$ and the evolution is captured by the *autonomous* recurrence equation

$$X_{n+1} = A_n \otimes X_n, \tag{3.12}$$

with initial condition X_0.

Bounded Multiprogramming. In case the total multiprogramming degree is bounded by N, then it is not enough that all subtasks of V_n^k have been completed by processor k and V_{n+1} has already 'arrived' for processor k to be able to start the execution of the subtasks of V_{n+1}^k. It is also required that all subtasks of V_{n-N+1} have been completed. In that case, the recurrence equations (stated here in terms of the Y_n variables) read

$$Y_{n+1} = A_{n-1} \otimes Y_n \oplus J \otimes A_{n-N} \otimes Y_{n-N+1} \oplus H \otimes T_{n+1} \tag{3.13}$$

where J is the square matrix with all its entries equal to e. The corresponding equation for X_n is obtained from the previous one and from the relation $X_n = A_{n-1} \otimes Y_n$, which yield the following *non-autonomous* recurrence equation of order N:

$$X_{n+1} = A_n \otimes X_n \oplus A_n \otimes J \otimes X_{n-N+1} \oplus B_{n+1} \otimes T_{n+1}. \tag{3.14}$$

Associated Stochastic Petri Net. When the topology of the task graphs is deterministic (in which case the randomness of V_n is limited to the execution times of subtasks), then the above system can be described by a stochastic marked graph. An example is illustrated in Figure 3.1. On this representation, the dashed arcs, places and transitions correspond to a maximum multiprogramming degree of 2. The saturated case could be represented within this framework by taking all the firing times of the source equal to 0.

3.4 Canonical Recurrence Equations

The general form of the equations we have established above is

– *Non autonomous case* (corresponds to the non-saturated case)

$$X_n = \bigoplus_{k=1}^{\mu} A_{n,k} \otimes X_{n-k} \oplus B_n \otimes T_n, \tag{3.15}$$

for some given matrices and with some initial conditions $X_0, X_1, \ldots, X_{\mu-1}$

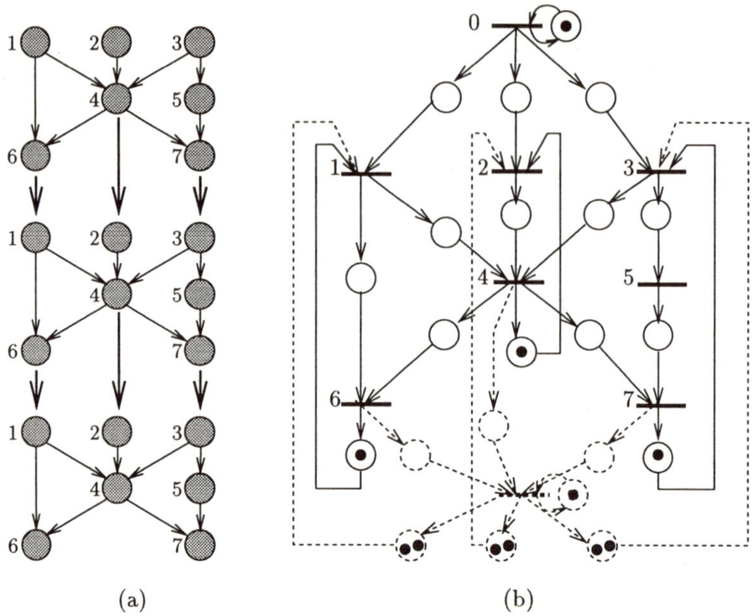

Fig. 3.1. Marked graph representation of the system.

– *Autonomous case* (corresponds to the saturated case)

$$X_n = \bigoplus_{k=1}^{\mu} A_{n,k} \otimes X_{n-k} \tag{3.16}$$

Note that $\mu = 1$ in the case with unbounded multiprogramming degree and $\mu \geq 1$ otherwise.

A more general case is that with k ranging from 0 to μ:

$$X_n = \bigoplus_{k=0}^{\mu} A_{n,k} \otimes X_{n-k}, \tag{3.17}$$

which can be reduced to the present case whenever $A_{n,0}$ is strictly lower (or upper) triangular in some basis; this reduction is actually exactly similar to the one performed above in order to get rid of the term $A(l,l) \otimes X_l$ in Equation (3.4) – see [4].

Equations (3.15-3.16) can always be rewritten as recurrences of order 1 of the type

$$\widetilde{X}_{n+1} = A_n \otimes \widetilde{X}_n \oplus \widetilde{B}_{n+1} \otimes T_{n+1} \tag{3.18}$$

and

$$\widetilde{X}_{n+1} = A_n \otimes \widetilde{X}_n, \tag{3.19}$$

respectively through the following (classical) state extension:

– A_n is the $\widetilde{K} = \mu \times K$ square matrix

$$A_n = \begin{pmatrix} A_{n+1,1} & A_{n+1,2} & \dots & \dots & A_{n+1,\mu} \\ E & \mathcal{E} & \dots & \mathcal{E} & \mathcal{E} \\ \mathcal{E} & E & \ddots & \vdots & \mathcal{E} \\ \vdots & \ddots & E & \mathcal{E} & \mathcal{E} \\ \mathcal{E} & \dots & \mathcal{E} & E & \mathcal{E} \end{pmatrix}. \tag{3.20}$$

– The $\widetilde{K} \times 1$ matrix $\widetilde{B}_n$ and the $\widetilde{K}$-dimensional vector $\widetilde{X}_n$ are given by

$$\widetilde{B}_n = \begin{pmatrix} B_n \\ \varepsilon \\ \vdots \\ \varepsilon \end{pmatrix}; \qquad \widetilde{X}_n = \begin{pmatrix} X_n \\ X_{n-1} \\ \vdots \\ X_{n-\mu+1} \end{pmatrix}. \tag{3.21}$$

Note that other constructions are possible for obtaining recurrence equations of order one with smaller matrices. This is the topic of Section 6.2.

3.5 Response Times

As mentioned above, in the non-saturated case, one is actually more interested in the difference

$$R_n^k = X_n^k - T_n \tag{3.22}$$

which represents the response time of the last subtask of V_n^k. Other variables of the same nature can of course be considered, leading to a similar analysis, like for instance the waiting time incurred by the first subtask of V_n^k defined by

$$W_n^k = Y_n^k - T_n. \tag{3.23}$$

We will only consider the model without limitation on the multiprogramming degree (the case of higher order recurrences can again be analyzed in similar terms – see [4] and [9]). Let $\tau_n = T_{n+1} - T_n$, $n \geq 0$. By subtracting T_{n+1} on both sides of (3.10), it is easily checked that the (new) state vectors R_n, defined by (3.22) satisfy the linear evolution equations

$$R_{n+1} = A_n \otimes C(\tau_n) \otimes R_n \oplus B_{n+1}, \tag{3.24}$$

where, for all $x \in \mathbb{R}$, $C(x)$ is the K - square matrix with all diagonal entries equal to $-x$ and all non-diagonal entries equal to $\varepsilon = -\infty$. Similarly

$$W_{n+1} = A_{n-1} \otimes C(\tau_n) \otimes W_n \oplus H. \tag{3.25}$$

4. Stability

For $x \in \mathbb{R}^K$ and $A \in \mathbb{R}_{max}^{K \times K}$, we use the notation $||x|| = \bigoplus_{i=1}^K x_i$ and $||A|| = \bigoplus_{i,j=1}^K A_{ij}$. The reference equation is $X_{n+1} = A_n \otimes X_n$ (the non-autonomous cases can be put in such a form by considering the input variable as one state variable). Within the framework of stability, we are interested in the existence of two kinds of asymptotic limits:

- First order limits like:

$$\lim_n \frac{||X_n||}{n}, \quad \lim_n \frac{X_n^i}{n},$$

  which give the existence of throughput (these limits can be understood in the almost sure sense or in expectation).
- Second order limits, on differences:

$$\lim_n X_{n+1}^i - X_n^i, \qquad \lim_n X_n^j - X_n^i, \ i \neq j,$$

  which give the existence of stationary regimes (these limits can be understood in the weak or the total variation sense for instance).

4.1 First Order Limits

Irreducible case. The following result is due to J.E. Cohen [16]

Theorem 4.1. *Let $\{A_n\}$ be a stationary and ergodic sequence of matrices. We suppose that $\forall i, j$, $P((A_0)_{ij} = \varepsilon) = 0$ and $+\infty > E((A_0)_{ij}) > \varepsilon$. There exists a constant $\gamma \in \mathbb{R}$ such that, for all initial conditions X_0 and for all $i \in \{1, \ldots, K\}$*

$$\lim_n \frac{X_n^i(X_0)}{n} = \lim_n E\left(\frac{X_n^i(X_0)}{n}\right) = \gamma, \quad P-a.s.$$

The constant γ is called the Lyapunov exponent of the stochastic matrix A_0.

This result can be extended to the case when some entries may be equal to ε, under the assumption that the matrices A_n are *irreducible.* By this, we mean that the *graph* of A_0 (the directed graph on $\{1, \ldots, K\}$ defined by $j \to k$ iff $P[(A_0)_{ij} > \varepsilon] > 0$) is strongly connected.

Different variants and generalizations of Theorem 4.1 are proposed in [12].

The Non-irreducible Case. We consider in this paragraph that matrix A_0 has a fixed structure. (a stochastic matrix $\{A(\omega),\ \omega \in \Omega\}$ has a fixed structure if $P(A(\omega)_{ij} = \varepsilon) = 1$ or $P(A(\omega)_{ij} = \varepsilon) = 0,\ \forall i, j$).

We decompose the graph of A_0 into its maximal strongly connected subgraphs (mscs). If we replace each mscs by one node, we obtain an associated *reduced graph* which is acyclic. With each node $\tilde{u}$ of the reduced graph (or equivalently to each mscs), we associate a constant $\gamma_{\tilde{u}}$ which is the Lyapunov exponent of the restrictions of A_n to this mscs (see Theorem 4.1). We denote by ${}^{\bullet}\tilde{u}$ the set of all ancestors of $\tilde{u}$ (including $\tilde{u}$) in the reduced graph. We have (see [2]):

Theorem 4.2. *Let $\{A_n\}$ be a stationary and ergodic sequence of matrices. We suppose that A_0 has a fixed structure. We suppose also that $E((A_0)_{ij}) < +\infty, \forall i, j$. Let us consider $i \in \{1, \ldots, K\}$, i belongs to the mscs $\tilde{u}$.*

$$\lim_n \frac{X_n^i(X_0)}{n} = \lim_n E\left(\frac{X_n^i(X_0)}{n}\right) = \bigoplus_{\tilde{v} \in {}^{\bullet}\tilde{u}} \gamma_{\tilde{v}},\ P-a.s.\,.$$

Intuitively, the Lyapunov exponent of a mscs has to be interpreted as the inverse of a throughput. The pace of the system is imposed by the mscs having the smallest throughput.

It is easy to check that in the parallel processing model considered in §2., the mscs of A_n coincide with the mscs of the graph $\mathcal{G}_n$, with nodes $\{1, \ldots, K\}$ (which can be identified with processors) and with arcs $l \to k$ if there exist two subtasks a and b of G_n, such that a is allocated to processor k and b to processor l and such that b is a predecessor of a in G_n. This decomposition result for parallel execution models was first established in [7].

More on First Order. If the sequence A_n is i.i.d., some additional results on convergence rates exist. In some special cases, a Central Limit Theorem is proved in [32]. Chapter 7 of [22] proposes results based on a martingale approach. Large deviation bounds have been proved in [6] and in [12].

4.2 Second Order Limits

Autonomous Systems. The results of this paragraph are borrowed from [87].

Definition 4.1. *The projective space $\mathbb{PR}^K_{max}$ is defined as the quotient of $\mathbb{R}^K_{max}$ by the parallelism relation :*

$$u, v \in \mathbb{R}^K_{max} \quad u \simeq v \Longleftrightarrow \exists a \in \mathbb{R}_{max} \setminus \{\varepsilon\} \text{ s.t. } u = a \otimes v\,.$$

Let π be the canonical projection of $\mathbb{R}^K_{max}$ into $\mathbb{PR}^K_{max}$. We define in a similar way $\mathbb{PR}^{K\times K}_{max}$ and $\mathbb{PR}^K = \{\pi(u),\ u \in \mathbb{R}^K\}$.

For example $(e, -1)'$ and $(1, e)'$ are in the same parallelism class, i.e. are two representatives of the same vector of $\mathbb{PR}^2_{max}$. It is easy to check that if $\alpha \in \mathbb{R}$ and if u is an eigenvector of a matrix A, then $\alpha \otimes u$ is also one. It is the motivation for the introduction of the projective space.

Definition 4.2. *A matrix A is said to be of* rank 1 *if all columns (resp. lines) are additively equivalent, i.e. if $\forall i, j$, $\pi(A_{.i}) = \pi(A_{.j})$ (resp. $\pi(A_{i.}) = \pi(A_{j.})$).*

Definition 4.3 (pattern). *Let $A : \Omega \to \mathbb{R}^{K \times K}_{max}$ be a random matrix. We say that $\tilde{A}$ is a pattern of A if $\tilde{A}$ is a deterministic matrix which belongs to the support of the random matrix A. This definition includes the cases where $\tilde{A}$ is only an accumulation point (A is a discrete r.v.) or a boundary point (A is a continuous r.v.) of the support.*

Theorem 4.3. *Let the sequence $\{A_n\}$ be stationary and ergodic. We suppose there is an integer N such that among the patterns of $A_{N-1} \otimes \cdots \otimes A_0$, there exists an irreducible matrix C of rank 1. Then $\pi(X_n)$ converges to a unique stationary distribution independently of the initial condition. If C is in the interior of the support, there is total variation convergence to the stationary distribution. Otherwise there is only weak convergence.*

We deduce from this theorem that a good way to show the stability of a system $X_{n+1} = A_n \otimes X_n$ is to extract some deterministic matrices from the support of A_0 and to build a rank-1 pattern with them. In most cases, an extracted model with two matrices will be enough to conclude, see [88].

Non-Autonomous Systems. In this paragraph, the reference equation is the non-autonomous recurrence equation (3.18):

$$X_{n+1} = A_n \otimes X_n \oplus B_{n+1} \otimes T_{n+1}. \tag{4.1}$$

Note that one can also see this as the following autonomous recurrence equation for the column vector (T_{n+1}, X_n):

$$\begin{pmatrix} T_{n+2} \\ X_{n+1} \end{pmatrix} = \begin{pmatrix} \tau_{n+1} & \varepsilon \\ B_{n+1} & A_n \end{pmatrix} \otimes \begin{pmatrix} T_{n+1} \\ X_n \end{pmatrix}.$$

To this equation, one can associate the vector $W_n = X_n - T_n$, which satisfies an equation of the type (3.24). Specific instances of such equations are waiting times and response times in our basic model. The following result is proved in Chapter 7 of [4]:

Theorem 4.4. *Assume that the sequence $\{A_n, B_n, \tau_n\}$ is stationary and ergodic, with all entries non identically equal to ε integrable. If $\rho < 1$, where $\rho = \lambda a$, $\lambda^{-1} = E(\tau_0)$, and a is the maximal Lyapunov exponent of the sequence of matrices $\{A_n\}$, then the sequence W_n converges in total variation to a unique stationary sequence. The stationary law of this sequence is that of the random variable W, which is given by the following matrix-series:*

$$W = B_0 \oplus \bigoplus_{n \geq 1} C(-T_{-n}) \otimes D_n \tag{4.2}$$

where

$$D_n = A_{-1} \otimes \ldots \otimes A_{-n} \otimes B_{-n}. \tag{4.3}$$

More general results on the case with multidimensional input processes are considered in [4].

Example. As mentioned above, a non-autonomous system can also be viewed as an autonomous one with an extended state including the input. We illustrate this and the above theorem by considering the autonomous system with deterministic matrix

$$A = \begin{pmatrix} 1 & \varepsilon \\ e & e \end{pmatrix}, \; A^n = \begin{pmatrix} n & \varepsilon \\ n-1 & e \end{pmatrix},$$

where $(\lambda^{-1} = 1) > (a = e)$. We put $X_0 = (u, v)'$. We have $A^n \otimes X_0 = (nu, (n-1)u \oplus v)'$. For n sufficiently big, we have

$$A^n X_0 = nu \otimes \begin{pmatrix} e \\ -1 \end{pmatrix} \Longrightarrow \pi(A^n X_0) = \pi \begin{pmatrix} e \\ -1 \end{pmatrix}.$$

We consider now a case where $(\lambda^{-1} = e) < (a = 1)$.

$$A = \begin{pmatrix} e & \varepsilon \\ e & 1 \end{pmatrix}, \; A^n = \begin{pmatrix} e & \varepsilon \\ n-1 & n \end{pmatrix},$$

we have

$$\pi(A^n X_0) = \pi \begin{pmatrix} e \\ (n-1) \oplus (v-u)n \end{pmatrix}.$$

We check that $X_n^2 - X_n^1 = (n-1) \oplus (v-u)n$ tends to $+\infty$ for all finite X_0.

For a stochastic model, the idea remains the same. If $\lambda a < 1$, the input process which is slower imposes its pace. If $\lambda a > 1$, everything happens asymptotically as if the system was saturated.

4.3 Multiple Stationary Regimes for Closed Systems

When all the timings are deterministic, a saturated model of task graphs is described by an equation of type $X_n = A \otimes X_{n-1} = A^n \otimes X_0$. Such a system may have several stationary regimes. More precisely, it can be proved that there is convergence in finite time of X_n to a vector x solution of $A^d x = \gamma x$ for some $d \in \mathbb{N}$. By analogy with conventional algebra, this equation is called a spectral equation, γ is called an eigenvalue and x an eigenvector of A^d. Let us provide some results of the spectral theory in the (max,+) algebra. For more details see [17, 4].

The graph of a square matrix A is a directed graph having a number of nodes equal to the dimension of A. This graph contains an arc from i to j

if and only if $A_{ji} \neq \varepsilon$. For each circuit $\zeta = \{t_1, t_2, \cdots, t_j, t_{j+1} = t_1\}$ in the graph, we define its average weight by $p(\zeta) = (A_{t_1 t_j} \otimes \cdots \otimes A_{t_3 t_2} \otimes A_{t_2 t_1})/j$.

Matrix $A = (A_{ij}, i, j = 1, \ldots, K)$ is irreducible if its graph is strongly connected, i.e. $\forall i, j\ \exists (i_1 = i, i_2, \ldots, i_n = j)$ s.t. $A_{ii_2} \otimes A_{i_2 i_3} \otimes \cdots \otimes A_{i_{n-1} j} > \varepsilon$.

Theorem 4.5. *If A is an irreducible matrix, it admits a unique (non ε) eigenvalue, γ. It is equal to the maximal average weight of the circuits of A, i.e. $\gamma = \max_\zeta p(\zeta)$. We call also γ the* Lyapunov exponent *of A.*

Theorem 4.1 is a generalization of Theorem 4.5 under stochastic assumptions.

We normalize a matrix by subtracting its eigenvalue to each coordinate. A normalized matrix has an eigenvalue of e. For a normalized matrix A of size K, we define $A^+ = A \oplus A^2 \oplus \cdots \oplus A^K$. We check that $A^+ \oplus A^{K+1} = A^+$.

Theorem 4.6. *Let A be a normalized matrix. If i is such that $A^+_{ii} = e$ then the index i belongs to a circuit ζ of maximal weight. Furthermore, the column $A^+_{.i}$ is an eigenvector of A. Every eigenvector of A can be expressed as a "linear" (in $\mathbb{R}_{max}$) combination of columns of A^+.*

If matrix A is of rank 1, it is also the case of A^+. We conclude by Theorem 4.6 that A has a unique eigenvector. Hence Theorem 4.3 has a very straightforward interpretation in the deterministic case. The vector $\pi(X_n) = \pi(A^n X_0)$ has a unique stationary regime iff A has a unique eigenvector.

The canonical projection π was defined in Definition 4.1. It can be interpreted geometrically as the orthogonal projection on the hyperspace orthogonal to the vector $\mathbf{1} = (1, \ldots, 1)'$. The projective space $\mathbb{PR}^K$ is isomorphic to $\mathbb{R}^{K-1}$. For irreducible matrices of size 3, a graphical representation of the set of eigenvectors is possible in $\mathbb{R}^2 \simeq \mathbb{PR}^3$ (see [86]).

Example. Let us consider the example of Equation (3.9) with the following service times :

$$\sigma_1 = 2,\ \sigma_2 = 1,\ \sigma_3 = 2,\ \sigma_4 = 1,\ \sigma_5 = 2,\ \sigma_6 = 1,\ \sigma_7 = 0\,.$$

We obtain the matrix :

$$A = \begin{pmatrix} 4 & 3 & 4 \\ 3 & 2 & 3 \\ 3 & 2 & 4 \end{pmatrix}.$$

The eigenvalue is $\gamma = A_{11} = A_{33} = 4$. It corresponds to the mean execution time of a task (the inverse of the throughput). It does not depend on the initial condition X_0. The set of eigenvectors of A in the projective space $\mathbb{PR}^3$ has been represented in Figure 4.1. The three dashed axes are the orthogonal projection of the basis of $\mathbb{R}^3$. The practical way of representing a point X of $\mathbb{PR}^3$ is to choose a vector ($\in \mathbb{R}^3$) in the parallelism class of X and to draw it in the three axes obtained by projection of the orthonormal basis of $\mathbb{R}^3$. It is easy to check that the point we obtain does not depend on the representative in the parallelism class.

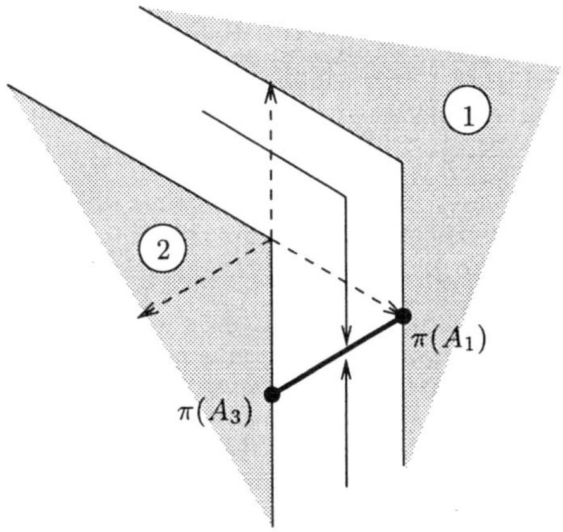

Fig. 4.1. Set of eigenvectors of matrix A.

The extremal eigenvectors of A are $\pi(A_1) = \pi(1,0,0)$ and $\pi(A_3) = \pi(1,0,1)$. The set of eigenvectors is the segment $[\pi(A_3), \pi(A_1)]$. For an initial condition in the gray zones 1 or 2, there is convergence to the eigenvectors $\pi(A_1)$ and $\pi(A_3)$ respectively. For an initial condition in the white strip, convergence occurs according to the arrows.

This multiplicity of eigenelements accounts for multiple possible operating modes of the task graph, depending on the initial condition X_0. Let us consider the difference δ between the completion dates of a task at processors 1 and 3, i.e. $\delta = X_n^1 - X_n^3$. We can have for example $\delta = 1$ (operating mode $\pi(A_1)$) or $\delta = 0$ (operating mode $\pi(A_3)$).

However for most values of the services σ_1 to σ_7, matrix A will be of rank 1. For instance, if we have $\sigma_4 > \sigma_5$, we obtain:

$$A = \sigma_4 \otimes \begin{pmatrix} \sigma_6 \\ 0 \\ \sigma_7 \end{pmatrix} \otimes \begin{pmatrix} \sigma_1 & \sigma_2 & \sigma_3 \end{pmatrix} .$$

The corresponding task graph has a unique operating mode. i.e. when A_n is a random matrix, it is very easy to get a rank 1 pattern, at least when the matrices are random enough.

5. Analytical Results

This section deals with methods for computing analytically the statistics.

5.1 Markovian Analysis

In this section, we address the problem of actually computing stationary or transient performance measures for dynamical systems described by stochastic recurrences of the form (3.19), *viz*: $X_{n+1} = A_n \otimes X_n$, by exploiting the underlying Markovian structure. Indeed, it turns out that under natural assumptions on the random driving sequences, the sequence of vectors $\{\pi(X_n)\}$ (see Section 4.2) is a Markov chain on the projective space $\mathbb{PR}^K_{max}$.

Before giving the details, note that Markovian analysis is routinely applied for analyzing the performances of stochastic Petri nets (and event graphs in particular). This standard approach is based on the analysis of the set of *reachable markings*. It usually applies when the distributions of firing times are exponential, and may be extended to handle coxian distributions. This technique is described for instance in [1].

The approach proposed here is different in that it uses as a state space the instants at which events occur (called *daters*). It allows to relax somewhat the restrictions on firing time distributions.

The Markovian technique based on daters was introduced by Resing *et al.* in [32] for solving (max, +) systems. It turns out to be applicable in the more general context of *recurrent homogeneous stochastic operators* [78, 57]. To illustrate this approach, consider the recurrence:

$$\left\{\begin{array}{lcl} X^1_{n+1} & = & (A_n)_{11} \otimes X^1_n \oplus (A_n)_{12} \otimes X^2_n \\ X^2_{n+1} & = & (A_n)_{21} \otimes X^1_n \oplus (A_n)_{22} \otimes X^2_n \,, \end{array}\right. \tag{5.1}$$

starting from some (X^1_0, X^2_0). Introducing the variable $Z_n = \pi(X^1_n, X^2_n) = X^2_n - X^1_n$, we obtain the following recurrences:

$$\left\{\begin{array}{lcl} Z_{n+1} & = & ((A_n)_{21} \oplus (A_n)_{22} + Z_n) - ((A_n)_{11} \oplus (A_n)_{12} + Z_n) \\ X^1_{n+1} & = & X^1_n \otimes ((A_n)_{11} \oplus (A_n)_{12} + Z_n) \,, \\ X^2_{n+1} & = & X^2_n \otimes ((A_n)_{21} - Z_n \oplus (A_n)_{22}) \,. \end{array}\right.$$

Assuming that the sequence $\{(A_n)_{ij}, i, j = 1, 2\}_{n=0}^{\infty}$ is i.i.d., it is clear that $\mathcal{Z} = \{Z_n, n \in \mathbb{N}\}$ and $\{(X^1_n, X^2_n, Z_n), n \in \mathbb{N}\}$ are homogeneous Markov chains. If $\mathcal{Z}$ admits a stationary distribution π, one readily obtains stationary performance measures in terms of π. Of course, the process $\{(X^1_n, X^2_n), n \in \mathbb{N}\}$ itself is a Markov chain, but this chain is transient, and the introduction of Z_n makes it clear that its growth depends on the behavior of another chain which, in most cases, turns out to have a stationary regime. The proper structure to describe this dependency is the class of *Markov Additive Processes* (MAP), discussed in particular in [14, 15]. Roughly speaking, a MAP is a Markov process with two components, such that the increments of the second component are independent given the values of the first component.

The practical consequences of this observation are summarized in the following theorems. For the sake of simplicity and numerical tractability, we restrict ourselves to the case of discrete random variables.

Theorem 5.1. *Let $\{(X_n, Z_n), n \in \mathbb{N}\}$ be a discrete time MAP on $\mathbb{N} \times \mathbb{N}^p$. Let $M(z)$ be the matrix:*

$$M(z)_{ij} = \mathbb{E}(z^{X_{n+1}-X_n} 1_{\{Z_n=j\}} \mid Z_{n-1}=i) , \quad i,j \in \mathbb{N}^p, |z|=1. \tag{5.2}$$

Then, the joint generating function of the X_n is given by:

$$\mathbb{E}\left(\prod_{n=0}^{N} s_i^{X_i}\right) = \pi_0 \; M(s_1 \dots s_N) \; M(s_2 \dots s_N) \; \dots \; M(s_{N-1} s_N) \; M(s_N) \; \mathbf{1} , \tag{5.3}$$

where $\pi_0^{(k)} = P(Z(0)=k)$. Alternately, let, for all $n \geq 1$, $d_n = X_n - X_{n-1}$. The joint generating function of the d_ns is given by:

$$\mathbb{E}\left(\prod_{n=1}^{N} s_n{}^{d_n}\right) = \pi_0 \; M(s_1) \; \dots \; M(s_N) \; \mathbf{1} . \tag{5.4}$$

The proof involves Markov chains techniques. The extension of this theorem when the component X is continuous and multidimensional is immediate; the corresponding definition of M involves Laplace transforms.

The central role played by the matrix $M(z)$ in the transient and asymptotic properties of the chain X_n has been known in the literature for a long time. See [33] for instance. Notice in particular that for z real and positive, $M(z)$ (where it is defined) satisfies the assumptions of the Perron-Frobenius theorem whenever $M(1)$ (which is the transition matrix of the chain $\mathcal{Z}$) does. This happens in particular when the state space of $\mathcal{Z}$ is finite and the chain satisfies the usual ergodicity conditions. In this case, we shall write: $\mathcal{Z}$ is PF.

Among the corollaries of Theorem 5.1, we have:

Corollary 5.1. *The generating function of the distribution of X_n is given by:*

$$\mathbb{E}(s^{X_n}) = \pi_0 \; M(s)^n \; \mathbf{1} .$$

Let $\gamma = \lim_{n\to\infty} \mathbb{E}X_n/n$ be the asymptotic growth rate *of the chain. We have:*

i/ if $\mathcal{Z}$ is stationary and ergodic with stationary distribution distribution π,

$$\gamma = \mathbb{E}_\pi X(1) = \pi M'(1)\mathbf{1} \tag{5.5}$$

ii/Assume $\mathcal{Z}$ is PF. Let $\lambda_1(z)$ be the Perron-Frobenius eigenvalue of the matrix $M(z)$, and $P(z,x) = det(M(z) - xI)$ be the characteristic polynomial of $M(z)$. Then

$$\gamma = \frac{d\lambda_1}{dz}(1) = -\frac{\partial P}{\partial z}(1,1) \; / \; \frac{\partial P}{\partial x}(1,1) . \tag{5.6}$$

It is therefore possible to compute the so called "first order" measures of these systems using either the stationary distribution with (5.5) or the characteristic polynomial (actually, only partial derivatives of it), with (5.6).

Theorem 5.1 also allows to address the computation of second order quantities, such as the limit behavior of the distribution of $d_n = X_{n+1} - X_n$ and its moments, as well as autocorrelations of the process $\{d_n, n \in \mathbb{N}\}$ and the central limit behavior of X_n. These questions are discussed in [78].

Applications of the technique described above to (max, +) and (min, max, +) systems above have been reported in [78, 26, 57].

5.2 Taylor Expansions for the M/G Case

Under certain integrability assumptions stated below, when the input process is Poisson, the expectation $\mathbb{E}W$ of the stationary state variable W given in (4.2) is finite and the components of $\mathbb{E}W$ can be expanded into a power series with respect to the arrival intensity λ. The results reported below apply to any recurrence equation of the type (4.1). However, for sake of simplicity, these results will be stated for waiting times W_n defined in (3.23). Their proof, which relies on Theorem 4.4 and on perturbation analysis techniques, can be found in [9].

Assumptions. We assume that each entry of A_n is either a.s. non-negative or a.s. equal to ε, and that all entries on the diagonal of A_n are non-negative, which holds true in our multiprocessing model.

We also assume that $\{T_n\}$ is a Poisson process with intensity λ, and that the execution times of the subtasks of different graphs are independent (we can allow dependencies of subtasks within a task). Finally, we assume that all execution times have finite moments of order $m+3$ for some $m \in \mathbb{N}$.

Expansion Theorem.

Theorem 5.2. *Under the above assumptions, if the stability condition of Theorem 4.4 holds, the following expansion holds for the expected value of the k-th coordinate of the stationary W variable defined in (4.2):*

$$\mathbb{E}W^i = \sum_{k=0}^{m} \lambda^k \mathbb{E}\; p_{k+1}(D_0^i, D_1^i, \ldots, D_k^i) \;+\; \mathcal{O}(\lambda^{m+1}). \tag{5.7}$$

The vectors D_n are defined in (4.3) The functions p_k are the following polynomials:

$$p_k(x_0, x_1, \ldots, x_{k-1}) = \sum_{(i_0,i_1,\ldots,i_{k-1}) \in S_k} (-1)^{q_k(i_0,i_1,\ldots,i_{k-1})} \frac{x_0^{i_0}}{i_0!}\frac{x_1^{i_1}}{i_1!}\cdots\frac{x_{k-1}^{i_{k-1}}}{i_{k-1}!}, \tag{5.8}$$

where $S_k = \{(i_0, i_1, ..., i_{k-1}) \in \mathbb{N}^k \,:\, i_0 + i_1 + ... + i_{k-1} = k$ and if $i_s = l > 1$, then $i_{s-1} = i_{s-2} = \ldots = i_{s-l+1} = 0\}$, (the $s-j$ are modulo k) and

$$q_k(i_0, i_1, \ldots, i_{k-1}) = 1 + \sum_{s=0}^{k-1} 1(i_s > 0).$$

In particular, we get

$$p_1(x_0) = x_0, \qquad p_2(x_0, x_1) = \frac{1}{2}\left[x_0^2 + x_1^2 - 2x_0x_1\right], \tag{5.9}$$

$$p_3(x_0, x_1, x_2) = \frac{1}{6}\left[x_0^3 + x_1^3 + x_2^3 - 3(x_0^2x_1 + x_1^2x_2 + x_2^2x_0) + 6x_0x_1x_2\right], \tag{5.10}$$

$$\begin{aligned} p_4(x_0, x_1, x_2, x_3) = \frac{1}{24}\big[&x_0^4 + x_1^4 + x_2^4 + x_3^4 \\ - \ & 4(x_0^3x_1 + x_1^3x_2 + x_2^3x_3 + x_3^3x_0) - 6(x_0^2x_2^2 + x_1^2x_3^2) \\ + \ & 12(x_0^2x_1x_2 + x_1^2x_2x_3 + x_2^2x_3x_0 + x_3^2x_0x_1) - 24x_0x_1x_2x_3\big] \end{aligned} \tag{5.11}$$

$$\begin{aligned} p_5(x_0, x_1, x_2, x_3, x_4) = \frac{1}{120}\big[&x_0^5 + x_1^5 + x_2^5 + x_3^5 + x_4^5 \\ - \ & 5(x_0^4x_1 + x_1^4x_2 + x_2^4x_3 + x_3^4x_4 + x_4^4x_0) \\ - \ & 10(x_0^3x_2^2 + x_1^3x_3^2 + x_2^3x_4^2 + x_3^3x_0^2 + x_4^3x_1^2) \\ + \ & 20(x_0^3x_1x_2 + x_1^3x_2x_3 + x_2^3x_3x_4 + x_3^3x_4x_5 + x_4^3x_0x_1) \\ + \ & 30(x_0^2x_2^2x_3 + x_1^2x_3^2x_4 + x_2^2x_4^2x_5 + x_3^2x_0^2x_1 + x_4^2x_1^2x_2) \\ - \ & 60(x_0^2x_1x_2x_3 + x_1^2x_2x_3x_4 + x_2^2x_3x_4x_5 + x_3^2x_4x_0x_1 + x_4^2x_0x_1x_2) \\ - \ & 120x_0x_1x_2x_3x_4\big]. \end{aligned} \tag{5.12}$$

The proof of Theorem 5.2 is given in [9].

5.2.1 Example. We apply the above analysis to the workload consisting of repetitions of the task depicted in Figure 5.1. The execution times of subtasks are assumed to be deterministic and their value is indicated inside the subtasks.

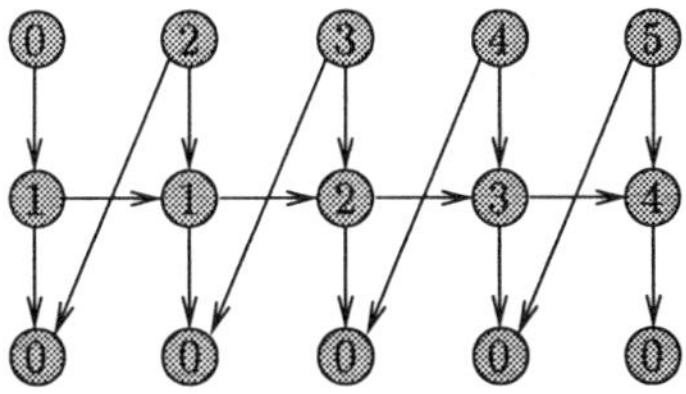

Fig. 5.1. A task to be executed on 5 processors.

An easy computation shows that this workload is characterized by the matrix:

$$A = \begin{pmatrix} 1 & 2 & \varepsilon & \varepsilon & \varepsilon \\ 2 & 3 & 3 & \varepsilon & \varepsilon \\ 4 & 5 & 5 & 4 & \varepsilon \\ 7 & 8 & 8 & 7 & 5 \\ 11 & 12 & 12 & 11 & 9 \end{pmatrix} .$$

In the case we consider (waiting times), $B_n = H$, where H is the column vector with all its entries equal to $e = 0$. Using this and a direct computation of the powers of A, we obtain

$$D_0 = \begin{pmatrix} 0 \\ 0 \\ 0 \\ 0 \\ 0 \end{pmatrix}, \quad D_1 = \begin{pmatrix} 2 \\ 3 \\ 5 \\ 8 \\ 12 \end{pmatrix}, \quad D_2 = \begin{pmatrix} 5 \\ 8 \\ 12 \\ 17 \\ 21 \end{pmatrix} \tag{5.13}$$

and

$$D_3 = \begin{pmatrix} 10 \\ 15 \\ 21 \\ 26 \\ 30 \end{pmatrix}, \quad D_4 = \begin{pmatrix} 18 \\ 24 \\ 30 \\ 35 \\ 39 \end{pmatrix}, \quad D_5 = \begin{pmatrix} 26 \\ 33 \\ 39 \\ 44 \\ 48 \end{pmatrix} \tag{5.14}$$

and $D^k_{n+1} = D^k_n + 9$ for all k and for all $n \geq 5$.

The case with random execution times can be handled within the same framework. In a first step, we have to compute the coefficients of D_n in function of the execution times, and in a second step, the expectation of the polynomials $p_k(D^i_0, \ldots D^i_{k-1})$ (see [9]). Taylor expansions are also available for Laplace transforms [5].

5.3 Transient and Stationary Distributions for the M/D Case

In this section, we derive a numerically effective way to compute the distribution of response times, in the transient and in the stationary regime, in the M/D case. Detailed results may be found in [80]

The assumptions on the system are as in the previous section. In addition, we assume that the execution times are deterministic; the formulas below may be useful in a more general context.

Consider a fixed i and let $d_n = D^i_n$, where D_n is defined in Equation (4.3).

From the analysis of Section 3., and in particular from a direct iteration of Equation (3.24), we obtain the following formula $\forall x \in \mathbb{R}$,

$$\begin{aligned} &\mathbb{P}(W_n \leq x) \\ &\quad = \mathbb{P}(d_0 \leq x, d_1 \leq x + \tau_n; d_2 \leq x + \tau_{n-1} + \tau_n; \ldots; d_n \leq x + \tau_1 + \ldots + \tau_n) \\ &\quad = \mathbb{P}(d_0 \leq x, d_1 \leq x + \tau_1; d_2 \leq x + \tau_1 + \tau_2; \ldots; d_{n-1} \leq x + \tau_1 + \ldots + \tau_n) \\ &\quad \triangleq H_n(d_0, d_1, d_2, \ldots, d_n; x) \end{aligned}$$

The function H_n is defined on $\mathbb{R}_+^n \times \mathbb{R}$. Among its properties, the one which is the basis of our analysis is: $\forall 0 \leq j \leq n-1, \forall x \in [d_j, d_{j+1}]$,

$$H_n(d_0, d_1, d_2, \ldots, d_n; x) = \int_0^\infty H_{n-j}(d_j, \ldots, d_n; x+t) \mathrm{d}E_j(t) , \quad (5.15)$$

where $\mathrm{d}E_j(t)$ is the density of the Erlang distribution with rate λ and $j \geq 0$ phases, that is: $\lambda e^{-\lambda t}(\lambda t)^{j-1}/(j-1)!$ if $j \geq 1$, and a Dirac mass at 0 if $j = 0$.

5.3.1 Transient Formulas. The distribution of W_n is characterized by the following theorem, easily proved by recurrence.

Theorem 5.3. *The function H_n can be rewritten as:*

$$H_n(d_0, d_1, d_2, \ldots, d_n; x) = e^{-\lambda(d_n - x)^+} L_n(d_0, d_1, d_2, \ldots, d_n; x) , \quad (5.16)$$

where the function L_n has the properties:

i/ $L_n(d_0, d_1, d_2, \ldots, d_n; x) = 1, \ \forall x \geq d_n$.
ii/ $L_n(d_0, d_1, d_2, \ldots, d_n; x) = 0, \ \forall x < d_0$.
iii/For all $0 \leq j \leq n-1$, L_n *is a polynomial of degree* j *on the interval* $[d_j, d_{j+1}]$, *given by:*

$$L_n(d_0, d_1, d_2, \ldots, d_n; x) = \sum_{s=0}^{j} \frac{\lambda^s}{s!}(d_{j+1} - x)^s L_{n-s}(d_s, \ldots, d_n; d_{j+1}) .$$

iv/ The numbers $\xi_{n,m,j} = L_{n-m}(d_m, \ldots, d_n; d_j)$, $0 \leq m \leq j < n$ *are given by the recurrence:*

$$\xi_{n,m,j} = \sum_{s=0}^{j-m} \frac{\lambda^s}{s!}(d_{j+1} - d_j)^s \xi_{n,m+s,j+1} , \quad 0 \leq m \leq j < n, \quad (5.17)$$

with $\xi_{n,m,n} = 1, \forall \ 0 \leq m \leq n$.

A first practical consequence of Theorem 5.3 is that quantities such as $\mathbb{P}(W_n \leq x)$ may be numerically computed with $\mathcal{O}(n^2)$ operations.

According to the following corollary, the moments of W_n may be computed with the same complexity.

Corollary 5.2. *The Laplace transform of W_n is given by:*

$$W^*(s) = e^{-sd_n} \left[\left(\frac{\lambda}{\lambda - s} \right)^{n+1} - \frac{s}{\lambda - s} \sum_{p=0}^{n} \xi_{n,p,p} e^{(\lambda - s)(d_p - d_n)} \left(\frac{\lambda}{\lambda - s} \right)^p \right] .$$

The first moment of W_n is given by:

$$\mathbb{E}\, W_n = d_n - \frac{n+1}{\lambda} + \frac{1}{\lambda} \sum_{p=0}^{n} \xi_{n,p,p} e^{\lambda(d_p - d_n)} .$$

5.3.2 Stationary behavior. Further analysis taking into account the asymptotic behavior of the sequence $\{d_n\}$ allows to derive stationary formulas. For instance, if there exists T and γ such that: $d_n = d_T + (n-T)\gamma, \forall n \geq T$ (like in the Example of Section 5.2, then the Laplace transform of the stationary distribution of the waiting time is:

$$W^*(s) = W_D^*(s) \left(\frac{\lambda}{\lambda - s}\right)^T e^{-sb_T} - \frac{s}{\lambda - s} \sum_{p=0}^{T-1} \tau_p \left(\frac{\lambda}{\lambda - s}\right)^p e^{-sb_p}.$$

In this formula, $W_D^*(s)$ is the transform of the waiting time in the $M/D/1$ with arrival rate λ and services γ, and the τ_p are coefficients correcting for the "transient period" of the sequence $\{d_n\}$. We omit the algorithm permitting to compute them.

5.3.3 Example. To illustrate the above analysis, we use consider the example of Section 5.2.1. We have $\gamma = 9$, and the sequence of vectors D_n was computed in (5.13-5.14). For processor number 1, the sequence $\{d_i\}$ will be: $\{0, 2, 5, 10, 17, 26, \ldots\}$ so that $T = 4$. For processor 5, the sequence is $\{0, 12, 21, \ldots\}$ so that we may take $T = 1$. Of course, the result is unchanged if we take a longer "transient". Figure 5.2 shows the value of the expected waiting times $\mathbb{E}W^k$, $1 \leq k \leq 5$ as a function of λ. The interrupted curves are the corresponding Taylor expansions (of order $m = 4$) obtained using Theorem 5.2.

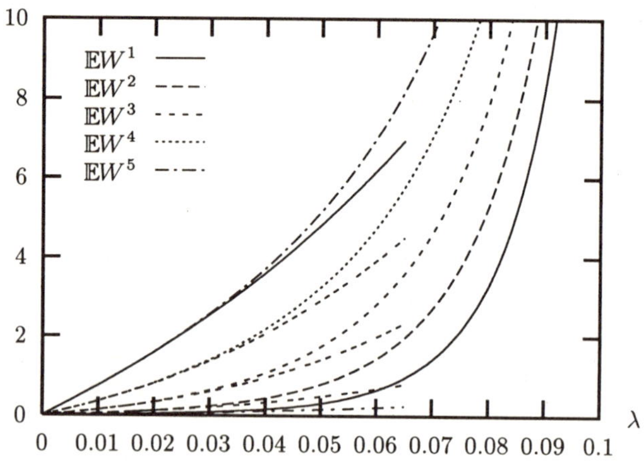

Fig. 5.2. Expected waiting times for the task of Figure 5.1

6. Parallel Simulation Issues

In this section, we are interested in ways of simulating the basic model using its evolution equations (rather than classical event-driven simulation based on the event list technique) and using parallel or distributed computers (rather than sequential ones). We propose several algorithms, compute their theoretical complexity and discuss various optimization issues.

The results obtained below are discussed in the context of stochastic event graphs, in which the case with task graphs with fixed topology was show to fall. More detailed results, extensions and proofs may be found in [3, 57, 58].

Our departure point will be the linear recurrence of order μ given in Equation (3.17):

$$X_n = A_{n,0} \otimes X_n \oplus \ldots \oplus A_{n,\mu} \otimes X_{n-\mu},$$

where the matrices $A_{n,k}, n \in \mathbb{N}, 0 \leq k \leq \mu$ are built from execution times in the system. In order to use this relation for simulating the system, one first has to transform this in a constructive recurrence of the type (3.16). This is done by multiplying by the "pseudo inverse" $A^{\star}_{n,0}$ defined in (3.5). This gives the form (3.16):

$$X_n = \overline{A}_{n,1} \otimes X_{n-1} \oplus \ldots \oplus \overline{A}_{n,\mu} \otimes X_{n-\mu}, \tag{6.1}$$

with $\overline{A}_{n,l} = A^{\star}_{n,0} \otimes A_{n,l}$.

In order to be able to perform the computations in parallel, it is useful to manipulate the canonical representation of (6.1) as defined in Section 3.4. This representation allows one to reduce the problem to the analysis of the equation

$$\widetilde{X}_n = A_n \otimes \widetilde{X}_{n-1}, \tag{6.2}$$

where the variables X_n are contained in the variables $\widetilde{X}_n$. The dimension $\widetilde{K}$ of such a representation is larger than that of the original system.

In Section 6.2.3, we show that there exist other transformations which yield similar representations of smaller dimension.

It is important to keep in mind that with a linear system of dimension K and order μ is associated an event graph, noted $\mathcal{E}$, with $T = K$ transitions and a maximum initial marking of μ (see [4]). This can be seen by building the dependency graph of the variables X^i_n (see Section 6.2.1) and by using the correspondence between periodic task graphs and event graphs, as in Figure 3.1. The associated recurrence of order 1 will be assumed to have dimension $\widetilde{T}$.

For sake of clear exposition, i is better to state our results at the level of the event graph rather than at that of the task graphs. We assume that the reader is acquainted with the basic notions and notations of Petri net theory, and in particular with the notion of *incidence matrix* I of the net, and the set $R(M_0)$ of *reachable markings* from some initial marking M_0, which satisfy the relation: $M = M_0 + I.x$, where x is a vector of integers [31].

For a Petri net $\mathcal{P}$, $t^\bullet$ will denote the set of arcs in $\mathcal{P}$ with starting node t and $^\bullet t$ the set of arcs in $\mathcal{P}$ with ending node t.

6.1 Parallel Simulation Algorithms

We present now two dual algorithms to simulate a linear system both based on the evolution equation (6.2). We analyze the complexity of each of them in terms of the parameters of the system. We then discuss (Section 6.2) the minimization of this complexity. See [3] for details on these algorithms.

6.1.1 Space Parallel Algorithm. This algorithm consists in computing the product $A_n \otimes \widetilde{X}_{n-1}$ in parallel using conventional linear algebra parallel algorithms. It can be efficiently implemented on a SIMD architecture. In the form proposed in [3], it uses the space extension of (3.20. It is called "space parallel" because for each n, the variables $\widetilde{X}_n^i, 1 \leq i \leq \widetilde{T}$ are computed by different processors.

An important step in this algorithm, is the computation of $A^\star_{n,0}$. The operation $\oplus$ being idempotent, we have $A^\star_{n,0} = (E \oplus A_{n,0})^L$, where L is the length of the longest path with no marks in the event graph representing the system.

Complexity. Assuming that the algorithm is run on a SIMD machine with a number K of processors less than μT^2, and which can transpose a matrix in polylog time, the asymptotic PRAM complexity for the computation of $\widetilde{X}_N$ turns out to be:

$$O\left((N/K)(\mu T^2(L \log T + T \log \mu))\right).$$

Using sparse matrix techniques for the multiplications gives a PRAM complexity of:

$$O\left((N/K)(\mu T^2(L \log T + D))\right), \tag{6.3}$$

where D is maximal indegree of a transition in the event graph.

6.1.2 Time Parallel Algorithm. A dual way to use parallelism to simulate Equation (6.2) is to rewrite it as:

$$\widetilde{X}_N = A_N \otimes \cdots \otimes A_1 \otimes \widetilde{X}_0,$$

and use the associativity of the matrix operation $\otimes$ to design a classical parallel prefix algorithm [10] to compute the vectors $\widetilde{X}_N, \cdots, \widetilde{X}_1$. This algorithm is "time parallel" because the computation of all vectors X_n is carried out in parallel.

Complexity. For this algorithm, matrices are multiplied sequentially on each processor. Combined with the complexity of the parallel prefix algorithm with K processors, this gives an asymptotic complexity of:

$$O\left((N/K)\widetilde{T}^2 D + \widetilde{T}^3 \log K\right).$$

Comparison. Because the PRAM model may be quite far from the actual computers, the complexity formulas above are not enough to compare the performances of practical implementations. However, they hint that that the space parallel is more suited for very large networks, and that the time parallel algorithm is limited to systems of moderate sizes.

6.2 Minimal Standard Representations

The formulas obtained in the preceding section show that the complexity of the parallel algorithms ultimately depends on the initial marking of the associated marked graph, through μ and L and the dimension of the standard representation. Therefore, changing the initial marking *before* deriving evolution equation may improve these algorithms.

We refer the interested reader to references [55, 58, 88] for the theorems showing how one may change the initial marking and the timings of an event graph without modifying its trajectories or its stationary behavior, thus allowing to start the simulation from any marking *structurally reachable* from the original one. In this paper, we shall instead discuss the algorithmic issues.

6.2.1 Dependency Graph. A useful object related to a linear system S is the *dependency graph*, $\delta(S)$, constructed from the dependence relations in S. This graph is also called the developed graph and is presented in [13] for example. Its nodes are the variables X_n^i. If there is a non-ε matrix coefficient relating X_n^i and X_m^j in S, then there is an arc between nodes X_m^j and X_n^i with this coefficient as weight.

Figure 6.1 depicts a dependency graph associated to a linear system of dimension $T = 4$ and order $\mu = 2$.

Dependency Graphs and the Event Graphs are strongly related. Let $\mathcal{E}$ be a marked graph and $\mathcal{D}$ its associated dependency graph. A marking M of $\mathcal{E}$ will be any integer vector (not necessarily positive) such that $M = M_0 + Ix$, $x \in \mathbb{N}^T$. Markings have the following properties:

- a marking M of $\mathcal{E}$ is associated with a *section* of $\mathcal{D}$, $S(M)$, which is a set of nodes with exactly one node per column;
- to each marking M is associated a certain *cut* of $C(M)$, which consists of $S(M)$ and all nodes that have successors "below" $S(M)$.

Figure 6.1 depicts the sets $S(M)$ and $C(M)$ for a (negative) marking $M = M_0 + I.(1,0,0,1)^t = (1,0,-1,2)$.

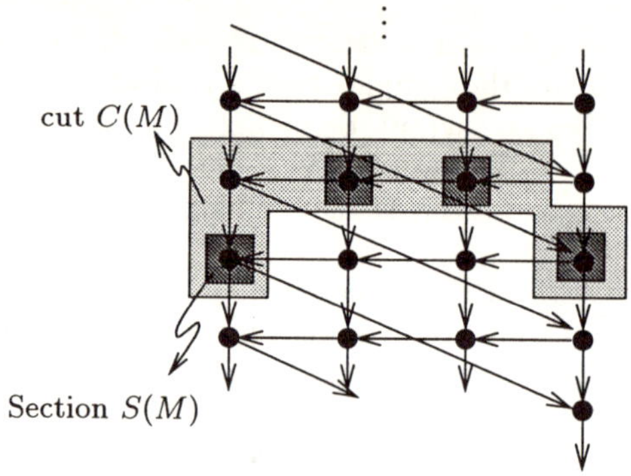

Fig. 6.1. The sets $S(M)$ and $C(M)$, with $M = (1, 0, -1, 2)$.

6.2.2 Optimization for Space Parallelism. In this section, we study the minimization of the parameters L and μ which appear in the complexity formula (6.3) of the space parallel algorithm.

Minimization of L. The parameter L depends on the marking M_0. We will denote it by $L(M_0)$ in the following. Let S be a linear system, $\delta(S)$ is its associated dependency graph. Let $\gamma(n)$ be length of the longest path in $\delta(S)$ from any node in the first row to any node in the n-th.

Definition 6.1 (sequentiality). *The sequentiality of a linear system S is* $\gamma = \lim_{n\to\infty} \gamma(n)/n$.

This limit is actually a *Lyapunov exponent* (Theorem 4.5). It can be computed in polynomial time using Karp's algorithm (see [4]).

The sequentiality of a linear system is a helpful criterion to measure the asymptotic complexity of the evaluation of the system when no particular properties are given on the dependencies between the state variables.

Theorem 6.1. $L^* = \lceil \gamma \rceil - 1$

In other words, L^* is the integer approximation of the sequentiality of the system. This remark gives an insight on the reason why the complexity of the parallel simulation of a linear system is linear in L^* in the best case.

In [55, 11], a "greedy algorithm" that computes a marking attaining L^* is proposed. It consists in repeatedly firing all transitions which are at the head of the longest empty paths in the event graph. It can be proved that this algorithm converges to a marking M with $L(M) = L^*$, and that its complexity is polynomial. Another algorithm to compute L^* and $M^{(L)}$ is given in [12].

Minimization of μ. Recall that μ is the maximal number of marks present in one place for the initial marking. For a given marking M, we will denote by $||M|| \stackrel{def}{=} \max_{p\in\mathcal{P}} M(p)$. Note that $\mu = ||M_0||$.

If we write this optimization under a linear program, we get:

$$\{\min b \ : \ M = M_0 + Ix, x \geq 0, M \geq 0, b \geq M_i, \forall i \in \mathcal{P} \ .\}$$

Let (b_r, M_r, x_r) be a solution of this linear program. Let $M^{(B)}$ be an optimal initial marking, *i.e.*, such that: $||M^{(B)}|| = \min_{M \in R(M_0)} ||M||$. One shows:

Theorem 6.2. $M^{(B)} = M_0 + I.\lfloor x_r \rfloor$ *and* $||M^{(B)}|| = \lceil b_r \rceil$.

As the computation of (M_r, x_r) is polynomial, being the solution of a linear program with constraint matrix of size $2.P \times T$, we obtain:

Corollary 6.1. *If* (G, M_0) *is a linear system, then the computation of a marking* $M^{(B)}$ *such that* $||M^{(B)}|| = \min_{M \in R(M_0)} ||M||$ *is polynomial in the size of* G.

6.2.3 Optimization for Time Parallelism. For the time parallel algorithm, the main quantity to minimize is $\widetilde{T}$, the dimension of the standard representation. As claimed above, it is possible to construct representations of dimension much smaller than the "classical" $\widetilde{T} = \mu \times T$.

A way to achieve this goal is to perform a *down tree* transformation of each transition in the event graph in the following way. For each transition t, we add $m = \max\{M_0(t^\bullet)\} - 1$ nodes, $a_1, \cdots, a_m$ and m places $b_1, \cdots, b_m$ with one mark. The original places get one mark if not originally marked.

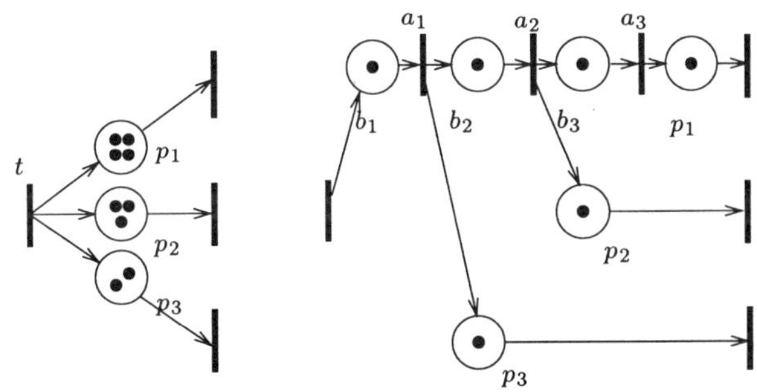

Fig. 6.2. Downstream tree-like transformation of transitions

This transformation is depicted in Figure 6.2. Note that the number of nodes of the new event graph G^d is

$$T^d = \sum_{1 \leq t \leq T} \max_{p \in t^\bullet} M_0(p). \tag{6.4}$$

This gives the size of the matrix $A_n^d(M_0)$ (which depends on M_0) involved in the linear system associated to G^d. This system is of order one. Moreover, the firing times in G^d may be easily defined in such a way that the evolution of the original transitions remains the same, so that G^d provides a standard representation the original system with a dimension equal to T^d.

Optimization of T^d. From Equation (6.4), the problem computing a marking $M^{(d)}$ which minimizes T^d can be formulated as a linear program:

$$\{\min \sum_{i \in T} N_i \ : \ M = M_0 + I.x, x \geq 0, M \geq 0, N_i \geq M(p), \ \forall p \in i^\bullet\} \ . \quad (6.5)$$

It turns out that this linear (integer) program is totally unimodular. Consequently, the computation of $M^{(d)}$ is polynomial in the size of the net. This follows from the fact that the basic optimal solution of a linear program which constraint matrix is totally unimodular is an integer valued vector [23]. A complete proof can be found in [55].

Cuts and the downstream decompositions are related by:

Lemma 6.1. *The size of* $C(M)$ *is* T^d *given by (6.4).*

According to this lemma, one may have the idea that the marking that minimizes (6.4) corresponds to a standard representation. This is true, but when this optimal marking, the matrices involved are not *disjoint*, that it, they are constructed using common variables. This is usually undesirable if random variables are involved, for then the matrices cannot be computed in parallel by different processors. However, in some cases, optimizing T^d without sign constraints on M may be of interest. This can be done by removing the constraint "$M \geq 0$" in (6.5).

6.2.4 Uniform Recurrence Equations. In this last paragraph, we briefly expose some concepts which give more insight on the problem of finding optimal standard representations for linear systems. This point of view is fully developed in [57, 58].

A linear system falls in the category of *uniform recurrence equations*, a formalism used in particular to model cyclic computation circuits with constant delays.

Let $\mathcal{G}$ be an oriented graph with T nodes. We attach to each node i a sequence of values $V_i(n)$ to be computed and an operator F_i. If nodes $j_1 \cdots, j_l$ are the predecessors of node i, There exists a sequence $k_{1,i}, \cdots k_{l,i}$ such that $V_i(n)$ is given by :

$$V_i(n) = F_i(V_{j_1}(\gamma^{k_{1,i}}(n)), \cdots, V_{j_l}(\gamma^{k_{l,i}}(n))),$$

where γ is a time shift operator *i.e.*, $\gamma(n) = n - 1$.

We denote by $k_i = \max_j k_{i,j}$, the maximal delay between node i and its successors. If we want to carry out the computation of $V_i(n)$ for $n \in \mathbb{N}$, we need registers for each node to store the values of $V_i(\gamma^{k_i}(n)), \cdots, V_i(\gamma(n))$, $V_i(n)$. The recurrence being uniform, it is possible to move delays around, which corresponds to changing the marking of $\mathcal{G}$. The optimal marking $M^{(d)}$

of paragraph 6.2.3 corresponds to a position of the delays such that the total number of registers necessary to carry out the computation is as small as possible.

References

1. M. Ajmone Marsan, G. Balbo and G. Conte, "Performance Models of Multiprocessor Systems", MIT Press, Cambridge, Mass., 1986.
2. F. Baccelli, "Ergodic theory of stochastic Petri networks", *Annals of Probability*, **20** (1), pp. 375–396, 1992.
3. F. Baccelli and M. Canales, "Parallel simulation of stochastic petri nets", *ACM Transactions on Modeling and Computer Simulation*, **3** (1), January 1993.
4. F. Baccelli, G. Cohen, G.-J. Olsder and J.-P. Quadrat, "Synchronization and Linearity", John Wiley & Sons, New York, 1992.
5. F. Baccelli, S. Hasenfuss and V. Schmidt, "Laplace Transforms for Poisson Driven (max, +)-Linear Systems", In preparation, 1995.
6. F. Baccelli and P. Konstantopoulos, "Estimates of cycle times in stochastic Petri nets", in Proc. of US-French Workshop on Applied Stochastic Analysis, I. Karatzas, D. Ocone (Eds), *Lecture Notes in Control and Information Sciences*, **177**, pp. 1–20, 1991.
7. F. Baccelli and Z. Liu, "On the executions of parallel programs on multiprocessor systems—a queueing theory approach", *Journal of the ACM*, **37**, pp. 373-414, 1990.
8. F. Baccelli and J. Mairesse, "Ergodic theory of stochastic operators and discrete event networks", In J. Gunawardena, editor, Idempotency. Cambridge Univ. Press, 1995. Submitted.
9. F. Baccelli and V. Schmidt, "Taylor Expansions for Poisson Driven (max, +)-Linear Systems", INRIA Report, RR #2494, Febr. 1995, Submitted to the Annals of Applied Probability.
10. G.E. Blelloch, "Synthesis of Parallel Algorithms (J.H. Reif Ed)", chapter Prefix Sums and Their Applications, Morgan Kaufmann Publishers, 1993.
11. M. Canales and B. Gaujal, "Marking Optimization and Parallelism of Marked Graphs", INRIA Technical report, RR #2049, September 1993.
12. C. S. Chang, "On the exponentiality of stochastic linear systems under the Max-Plus algebra", Working paper, 1995.
13. P. Chretienne, "Les Réseaux de Petri Temporisés", PhD thesis, Université Paris VI, Paris, 1983.
14. E. Çinlar, "Markov additive processes I", *Z. Wahrsheinlichktheorie verw. Geb.*, **24**, pp. 85–93, 1972.
15. E. Çinlar, "Markov additive processes II", *Z. Wahrsheinlichktheorie verw. Geb.*, **24**, pp. 95–121, 1972.
16. J.E. Cohen, "Subadditivity, generalized product of random matrices and operations research", *SIAM Review*, **3** (1), pp. 69–86, 1988.
17. G. Cohen, D. Dubois, J.-P. Quadrat and M. Viot, "A linear system-theoretic view of discrete-event processes and its use for performance evaluation in manufacturing", *IEEE Trans. Automatic Control*, **AC-30**, pp. 210–220, 1985.

18. N. Götz, U. Herzog and M. Rettelbach (eds.), "Guidelines for the QMIPS Workshop: Formalisms, Principles and State-of-the Art", Proc. QMIPS workshop on Formalisms — Principles and State-of-the-Art, *Arbeitsberichte des IMMD*, **26** University of Erlangen, September 1993.
19. B. Gaujal, "Parallélisme et simulation des systèmes à événements discrets", PhD thesis, University of Nice Sophia Antipolis, June 1994.
20. B. Gaujal and A. Jean-Marie, "Computational Issues in Recursive Stochastic Systems", In Idempotency, J. Gunawardena (ed.), Cambridge Univ. Press, 1995. Submitted.
21. B. Gaujal, A. Jean-Marie and J. Mairesse, "Minimal Representation of Uniform Recurrence Equations". INRIA RR #2568, June 1995.
22. P. Glasserman and D. Yao, "Monotone Structure in Discrete-Event Systems", John Wiley & Sons, 1994.
23. A.J. Hoffman and J.B. Kruskal, "Integral boundary points of convex polyhedra", *Annals of Math. Studies, Princeton*, **38**, pp. 223, 1956.
24. A. Jean-Marie, "Analytical computation of Lyapunov exponents in stochastic event graphs", In O. Boxma and G. Koole, editors, Third QMIPS Workshop, CWI Tracts #106, 1994.
25. A. Jean-Marie, "On Queueing Systems with Poisson Inputs and Known Services", in preparation, 1995.
26. A. Jean-Marie and G. J. Olsder, "Analysis of stochastic min-max systems: results and conjectures", Technical Report #93-94, Delft University of Technology, 1993.
27. C.E. Leiserson and J.B. Saxe, "Retiming synchronous circuitry", *Algorithmica*, **6**, pp. 5–35, 1991.
28. J. Mairesse, "Products of irreducible random matrices in the (max,+) algebra", Technical Report #1939, INRIA, Sophia Antipolis, France, 1993. To appear in *JAP*.
29. J. Mairesse, "A graphical approach of the spectral theory in the (max,+) algebra", *IEEE Trans. Automatic Control*, September 1995. To appear.
30. J. Mairesse, "Stabilité des systèmes à événements discrets stochastiques", PhD thesis, Ecole Polytechnique, Paris, June 1995.
31. T. Murata, "Petri nets: Properties, analysis and applications", *Proceedings of the IEEE*, **77** (4), pp. 541–580, 1989.
32. J. Resing, R.E. de Vries, M.S. Keane, G. Hooghiemstra and G.J. Olsder, "Asymptotic behavior of random discrete event systems", *Stochastic Processes and their Applications*, **36**, pp. 195–216, 1990.
33. I. S. Volkov, "On the distribution of sums of random variables defined on a homogeneous Markov chain with a finite number of states", *SIAM J. Theory Prob. Applications*, **3**, pp. 384–399, 1958.

TIPP and the Spectral Expansion Method

I. Mitrani[1], A. Ost[2], and M. Rettelbach[2]

[1] University of Newcastle upon Tyne, UK
[2] University of Erlangen-Nürnberg, Germany

Summary. Stochastic Process Algebras (SPA) like TIPP are a means for functional, performance and dependability modelling of concurrent systems in a modular fashion. Until now their applicability has been restricted by the requirement that the process state space should be finite. This was due to the solution algorithms that were employed. In this paper we present a variant of SPA which enables the Spectral Expansion solution method (SE) to be used, thus allowing the modelling of processes with infinite state space. Whether SE is applicable to a given problem can be decided *before* generating a detailed description of the state space. The mapping from the SPA to the SE formalisms can be automated and the technicalities of the solution can be hidden from the user. This approach is illustrated on a small but non-trivial example.

1. Introduction

Stochastic Process Algebras provide an "*easy-to-use*" interface for the description of stochastic processes. They support modular design in a natural way by providing operators for the construction of complex systems from smaller ones. A particular SPA called TIPP, dealing with Markov processes only, was introduced in [2]. In common with other SPA's, the current version of TIPP requires that the system to be modelled has a finite number of states. The TIPP description is transformed into a finite Markov chain; the latter is then solved numerically in order to determine the steady-state probabilities.

The purpose of this paper is to demonstrate the flexibility of the SPA approach by showing how a small modification of the syntax, combined with appropriate new semantics, can extend the modelling power considerably. The target Markov process can now be two-dimensional, finite in one direction and infinite in the other. The model description in terms of the modified TIPP (called SE-TIPP) is transformed into a collection of matrices which are then fed into the Spectral Expansion solution procedure [10]. The infinite Markov chain is solved exactly by exploiting the inherent regularity.

The semantic concepts introduced in this paper may appear complex but it must be emphasized that most of the technical details are hidden for a normal user. Thus one can model a system with the SPA formalism (following a few simple rules) and apply SE to the problem. The matrices necessary for the SE solution are generated automatically.

The models that are being considered are defined in section 2, which also provides a reasonably self-contained introduction to the SE solution method. Section 3 describes the modified Stochastic Process Language SE-TIPP and defines the special semantic rules for generating the SE matrices. In Section 4, the schema is applied to an example taken from the area of ATM/B-ISDN networks.

2. The Spectral Expansion solution method

There is a large class of models which involve two-dimensional Markov processes on semi-infinite lattice strips. That is, the system state is described by two integer random variables, I and J; one of these has a finite range, and the other can take any non-negative value. Often these models are cast in the framework of a Markov-modulated queue: then the bounded variable, I, indicates the state of the Markovian environment, while the unbounded one, J, represents the number of jobs in the system (a recent survey can be found in Prabhu and Zhu [8]).

We are interested in a sub-class of the above processes, characterised by the following two properties:

(i) the instantaneous transition rates out of state (i,j) do not depend on j when the latter is sufficiently large;
(ii) the jumps of the random variable J are limited in size.

To keep the presentation simple, we shall describe the Spectral Expansion solution method in the context of a skip-free Markov-modulated queue (i.e., the jobs arrive and depart singly). For a more general treatment, and a comparison with other solution methods, see [1, 10].

Suppose that the Markovian environment can be in N possible states, numbered $0, 1, \ldots, N-1$. Let $I(t)$ and $J(t)$ be the random variables representing the state of the environment at time t, and the number of jobs in the system at time t, respectively. We shall sometimes refer to $I(t)$ as the *operative state*. It is assumed that $X = \{[I(t), J(t)] \; ; \; t \geq 0\}$ is an irreducible Markov process with state space $\{0, 1, \ldots, N-1\} \times \{0, 1, \ldots\}$. The evolution of that process proceeds according to the following set of possible transitions:

(a) From state (i,j) to state (k,j) $(0 \leq i,k \leq N-1 \; ; \; i \neq k)$;
(b) From state (i,j) to state $(k,j+1)$ $(0 \leq i,k \leq N-1)$;
(c) From state (i,j) to state $(k,j-1)$ $(0 \leq i,k \leq N-1)$.

We assume further that there is a threshold, M, $(M \geq 1)$ such that the instantaneous transition rates do not depend on j when $j \geq M$. In other words, if we denote the transition rate matrices associated with (a), (b) and (c) by $A_j^{(0)}$, $A_j^{(1)}$ and $A_j^{(-1)}$ respectively (the main diagonal of $A_j^{(0)}$ is zero by definition; also, $A_0^{(-1)} = 0$ by definition), then we have

$$A_j^{(0)} = A_M^{(0)} \; ; \; A_j^{(1)} = A_M^{(1)} \; ; \; A_j^{(-1)} = A_M^{(-1)} \; , \; j \geq M \; . \tag{2.1}$$

In the above notation, the superscript denotes the jump in the number of jobs present. Transitions (a) correspond to changes in the environment only.

A transition of type (b) represents a job arrival which may coincide with such a change. If these coincidences do not occur, then the matrices $A_j^{(1)}$ and $A_M^{(1)}$ are diagonal. Similarly, a transition of type (c) represents a job departure coinciding with a change in the environment. Again, if such coincidences do not occur, then the matrices $A_j^{(-1)}$ and $A_M^{(-1)}$ are diagonal.

As well as these matrices, it is convenient to define the diagonal matrices $D_j^{(0)}$, $D_j^{(1)}$ and $D_j^{(-1)}$, whose i^{th} diagonal element is the ith row sum of $A_j^{(0)}$, $A_j^{(1)}$ and $A_j^{(-1)}$, respectively. Those row sums are the total rates at which the process X leaves state (i,j), due to (a) changes in the environment, (b) job arrivals (perhaps accompanied by such a change) and (c) job departures (ditto), respectively. The j-independent versions of these diagonal matrices are denoted by $D_M^{(0)}$, $D_M^{(1)}$ and $D_M^{(-1)}$, respectively.

The object of the analysis is to determine the joint steady-state distribution of the state of the environment and the number of jobs in the system:

$$p_{i,j} = \lim_{t\to\infty} P(I(t) = i, J(t) = j) \; ; \; i = 0,1,\ldots,N-1 \; ; \; j = 0,1,\ldots \; . \qquad (2.2)$$

That distribution exists for an irreducible Markov process if, and only if, the corresponding set of balance equations has a unique normalisable solution.

Rather than working with the two-dimensional distribution $\{p_{i,j}\}$, we shall introduce the row vectors,

$$v_j = (p_{0,j}, p_{1,j}, \ldots, p_{N-1,j}) \; ; \; j = 0,1,\ldots \; , \qquad (2.3)$$

whose elements represent the states with j jobs in the system.

The balance equations satisfied by the probabilities $p_{i,j}$ can be written in terms of the vectors v_j:

$$v_j[D_j^{(0)} + D_j^{(1)} + D_j^{(-1)}] = v_{j-1}A_{j-1}^{(1)} + v_jA_j^{(0)} + v_{j+1}A_{j+1}^{(-1)} \; ; \; j \geq M \; , \qquad (2.4)$$

(where $v_{-1} = 0$ by definition), and

$$v_j[D_M^{(0)} + D_M^{(1)} + D_M^{(-1)}] = v_{j-1}A_M^{(1)} + v_jA_M^{(0)} + v_{j+1}A_M^{(-1)} \; ; \; j > M \; . \qquad (2.5)$$

In addition, all probabilities must sum up to 1:

$$\sum_{j=0}^{\infty} v_j e = 1 \; , \qquad (2.6)$$

where e is a column vector with N elements, all of which are equal to 1.

The first step is to find the general solution of equation (2.5). That equation has the nice property that its coefficients do not depend on j. It can be rewritten in the form

$$v_jQ_0 + v_{j+1}Q_1 + v_{j+2}Q_2 = \mathbf{0} \; ; \; j = M, M+1, \ldots \; , \qquad (2.7)$$

where $Q_0 = A_M^{(1)}$, $Q_1 = A_M^{(0)} - D_M^{(0)} - D_M^{(1)} - D_M^{(-1)}$ and $Q_2 = A_M^{(-1)}$. This is a homogeneous vector difference equation of order 2, with constant coefficients. Associated with it is the characteristic matrix polynomial, $Q(\lambda)$, defined as

$$Q(\lambda) = Q_0 + Q_1\lambda + Q_2\lambda^2 . \tag{2.8}$$

Denote by λ_k and $\boldsymbol{\psi_k}$ the eigenvalues and corresponding left eigenvectors of $Q(\lambda)$. In other words, these are quantities which satisfy

$$\boldsymbol{\psi_k} Q(\lambda_k) = \mathbf{0} \; ; \; k = 1, 2, \ldots, d \, , \tag{2.9}$$

where $d = degree\{det[Q(\lambda)]\}$.

The eigenvalues do not have to be simple, but we shall assume that if λ_k has multiplicity m, then it also has m linearly independent left eigenvectors. This is invariably observed to be the case in practice.

Suppose that c of the eigenvalues of $Q(\lambda)$ are strictly inside the unit disk (each counted according to its multiplicity), while the others are on the circumference or outside. Let the numbering be such that $|\lambda_k| < 1$ for $k = 1, 2, \ldots, c$. The corresponding independent eigenvectors are $\boldsymbol{\psi_1}$, $\boldsymbol{\psi_2}$, ..., $\boldsymbol{\psi_c}$. Then any solution of equation (2.5) which can be normalised to a probability distribution is of the form

$$v_j = \sum_{k=1}^{c} x_k \boldsymbol{\psi_k} \lambda_k^j \quad ; \; j = M, M+1, \ldots \, , \tag{2.10}$$

where x_k $(k = 1, 2, \ldots, c)$, are arbitrary (complex) constants.

So far, we have obtained expressions for the vectors $v_M, v_{M+1}, \ldots$, which contain c unknown constants. Now it is time to consider equations (2.4), for $j = 0, 1, \ldots, M$. This is a set of $(M+1) \times N$ linear equations with $M \times N$ unknown probabilities (the vectors v_j for $j = 0, 1, \ldots, M-1$), plus the c constants x_k. However, only $(M+1) \times N - 1$ of these equations are linearly independent, since the generator matrix of the Markov process is singular. On the other hand, an additional independent equation is provided by (2.6).

This set of $(M+1) \times N$ equations with $M \times N + c$ unknowns has a unique solution when $c = N$. In other words, the ergodicity condition for the Markov process X is that the number of eigenvalues of $Q(\lambda)$ strictly inside the unit disk is equal to the number of operative states.

In summary, the SE solution procedure consists of the following steps:

(1) Compute the eigenvalues, λ_k, and the corresponding left eigenvectors, ψ_k, of $Q(\lambda)$. If $c < N$, stop; a steady-state distribution does not exist.
(2) Solve the finite set of linear equations (2.4) and (2.6), with v_M and v_{M+1} given by (2.10), to determine the constants x_k and the vectors v_j for $j < M$.
(3) Use the obtained solution for the purpose of determining various moments, marginal probabilities, percentiles and other system performance measures that may be of interest.

The numerical implementation of step 1 is best done by reducing the quadratic eigenvalue-eigenvector problem (2.9) to a linear one of the form $yQ = \lambda y$, where Q is a matrix whose dimensions are twice as large as those of Q_0, Q_1 and Q_2 (see [1]). The latter problem is normally solved by applying various transformation techniques. Efficient routines for linear eigenvalue-eigenvector problems are available in most numerical packages.

The generalisation of the Spectral Expansion method to models with batch arrivals and/or departures is quite straightforward. The matrices $A_j^{(\ell)}$ are defined for superscripts in some range $-S_1 \leq \ell \leq S_2$, where S_1 and S_2 are the largest possible downward and upward jumps of the random variable J, respectively. Again, these are assumed to be independent of j above some threshold, M. The equilibrium probabilities satisfy a vector difference equation of order $S_1 + S_2$. The eigenvalues in the interior of the unit disk, and the left eigenvectors, of the corresponding characteristic polynomial, provide the Spectral Expansion solution.

3. SE–TIPP

The standard TIPP language was designed to model systems with a finite number of states. The description of infinite state systems using TIPP involves recursion over static operators [3] which will lead to a unsuitable structure of the state space. Therefore, in order to allow such descriptions, we propose a dialect of TIPP which will be referred to as SE-TIPP and allows to specify infinitely long process terms. It has the following features:

- Subsystems which involve an infinite number of states (such as unbounded queues) can be modeled in a very intuitive way.
- The specification scheme for these subsystems leads to an economic representation of an infinite Markov process which can be solved by the Spectral Expansion method.

We will present a compositional approach to determine the semantics of systems which involve such infinite subsystems.

3.1 Syntax

Subsystems involving finite state spaces can be specified by using standard TIPP-syntax:

$$P ::= 0 \mid X \mid (a,\lambda).P \mid P+P \mid P \parallel_S P \mid P \backslash L \mid recX : P \qquad (3.1)$$

X is from a set of variables Var, $a \in Act$ denotes an action, λ its rate, and S is a set of actions to synchronise on.

To guarantee the finite state property of such processes, we restrict to the class of so called *rs-free*[1] processes, i.e., each subterm of the form $recX : P$ must not contain either hiding or parallel operator [3].

A process which involves an infinite state space may be specified by an infinite number of process definitions having the form

$$\begin{aligned} Q_0 &:= \ldots \\ Q_1 &:= \ldots \\ &\vdots \\ Q_i &:= \ldots \qquad i \geq M. \end{aligned} \tag{3.2}$$

Each process Q_i may contain references to process variables Q_j in order to reference the behaviour of another process Q_j. Thus, this system of process terms can be considered as an equation system, recursively defining *one* process Q of infinite length. Using such equation systems, the definition of, for example, an unbounded queue is quite easy:

$$\begin{aligned} Q = Q_0 &:= (arr, \lambda).Q_1 \\ Q_i &:= (arr, \lambda).Q_{i+1} + (deq, \mu).Q_{i-1} \qquad i \geq 1 \end{aligned} \tag{3.3}$$

The infinite number of reachable states in this system is due to the infinite length of the process term Q, and is *not* caused by replicating static operators, as it would be the case when modelling the queue in standard TIPP.

The compact structure of the state-space of a so-defined process can only be guaranteed if all processes Q_i themselves are rs-free. For simplicity, we restrict in this paper to Q_i having the form

$$P ::= (a, \lambda).Q_j \mid P + P. \tag{3.4}$$

The language SE–TIPP (which will be denoted as the set $\mathcal{L}^\infty$ of process terms) holds all processes which result from parallel composition of an arbitrary number of finite-state processes and at most *one* process which involves an infinite state space, i.e.

$$System := P_1 \parallel_{S_1} \cdots \parallel_{S_{n-1}} P_n \parallel_{S_n} Q, \tag{3.5}$$

where $P_1, \ldots, P_n$ are finite processes, and Q is either a finite state process or a infinite-state process specified by an equation system as mentioned above.

3.2 Semantic model

Normally, the semantics of both finite- and infinite-state processes are formally represented by labelled transition systems. However, transition systems do not impose any structure upon their state space, and thus the application of the Spectral Expansion solution method to their underlying Markov

[1] 'rs' abbreviates 'recursion through static operators'.

chain would represent a difficult task. To avoid this problem, we introduce the notion of *generator systems*. Generator systems will be used as an alternative way for describing the formal semantics of a process, essentially holding the same information as labelled transition systems, but providing additional information about the structure of the state space. Generator systems are closely related to the infinitesimal generator matrices of the underlying Markov chains, thus their name.

According to the division of processes in finite and infinite state we come up with finite and infinite generator systems.

Finite generator systems reflect the semantics of finite-state processes. A finite generator system of order N for a finite-state process P is a pair

$$(\underline{P}, m), \tag{3.6}$$

where $\underline{P} \in \left(2^{Act \times Rate \times Lab}\right)^{N \times N}$ is a matrix holding sets of transitions between reachable states in the transition system of process P. The bijective function $m : \{0, \ldots, N-1\} \to reach(P)$ associates rows and columns of this matrix with the corresponding states in the transition system. The matrix $\underline{P}$ has to hold exactly the transitions between reachable states in the transition system, i.e.[2]

$$\forall i, j \in \{0, \ldots, N-1\} : [\underline{P}]_{i,j} = \{(a, \lambda, w) \mid m(i) \xrightarrow{a,\lambda,w} m(j)\}. \tag{3.7}$$

Since we intended to hold *all* information which is given in the labelled transition system, we also have to keep track of its starting state. This is accomplished by requiring

$$m(0) = P. \tag{3.8}$$

Infinite generator systems To describe the behaviour of infinite-state processes, we could extend the notion of finite generator systems to hold infinite matrices. However – having in mind a later analysis using the Spectral Expansion method – we propose a different description scheme, which is closely related to the matrices $A_j^{(d)}$ presented in section 2. Infinite generator systems

$$(\{\underline{Q}_j^{(d)} \mid j \in \mathbb{N}_0, d \in \mathbb{Z}\}, n) \tag{3.9}$$

of order N hold an infinite number of matrices $\underline{Q}_j^{(d)} \in \left(2^{Act \times Rate \times Lab}\right)^{N \times N}$ and an injective function $n : \{0, \ldots, N-1\} \times \mathbb{N}_0 \to \mathcal{L}^\infty$ for which $img(n) \subseteq reach(Q)$ holds. This function associates each reachable state in the transition system with an ordered pair (i, j). All transitions between states (i_1, j_1) and (i_2, j_2) are kept in the matrix element $[\underline{Q}_{j_1}^{(j_2 - j_1)}]_{i_1, i_2}$, that is,

$$\begin{aligned} &\forall i_1, i_2 \in \{0, \ldots, N-1\}, \forall j \in \mathbb{N}_0, \forall d \in \mathbb{Z} : \\ &\qquad [\underline{Q}_j^{(d)}]_{i_1, i_2} = \{(a, \lambda, w) \mid n(i_1, j) \xrightarrow{a,\lambda,w} n(i_2, j+d)\}. \end{aligned} \tag{3.10}$$

[2] $[A]_{i,j}$ denotes the entry in row i and column j of matrix A, where counting starts with 0.

Again, to keep track of the transition system's starting state, we require

$$n(0,0) = Q. \tag{3.11}$$

3.3 Construction schema

We will present a compositional approach to derive the generator system semantics of a valid SE-TIPP process as given in (3.5). Thus, we describe how to get generator systems for the finite and infinite components composed in (3.5), as well as an algorithm for deriving the generator system of a composed process from the generator systems of the processes involved in the composition.

3.3.1 Component generator systems.

Finite state processes The generator system $(\underline{P}, m)$ of a finite state process P is immediately given by its transition system. The function m may be defined arbitrarily as long as $m(0) = P$ and $img(m) = reach(P)$ hold. Given this function, the construction of the matrix $\underline{P}$ is obvious.

Infinite state processes If the specification of an infinite state process Q is given by an equation system consisting of processes which comply to (3.4), the corresponding generator system $(\{\underline{Q}_j^{(d)} \mid j \in \mathbb{N}_0, d \in \mathbb{Z}\}, n)$ is constructed as follows:

- Since all processes Q_i *only* contain transitions to processes Q_j the condition $reach(Q) \subseteq \{Q_0, Q_1, \ldots\}$ holds. Thus we set the order of the infinite generator system to 1, and define

$$n(0,i) = Q_i. \tag{3.12}$$

- The matrices $\underline{Q}_i$ have to hold all transitions of the process Q. Since all states in the transition system of Q have the form Q_i, and all transitions leaving a state Q_i are defined in the equation corresponding to Q_i, all transitions are included if the matrices $\underline{Q}_i$ fulfil

$$\forall i \in \{0,1,\ldots\} : Q_i \xrightarrow{(a,\lambda,w)} Q_j \Longrightarrow (a,\lambda,w) \in [\underline{Q}_i^{(j-i)}]_{0,0}. \tag{3.13}$$

3.3.2 Parallel composition. As shown in (3.5), the complete system description emerges from a parallel composition of finite and infinite subsystems. In the following, we present a compositional approach to determine the generator system of a process $R = P \parallel_S Q$, given the finite generator system $(\underline{P}, m)$ of order N_P of process P and Q's infinite generator system $(\{\underline{Q}_j^{(d)} \mid j \in \mathbb{N}_0, d \in \mathbb{Z}\}, n)$ of order N_Q.

Originally, the state space structure of $R = P \parallel_S Q$ is three-dimensional, due to the fact that both process P and Q can act independent of each other in parallel composition. However, this three-dimensional structure can be reduced to a two dimensional one.

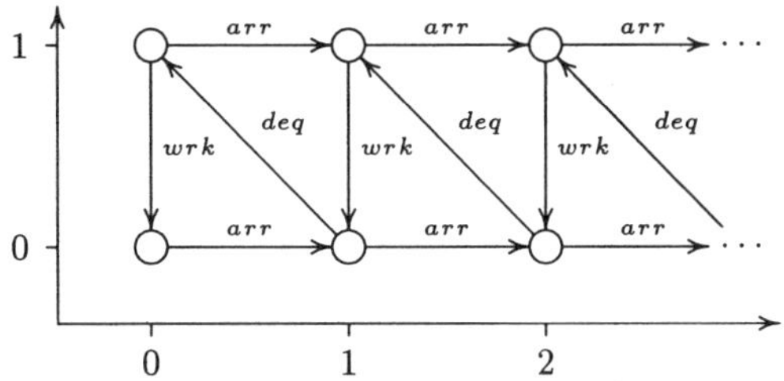

Fig. 3.1. Parallel composition of a finite and an infinite generator system.

The idea is to combine the finite number of states in *reach*(P) with the states in the finite component of the state space in Q's generator system. Thus, the dimension N_R of the resulting (infinite) generator system $(\{\underline{R}_j^{(d)} \mid j \in \mathbb{N}_0, d \in \mathbb{Z}\}, o)$ is $N_P \cdot N_Q$. Figure 3.1 illustrates this idea for $P = recX : (deq, 1).(wrk, \nu).X$ (thus $N_P = 2$) and the infinite queue Q modelled in (3.3) ($N_Q = 1$), synchronised by action *deq*. The lower half of the state space corresponds to those states where process P is in state P, the upper half corresponds to those states where process P is in state $(wrk, \nu).P$.

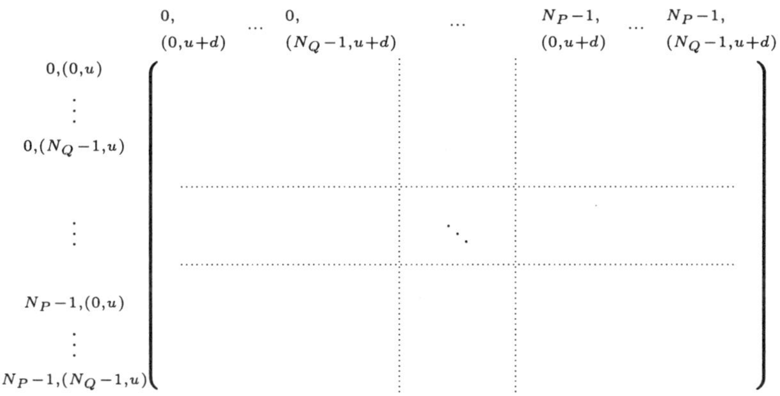

Fig. 3.2. Structure of the matrices $\underline{R}_u^{(d)}$.

Figure 3.2 shows the structure of the matrices $\underline{R}_u^{(d)}$ and the states of P and Q associated with their rows and columns (separated by comma). Depending on whether a transition of process R is due to an unsynchronised action in P, an unsynchronised action in Q, or a synchronised action which has to occur in both P and Q, three cases have to be considered in the construction of the matrices $\underline{R}_j^{(d)}$. First, we introduce some abbreviations needed in the treatment of these cases.
Let $\underline{A}, \underline{B} \in \left(2^{Act \times Rate \times Lab}\right)^{N \times N}$ and $S \subseteq Act$. Then

– $\underline{A}:S$ denotes the *limitation* of $\underline{A}$ on S, with

$$[\underline{A}:S]_{i,j} := \{(a,\lambda,w) \mid (a,\lambda,w) \in [\underline{A}]_{i,j} \ \wedge \ a \in S\}. \tag{3.14}$$

– $\underline{A} \backslash S := \underline{A}:(Act \backslash S)$.
– $u \cdot \underline{A}$ denotes *labelprefixing*, with

$$[u \cdot \underline{A}]_{i,j} := \{(a,\lambda,w) \mid (a,\lambda,v) \in [\underline{A}]_{i,j} \ \wedge \ w = uv\}. \tag{3.15}$$

– $\underline{A} \cap_{\|} \underline{B}$ denotes *parallel intersection* of $\underline{A}$ and $\underline{B}$. Parallel intersection combines rates and labels according to the SOS-rules for the parallel operator:

$$[\underline{A} \cap_{\|} \underline{B}]_{i,j} := \{(a,\gamma,w) \mid \begin{array}{l} (a,\lambda,u) \in [\underline{A}]_{i,j} \ \wedge \\ (a,\mu,v) \in [\underline{B}]_{i,j} \ \wedge \\ \gamma = \lambda\mu \ \wedge \ w = (u,v)\}. \end{array} \tag{3.16}$$

The relation $\subseteq$ between matrices in $\left(2^{Act \times Rate \times Lab}\right)^{N \times N}$ is fulfilled if the corresponding element-wise comparisons are fulfilled. $full_N(M)$ denotes a matrix holding M in all its elements, and $diag_N(M)$ contains the set M on its main diagonal.

The construction of the matrices $\underline{R}_u^{(d)}$ handles the three cases mentioned above[3]:

1. Unsynchronised transitions in process Q are independent of transitions in P, thus

$$\begin{array}{l} \forall u \in \mathbb{N}_0, \forall d \in \mathbb{Z}, \forall p \in \{0,\ldots,N_P-1\}: \\ \qquad (\|_r \cdot (\underline{Q}_u^{(d)} \backslash S)) \subseteq \underline{R}_u^{(d)[p,p]}. \end{array} \tag{3.17}$$

2. Unsynchronised transitions in process P occur without changing the state of Q, thus they appear in all matrices $\underline{Q}_u^{(0)}$:

$$\begin{array}{l} \forall u \in \mathbb{N}_0 : \forall p_1, p_2 \in \{0,\ldots,N_P-1\}: \\ \qquad (\|_l \cdot diag_{N_Q}([\underline{P} \backslash S]_{p_1,p_2})) \subseteq \underline{R}_u^{(0)[p_1,p_2]}. \end{array} \tag{3.18}$$

3. Transitions with synchronising actions must occur in both processes P and Q, thus

$$\begin{array}{l} \forall u \in \mathbb{N}_0 : \forall d \in \mathbb{Z} : \forall p_1, p_2 \in \{0,\ldots,N_P\}: \\ \qquad (full_{N_Q}([\underline{P}:S]_{p_1,p_2}) \cap_{\|} (\underline{Q}_u^{(d)}:S)) \subseteq \underline{R}_u^{(d)[p_1,p_2]}. \end{array} \tag{3.19}$$

[3] For simplicity, the notation $\underline{R}_u^{(d)[p_1,p_2]}$ is used for the N_Q-dimensional submatrix in row p_1 and column p_2 of the matrix $\underline{R}_u^{(d)}$. These submatrices correspond to the dotted areas in Figure 3.2.

4. Application example

In this section, we will apply the presented specification and evaluation techniques to a problem originating from an ATM/B-ISDN-based communication infrastructure, which was also investigated in [5] using Stochastic Petri Nets. There, the AAL-(ATM adaption-) layers offer connectionless traffic over a connection oriented communication system [7].

When packets arrive at the AAL service access points, they may suffer possible delays if the connection has to be established. Once it has been established, all packets remaining in the buffer can be transmitted without further connection-setup delay. When all packets are transmitted (i.e., the buffer is empty), the connection can be released after a certain time.

This release time heavily influences the cost/performance ratio of the offered connectionless service: if the connection is released too quick, it has to be established again for packets arriving soon after the release timeout. If the release rate is too low, connections are maintained when they are not needed, thus causing unnecessary costs.

4.1 System description

Arrival Process A We suppose that packets arrive in *bursts*, occuring with rate α and ending with rate β. When in burst mode, packets arrive with rate λ. Associating the actions *on*, *off* and *arr* with these events, the arrival process can be modelled as

$$\begin{aligned} A = A_0 \quad &:= \quad (on, \alpha).A_1 \\ A_1 \quad &:= \quad (off, \beta).A_0 + (arr, \lambda).A_1 . \end{aligned} \tag{4.1}$$

Buffer Q We assume an infinite buffer, whose specification is similar to the one given in (3.3). However, we model the rates passive with rate 1, so they can be determined by the other system components. Furthermore, since the behaviour of the AAL-layer depends on whether the queue is empty, the buffer process indicates a non-empty queue by offering immediate transitions with action *ne*:

$$\begin{aligned} Q = Q_0 \quad &:= \quad (arr, 1).Q_1 \\ Q_i \quad &:= \quad (arr, 1).Q_{i+1} + (deq, 1).Q_{i-1} + (ne, \infty).Q_i \qquad i \geq 1. \end{aligned} \tag{4.2}$$

AAL-layer L The behaviour of the AAL-layer is as follows: if the buffer is non-empty, connections are established with rate c (action name *con*). If a connection is established, packets from the buffer are dequeued (action *deq*) and then delivered at rate μ (action *del*). Once the buffer is empty, the connection is released with rate r (action *rel*).

$$\begin{aligned} L = \quad L_{empty} &:= (ne,\infty).L_{nonempty} \\ L_{nonempty} &:= (con,\mu).L_{connected} \\ L_{connected} &:= (deq,\infty).(del,\mu).L_{connected} + (rel,r).L_{empty}. \end{aligned} \tag{4.3}$$

Since packets from the buffer are dequeued with an infinite rate, a release action can only occur if there are no packets in the buffer.

Composition The complete system description is given by composing all three components:

$$System := A \parallel_{\{arr\}} Q \parallel_{\{ne,deq\}} L. \tag{4.4}$$

4.2 System semantics

First, we demonstrate the construction scheme for $R := A \parallel_{\{arr\}} Q$. Process A_0 has to be associated with row 0 of its corresponding generator system matrix, and we associate process A_1 with row 1. Therefore, the matrix $\underline{A}$ is as follows[4]:

$$\underline{A} = \begin{bmatrix} \emptyset & \{on\} \\ \{off\} & \{arr\} \end{bmatrix}. \tag{4.5}$$

The matrices of the infinite generator system for process Q are

$$\begin{array}{lll} \underline{Q}_0^{(-1)} = [\emptyset] & \underline{Q}_0^{(0)} = [\emptyset] & \underline{Q}_0^{(1)} = [\{arr\}] \\ \underline{Q}_i^{(-1)} = [\{deq\}] & \underline{Q}_i^{(0)} = [\{ne\}] & \underline{Q}_i^{(1)} = [\{arr\}], \end{array} \tag{4.6}$$

where $i \geq 1$. Their composition with $\underline{A}$ results in an infinite generator system for process R, with matrices

$$\begin{array}{lll} R_0^{(-1)} = \begin{bmatrix} \emptyset & \emptyset \\ \emptyset & \emptyset \end{bmatrix} & R_0^{(0)} = \begin{bmatrix} \emptyset & \{on\} \\ \{off\} & \emptyset \end{bmatrix} & R_0^{(1)} = \begin{bmatrix} \emptyset & \emptyset \\ \emptyset & \{arr\} \end{bmatrix} \\ R_i^{(-1)} = \begin{bmatrix} \{deq\} & \emptyset \\ \emptyset & \{deq\} \end{bmatrix} & R_i^{(0)} = \begin{bmatrix} \{ne\} & \{on\} \\ \{off\} & \{ne\} \end{bmatrix} & R_i^{(1)} = \begin{bmatrix} \emptyset & \emptyset \\ \emptyset & \{arr\} \end{bmatrix} \end{array} \tag{4.7}$$

Similarly, the infinite generator system for the complete system specification can be obtained by combining the generator system in (4.7) with the generator system for process L. This results in an infinite generator system of order $N = 8$.

4.3 System evaluation

Two steps have to be accomplished in order to derive the Spectral Expansion matrices $A_j^{(d)}$ from the system's infinite generator system:

- Markov chains only allow finite transition rates. Thus, instantaneous transitions have to be eliminated. This is easily done by applying the corresponding TIPP-axioms to the system (see [4] for a discussion of immediate transitions).

[4] For shortness, labels and rates were omitted in the following matrices.

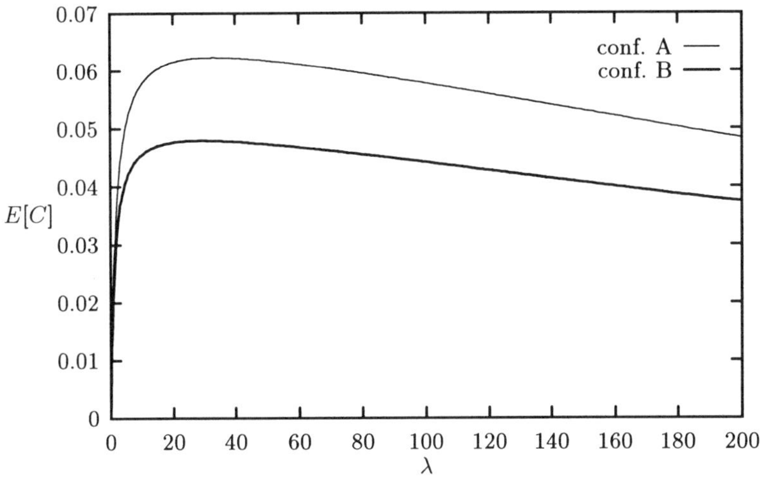

Fig. 4.1. The mean connection setup rate as a function of the arrival rate λ.

- Multiple transitions between states of the generator system have to be replaced by one transition with the sum of all rates in the Markov chain.

The elimination of instantaneous transitions, and the parallel composition over a non-empty set of synchronising actions may lead to unreachable states in the Markov chain. Due to the regular structure of the Markov chain, unreachable states can be removed easily. In the present example, we reduced the system from $N = 8$ to $N = 4$, with $M = 1$.

Two system characteristics were investigated:

- The mean connection setup rate $E[C]$.
- The mean number of packets in the buffer, $E[P]$.

All experiments were carried out with $\alpha = 0.04$, $\beta = 1.0$ and $c = 10$. Two different configurations were chosen for the other parameters. Configuration A ($\mu = 336, r = 1$) gives preference to high transmission speeds, while configuration B ($\mu = 236, r = 0.5$) favours a low connection release rate. The results for the above mentioned measures are shown in Figures 4.1 and 4.2.

5. Conclusion

We presented a convenient means to model the behaviour of infinite-state systems using the Stochastic Process Algebra TIPP. The approach allows the analysis of the system's underlying Markov chain with the SE solution method, thus providing an efficient solution algorithm for the presented class of systems. It has been shown that the modular design approach of Stochastic

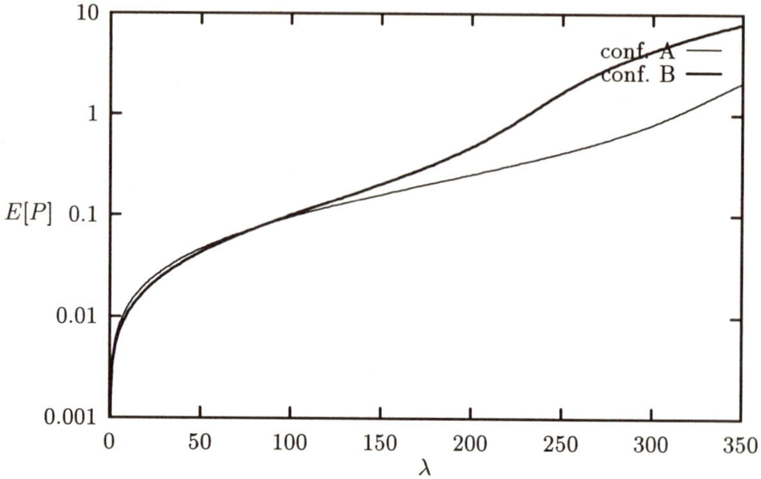

Fig. 4.2. Mean number of packets in buffer as a function of the arrival rate λ.

Process Algebras not only facilitates the specification of complex systems, but also simplifies the application of certain solution algorithms.

Concerning system specification, further work will focus on the extension of SE-TIPP to a larger class of processes by providing a completely compositional generator system semantic.

Concerning system evaluation, there are several ways to improve the SE method, e.g. by allowing an arbitrary structure of the Markov chain below the limit M. This way, the problem of special treatment for unreachable states in the Markov chain can be solved.

References

1. R. Chakka and I. Mitrani, "Spectral Expansion Solution for a Class of Markov models: Application and Comparison with the Matrix-Geometric Solution", *Performance Evaluation*, **23**, 1995.
2. N. Götz, H. Hermanns, U. Herzog, V. Mertsiotakis and M. Rettelbach, "Stochastic Process Algebras – Constructive Specification Techniques Integrating Functional, Performance and Dependability Aspects" in F. Bacelli, I. Mitrani, editors, Quantitative Modelling in Parallel Systems, Springer, 1995.
3. H. Hermanns and M. Rettelbach, "Syntax, Semantics, Equivalences and Axioms for MTIPP", in U. Herzog, M. Rettelbach, editors, Proc. of the 2nd Workshop on Process Algebra and Performance Modelling. University of Erlangen-Nürnberg, IMMD, 1994.
4. H. Hermanns, M. Rettelbach and T. Weiß, "Formal Characterisation of Immediate Actions in SPA with Nondeterministic Branching", in S. Gillmore, J.

Hillston, editors, Proc. of the 3rd Workshop on Process Algebra and Performance Modelling, Springer, 1995.
5. B. M. Haverkort, "Matrix-Geometric Solution of Infinite Stochastic Petri Nets", In Proc. IEEE International Computer Performance and Dependability Symposium. Erlangen, 1995.
6. I. Mitrani and D. Mitra, "A Spectral Expansion Method for Random Walks on Semi-Infinite Strips", IMACS Symposium on Iterative Methods in Linear Algebra, Brussels, 1991.
7. R. O. Onvural, "Asynchronous Transfer Mode: Performance Issues", Artech House, 1994.
8. N.U. Prabhu and Y. Zhu, "Markov-Modulated Queueing Systems, QUESTA, **5**, pp. 215–246, 1989.

G-Networks: A Survey of Results, a Solver and an Application

S. Chabridon[1], E. Gelenbe[2], M. Hernández[3], and A. Labed[1]

[1] EHEI, Université René Descartes, France
[2] Department of Electrical Engineering, Duke University, USA
[3] LAMIFA, Université d'Amiens, France

Summary. In this paper, we first present a brief survey of the main theoretical results providing product forms for networks of queues with positive and negative customers and with signals (G-networks). Then we present a graphical tool for solving a G-network model in steady state, i.e. for finding the steady-state probabilities of the number of positive customers in a G-network. The user will draw a G-network on the screen and input the parameters of each queue (mean service time, arrival rates, routing probabilities, etc.). Then the solver will provide the user with the solution of the system of non-linear traffic equations, and the stationary distribution of queue length, and performance measures such as sojourn times, mean number of customers in the system. Finally we show how these theoretical results and the tool we describe can be used to obtain an analytical solution to a problem which until now has resisted to such a treatment: the performance evaluation of receiver initiated load balancing algorithms in distributed systems.

1. Introduction

A new class of queueing networks has been recently introduced by Gelenbe [17, 21, 22] which unify different stochastic networks such as queueing networks and neural nets [13, 14, 15, 18, 20]. The G-network model was initially motivated by the analogy with neural networks [15]. The theory of the random neural network is developed by Gelenbe [14, 15, 19, 23]. G-networks have been widely used as neural networks, in particular with applications to the traveling salesman problem [30], minimum graph covering [25], graph partitioning [1], load balancing [2] and task assignment in a distributed system subject to failures [40]. Other applications concern problems of supervised learning of images [42], image and pattern recognition [44], texture generation [4, 3] and associative memory [28]. G-networks have been applied to evaluate the performance of unreliable flow systems [41] and to model virus behavior in a computer network [39]. In [24], it has been proved that the solution of a G-network provides a local minimum to a quadratic cost function.

When viewed as queueing networks, these new models called G-networks have essentially two types of customers: positive and negative. Positive customers have the same behavior as ordinary queueing network customers. If a positive customer joins a queue it waits until it receives service or it can be destroyed by a negative customer arriving to the queue. A negative customer joining a *non-empty* queue has the power to move or destroy a positive customer, or it will vanish immediately if the queue is empty. Negative customers will not be stored in a queue and will disappear as soon as they have accomplished their task. In the literature these negative customers are referred to as signals if their role is to displace a normal customer from one queue to another. They are referred to as negative customers if their role is to destroy one normal customer or a batch [22] of normal customers at some queue. Negative customers do not receive service and their actions are supposed to be taken instantaneously, that is, they do not consume any time. A positive customer leaving a queue after service can join another queue remaining positive or it can become a negative customer according to some probability. Although these networks have product form, their solution is quite different from that of usual BCMP models [5]. Specifically, the traffic equations for these networks, which allow one to calculate the rate of arrival of all types of customers to each queue, are non-linear. Furthermore, the probability intensity at each queue will have in its denominator the arrival rate of negative customers to that queue, while its denominator will contain the arrival rates of positive and negative customers. Even though G-networks have appeared recently, they have already motivated a substantial amount of research. Product form solutions have been characterized in [6, 7, 32, 33, 34, 36]. In [21], an extension of the previous work is presented where a different behavior of negative customers is considered. That is, the effect of a negative customer, now considered as a signal, arriving to a non-empty queue is to move a positive customer to another queue instead of just destroying it. This is called triggered customer movement. G-networks with signals also have product form solution [21]. In [22] the model is extended to networks where negative customers destroy batches of positive customers. Stability conditions are provided in [16].

Gelenbe, Glynn and Sigman [27] have studied several single server policies related to the arrival of negative customers to a non-empty queue, like removal of the customer in service and removal of the customer in the tail. Several extensions to this model have then been considered. In [9, 10], an extension of G-networks has been discussed where positive customers could have different classes. Henderson et al. have proposed several extensions allowing state-dependent rate and batch transitions [35, 36, 37, 38]. [11] considers multiple class G-networks with jumps back to zero and [12] proposes G-networks with triggered batch state-dependent movement.

This paper begins with a survey of theoretical results on G-networks. Then we describe a simple software tool which allows the user to draw a G-network on the screen and to input the parameters of each queue (mean service time, external arrival rates, routing probabilities, etc.) for positive and negative customers. Then the solver will provide the user with the solution of the system of non-linear traffic equations, and of the stationary distribution of queue length, and performance measures such as sojourn times, mean number of customers in the system, etc. Finally, we will show how this class of models can be applied to one important problem in system performance modeling:

the evaluation of the performance of a distributed system under the effect of receiver initiated load balancing.

In the rest of this paper, Sections 2 to 4 are devoted to the G-networks formalism for the cases mentioned above: positive and negative customers, signals, batch removals. Section 5 describes the tool we have designed for solving G-networks. In section 6 we present the numerical solution algorithm which is used and discuss some numerical aspects involved on it and its convergence. In section 7 an example of the use of G-networks for load balancing in distributed systems is presented. This example addresses and provides a first solution to one of the classical unsolved problems in system performance modeling: the analysis of systems with explicit on-line controls.

2. G-networks with positive and negative customers

In the simplest G-network model, customers are either *negative* or *positive.* Positive customers behave like ordinary queueing network customers. If a positive customer joins a queue it could wait until it receives service or it could be destroyed by a negative customer arriving to the queue. An arriving negative customer joining the queue instantaneously destroys a positive customer, if there is any in the queue, or it would vanish immediately if the queue is empty. Negative customers do not receive service and their actions are supposed to be taken instantaneously, that is, they do not consume any time. External positive or negative customer arrivals to queue i constitute independent Poisson processes with rate Λ_i for positive customers and rate λ_i for negative customers. Positive customers have iid exponential service distribution times with rate r_i at queue i. Positive customers leaving a queue after the completion of their service may join another queue either as a negative or as a positive customer. That is, a positive customer could become negative after its service is completed. The movement of customers between queues is represented by a Markov chain. A positive customer leaving queue j (after finishing service) joins queue i as a positive customer with probability $P^+_{j,i}$, or as a negative customer with probability $P^-_{j,i}$. It may leave the network with probability d_i. Let $P_{i,j} = P^+_{i,j} + P^-_{i,j}$; it represents the transition probability of a Markov chain modeling the movement of customers between queues. Therefore, we have for n such queues the following relation:

$$\Sigma^n_{j=1} P^+_{i,j} + \Sigma^n_{j=1} P^-_{i,j} + d_i = 1 \qquad 1 \le i \le n$$

G-networks have a non standard product form solution for the distribution of the queue length ($P(x)$) which is given in the following theorem.

Theorem 2.1. *[14, 17] Consider a G-network with N queues or nodes and positive and negative customers. If the system of non-linear equations*

$$q_i = \frac{\Lambda_i + \sum_{j=1}^{n} r_j q_j P_{j,i}^{+}}{r_i + \lambda_i + \sum_{j=1}^{n} r_j q_j P_{j,i}^{-}} \tag{2.1}$$

has a positive solution, such that for any queue i, $q_i < 1$ *holds, then the stationary distribution* $P(\boldsymbol{x})$ *for the queue length at each station i of the network exists and has the following product form solution:*

$$P(\boldsymbol{x}) = \prod_{i=1}^{n} p_i(x_i = k_i) \quad \textit{where} \quad p_i(x_i = k_i) = (1 - q_i)(q_i)^{k_i}$$

This model has been extended in [9, 10], to networks with multiple classes of positive customers and just one class of negative customers and three types of service policies (Processor Sharing, FIFO, LIFO). Note that the only customers which sojourn, i.e. actually spend any length of time, in G-networks are positive ones because negative customers have the strange property of appearing and disappearing instantaneously even though during this infinitesimal time they do have an important effect in the network. It is easy however to represent situations where negative customers would actually spend time traveling through a network, queueing up at some servers, etc.: during these activities they would be represented as normal positive customers and only change nature when they reach a queue where their "negative" behavior is effectively carried out. Thus the measures considered (sojourn time, number of customers, etc.) correspond to positive customers. Positive customer departures take place when:

- a service is completed,
- a negative customer arrives to a non empty line and destroys a positive customer.

Thus the mean sojourn time W of positive customers in the system is given by Little's formula (where q_i is given by (2.1)):

$$W = \frac{1}{\lambda_i^{+}} N_i \qquad N_i = \Sigma_{i=1}^{n} \frac{q_i}{1 - q_i}$$

3. G-networks with signals

In [21] an important extension of the previous model is shown to have a product form solution. This is the extension which allows us to model important effects such as traffic re-routing in computer networks or load balancing in distributed systems. Here, an arriving negative customer which is now denoted a signal, may either destroy a customer, or it may move a positive customer to another queue instead of destroying it. These movements are Markovian, with transition matrix is denoted as $Q = (Q_{i,j})$ where $Q_{i,j}$ is the probability that a negative customer arriving to queue i displaces a positive customer residing in that queue towards queue j. The following theorem establishes the solution of their distribution and is proved in [21].

Theorem 3.1. *Consider a G-network with signals. If the system of non-linear equations*

$$q_i = \frac{\Lambda_i + \sum_{j=1}^{n} r_j q_j P_{j,i}^{+} + \sum_{m=1}^{n} (\lambda_m + \sum_{j=1}^{n} r_j q_j P_{j,m}^{-}) Q_{m,i} q_m}{r_i + \lambda_i + \sum_{j=1}^{n} r_j q_j P_{j,i}^{-}} \tag{3.1}$$

has a positive solution such that for any queue i, $q_i < 1$ holds, then the stationary distribution $P(\boldsymbol{x})$ of the network exists and has the standard product form of Theorem 1.1 in which the value of q_i given here is substituted.

4. G-networks with signals and batch removals

The preceding work has been generalized in [22] to allow the destruction of a batch of positive customers, in addition to the motions of customers with the use of signals. In this extension, a signal arriving to an empty queue will have no effect and will just disappear. However if a signal arrives to queue i which is non-empty, then one of the following two events occur:

- The arriving signal triggers the instantaneous passage of a customer from queue i to some other queue j with probability $Q_{i,j}$.
- With probability $D(i) = 1 - \Sigma_j Q_{i,j}$, it forces a batch of customers of random size to leave the network. Let the length of queue i be k_i at the instant of arrival of the trigger; if $k_i \geq B_i$, then its length is reduced by B_i (batch size) and if $k_i < B_i$, the queue length becomes zero. The batch removal size distribution at queue i is given by: $P[B_i = m] = \pi_{im}, m \geq 1$.

Thus, a signal acts as an external trigger that instantaneously moves a customer from one queue to another or a batch to the outside world.

Theorem 4.1. *Define the function $f_i(x) = \frac{1-\Sigma_{m=1}^{\infty}\pi_{i,m}x^m}{1-x}$. If the system of non-linear equations:*

$$q_i = \frac{\Lambda_i + \sum_{j=1}^{n} r_j q_j P_{j,i}^{+} + \sum_{m=1}^{n} (\lambda_m + \sum_{j=1}^{n} r_j q_j P_{j,m}^{-}) Q_{m,i} q_m}{r_i + (\lambda_i + \sum_{j=1}^{n} r_j q_j P_{j,i}^{-}) D_i f_i(q_i)} \tag{4.1}$$

has a solution with $q_i < 1$, then the G-network with signals and batch removal has the standard product form solution in steady-state.

Clearly, if the batch is of size 1 and the matrix Q is a null matrix, we obtain the simplest G-network with positive and negative customers described in Section 2, while if the batch is of size 1 then we will simply have the model of Section 3. Note also that the destruction of *all* customers in the queue by the arrival of a negative customer is also very easy to achieve. Note that a batch of infinite size at queue i may simply be represented by:

$$\pi_{i,m} = 0 \quad \text{for } m < \infty, \qquad \Sigma_{m=0}^{\infty} \pi_{i,m} = 1,$$

which will give:

$$f_i(x) = \frac{1}{1-x}$$

Thus to analyze this case it will suffice to introduce this particular form of $f_i(x)$ in the formulae for the q_i.

5. The solver tool

The solver tool for G-networks which we have implemented is composed of a user interface and of a numerical solver. To the best of our knowledge, this is the first tool developed for solving queueing network models which use positive and negative customers, although there exist already various tools for solving standard queueing networks: QNAP2 [43, 48], PAWS [45], RESQ [47], SIMAN V [46], etc. Let us first briefly describe its user interface.

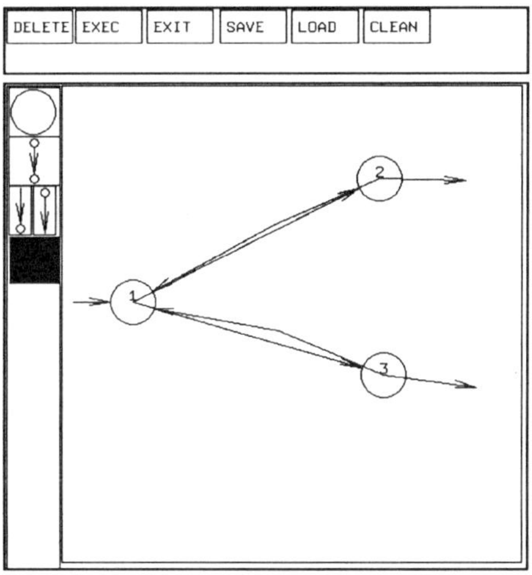

Fig. 5.1. The solver graphical interface

The tool is written in C and runs on any Unix workstation provided with X-windows (the version X11R5 or a later version) and allows the user to draw on the screen the G-network that is to be solved. Once it is drawn, parameters must be entered for each arc and each queue, including the routing probabilities for each type of customer and the service rates. It is called with the command: *solver*. No arguments are necessary. A single window (see Figure 1) will appear on the screen. This window has three areas:

- Main Menu (at the top)
- Icons (on the left)

- The window itself which is a drawing area

We now describe how to use each of these areas. Clicking a mouse button simply consists in pressing the button and immediately releasing it. To drag with a mouse button, move the cursor over an object, then press a mouse button and hold it down. Move the mouse by continuing to hold down the mouse button and complete the drag by releasing the mouse button.

The Main Menu is localized at the top of the window. It has the following options which are selected by clicking the left button of the mouse. There are seven possible operations. Six operations only are displayed in the main menu. The option CREATION is the default and corresponds to the case where no operation is actually in inverse video.

- CREATION : This option allows the user to create a new G-network. This is the default option of the tool.
- LOAD : It is used to load on the screen a G-network which has been previously created. A small window appears on the screen to allow the user to give the name of the file to be loaded.
- SAVE : Once created, the G-network and its corresponding parameters are saved in a file. A dialog box is displayed to ask for a file name.
- DELETE : In the process of the construction of a G-network, the user may want to delete an object. Deleting a queue will automatically delete the arrows connecting it with other queues.
- CLEAN : This option allows the user to clear what has already been drawn and to start the drawing of a new G-network.
- EXEC : This option will run the program to solve the network. The corresponding results or errors are reported in a file called "results".
- EXIT : Its purpose is to exit the solver environment.

The Icons area is placed vertically on the left of the window; it indicates the current selected icon. There are currently four possible icons :

- node : corresponds to a service station and its associated queue; it is represented by a circle.
- connect line : corresponds to a link between two nodes; it is represented by an arrow with one circle at both end points.
- entry line : corresponds to an external arrival to a node; it is represented by an arrow with a circle at its end point.
- out line : corresponds to an external departure from a node; it is represented by an arrow with a circle at its beginning point.

The Drawing Area contains the result of mouse operations as a function of the currently selected operation in the main menu.

- CREATE When the creation mode is active, the user simply has to select an icon with the left mouse button and then click it in the drawing area at the position where the user wants the object to be drawn. To draw an

arc from one node to another, drag from one node to another with the left mouse button.
- DELETE When the DELETE operation is selected in the main menu, clicking with the left mouse button on an object in the drawing area will automatically delete it.

When the middle mouse button is clicked on an object, a dialog box is displayed. It contains edit fields for the parameters corresponding to the type of the clicked object:

- Parameters of node i:
  Mu : Service rate of node i (r_i in the formulas).

- Parameters of arcs reaching node i:
  LAMBDA : Arrival rate of positive external customers (Λ_i in the formulas),
  lambda : Arrival rate of negative external customers (λ_i in the formulas).

- Parameters of arcs leaving node i:
  d : Probability for a customer to leave node i ($d(i)$ in the formulas).

- Parameters of an arc connecting nodes i and j:
  P^+ : corresponds to $P^+_{i,j}$ in the formulas,
  P^- : corresponds to $P^-_{i,j}$ in the formulas,
  Q : corresponds to $Q_{i,j}$ in the formulas.

Since this is the first version of this tool, additional features will be implemented in the future. Batch removals cannot be specified so that all the destructions are equivalent to the destruction of a batch of size 1. The size of the G-network is limited by the size of the window screen since there is no scrolling implemented. Thus the G-network can only contain as many queues as can been drawn on one screen. Drawing arrows is not very flexible; an arrow is formed by only one straight line. However, when there are two arrows between two queues in opposite directions, the second arrow is automatically represented by two lines.

Let us briefly discuss some numerical considerations. In [15, 21, 22] the existence of the solution of the nonlinear customer flow equations was established using Brouwer's fixed-point theorem. This is valid for stable and unstable systems, as long as the numerical procedure for computing the probabilities q_i makes sure that their value can never exceed 1. Once the q_i's are numerically obtained, all the other parameters of interest, including the joint queue length probabilities in steady-state, follow directly. Heuristic methods for finding a solution for G-networks have also been proposed in [8]. The following algorithm is used by the solver to compute a solution for the system of non-linear equations for the q_i's of the G-network:

1. Initialize the error ε which is the iteration's stopping criterion based on the square of the difference of two successive computations of q_i:

$$E^k = \sum_{i=1}^{n} (q_i^k - q_i^{k-1})^2 \tag{5.1}$$

2. Set $k = 0$. For $i = 1, ..., n$, initialize q_i^0 with random values in the interval $[0, 1]$ using a uniform distribution.
3. Compute the new value of q_i^k using the appropriate non-linear equation ((2.1), (3.1) or (4.1) according to which specific model is considered). If $q_i^k > 1$ set $q_i^k = 1$.
4. Compare the value of q_i^k at iteration k, to its value at the previous iteration q_i^{k-1} and go to Step 3 if $E^k = \sum_{i=1}^{n} (q_i^k - q_i^{k-1})^2 > \varepsilon$.

In [26] the convergence of this iteration to the steady-state probabilities q_i of the model is proved, for any set of initial probabilities q_i^0 in $[0, 1]$.

6. An example: Performance evaluation of receiver initiated load balancing

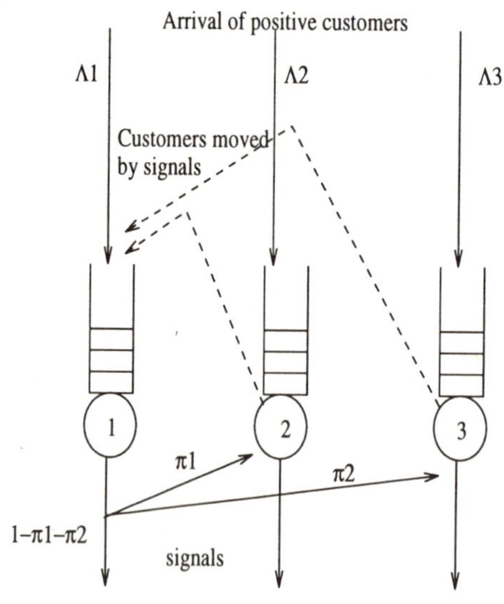

Fig. 6.1. System with load balancing

Dynamic load balancing occurs explicitly (by design) or implicitly (as a result of spontaneous system actions) in distributed systems. It has a profound effect on the performance of a distributed system for obvious reasons: a poorly balanced system may concentrate all the work at a few processors and leave other processing units idle, as a result of which system performance may be very bad. A well balanced system will fully exploit parallelism and therefore provide the best performance that the workload can expect. Static load balancing may be carried out for a given workload on a given system prior to execution, while dynamic load balancing is carried out continuously during execution as a function of the observed load throughout the system. Because of its importance, there has been much research on the subject, and it is still a matter of ongoing investigation. Here we will not survey the abundant literature on load balancing but simply present a specific example using G-networks. In this example we consider receiver initiated load balancing, where any processing unit is allowed to request work from other units whenever it considers that it can assume more work. In order to simplify the discussion we consider a distributed system with three processors where the goal is to balance the processors load. The discussion and analysis presented here can be extended to a system containing an arbitrary number of processing units.

The system is depicted in Figure 6.1. The three processors are assumed to be connected by a perfect communication network which transfers jobs in zero time and in a perfectly reliable manner. Similarly, messages used to control the system are also assumed to transit instantaneously through the network. We wish to point out that it is quite easy to model the effect of an imperfect network with substantial transit times for messages and jobs using a very similar approach. Each processing unit receives a stream of jobs from the outside world. However in addition, it may request jobs from other processing units. Receiver initiated load balancing proceeds in the following manner. As soon as processing unit i finishes a job, it may request that a job be transferred to it from one of the other processing units, say j. If it does so, then j will transfer a job to i if it has one in its queue. This request is represented by a signal which leaves processing unit i to go to j as soon as i finishes work. This is modeled by a probability $\pi_{i,j}$ for a signal to be sent to processor j by i when at the end of a service epoch. Clearly, even if a processing unit is unaware of the actual load at other units, the fact that it will have a tendency to request work of others whenever it finishes work will have a tendency to move more work to those processors which are serving jobs at a higher rate, while slow or relatively inactive processors will become less active.

In this model no ordinary negative customers arrive or exist in the system, and therefore $\boldsymbol{\lambda} = \mathbf{0}$. We use the previous notation so that the external arrivals of jobs to processor i are represented by a Poisson process of rate Λ_i, and it serves jobs at rate r_i. In the numerical example given below we assume that the receiver initiated load balancing requests are carried out *only* by processor 1 so that $\pi_{1,j} = \pi$ for $j = 2, 3$. We consider that queues 2 and 3 are identical; they have the same arrival rate Λ, the same service rate r, and the same probability π of receiving a signal from 1. The transition matrices of the corresponding G-network model are then:

$$P^+ = \begin{pmatrix} 0 & 0 & 0 \\ 0 & 0 & 0 \\ 0 & 0 & 0 \end{pmatrix} \qquad P^- = \begin{pmatrix} 0 & \pi & \pi \\ 0 & 0 & 0 \\ 0 & 0 & 0 \end{pmatrix} \qquad Q = \begin{pmatrix} 0 & 0 & 0 \\ 1 & 0 & 0 \\ 1 & 0 & 0 \end{pmatrix}$$

Using the G-network solver presented in Section 5, we computed the values of the loads q_i with the following parameters: $\Lambda_1 = 3.0$ and $\Lambda = 1.6$, $r_1 = 10.0$, $r = r_2$, r_3 varies in the range $[1, 10]$, while π varies in $[0.1, 0.5]$. Equal loads were obtained for values of r in the interval $[2, 5]$. In Figure 6.2, we show the variation of the q_i's versus π for the four values of r. On Figure 6.3, we give the average sojourn time of jobs in the system as a function of r for the case with no load balancing, i.e. with $\pi = 0$, and for π in $[0.1, 0.5]$. As expected, when the service rate of processor 1 is much higher than that of 2 and 3, load balancing is very useful and results in much smaller sojourn times than without load balancing. However, beyond the intuitive relationship betwen the different parameter values and the results observed, this analysis allows us to quantify the conditions under which load balancing would make sense, and the order of magnitude of the performance improvement that can be expected.

7. Conclusions

The purpose of this paper has been to summarize the main theoretical results concerning G-networks which have been obtained in the context of the QMIPS project, to describe a convenient and portable software tool which we have developed for specifying and then solving the model in steady state, and to describe its use via a simple example.

Due to the fact that this formalism can be used in many applications, a tool such as the one we have described facilitates the task of modeling practical applications. We expect that a variety of new applications will be addressed using G-networks, and that these will lead to further generalizations and extensions.

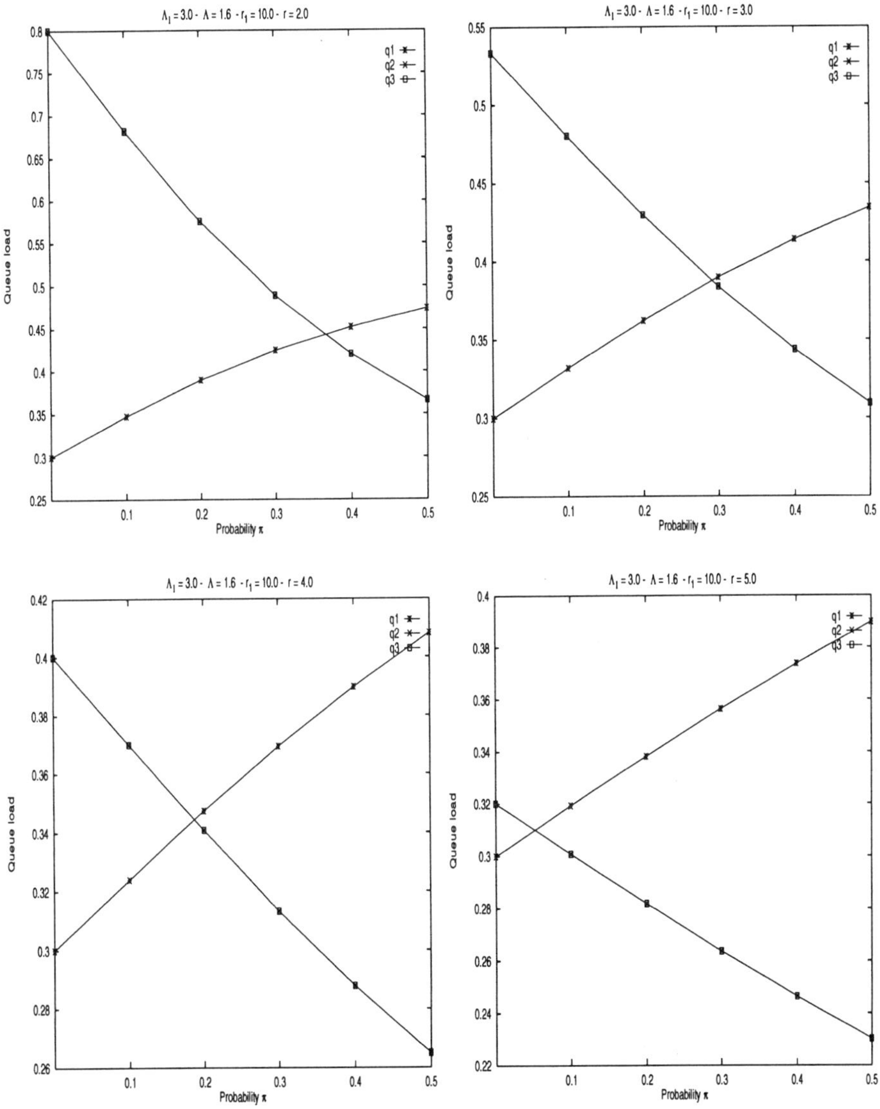

Fig. 6.2. Cases with balanced loads at each queue

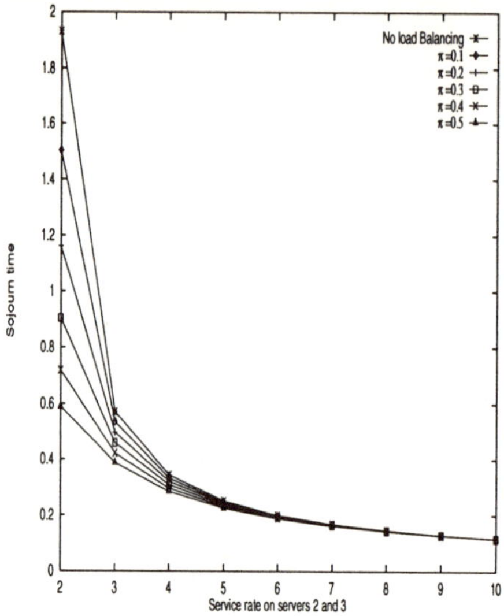

Fig. 6.3. Average sojourn time in the system

References

1. J. Aguilar, "Comparison between the Random Neural Network Model and other Optimization Combinatorial Methods for the Large Acyclic Graph Partitioning Problem", Proc. 7th Int. Symp. on Computer and Information Sciences (ISCIS), Antalya, Turkey, 1992.
2. J. Aguilar, "L'allocation de tâches, l'équilibrage de charge et l'optimisation combinatoire", PhD Thesis, University of Paris V, France, 1995.
3. V. Atalay, "Réseaux de neurones aléatoires et textures d'images", PhD Thesis, University of Paris V, France, Nov. 1993.
4. V. Atalay, E. Gelenbe and N. Yalabik, "Image Texture Generation with the Random Neural Network Model", Int. Conf. on Artificial Neural Networks (ICANN-91), Helsinki (Kohonen T. ed.), Elsevier, 1991.
5. F. Baskett, K.M. Chandy, R.R. Muntz and F.G. Palacios, "Open, Closed and Mixed Networks of Queues with Different Classes of Customers", *Journal of ACM*, **22** (2), pp. 248–260, Apr. 1975.
6. R. Boucherie, "Product-form in queueing networks", PhD thesis, Vrije Universiteit, North-Holland, May 1992.
7. R. Boucherie and N. Van Dijk, "Local Balance in queueing networks with negative customers", Research memorandum 1992-1, Free University of Amsterdam, North-Holland, 1992.
8. J-M. Fourneau, "Computing the Steady-state Distribution of Networks with Positive and Negative Customers", LRI Report, $13^{th} XS$ IMACS World Congress on Computation and Applied Mathematics, Dublin, Ireland, 1991.
9. J-M. Fourneau and E. Gelenbe, "G-Networks with Multiple Classes of Signals", Proceedings ORSA Computer Science Technical Committee Conference, Williamsburgh, VA, USA, Jan. 8-10, Pergamon Press, 1992.
10. J-M. Fourneau and E. Gelenbe, "Multiclass G-Networks", ORSA Conference: Computer Science and operation Research : new developments in their interface, Williamsburg, USA, Jan. 1992.

11. J-M. Fourneau, L. Kloul and F. Quessette, "Multiple Class G-Networks with Jumps back to Zero", Proc. of the 3d Int. Workshop on Modeling, Analysis and Simulation of Computer and Telecommunication Systems (MASCOTS'95), Durham, NC, USA, pp. 28–32, Jan. 1995.
12. J-M. Fourneau and D. Verchère, "G-Networks with Triggered Batch State Dependent Movement", Proc. of the 3d Int. Workshop on Modeling, Analysis and Simulation of Computer and Telecommunication Systems (MASCOTS'95), Durham, NC, USA, pp. 33–37, Jan. 1995.
13. E. Gelenbe, "Random Neural Networks with Negative and Positive Signals and Product Form Solution", *Neural Computation*, **1** (4), pp. 502–510, 1989.
14. E. Gelenbe, "Réseaux Stochastiques avec Clients Négatifs et Positifs et Réseaux Neuronaux", Comptes-Rendus Académie des Sciences, **309**, Série II, Paris, France, pp.979–982, 1989.
15. E. Gelenbe, "Réseaux Neuronaux Aléatoires Stables", Comptes-Rendus Académie des Sciences, Paris, France, pp. 310–313, 1990.
16. E. Gelenbe, "Stability of the Random Neural Network Model", *Neural Computation*, **2** (2), pp. 239–247, 1990.
17. E. Gelenbe, "Product Form Queueing Networks with Positive and negative customers", *Journal of Applied Probability*, **28**, pp. 656–663, 1991.
18. E. Gelenbe, "Theory of the Random Neural Network Model", Neural Networks: Advances and Applications (E. Gelenbe ed.), North-Holland, 1991.
19. E. Gelenbe, "G-Nets and Learning Recurrent Random Networks", Proc. Int. Conf. on Artificial Neural Networks, Brighton, England, 1992.
20. E. Gelenbe, "G-Networks: A Unifying Model for Neural Nets and Queueing Networks", Proc. of the 1st Int. Workshop on Modeling, Analysis and Simulation of Computer and Telecommunication Systems (MASCOTS'93), San Diego, CA, USA, *Simulation Series*, **25** (1), pp. 3–8, 1993.
21. E. Gelenbe, "G-Networks with Triggered Customer Movement", *Journal of Applied Probability*, **30**, pp. 742–748, 1993.
22. E. Gelenbe, "G-Networks with Signals and Batch Removals", Probability in Engineering and Informational Sciences, *Cambridge University Press*, England, **7**, pp. 335–342, 1993.
23. E. Gelenbe, "Learning in the Recurrent Random Neural Network", *Neural Computation*, **5** (5), pp. 154–164, 1993.
24. E. Gelenbe, "G-networks and Minimum Cost Functions", Proc. of the 3d Int. Workshop on Modeling, Analysis and Simulation of Computer and Telecommunication Systems (MASCOTS'95), pp. 135–141, Durham, NC, USA, 1995.
25. E. Gelenbe and F. Batty, "Application of the Random Neural Network Model to the Minimum Graph Covering", Neural Networks: Advances and Applications 2 (E. Gelenbe ed.) North-Holland, 1992.
26. E. Gelenbe and W. Jin, "Convergence of the numerical iteration for the steady-state distribution of G-networks", submitted for publication, May 1995.
27. E. Gelenbe, P. Glynn and K. Sigman, "Queues with Negative Arrivals", *Journal of Applied Probability*, **28**, pp. 245–250, 1991.
28. E. Gelenbe, A. Stafylopatis and A. Likas, "Associative Memory Operation of the Random Network Model", *Proc. Int. Conf. on Artificial Neural Networks*, Amsterdam, North-Holland, 1991.
29. E. Gelenbe and P. Schassberger, "Stability of Product Form G-Networks", *Probability in Engineering and Informational Sciences*, Cambridge University Press, England, **6**, pp. 271–276, 1992.
30. E. Gelenbe, V. Koubi and F. Pekergin, "Dynamical Random Neural Network Approach to the Traveling Salesman Problem", Proc. Conf. on Systems, Man and Cybernetics, Illinois, USA, 1993.

31. E. Gelenbe, O.W. Boxma, J.M. Fourneau, P.G. Harrison, M. Hernandez and E. Pitel, "G-networks", Hot Topics Session, ACM-SIGMETRICS/ IFIP WG 7.3 Symposium on System Performance Evaluation, Ottawa, May 1995.
32. P.G. Harrison and E. Pitel, "Sojourn Times in Single Server Queues with Negative Customers", *Journal of Applied Probability*, **30**, pp. 943–963, 1993.
33. P.G. Harrison and E. Pitel, "The M/G/1 Queue with Negative Customers", Proceedings of the 4th QMIPS (Queueing Modeling in Parallel Systems) Workshop, London, England, pp. 185–213, Apr. 1994.
34. P.G. Harrison and E. Pitel, "Response Time Distributions in Tandem G-networks", to appear in *Journal of Applied Probability*, Mar. 1995.
35. W. Henderson, "Queueing networks with negative customers and negative queue lengths", *Journal of Applied Probability*, **30**, pp. 931–942, 1993.
36. W. Henderson, B.S. Northcote and P.G. Taylor, "Modeling using queueing networks with signals", ITC 13, 1991.
37. W. Henderson, B.S. Northcote and P.G. Taylor, "Geometric equilibrium distributions for queues with interactive batch departures", *Annals of Operations Research*, **48**, pp. 493–511, 1994.
38. W. Henderson, B.S. Northcote and P.G. Taylor, "Networks of customer queues and resource queues", ITC 14, 1994.
39. M. Hernández, "Virus Transmission in a Computer Network", Research Report LAMIFA, Université d'Amiens, France, to appear, 1995.
40. M. Hernández and J. Aguilar, "A Simulator for Task Assignment in a Distributed System Subject to Failures", Proc. of the 4th QMIPS (Queueing Modeling in Parallel Systems) Workshop, London, England, pp. 89–106, Apr. 1994.
41. M. Hernández and J-M. Fourneau, "Modeling Defective Parts in a Flow System using G-Networks", Proc. Workshop on Performability Modeling of Computer and Communication Systems, Le Mont St-Michel, France, Jun. 1993.
42. C. Hubert, "Supervised Learning and Retrieval of Simple Images with the Random Neural Network", Proc. 7th Int. Symp. on Computer and Information Sciences (ISCIS), Antalya, Turkey, 1992.
43. D. Merle, D. Potier and M. Véran, "A Tool for Computer Systems Performance Analysis", Performance of Computer Installations, Ed. Ferrari D., Amsterdam, North-Holland, pp. 195–213, 1978.
44. M. Mokhtari, "Réseau Neuronal Aléatoire: Applications à l'apprentissage et à la reconnaissance d'images", PhD Thesis, Univ. Paris V, France, Jan. 1994.
45. "PAWS: A User Guide", Information Research Ass., Austin, TX, USA, 1983.
46. C.D. Pegden, "Introduction to Siman", Systems Modeling Corp., State College, PA, USA, 1984.
47. C.H. Sauer and E.A. MacNair, "Simulation of Computer Communication Systems", Englewood Cliffs, Prentice-Hall, USA, 1983.
48. M. Véran and D. Potier, "QNAP2: A Portable Environment for Queueing Systems Modeling" Int. Conf. on Modeling Techniques and Tools for Performance Analysis, North-Holland, pp. 25–63, 1984.

Polling Models with Threshold Switching

O.J. Boxma[1], G.M. Koole[2], and I. Mitrani[3]

[1] CWI, The Netherlands
[2] INRIA Sophia Antipolis, France
[3] Computing Science Department, University of Newcastle, UK

Summary. We consider a model of two $M/M/1$ queues, served by a single server. The service policy for this polling model is of threshold type: the server serves queue 1 exhaustively, and does not remain at an empty queue if the other one is non-empty. It switches from queue 2 to queue 1 when the size of the latter queue reaches some level T, either preemptively or non-preemptively. All switches are instantaneous.

We determine the joint queue length distribution, both using analytic techniques and using the power series algorithm.

1. Introduction

In this paper we consider a model of two $M/M/1$ queues, which are served by a single server. The service policy for this polling model is of the threshold type: the server serves queue 1 exhaustively, and does not remain at an empty queue if the other one is non-empty. It immediately switches from queue 2 to queue 1 when the size of the latter queue reaches some level T. Both the preemptive and the non-preemptive model are considered. All switches are instantaneous. The arrival rates are λ_1, λ_2, and the service rates μ_1, μ_2. The ergodicity condition is satisfied if we assume that the traffic load $\rho := \lambda_1/\mu_1 + \lambda_2/\mu_2 < 1$.

We are interested in the two-dimensional steady-state queue length process, our ultimate goal being to obtain insight into the influence of thresholds on system performance, and into the quality of threshold policies for polling models.

The motivation for this work is two-fold. The first one is application-oriented. Polling models like the present one find wide applicability in computer-communications, manufacturing, road traffic, etc. In particular, in modern telecommunication networks a key problem is to be able to meet the quality-of-service requirements for different types of traffic. One way of accomplishing this is to assign different priorities to real-time traffic (voice, video) and non-real-time traffic (data). The stringent delay requirements for real-time traffic dictate the assignment of a higher priority to it, but one would like to be able to meet those delay requirements while simultaneously giving the best possible service to non-real-time traffic. Threshold-type service disciplines seem appropriate for this purpose; thus one would like to obtain insight into their performance. Some threshold-based priority systems have recently been proposed and analysed by Lee and Sengupta [11, 12]. In

[11] Lee considers a single-server two-queue model where the high-priority queue is served exhaustively; the low-priority queue receives k-limited service. In [12] a customer of each queue is served alternately unless the queue length of the real-time-traffic queue exceeds a certain threshold level; then only customers from that queue are served. This is similar to our model, in which queues are served *exhaustively* unless a threshold level is reached.

A second motivation for the present study is the interesting feature that the server behaviour is not only determined by the situation at the queue that is presently being visited, but also by the situation at the other queue. [4, 6, 8, 12, 14, 17] are among the few polling papers that take this possibility into consideration. Hofri and Ross [6] have studied the optimal switching policy for a two-queue polling model with holding costs and switchover times and costs. They have shown that, for the case of identical service time distributions and equal holding costs at both queues, the optimal policy w.r.t. the long-run discounted costs is to serve each queue exhaustively (see also Liu et al. [10] for a model with an arbitrary number of queues). Hofri and Ross furthermore conjecture that, once the server has exhausted a queue, it is optimal to switch to the other queue only if its queue length exceeds a certain level.

Koole [8] presents results on a model with exponential service times, but with unequal parameters. In this case the low priority queue should not always be served exhaustively. For all queue length combinations in a truncated state space he determines via dynamic programming whether the server should switch to the other queue. The optimal switching curve appears not to have a simple form, but it is closely approximated by a threshold policy: the queue with the highest μc-value should be served exhaustively, and if the number of customers in that queue exceeds a certain threshold level, then it pays to switch to it when serving the other queue. More limited results, but for general service times, were obtained by Duenyas and Van Oyen [4]. For the same model, Reiman and Wein [14] arrive at a similar policy using heavy traffic analysis. Yadin [17] presents an exact analysis of several threshold policies, including the present one. However, he limits his discussion to the behaviour of the queue length process during one visit to a queue. His analysis is based on elegant random walk considerations and the method of collective marks.

For the preemptive model, we obtain the joint queue length distribution under the threshold policy in Section 2., via an analytic approach. In Section 3. we apply the same method to the non-preemptive model. This analytic approach will generally break down when there are more than two queues. Hence, in Section 4., we develop a numerical approach, which is also applicable to the case of multiple queues. It is based on the power series algorithm (cf. [1, 81]). Some numerical results are presented to indicate the effect of the threshold level on the mean queue lengths.

Note. This paper builds upon and extends [3], in which we restricted ourselves to the preemptive case.

2. Analytic Solution for the preemptive model

Let X_1 and X_2 be the numbers of jobs in queue 1 and queue 2, respectively. Also, let S be a random variable which is equal to 1 if the server is at queue 1, and to 2 if it is at queue 2. Define the steady-state probabilities

$$\begin{aligned} p_{ij} &= P(X_1 = i, X_2 = j, S = 1), \; i \geq 1, j \geq 0, \\ q_{ij} &= P(X_1 = i, X_2 = j, S = 2), \; 0 \leq i \leq T-1, j \geq 1, \\ r_{00} &= P(X_1 = 0, X_2 = 0). \end{aligned}$$

These probabilities satisfy the following balance equations:

$$\begin{aligned} p_{ij}(\lambda_1 + \lambda_2 + \mu_1) &= \lambda_1 p_{i-1,j}\delta(i > 1) + \lambda_2 p_{i,j-1}\delta(j > 0) \\ &\quad + \mu_1 p_{i+1,j} + \lambda_1 r_{00}\delta(i = 1, j = 0) + \lambda_1 q_{T-1,j}\delta(i = T, j > 0) \\ &\quad + \mu_2 q_{i1}\delta(i < T, j = 0), \; i \geq 1, j \geq 0, \qquad (2.1) \\ q_{ij}(\lambda_1 + \lambda_2 + \mu_2) &= \lambda_1 q_{i-1,j}\delta(i > 0) + \lambda_2 q_{i,j-1}\delta(j > 1) \\ &\quad + \mu_2 q_{i,j+1} + \lambda_2 r_{00}\delta(i = 0, j = 1) \\ &\quad + \mu_1 p_{1j}\delta(i = 0), \; 0 \leq i \leq T-1, j \geq 1, \qquad (2.2) \\ r_{00}(\lambda_1 + \lambda_2) &= \mu_1 p_{10} + \mu_2 q_{01}, \qquad (2.3) \end{aligned}$$

where $\delta(A) = 1$ if the condition A holds, and 0 otherwise. In addition,

$$r_{00} + \sum_{i=1}^{\infty}\sum_{j=0}^{\infty} p_{ij} + \sum_{i=0}^{T-1}\sum_{j=1}^{\infty} q_{ij} = 1. \qquad (2.4)$$

Introduce the generating functions

$$\begin{aligned} P(x, y) &= \sum_{i=1}^{\infty}\sum_{j=0}^{\infty} p_{ij} x^{i-1} y^j, \\ Q_i(y) &= \sum_{j=1}^{\infty} q_{ij} y^{j-1}, \; 0 \leq i \leq T-1, \end{aligned}$$

and define

$$\begin{aligned} K(x, y) &= \lambda_1(1 - x) + \lambda_2(1 - y) + \mu_1(1 - \frac{1}{x}), \\ a(y) &= \lambda_1 + \lambda_2(1 - y) + \mu_2(1 - \frac{1}{y}). \end{aligned}$$

Then the equations (2.1), (2.2) and (2.3) imply

$$\begin{aligned}
P(x,y)K(x,y) &= -\frac{\mu_1}{x}P(0,y) + \lambda_1 r_{00} + \lambda_1 x^{T-1} y Q_{T-1}(y) \\
&\quad + \mu_2 \sum_{i=1}^{T-1} x^{i-1} Q_i(0), \qquad (2.5) \\
Q_0(y)a(y) &= -\frac{\mu_2}{y}Q_0(0) + \lambda_2 r_{00} + \frac{\mu_1}{y}\Big(P(0,y) - P(0,0)\Big), \qquad (2.6) \\
Q_i(y)a(y) &= \lambda_1 Q_{i-1}(y) - \frac{\mu_2}{y}Q_i(0), \; 1 \le i \le T-1. \qquad (2.7)
\end{aligned}$$

For every y in the interior of the unit disk, the kernel $K(x,y)$ has a unique zero, $x = \alpha(y)$, in the same region. It can be shown (see [15]), that that zero satisfies

$$\alpha(y) = E\big[e^{-\lambda_2(1-y)B_1}\big],$$

where B_1 is the busy period of queue 1 in isolation.

Since $P(x,y)$ is analytic in the polydisk $|x| \le 1$, $|y| \le 1$, the right-hand side of (2.5) must vanish for all zeros $x = \alpha(y)$ of $K(x,y)$ in $|y| \le 1$. This gives

$$\begin{aligned}
P(0,y) &= \frac{\lambda_1}{\mu_1} r_{00}\alpha(y) + \frac{\lambda_1}{\mu_1}\alpha^T(y) y Q_{T-1}(y) \\
&\quad + \frac{\mu_2}{\mu_1}\sum_{i=1}^{T-1} \alpha^i(y) Q_i(0). \qquad (2.8)
\end{aligned}$$

Remark. It should be noted that $\alpha(y)$ is the generating function of the number of arrivals at queue 2 during one busy period at queue 1. The appearance of this term is natural. For example, the ith term in the sum in (2.8) corresponds to the following situation. The server leaves queue 2 behind empty, finding i customers at queue 1. The next time that he leaves queue 1, after i 'busy periods', the number of customers that he will find at queue 2 has generating function $\alpha^i(y)$.

Successive substitutions of (2.7) yield:

$$Q_{T-1}(y) = \left(\frac{\lambda_1}{a(y)}\right)^{T-1} Q_0(y) - \frac{\mu_2}{ya(y)}\sum_{i=1}^{T-1}\left(\frac{\lambda_1}{a(y)}\right)^{T-1-i} Q_i(0).$$

Equation (2.8) can now be rewritten as

$$P(0,y) = \frac{\lambda_1}{\mu_1} r_{00}\alpha(y)$$

$$+\frac{\lambda_1}{\mu_1}\alpha^T(y)y\left(\left(\frac{\lambda_1}{a(y)}\right)^{T-1} Q_0(y) - \frac{\mu_2}{ya(y)}\sum_{i=1}^{T-1}\left(\frac{\lambda_1}{a(y)}\right)^{T-1-i} Q_i(0)\right)$$

$$+\frac{\mu_2}{\mu_1}\sum_{i=1}^{T-1}\alpha^i(y)Q_i(0). \tag{2.9}$$

By using (2.3), equation (2.6) can be simplified to

$$Q_0(y)a(y) = \frac{\mu_1}{y}P(0,y) + \Big(\lambda_2 - \frac{\lambda_1+\lambda_2}{y}\Big)r_{00}. \tag{2.10}$$

Eliminating $P(0,y)$ from (2.9) and (2.10) allows us to write

$$u(y)Q_0(y) = \mu_2\sum_{i=1}^{T-1}\alpha(y)^i[(ya(y))^{T-1} - (\lambda_1\alpha(y))^{T-i}a(y)^{i-1}y^{T-1}]Q_i(0)$$

$$- r_{00}[\lambda_1(1-\alpha(y)) + \lambda_2(1-y)](ya(y))^{T-1}, \tag{2.11}$$

where

$$u(y) := (ya(y))^T - (\lambda_1 y\alpha(y))^T. \tag{2.12}$$

It only remains now to determine the T unknown constants $Q_i(0)$, $i = 1,2,\ldots,T-1$, and r_{00}. The last of these is given by $r_{00} = 1-\rho$ (this follows from first principles, but can also be obtained from the normalizing equation). Additional equations for the other unknowns are obtained by noting that the right-hand side of (2.11) must vanish whenever $u(y) = 0$ and $|y| \le 1$. When the ergodicity condition $\rho < 1$ is fulfilled, the function $u(y)$ has exactly T zeros in the unit disc, of which one is at $y = 1$ (this is seen directly), and the other $T-1$ are strictly in the interior. Indeed, consider the two functions in the right-hand side of (2.12), $v(y) := (ya(y))^T$ and $w(y) := (\lambda_1 y\alpha(y))^T$. These functions are analytic in the unit disc, and satisfy $|v(y)| \ge |w(y)|$ when $|y| = 1$. Moreover, that inequality is strict everywhere on the circle except at $y = 1$. At this last point, the derivative of $u(y)$ is given by

$$u'(1) = T\lambda_1^{T-1}\mu_2\frac{1-\rho}{1-\lambda_1/\mu_1}.$$

Thus, when $\rho < 1$, this derivative is positive at $y = 1$. Hence, if the unit circle is deformed slightly in the region of unity, by making it pass through a point $y = 1+\epsilon$ for some small ϵ, then on the modified contour there would be a strict inequality $|v(y)| > |w(y)|$. Applying Rouché's theorem to those two functions, and noting that $v(y)$ has exactly one (real) zero of multiplicity T in the unit disc, establishes the desired proposition.

Let us now study the $T-1$ zeros inside the unit disc in some more detail. Let e_k, $k = 0,1,\ldots,T-1$ be the T roots of unity of order T: $e_k = e^{2ki\pi/T}$. For $k = 1,2,\ldots,T-1$, the equation $e_k ya(y) = \lambda_1 y\alpha(y)$ has a single root, y_k, strictly inside the unit disk. Indeed, that equation is equivalent to

$$\lambda_2 y^2 - \big[\lambda_1\big(1-\frac{\alpha(y)}{e_k}\big) + \lambda_2 + \mu_2\big]y + \mu_2 = 0$$

; one can in fact apply Rouché's theorem to the two functions $f(y) = [\lambda_1(1 - \frac{\alpha(y)}{e_k}) + \lambda_2 + \mu_2]y$ and $g(y) = \lambda_2 y^2 + \mu_2$. It can also be seen that

$$y_k = E\left[e^{-\lambda_1(1-\alpha(y_k)/e_k)B_2}\right],$$

where B_2 is the busy period of queue 2 in isolation.

Substituting $y = y_1, y_2, \ldots, y_{T-1}$ into the right-hand side of (2.11) and equating to 0 yields $T-1$ linear relations for the unknown $Q_i(0)$. Setting $y = y_0 = 1$ leads to an identity and does not supply any new information. It should be noted that the roots y_k are either real, or come in complex-conjugate pairs, $y_k = \overline{y_{T-k}}$. Since each such pair provides two real linear equations, there are exactly $T-1$ equations for the $T-1$ unknowns.

Having found the constants $Q_i(0)$, the generating functions $P(0, y)$, $Q_i(y)$ and $P(x, y)$ are completely determined, and can be used to calculate performance measures of interest.

We have not formally verified (apart from some special cases) that the equations for $Q_i(0)$ are independent of each other when $\rho < 1$. However, an intuitive argument for independence is provided by the remark that if that set of equations has more than one solution, then the Markov process would have more than one equilibrium distribution, which is impossible.

As an example, we have computed the expected queue length EX_1 using a symbolic manipulation package. It is readily seen that

$$EX_1 = \frac{d}{dx} xP(x,1)\Big|_{x=1} + \sum_{i=0}^{T-1} iQ_i(1).$$

The only time consuming part is the numerical computation of the $Q_i(0)$'s, which takes a few seconds on a workstation. The results are equal to those in tables 1 to 3 (as found using the power series algorithm), and their imaginary parts are in the order of 10^{-10}, giving an indication of the accuracy of the final results.

Remark. When $T = 1$, this model is equivalent to the M/M/1 queue with two customer classes and preemptive-resume priority for class 1. Indeed, our results for $T = 1$ agree with those in Ch. 4 of Jaiswal [7]. Similarly, when $T = \infty$, the model reduces to the classical two-queue model with exhaustive service at both queues, cf. Takács [16].

3. Analytic Solution for the non-preemptive model

In some applications, it may be undesirable or impossible to interrupt a service which is in progress. It is then of interest to consider a non-preemptive threshold policy: the server switches from queue 2 to queue 1 only at service completion instants, if the current size of queue 1 is greater than or equal to T. The analysis proceeds along similar lines to that in Section 2.

The probabilities p_{ij} and q_{ij} are defined as before, except that q_{ij} can now have non-zero values for all $i \geq 0$ and $j \geq 1$. The new balance equations corresponding to (2.1) and (2.2) have the form:

$$\begin{aligned} p_{ij}(\lambda_1 + \lambda_2 + \mu_1) &= \lambda_1 p_{i-1,j}\delta(i > 1) + \lambda_2 p_{i,j-1}\delta(j > 0) \\ &+\lambda_1 r_{00}\delta(i = 1, j = 0) + \mu_1 p_{i+1,j} + \mu_2 q_{i1}\delta(i < T, j = 0) \\ &+\mu_2 q_{i,j+1}\delta(i \geq T), \ i \geq 1, j \geq 0, \end{aligned} \tag{3.1}$$

$$\begin{aligned} q_{ij}(\lambda_1 + \lambda_2 + \mu_2) &= \lambda_1 q_{i-1,j}\delta(i > 0) + \lambda_2 q_{i,j-1}\delta(j > 1) \\ &+\lambda_2 r_{00}\delta(i = 0, j = 1) + \mu_2 q_{i,j+1}\delta(i < T) \\ &+\mu_1 p_{1j}\delta(i = 0), \ i \geq 0, j \geq 1. \end{aligned} \tag{3.2}$$

Equation (2.3) remains unchanged, and the normalizing equation becomes

$$r_{00} + \sum_{i=1}^{\infty}\sum_{j=0}^{\infty} p_{ij} + \sum_{i=0}^{\infty}\sum_{j=1}^{\infty} q_{ij} = 1 \, . \tag{3.3}$$

In addition to the generating functions $P(x, y)$ and $Q_i(y)$ $(i = 1, 2, \ldots, T-1)$, introduced in Section 2, define

$$Q(x, y) = \sum_{i=T}^{\infty}\sum_{j=1}^{\infty} q_{ij} x^{i-T} y^{j-1}.$$

Then equations (3.1) are transformed into

$$\begin{aligned} P(x, y)K(x, y) &= -\frac{\mu_1}{x}P(0, y) + \lambda_1 r_{00} \\ &+\mu_2 \sum_{i=1}^{T-1} x^{i-1}Q_i(0) + \mu_2 x^{T-1}Q(x, y), \end{aligned} \tag{3.4}$$

where $K(x, y)$ is the same kernel as in (2.5). Equations (3.2) imply

$$Q(x, y)[\lambda_1(1 - x) + \lambda_2(1 - y) + \mu_2] = \lambda_1 Q_{T-1}(y). \tag{3.5}$$

Equations (2.6) and (2.7) remain unchanged.

Setting, as before, $x = \alpha(y)$ in (3.4) and using the fact that the right-hand side must vanish, yields a relation similar to (2.8):

$$\mu_1 P(0, y) = \lambda_1\alpha(y)r_{00} + \mu_2 \sum_{i=1}^{T-1} \alpha(y)^i Q_i(0) + \mu_2\alpha(y)^T Q(\alpha(y), y). \tag{3.6}$$

Next, substitute (3.5) into (3.6), express $Q_{T-1}(y)$ in terms of $Q_0(y)$ and eliminate $P(0, y)$ from the resulting expression and from (2.6). This leads to

$$Q_0(y)h(y) =$$
$$y^{T-1}\sum_{i=1}^{T-1}[\mu_2 a(y)^{T-1}\alpha(y)^i - \lambda_1^{T-i}y^{-1}\alpha(y)^T a(y)^{i-1}c(\alpha(y),y)]Q_i(0)$$
$$-r_{00}y^{T-1}a(y)^{T-1}[\lambda_1(1-\alpha(y))+\lambda_2(1-y)], \tag{3.7}$$

where

$$c(x,y) = \frac{\mu_2}{\lambda_1(1-x)+\lambda_2(1-y)+\mu_2},$$

and

$$h(y) = y^T a(y)^T - \lambda_1^T y^{T-1}\alpha(y)^T c(\alpha(y),y). \tag{3.8}$$

Again it remains to determine the T unknown constants $Q_i(0)$, $i = 1,2,\ldots,T-1$, and r_{00}. The last of these is still equal to $1-\rho$, since the probability of an empty system does not depend on the scheduling strategy. Additional equations for the other unknowns are obtained by noting that the right-hand side of (3.7) vanishes whenever $h(y) = 0$ and $|y| \leq 1$.

When the ergodicity condition $\rho < 1$ is satisfied, the function $h(y)$ has exactly T zeros in the unit disc, of which one is at $y = 1$ (this is seen directly), and the other $T-1$ are strictly in the interior. Indeed, consider the two functions in the right-hand side of (3.8), $f(y) := y^T a(y)^T$ and $g(y) := \lambda_1^T y^{T-1}\alpha(y)^T c(\alpha(y),y)$. These functions are analytic in the unit disc, and satisfy $|f(y)| \geq |g(y)|$ when $|y| = 1$. Moreover, that inequality is strict everywhere on the circle except at $y = 1$. At this last point, the derivative of $h(y)$ is given by

$$h'(1) = \lambda_1^{T-1}(\lambda_1 + T\mu_2)\frac{1-\rho}{1-\lambda_1/\mu_1}.$$

Thus, when $\rho < 1$, this derivative is positive at $y = 1$. Hence, if the unit circle is deformed slightly in the region of unity, by making it pass through a point $y = 1+\epsilon$ for some small ϵ, then on the modified contour there would be a strict inequality $|f(y)| > |g(y)|$. Applying Rouché's theorem to those two functions, and noting that $f(y)$ has exactly one (real) zero of multiplicity T in the unit disc, establishes the desired proposition.

The $T-1$ zeros of $h(y)$ in the interior of the unit disc provide the necessary equations for determining the unknown probabilities $Q_i(0)$, $i = 1,2,\ldots,T-1$.

Remark. When $T = 1$, this model is equivalent to the M/M/1 queue with two customer classes and nonpreemptive priority for class 1. Indeed, our results for $T = 1$ agree with those of Miller [13]. Similarly, when $T = \infty$, the model reduces to the classical two-queue model with exhaustive service at both queues, cf. Takács [16].

4. Power series algorithm

The method of Sections 2. and 3. cannot be readily extended to the case of three or more queues. The power series algorithm is a recently developed method that enables the numerical solution of multi-dimensional Markov processes (cf. the survey [1]). Below we apply this method to our two-queue models, but its extension to more than two queues is immediate.

Introduce an artificial parameter ζ in the transition rates by replacing λ_1 by $\zeta\lambda_1$ and λ_2 by $\zeta\lambda_2$. The service parameters μ_1 and μ_2 remain unchanged. Formally we can write

$$\begin{aligned} p_{ij} &= \sum_{k=0}^{\infty} \tilde{p}_{kij}\zeta^{i+j+k}, \\ q_{ij} &= \sum_{k=0}^{\infty} \tilde{q}_{kij}\zeta^{i+j+k}, \\ r_{00} &= \sum_{k=0}^{\infty} \tilde{r}_{k00}\zeta^{k}, \end{aligned}$$

because p_{ij} and q_{ij} are $\mathcal{O}(\zeta^{i+j})$ (as follows from the theory developed in [81]).

The power series algorithm approximates the stationary distribution of a given Markov process by computing its partial sums, the coefficients of which can be computed by a simple recursion assuming that ζ is introduced correctly in the transition rates. It follows from [81] that the above choice is a good one for the model at hand.

Consider first the preemptive model. By equating terms with equal power of ζ in (2.1) and (2.2) we get

$$\begin{aligned} &\mu_1\tilde{p}_{kij} + (\lambda_1+\lambda_2)\tilde{p}_{k-1,i,j}\delta(k>0) = \\ &\qquad \lambda_1\tilde{q}_{k,T-1,j}\delta(i=T, j>0) + \lambda_1\tilde{p}_{k,i-1,j}\delta(i>1) \\ &\qquad +\lambda_1\tilde{r}_{k00}\delta(i=1, j=0) + \lambda_2\tilde{p}_{k,i,j-1}\delta(j>0) + \mu_1\tilde{p}_{k-1,i+1,j}\delta(k>0) \\ &\qquad +\mu_2\tilde{q}_{k-1,i,1}\delta(i<T, j=0, k>0), \; i>0, \qquad (4.1) \\ &\mu_2\tilde{q}_{kij} + (\lambda_1+\lambda_2)\tilde{q}_{k-1,i,j}\delta(k>0) = \\ &\qquad \lambda_1\tilde{q}_{k,i-1,j}(i>0) + \lambda_2\tilde{q}_{k,i,j-1}\delta(j>1) \\ &\qquad +\lambda_2\tilde{r}_{k00}\delta(i=0, j=1) + \mu_1\tilde{p}_{k-1,1,j}\delta(i=0, k>0) \\ &\qquad +\mu_2\tilde{q}_{k-1,i,j+1}\delta(k>0), \; i<T, j>0. \qquad (4.2) \end{aligned}$$

From the normalizing equation it follows that $\tilde{r}_{000} = 1$ and

$$\tilde{r}_{l00} + \sum_{i+j+k=l} (\tilde{p}_{kij} + \tilde{q}_{kij}) = 0, \; l \geq 1.$$

Combining these results with (4.1) and (4.2) enables us to derive all coefficients recursively. Taking $\zeta = 1$ returns us to the original model. We restrict the computation to all coefficients with the power of ζ up to a number K, i.e., all coefficients with $k+i+j \leq K$. The resulting partial sums are used as approximations for the steady-state probabilities. Note that if $K \geq 1$, then the approximation of r_{00} is exact, as $r_{00} = 1 - \zeta\lambda_1/\mu_1 - \zeta\lambda_2/\mu_2 = 1 - \zeta\rho$.

Below are three tables containing the average queue lengths for queue 1 and queue 2, for various parameter combinations. The tables also contain the queue lengths for the non-preemptive case, denoted by EX_1' and EX_2', which can be computed in an analogous way. The ϵ-algorithm (see [1]) was applied, and the results are based on the terms with power of ζ smaller than 60.

T	EX_1	EX_2	EX_1'	EX_2'
1	0.5000	1.5000	0.6667	1.3333
2	0.6607	1.3393	0.7522	1.2478
3	0.7711	1.2289	0.8254	1.1746
4	0.8457	1.1543	0.8794	1.1206
5	0.8960	1.1040	0.9175	1.0825
10	1.0000	1.0000	1.0000	1.0000

Table 1: Average queue sizes for different thresholds;
$\lambda_1 = \lambda_2 = 1$, $\mu_1 = \mu_2 = 3$.

T	EX_1	EX_2	EX_1'	EX_2'
1	1.0000	5.0000	1.2222	4.6667
2	1.2587	4.6119	1.3999	4.4001
3	1.4671	4.2993	1.5669	4.1497
4	1.6343	4.0485	1.7084	3.9374
5	1.7686	3.8471	1.8252	3.7622
10	2.1372	3.3020	2.1543	3.2351
15	2.2692	3.0944	2.2759	3.0873
20	2.3326	3.0008	2.3328	3.0004
30	2.3333	3.0000	2.3333	3.0000

Table 2: Average queue sizes for different thresholds;
$\lambda_1 = \lambda_2 = 1$, $\mu_1 = 2$ and $\mu_2 = 3$.

T	EX_1	EX_2	EX_1'	EX_2'
1	0.5000	4.0000	0.8750	3.7500
2	0.8177	3.7882	1.0801	3.6133
3	1.0950	3.6033	1.2971	3.4686
4	1.3364	3.4424	1.4994	3.3337
5	1.5467	3.3022	1.6815	3.2124
10	2.2574	2.8236	2.3188	2.7912
15	2.6393	2.5911	2.6671	2.5679
20	2.7836	2.4955	2.8114	2.4669
30	3.0000	2.3333	3.0000	2.3333

Table 3: Average queue sizes for different thresholds;
$\lambda_1 = \lambda_2 = 1$, $\mu_1 = 3$ and $\mu_2 = 2$.

Remark. The conservation law for this model states that (cf. Gelenbe & Mitrani [5], Ch. 6)

$$\frac{EX_1}{\mu_1} + \frac{EX_2}{\mu_2} = \frac{EX_1'}{\mu_1} + \frac{EX_2'}{\mu_2} = \frac{\lambda_1/\mu_1^2 + \lambda_2/\mu_2^2}{1-\rho}.$$

The results in the tables satisfy this conservation law almost exactly in all cases.

Remark. Based on the numerical results and our intuition, we conjecture that EX_1 and EX_1' are mononically increasing in T. We have not been able to prove this.

Comments on the analytic and power series solutions. For a given threshold, T, the analytic approach involves the determination of $T-1$ zeros in the interior of the unit disk, plus the solution of $T-1$ simultaneous linear equations. The complexity of that solution is therefore on the order of $O(T^3)$. The accuracy of the results is limited only by the numerical precision of the software that is used. On the other hand, both the complexity and the accuracy of the power series algorithm depend on the number of terms in the expansion that are computed. There is no guarantee that any fixed number of terms will achieve a given accuracy. However, the experimental results are quite impressive: a relative error of less than 1% is achieved with 4 terms for T=1, 30 terms for $T = 5$ and 12 terms for $T = 30$.

Remark. In a forthcoming paper [2], the case of general service time distributions at both queues, switchover times and nonpreemptive switching rule will be analyzed. In that study the joint queue length distribution at imbedded epochs of service completions is determined.

Acknowledgement. The research of the authors was supported by the European Grant BRA-QMIPS of CEC DG XIII.

References

1. J.P.C. Blanc, "Performance analysis and optimization with the power-series algorithm", in: *Performance Evaluation of Computer and Communication Systems* (eds. L. Donatiello and R.D. Nelson), Springer, New York, pp. 53–80, 1993.
2. O.J. Boxma and D.G. Down, "A two-queue polling model with threshold switching", in preparation
3. O.J. Boxma, G.M. Koole and I. Mitrani, "A two-queue polling model with a threshold service policy", in: Proceedings MASCOTS '95 (eds. P. Dowd and E. Gelenbe), *IEEE Computer Society Press*, Los Alamitos (CA), pp. 84–89, 1995.
4. I. Duenyas and M.P. Van Oyen, "Stochastic scheduling of parallel queues with set-up costs", Technical Report 93–09, Northwestern University, 1993.

5. E. Gelenbe, I. Mitrani, "Analysis and Synthesis of Computer Systems", Academic Press, London 1980.
6. M. Hofri, K.W. Ross, "On the optimal control of two queues with server setup times and its analysis", *SIAM Journal on Computing*, **16**, pp. 399–420, 1987.
7. N.K. Jaiswal, "Priority Queues", Academic Press, New York, 1968.
8. G.M. Koole, "Assigning a single server to inhomogeneous queues with switching costs", CWI Report BS-R9405, 1994.
9. G.M. Koole, "On the power series algorithm", in: Performance Evaluation of Parallel and Distributed Systems, Part 1 (eds. O.J. Boxma and G. M. Koole), CWI Tract 105, Amsterdam, pp. 139–155, 1994.
10. Z. Liu, P. Nain, D. Towsley, "On optimal polling policies", *Queueing Systems*, **11**, pp. 59–83, 1992.
11. D-S. Lee, "A two-queue model with exhaustive and limited service disciplines", Report C & C Research Laboratories, NEC USA Inc., 1993.
12. D-S. Lee, B. Sengupta, "Queueing analysis of a threshold based priority scheme for ATM networks", *IEEE/ACM Transactions on Networking*, **1**, pp. 709–717, 1993.
13. R.G. Miller, "Priority queues", *Ann. Math. Statistics*, **31**, pp. 86–103, 1960.
14. M.I. Reiman, L.M. Wein, "Dynamic scheduling of a two-class queue with setups", Working paper, 1994.
15. L. Takács, "Introduction to the Theory of Queues", Oxford University Press, New York, 1962.
16. L. Takács, "Two queues attended by a single server", Operations Research, **16**, pp. 639–650, 1968.
17. M. Yadin, "Queueing with alternating priorities, treated as random walk on the lattice in the plane", *Journal of Applied Probability*, **7**, pp. 196–218, 1970.

Two-Dimensional Nearest-Neighbour Queueing Models, a Review and an Example

J.W. Cohen

CWI, The Netherlands

Summary. Several queueing problems can be modelled as two-dimensional nearest-neighbour random walks, the shortest two-server queueing model is a well-known example. By means of uniformisation or by formulating the inherent problem as a Boundary Value Problem these random walks can be analysed. Recently, a fairly simple analytic approach has been developed for nearest-neighbour random walks without one-step transitions to the North, the North-East and the East. This approach is exposed here for the symmetric shortest two-server queue.

Keywords: queueing models, nearest-neighbour random walks, symmetrical shortest queue.

1. A review

In present day teletraffic analysis the performance models may be roughly divided into macro- and micro-models. The macro-models concern queueing networks and are applied for the analysis of traffic streams which pass successively a series of service and/or switching points. The micro-models concern the study of the performance characteristics of traffic processes at a single switching node.

The M/G/1 model is a classical micro-model. In a basic paper Kendall [18] showed that its embedded process at successive departure epochs is a discrete time parameter Markov chain with state space $S = \{0, 1, 2, ...\}$; actually it is a random walk on S with one-step displacement $\boldsymbol{\xi} \in \{-1, 0, 1, 2, ...\}$. Presently many micro-models have to be described in terms of random walks on a two- or higher dimensional state space S. For such random walks information concerning its stationary distribution is usually the most important source for judging the performance characteristics. Its determination is generally not a simple analytic problem, and presently effective analytical(theoretical) techniques are hardly available for random walks with state space of dimension three or higher.

However, for the two-dimensional case the research of the last two decades led to powerful techniques for the analysis of random walks with state space S the set of lattice points $S = \{0, 1, 2, ...\} \times \{0, 1, 2, ...\}$ and one-step displacement vector $\{\boldsymbol{\xi}, \boldsymbol{\eta}\} \in \{-1, 0, 1, 2, ...\} \times \{-1, 0, 1, 2, ...\}$ at interior points of S. Here the involved analytic problem may be formulated as a Riemann-Hilbert Boundary Value Problem, and as such it can be solved, cf. [4]. This approach requires generally the construction of a conformal mapping. An explicit representation of this mapping is generally quite difficult to obtain and so it has to be numerically evaluated, but this is not a serious problem. For a review concerning the analysis of random walks in terms of boundary value problems see [5], for conditions concerning the existence of stationary distributions, see [6].

A conformal mapping is not needed in the analysis of the so-called nearest-neighbour random walks (NNRW), which are characterised by the restriction that for the one-step-displacement vector (ξ, η) is restricted to the set $\{-1,0,1\} \times \{-1,0,1\}$, see FIGURE 1.

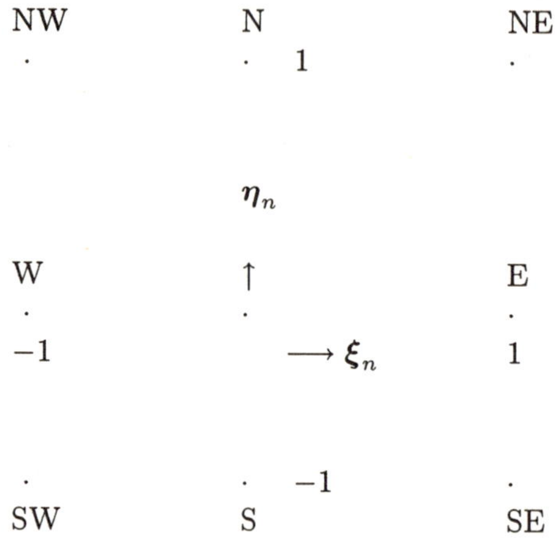

FIGURE 1.

Recent research of NNRW led to quite some information concerning the character of the generating function of the bivariate stationary distribution, i.e., of $\mathrm{E}\{r_1^{x_1} r_2^{x_2}\}, |r_1| \le 1, |r_2| \le 1$; here $(x_1, x_2) \in S$ stands for a stochastic vector with joint distribution the stationary distribution of the random walk. This generating function can be continued analytically into $|r_1| \ge 1, |r_2| \ge 1$. The type of this continuation depends on the nature of the one-step transition distribution.

Whenever the one-step transitions to the North, North-East and East are not possible, i.e., they all have zero probability, then $\mathrm{E}\{r_1^{x_1} r_2^{x_2}\}$ is for every fixed r_2 with $|r_2| \le 1$ a meromorphic function of r_1, all its poles are independent of r_2; similarly with r_1 and r_2 interchanged. Note that a meromorphic function is a regular function, except for at most a finite number of poles in every finite domain. Random walks with one-step transitions to the N, NE and E occur in the studies [1], [2], [7], [8], [9], [11], [12], [14], [17].

In [15] a NNRW is analysed for the case that only one-step tansitions can occur to the NE, the W and the S. The bivariate generating function when continued analytically for $|r_1| \ge 1$, and fixed $r_2, |r_2| \le 1$, appears to be an algebraic function on a two-sheeted Riemann surface, it has two poles. A similar result is obtained in [10] for the case with only one-step transitions to the N, the E and the SW. Whenever next to the one-step transitions to the NE, the W, the S also those to the N and the E are possible then the bivariate generating function is no longer algebraic, it is a transcendental function as it appears from the results in [19], see also [13].

In the analysis of random walks the kernel

$$K(r_1, r_2) := r_1 r_2 - \mathrm{E}\{r_1^{\xi+1} r_2^{\eta+1}\},$$

characterises the bivariate generating function of the distribution of the one-step transitions. For a NNRW this kernel is a biquadratic polynomial in r_1 and r_2, and a zero r_1 as a function of r_2 has in general four branch points, they are all real and two are located inside, the other two outside the unit disk. Generally, the uniformisation technique is used to describe the manifold $K(r_1, r_2) = 0$. Recently, it appeared that the uniformisation can be avoided in the analysis of NNRW without one-step transitions to the N, NE and E, cf. [7], and as a consequence the analysis becomes much simpler; in particular this approach has led to a complete description of the stationary distribution for the asymmetrical shortest queue, cf. [11]. In the next section we shall outline this approach for the symmetrical shortest queueing model.

As already mentioned above analytical results are not yet available for higher dimensional random walks (≥ 3), but the approaches described in [1], [2], [3] and [16] appear to lead to quite accurate numerical results. In [3] and [16] the stationary state probabilities are expressed as power series of a suitably chosen function of the traffic intensity. Substitution of these series in the Kolmogorov equations leads to equations for the coefficients, these equations can be solved recursively. For some cases it has been proved that the series converge to the exact solution. In [1] and [2] the stationary state probabilities are represented by infinite series of which the terms are recursively calculated via the Kolmogorov equations. The structure of these series resembles those of the exact solution for the two-dimensional case, cf. (2.50) below. In [1] and [2] it is claimed that the approach there exposed yields the correct solution. Unfortunately, that claim is not correct.

2. The symmetrical shortest queueing model

In this section we shall sketch the analysis of the two-server symmetrical shortest queueing model and present the main results obtained from this analysis. Generally all proofs will be omitted, for such proofs the reader is referred to [8] and [12]; however, the main points of the proofs needed to understand the analysis will be elucidated.

In the symmetrical shortest queue model the arrival process of the customers is a Poisson process with arrival rate λ. The system consists of two servers each with its own queue. The service times of the customers are independent, negative exponentially distributed stochastic variables with first moment β. An arriving customer joins the shorter queue, if both queues are equal he chooses a queue with probability 1/2. The queue length has a unique stationary distribution if and only if

$$a := \lambda\beta < 2, \tag{2.1}$$

this condition is assumed to hold.

Denote by (x_1, x_2) a stochastic vector with distribution the stationary distribution of the queue lengths $x_i, i = 1, 2,$ of queue i.

Put

$$\begin{aligned} \Omega(r) &:= \mathrm{E}\{r^{x_1}(x_2 = 0)\}\,, \quad |r| \le 1, \\ \Phi(t) &:= \mathrm{E}\{t^{x_1}(x_1 = x_2)\}\,, \quad |t| \le 1. \end{aligned} \tag{2.2}$$

It is shown that for $|r| \le 1,\ |t| \le 1,$

$$\begin{aligned} &k_1(r,t)\mathrm{E}\{t^{x_1}r^{x_2-x_1}(x_2 \ge x_1)\} = k_1(r,t)\Phi(t) + \\ &r[(r-t)\Omega(r) - \{r + \tfrac{1}{2}art - \tfrac{1}{2}(2+a)t\}\Phi(t)], \end{aligned} \tag{2.3}$$

here

$$k_1(r,t) = at^2 + [1 - (2+a)r]t + r^2. \tag{2.4}$$

For fixed r the two zeros $t_1(r)$ and $t_2(r)$ of $k_1(r,t)$ may be so defined that

$$\begin{aligned} &|t_1(r)| < |r| < |t_2(r)| \quad \text{for} \quad |r| \ge 1, \quad r \ne 1, \\ &t_1(1) = \min(1, \tfrac{1}{a}), \qquad\qquad t_2(1) = \max(1, \tfrac{1}{a}). \end{aligned} \tag{2.5}$$

The branch points $\rho_1,\ \rho_2$ of these zeros are given by

$$\rho_{1,2} = [1 + (1 \pm \sqrt{a})^2]^{-1}, \quad 0 < \rho_1 < \rho_2 \le 1. \tag{2.6}$$

For any zero-tuple $(\hat{r}, \hat{t})$ of $k_1(r,t)$ with $|\hat{r}| \le 1,\ |\hat{t}| \le 1$, the righthand-side of (2.3) should be zero because $x_1 \ge 0,\ x_2 \ge 0$ implies

$$|\mathrm{E}\{\hat{t}^{x_1}\hat{r}^{x_2-x_1}(x_2 \ge x_1)\}| \le 1. \tag{2.7}$$

In particular a simple calculation shows that the condition (2.7) implies that

$$\Omega(r) + k_2(r, t_1(r))\Phi(t_1(r)) = 0 \quad \text{for} \quad |r| = 1, \tag{2.8}$$

with

$$k_2(r,t) := -1 + \frac{1}{2}a^2t - \frac{1}{2}ar. \tag{2.9}$$

Obviously, the functions $\Phi(t)$ and $\Omega(r)$, cf.(2.2), should further satisfy the conditions:

$\Phi(t)$ is regular for $|t| < 1$, continuous for $|t| \leq 1$, and its series expansion in powers of t, $|t| \leq 1$, has nonnegative *coefficients* of which at least one is positive, similarly for $\Omega(t)$.

Let $\mathcal{L}$ be a simple smooth closed contour which has only one point R_0, say, in common with the unit circle, $|R_0| = 1$, $R_0 \neq 1$, and $r \in \mathcal{L} \Rightarrow |r| < 1$, and which intersects the interval $[\rho_1, \rho_2]$, cf.(2.6), only once, say at the point R_p. Because of (2.10) and the structure of $k_2(r,t)$, cf.(2.9), it is readily seen that (2.8) can be continued analytically along the part R_0R_p of $\mathcal{L}$. At $r = R_p$ it is seen that $t_1(R_p)$ and $t_2(R_p)$ are complex conjugated, and so by continuing the relation (2.8) along $\mathcal{L}$, $t_1(R_p)$ has to be replaced by $t_2(R_p)$ when passing the point R_p. Therefore it is seen that by continuation from R_p to R_0 along $\mathcal{L}$ the relation (2.8) holds with $t_1(R_0)$ replaced by $t_2(R_0)$. Because $R_0 \neq 1$ is an arbitrary point of $|r| = 1$ it follows that we have

$$\Omega(r) + k_2(r, t_j(r))\Phi(t_j(r)) = 0, \quad \text{for} \quad |r| = 1,\ j = 1, 2, \tag{2.10}$$

the fact that (2.11) also holds for $r = 1$ follows from that for $|r| = 1$, $r \neq 1$ by continuity. Further it is readily seen that (2.11) is equivalent with the condition (2.7). Consequently, the functions $\Omega(r)$ and $\Phi(t)$ should satisfy the conditions (2.10) and (2.11).

Because $|t_2(r)| > 1$ for $|r| = 1$, cf.(2.5), it is seen from the arguments above that $\Phi(t)$ is regular in some domain contained in $|t| \geq 1$. Because the two branch points of the zeros $r(t)$ of $k_1(r,t)$ are also located inside $|t| < 1$, a similar argument as used above shows that also $\Omega(r)$ is regular in some domain contained in $|r| \geq 1$. Starting from out these domains and by using (2.11) alternatingly for $j = 1$ and $j = 2$ it is not difficult to show by analytic continuation that (2.11) should hold for all $|r| \geq 1$, and that $\Omega(r)$ has an analytic continuation in $|r| \geq 1$ except possibly for singularities, similarly for $\Phi(t)$ in $t \geq 1$. Because $k_2(r,t)$ is a polynomial and the branch points of the zeros of $k_1(r,t)$ are located in the unit disk these singularities can be only poles. These poles are obviously generated by those r for which $k_2(r, t(r)) = 0$. It is readily verified that

$$(r_0^-, t_0^-) = (-1 - \frac{2}{a}, -\frac{1}{a}) \quad \text{and} \quad (r_0, t_0) = (\frac{2}{a}, \frac{4}{a^2}), \tag{2.11}$$

are the only common zero-tuples of $k_1(r,t)$ and $k_2(r,t)$.

Consider the sequence

$$r_0 < t_0 < r_1 < t_1 < r_2 < \ldots < t_{n-1} < r_n < t_n < \ldots, \tag{2.12}$$

with

$$t_{n-1} = t_1(r_n),\ n = 1, 2, \ldots, \qquad t_n = t_2(r_n), \quad n = 0, 1, 2, \ldots,$$

so that (r_n, t_{n-1}) and (r_n, t_n) are zero-tuples of $k_1(r,t)$.

From (2.11) we have

$$\Omega(r_0) + k_2(r_0,t_0)\Phi(t_0) = 0, \quad k_2(r_0,t_0) = 0, \tag{2.13}$$

and so because of (2.10) and $r_0 > 1$, $t_0 > 1$, it follows from (2.12) and (2.14) that

$$0 < \Omega(r_0) < \infty \Rightarrow \Phi(t_0) = \infty. \tag{2.14}$$

Obviously $\Omega(r_0) > 0$. The supposition $\Omega(r_0) = \infty$ leads to a contradiction, since by extending the sequence (2.13) to the left it results from (2.11) that there exists an r with $0 < r < 1$ for which $\Omega(r) = \infty$ or a t with $0 < t < 1$ for which $\Phi(t) = \infty$; both results violate (2.10). Hence t_0 is a pole of $\Phi(t)$, and actually a simple pole. From (2.11), (2.12) and (2.13) it follows that r_1 is a simple pole. Successively applying the latter argument it follows that

$$\begin{aligned} &t_n,\ n = 0,1,2,\dots, && \text{are simple poles of } \Phi(t), \\ &r_n,\ n = 1,2,\dots, && \text{are simple poles of } \Omega(r). \end{aligned} \tag{2.15}$$

Next consider the sequence

$$\begin{aligned} &t_0^- > r_0^- > t_1^- > r_1^- > t_2^- \dots > r_{n-1}^- > t_n^- > r_n^- > \dots, \\ &\text{with} \\ &t_{n+1}^- = t_1(r_n^-),\ n = 1,2,\dots,\quad t_n^- = t_2(r_n^-),\ n = 0,1,\dots . \end{aligned} \tag{2.16}$$

Obviously (2.11) with $r_0^-, t_0^- = t_2(r_0^-)$ and (2.12) imply that

$$|\Phi(t_0^-)| < \infty \Rightarrow \Omega(r_0^-) = 0. \tag{2.17}$$

The supposition $|\Phi(t_0^-)| = \infty$ leads via extending the sequence (2.17) to the left and by using (2.11) to the conclusion that an r exists with $0 > r > -1$ for which $|\Omega(r)| = \infty$ or that a t exists with $-1 < t < 0$ for which $|\Omega(t)| = \infty$; this violates (2.10). Hence r_0 is a zero of $\Omega(r)$, and it is a simple zero. From (2.11) it now results that t_1 is a simple zero of $\Phi(t)$. Repeating this argument it is seen by using (2.11) that

$$\begin{aligned} &r_n^-,\ n = 0,1,2,\dots, && \text{are simple zeros of } \Omega(r), \\ &t_n^-,\ n = 1,2,\dots, && \text{are simple zeros of } \Phi(t). \end{aligned} \tag{2.18}$$

It is readily shown that the supposition that $\Omega(r)$ and/or $\Phi(t)$ have other poles and zeros then those listed above leads again to a violation of (2.10).

It is not difficult to verify that for $n \to \infty$,

$$\begin{aligned} &r_n \to \infty,\ t_n \to \infty,\ r_n^- \to -\infty,\ t_n^- \to -\infty, \\ &\tfrac{t_{n+1}}{t_n} \to a\delta^2,\ \tfrac{t_{n+1}^-}{t_n^-} \to a\delta^2,\ \tfrac{r_{n+1}}{r_n} \to a\delta^2,\ \tfrac{r_{n+1}^-}{r_n^-} \to a\delta^2, \\ &\text{with} \\ &\delta := \tfrac{1}{2a}[2 + a + \sqrt{a^2+4}] > \tfrac{2}{a} > 1. \end{aligned} \tag{2.19}$$

Obviously (2.20) implies

$$\sum_{n=0}^{\infty} |\frac{1}{t_n}| < \infty, \; \sum_{n=1}^{\infty} |\frac{1}{r_n}| < \infty, \; \sum_{n=1}^{\infty} |\frac{1}{t_n^-}| < \infty, \; \sum_{n=0}^{\infty} |\frac{1}{r_n^-}| < \infty, \tag{2.20}$$

so that $\Phi(t)$ and $\Omega(r)$ are both meromorphic functions, of which all zeros and poles are known. It follows from the theory of entire functions, cf.[20], chapter VII, that

$$\begin{aligned} \Phi(t) &= \Phi(1)\{\prod_{n=1}^{\infty} \frac{1-\frac{t}{t_n^-}}{1-\frac{1}{t_n^-}}\}\{\prod_{n=0}^{\infty} \frac{1-\frac{1}{t_n}}{1-\frac{t}{t_n}}\}, \\ \Omega(r) &= \Omega(1)\{\prod_{n=0}^{\infty} \frac{1-\frac{r}{r_n^-}}{1-\frac{1}{r_n^-}}\}\{\prod_{n=1}^{\infty} \frac{1-\frac{1}{r_n}}{1-\frac{r}{r_n}}\}, \end{aligned} \tag{2.21}$$

note that the infinite products all converge absolutely. From the norming condition and (2.11) it follows that

$$\Omega(1) = 1 - \frac{1}{2}a, \quad \Phi(1) = \frac{1}{1+a}. \tag{2.22}$$

With the construction of $\Phi(t)$ and $\Omega(r)$, cf.(2.22) and (2.23), the analytical problem formulated by (2.10) and (2.11) has been solved.

Next we derive some relations for the performance characteristics. From (2.22) and (2.23) the bivariate generating function $\mathrm{E}\{t^{x_1} r^{x_2 - x_1}(x_2 \geq x_1)\}$ is readily calculated.

Denoting by

$$x_s := \min(x_1, x_2), \quad x_l := \max(x_1, x_2), \tag{2.23}$$

so that x_s is the length of the shorter queue and x_l that of the longer one; it follows that

$$\begin{aligned} &\mathrm{E}\{r^{x_1+x_2}\} = \tfrac{2}{2-ar}\Omega(r), \\ &\mathrm{E}\{t^{x_1}(x_2 > x_1)\} = \tfrac{1}{1-at}[1 - \tfrac{1}{2}a - \Phi(t)], \quad \Phi(\tfrac{1}{a}) = 1 - \tfrac{1}{2}a, \\ &\mathrm{E}\{t^{x_2}(x_2 > x_1)\} = \tfrac{1}{2} \text{ at } \Phi(t), \\ &\mathrm{E}\{t^{x_l}\} = (1+at)\Phi(t), \\ &\mathrm{E}\{t^{x_s}\} = \tfrac{2-a-(1+at)\Phi(t)}{1-at}. \end{aligned} \tag{2.24}$$

Further

$$
\begin{aligned}
\Pr\{x_1 = x_2\} &= \tfrac{1}{1+a}, \quad \Pr\{x_1 > x_2\} = \tfrac{1}{2}\tfrac{a}{1+a}, \\
\mathrm{E}\{x_2(x_2 > x_1)\} &= \tfrac{a}{2(1+a)}[1 + \tfrac{\Phi^{(')}(1)}{\Phi(1)}], \\
\mathrm{E}\{x_1(x_2 > x_1)\} &= \tfrac{1}{1-a^2}[\tfrac{1}{2}a^2 - \tfrac{\Phi^{(')}(1)}{\Phi(1)}] && \text{for } a \neq 1, \\
&= \tfrac{1}{4}\tfrac{\Phi^{('')}(1)}{\Phi(1)} && \text{for } a = 1, \\
\mathrm{E}\{x_1(x_1 = x_2)\} &= \tfrac{1}{1+a}\tfrac{\Phi^{(')}(1)}{\Phi(1)}, && (2.25) \\
\mathrm{E}\{x_1\} &= \tfrac{a}{2(2-a)} + \tfrac{1}{2}\tfrac{\Omega^{(')}(1)}{\Omega(1)}, \\
\mathrm{E}\{x_s\} &= \tfrac{1}{1-a^2}[a^2 - (1+a)\tfrac{\Phi^{(')}(1)}{\Phi(1)}] && \text{for } a \neq 1, \\
&= \tfrac{1}{4} + \tfrac{1}{2}\tfrac{\Phi^{('')}(1)}{\Phi(1)} && \text{for } a = 1, \\
\mathrm{E}\{x_l\} &= \tfrac{a}{a+1}[1 + \tfrac{\Phi^{('')}(1)}{\Phi(1)}].
\end{aligned}
$$

$$
\mathrm{E}\{e^{-\rho w}\} = \mathrm{E}\{[\beta(\rho)]^{x_s}\} = \frac{2 - a + (1 + a\beta(\rho))\Phi(\beta(\rho))}{1 - a\beta(\rho)}, \ \mathrm{Re}\,\rho \geq 0, \quad (2.26)
$$

here $\beta(\rho) = [1 + \rho\beta]^{-1}$ and w is a stochastic variable with distribution the stationary distribution of the waiting time of a customer. Concerning the calculation of the moments note that

$$
\frac{\Phi^{(')}(t)}{\Phi(t)} \Big|_{t=1} = \frac{\mathrm{d}}{\mathrm{d}t} \log \Phi(t) \Big|_{t=1} = \frac{1}{t_0 - 1} + \sum_{n=1}^{\infty}\{\frac{1}{1 + |t_n^-|} + \frac{1}{t_n - 1}\}, \quad (2.27)
$$

and concerning the calculation of $\Phi(0) = \Omega(0) = \Pr\{x_1 = x_2 = 0\}$ see [8].

The explicit expressions for $\Omega(r)$ and $\Phi(t)$ obtained above, cf.(2.22), could be derived because the poles as well as the zeros of these functions are readily obtained from the functional equations (2.11). The recent research of NNRW has learned that generally the location of the poles of the functions to be derived can be rather easily obtained from the relevant functional equation, however, the determination of the zeros is quite often not possible. We, therefore, discuss below the technique to find $\Omega(r)$ and $\Phi(t)$ without using information concerning their zeros. This approach is based on the calculation of the residues of $\Phi(t)$ and $\Omega(r)$. Put, cf.(2.16),

$$
\begin{aligned}
\phi_n &:= \lim_{t \to t_n}(t - t_n)\Phi(t), \quad n = 0, 1, 2, \ldots, \\
\omega_n &:= \lim_{r \to r_n}(r - r_n)\Omega(r), \quad n = 1, 2, \ldots.
\end{aligned} \quad (2.28)
$$

From (2.11) we have for $j = 1, 2$,

$$\begin{aligned} &i. \quad \Omega(r) + k_2(r, t_j(r))\Phi(t_j(r)) = 0, && \text{for all } r \neq r_n, \\ &ii. \quad \lim_{r\to r_n}[\Omega(r) + k_2(r, t_j(r))]\Phi(t_j(r)) = 0, && \text{for all } n = 0, 1, 2, \ldots . \end{aligned} \tag{2.29}$$

Next note that

$$\begin{aligned} \lim_{r\to r_n}(r - r_n)\Phi(t_2(r)) &= \phi_n \left[\frac{\mathrm{d}t_2(r)}{\mathrm{d}r}\right]^{-1}_{r=r_n}, && n = 0, 1, \ldots, \\ \lim_{r\to r_n}(r - r_n)\Phi(t_1(r)) &= \phi_{n-1} \left[\frac{\mathrm{d}t_1(r)}{\mathrm{d}r}\right]^{-1}_{r=r_n}, && n = 1, 2, \ldots, \\ \frac{\mathrm{d}t_j(r)}{\mathrm{d}r} = -\frac{2r-(2+a)t_j(r)}{2at_j(r)-1+(2+a)r} &= \frac{r_n - r_{n+1}}{t_n - t_{n-1}} && \text{for } j = 2, \\ &= \frac{r_n - r_{n-1}}{t_{n-1} - t_n} && \text{for } j = 1. \end{aligned} \tag{2.30}$$

From (2.29), ..., (2.31), we obtain for $n = 1, 2, \ldots$,

$$\begin{aligned} \omega_n &= -k_2(r_n, t_n)\frac{t_n - t_{n-1}}{r_n - r_{n+1}}\phi_n, \\ &= -k_2(r_n, t_{n-1})\frac{t_{n-1} - t_n}{r_n - r_{n-1}}\phi_{n-1}, \end{aligned} \tag{2.31}$$

and so for $n = 1, 2, \ldots$,

$$\begin{aligned} \frac{\phi_n}{\phi_{n-1}} &= \frac{-1+\frac{1}{2}a^2t_{n-1}-\frac{1}{2}ar_n}{-1+\frac{1}{2}a^2t_n-\frac{1}{2}ar_n}\,\frac{r_{n+1}-r_n}{r_n-r_{n-1}}, \\ \frac{\omega_{n+1}}{\omega_n} &= \frac{-1+\frac{1}{2}a^2t_n-\frac{1}{2}ar_{n+1}}{-1+\frac{1}{2}a^2t_n-\frac{1}{2}ar_n}\,\frac{t_{n+1}-t_n}{t_n-t_{n-1}}. \end{aligned} \tag{2.32}$$

The norming condition yields $\Omega(1) = 1 - \frac{1}{2}a$, and so by starting with $r = 1$ we can calculate from (2.11) $\Omega(\frac{2}{a})$ and ϕ_0, it is found that

$$\Omega(\frac{2}{a}) = \frac{1}{4}(2-a)(4-a), \quad \phi_0 = -\frac{4}{a^2}\frac{(2-a)(4-a)}{4+a}, \tag{2.33}$$

and consequently from (2.32) and (2.33) the ϕ_n and ω_n can be determined recursively. From (2.20) and (2.33) it is readily derived that for $n \to \infty$,

$$\lim_{n\to\infty} \frac{-\phi_n}{\phi_{n-1}} = a\delta\frac{\delta-1}{a\delta-1} > 1, \; \lim_{n\to\infty} \frac{-\omega_{n+1}}{\omega_n} = a^2\delta^3\frac{\delta-1}{a\delta-1}. \tag{2.34}$$

Consider the series

$$\sum_{n=0}^{\infty} \frac{\phi_n}{t-t_n}(\frac{t}{t_n})^\mu, \quad \mu \in \{0, 1, 2, \ldots\}. \tag{2.35}$$

Because

$$0 < \frac{1}{\delta}\frac{\delta-1}{a\delta-1} < 1, \tag{2.36}$$

it is readily verified by using (2.35) and (2.37) that the series in (2.36) converges absolutely for every finite $t \neq t_n$ and every μ. Put

$$\tilde{\Phi}(t) := \sum_{n=0}^{\infty} \frac{\phi_n}{t - t_n}, \quad \tilde{\Omega}(r) := \sum_{n=1}^{\infty} \frac{\omega_n}{r - r_n} \frac{r}{r_n}, \tag{2.37}$$

note that the second series converges also absolutely for every $r \neq r_n$. Hence the functions in (2.38) are well-defined meromorphic functions, so we write

$$\begin{aligned} \Phi(t) &= \hat{\Phi}(t) + \tilde{\Phi}(t), \\ \Omega(r) &= \hat{\Omega}(r) + \tilde{\Omega}(r), \end{aligned} \tag{2.38}$$

with $\hat{\Phi}(\cdot)$ and $\hat{\Omega}(\cdot)$ entire functions. Obviously (2.39) satisfies (2.30)ii, but (2.39) should also satisfy (2.30)i. Because $k_2(r, t_j(r))$ behaves as r for $r \to \infty$, and (2.11) should hold for all r, simple functional theoretical arguments show that $\hat{\Phi}(t)$ should be a constant and $\hat{\Omega}(r)$ a first degree polynomial, see for details [5], [11], [12]. So we have

$$\begin{aligned} \Phi(t) &= \Phi(0) + \textstyle\sum_{n=0}^{\infty} \frac{\phi_n}{t_n} + \sum_{n=0}^{\infty} \frac{\phi_n}{t - t_n}, \\ \Omega(r) &= \Omega(0) + [\Omega^{(')}(0) + \textstyle\sum_{n=1}^{\infty} \frac{\omega_n}{r_n^2}]r + \sum_{n=1}^{\infty} \frac{\omega_n}{r - r_n} \frac{r}{r_n}. \end{aligned} \tag{2.39}$$

Because $\Phi(0) = \Omega(0)$ and since $\Omega(1) = 1 - \frac{1}{2}a$, $\Phi(1) = (1 + a)^{-1}$, cf.(2.23), the remaining constants in (2.40) are determined. Actually, it may be shown that

$$\Omega(0) = \Phi(0) = -\sum_{n=0}^{\infty} \frac{\phi_n}{r_n}. \tag{2.40}$$

By using Foster's criterion it is not difficult to prove that the functional equations (2.11) have a unique solution under the conditions (2.10), and so (2.40) represents that solution.

From the result obtained we derive the explicit expressions for

$$p_{km} := \Pr\{x_1 = k, x_2 - x_1 = m\}, \quad k = 0, 1, 2, \ldots; \quad m = 0, 1, 2, \ldots . \tag{2.41}$$

From (2.3) we have for $|t| = 1$, $m = 1, 2, \ldots$,

$$\begin{aligned} \textstyle\sum_{k=0}^{\infty} p_{km} t^k &= \frac{1}{2\pi i} \int_{|r|=1} \frac{\mathrm{d}r}{r^m} \frac{(r-t)\Omega(r) - [r + \frac{1}{2}art - \frac{1}{2}(2+a)t]\Phi(t)}{k_1(r,t)} \\ &+ \frac{1}{2\pi i} \int_{|r|=1} \frac{\mathrm{d}r}{r^{m+1}} \Phi(t) . \end{aligned} \tag{2.42}$$

Note that the last integral in (2.43) is zero for $m \geq 1$. To evaluate the first integral in (2.43) note that the zeros of $k_1(r, t)$ with $|t| = 1$ are no poles of the integrand so that its only poles in $|r| \geq 1$ are those of $\Omega(r)$. Put

$$R_N := \frac{1}{2}(r_N + r_{N+1}), \tag{2.43}$$

and note that, cf.(2.5),

$$k_1(r,t) = a[t - t_1(r)][t - t_2(r)]. \tag{2.44}$$

By applying Cauchy's theorem we obtain from (2.43) for $|t| = 1,\ m = 1, 2, \ldots,$

$$\begin{aligned}\sum_{k=0}^{\infty} p_{km} t^k &= \sum_{n=1}^{N} \lim_{r \to r_n} (r - r_n) \frac{-(r-t)\Omega(r) + [r + \frac{1}{2}art - \frac{1}{2}(2+a)t]\Phi(t)}{a(t-t_1(r))(t-t_2(r))r^m} \\ &+ \frac{1}{2\pi i} \int_{|r|=R_N} \frac{\mathrm{d}r}{r^m} \frac{(r-t)\Omega(r) - [r + \frac{1}{2}art - \frac{1}{2}(2+a)t]\Phi(t)}{a(t-t_1(r))(t-t_2(r))} .\end{aligned} \tag{2.45}$$

From (2.40) it may be shown that for $N \to \infty$,

$$\Omega(R_N) = R_N[\Omega^{(')}(0) + \sum_{n=1}^{\infty} \frac{\omega_n}{r_n^2}] + O(1). \tag{2.46}$$

Because $t_j(r)/r, j = 1, 2$, has a finite limit for $r \to \infty$, it is seen that the integrand of the last integral behaves as R_N^{-m} for $N \to \infty$; hence the limit of this integral for $N \to \infty$ is zero if $m \geq 2$. So we obtain for $|t| = 1,\ m \geq 2$,

$$\begin{aligned}\sum_{k=0}^{\infty} p_{km} t^k &= \sum_{n=1}^{\infty} \frac{\omega_n}{r_n^m} \frac{t - r_n}{a(t-t_1(r_n))(t-t_2(r_n))} \\ &= \frac{1}{a} \sum_{n=1}^{\infty} \frac{-\omega_n}{t_n - t_{n-1}} [\frac{t_n - r_n}{t_n - t} - \frac{t_{n-1} - r_n}{t_{n-1} - t}] \frac{1}{r_n^m}.\end{aligned} \tag{2.47}$$

Calculation of the limit for $N \to \infty$ of the integral in (2.46) for the case $m = 1$ leads to: for $|t| = 1$,

$$\begin{aligned}\sum_{k=0}^{\infty} p_{k1} t^k &= \frac{1}{a} \sum_{n=1}^{\infty} \frac{\omega_n}{r_n} \frac{1}{t_n - t_{n-1}} [\frac{t_{n-1} - r_n}{t_{n-1} - t} - \frac{t_n - r_n}{t_n - t}] \\ &+ [\Omega^{(')}(0) + \sum_{n=1}^{\infty} \frac{\omega_n}{r_n^2}] = \frac{-2\Omega(0) + (2+a)\Phi(t)}{2(1+at)},\end{aligned} \tag{2.48}$$

here the second expression is obtained from (2.43) with $m = 1$ as the sum of the residues in $|t| < 1$, i.e. the residue at $r = 0$.

From (2.40), (2.48) and (2.49) the explicit expressions for p_{km} are easily obtained. They read

$$\begin{aligned}p_{km} &= \frac{1}{a} \sum_{n=1}^{\infty} \frac{\omega_n}{r_n^m} [\frac{t_n - r_n}{t_n - t_{n-1}} t_n^{-(k+1)} + \frac{r_n - t_{n-1}}{t_n - t_{n-1}} t_{n+1}^{-(k+1)}], && k \geq 0, \quad m \geq 2, \\ p_{k1} &= \frac{1}{2}(2 + a) \sum_{n=0}^{\infty} \frac{-\phi_n}{1 + at_n} t_n^{-(k+1)}, && k \geq 0, \\ p_{k0} &= \sum_{n=0}^{\infty} (-\phi_n) t_n^{-(k+1)}, && k \geq 0, \\ p_{0m} &= 2 \sum_{n=1}^{\infty} (-\omega_n) r_n^{-(m+1)}, && m \geq 2 .\end{aligned} \tag{2.49}$$

Acknowledgement. This work was supported in part by the European Grant BRA-QMIPS of CEC DG XIII.

References

1. I.J.B.F. Adan, J. Wessels and W.H.M. Zijm, "Analysis of the symmetric shortest queueing problem, Stochastic Models", **6**, pp. 691–713, 1990.
2. I.J.B.F. Adan, "A Compensation Approach for Queueing Problems", CWI Tracts, # 104. Math. Center Amsterdam, 1994.
3. J.P.C. Blanc, "The power-series algorithm applied to the shortest queueing problem", Op. Res. **40**, pp. 157–167, 1992.
4. J.W. Cohen and O.J. Boxma, "Boundary Value Problems in Queueing System Analysis", North-Holland Publ. Co., Amsterdam, 1983.
5. J.W. Cohen, "Boundary value problems in queueing theory", QUESTA **3**, pp. 97–128, 1988 .
6. J.W. Cohen, " Analysis of Random Walks", IOS Press, Amsterdam, 1992.
7. J.W. Cohen, "On a class of two-dimensional nearest-neighbour random walks", Studies in Appl. Prob. Papers in honour of LAJOS TAKÁCS ed., J. GALAMBOS, J. GANI, A.P.T. Journ. Appl. Prob. $\mathbf{31}^A$, pp. 207–237, 1994.
8. J.W. Cohen, "On the analysis of the symmetrical shortest queue", CWI Report BS-R9420, Amsterdam, 1994.
9. J.W. Cohen, "On the determination of the stationary distribution of a symmetric buffered switch", CWI Report BS-R9427, Amsterdam, 1994.
10. J.W. Cohen, "Analysis of a two-dimensional algebraic nearest-neighbour random walk. (Queue with paired services)", CWI Report BS-R9437, Amsterdam, 1994.
11. J.W. Cohen, "Analysis of the asymmetrical shortest two-server queueing model", CWI Report BS-R9509, Amsterdam, 1995.
12. J.W. Cohen, "On the symmetrical shortest queue and the compensation approach", to appear as CWI Report, Amsterdam, 1995.
13. G. Fayolle, R. Iasnogorodski and V.A. Malyshev, "Algebraic generating functions for two-dimensional random walks", Report INRIA, Rocquencourt, France, 1990.
14. L. Flatto and H.P. McKean, "Two queues in parallel", Pure and Appl. Math. **30**, pp. 255–263, 1977 .
15. L. Flatto and S. Hahn, "Two parallel queues created by arrivals with two demands", SIAM J. Appl. Math. **44**, pp. 1041–1054, 1984, see also SIAM J. App. Math. **45**, pp. 861–878, 1985.
16. G. Hooghiemstra, M. Keane and S. Van de Ree, "Power series for stationary distributions of coupled processor models", SIAM J. Appl. Math. **48**, pp. 1159–1166, 1988.
17. S. Jaffe, "The equilibrium distribution for a clocked buffered switch", Prob. Engin. Inform. Sc. **6**, pp. 425–438, 1992.
18. D.G. Kendall, "Stochastic processes in the theory of queues and their analysis by the method of the imbedded Markov chain", Ann. Math. Stat. **24**, pp. 338–354, 1953.
19. P.E. Wright, "Two parallel processors with coupled inputs", Adv. Appl. Prob. **24**, pp. 986–1007, 1992.
20. S. Saks and A. Zygmund, "Analytic Functions", Nakladem Polskiego, Warshaw, 1952.

M/G/1 Queues with FCFS Negative Arrivals

P.G. Harrison and E. Pitel*

Department of Computing, Imperial College, UK

Summary. The generating function of the equilibrium queue length probability distribution in a single server queue with general service times and independent Poisson arrival streams of both positive and negative customers is investigated. The queueing discipline first come first served is chosen for the positive customers together with a killing strategy in which the last customer in the queue is removed by a negative customer. This killing strategy leads to complex mathematical analysis and, ultimately, to a Fredholm integral equation of the first kind. This type of equation has no known reliable numerical solution method except in special cases. We derive an alternative, iterative method involving the numerical inversion of Laplace transforms.

1. Introduction

The arrival of a negative customer to a queue causes one ordinary (or 'positive') customer to be removed (or 'killed'), if any is present. Negative arrivals to an empty queue depart immediately with no effect. A negative customer therefore represents some kind of work cancelling signal and can be thought of as modelling inhibitor signals in neural networks, killing signals in speculative parallelism, and breakdowns, amongst other applications.

However, work to date has related only to Markovian queues (M/M/1), e.g. [5], and networks thereof, e.g. [3], apart from the stability analysis of the M/G/1 queue in [2]. Notice that the killing strategy and queueing discipline are immaterial in M/M/1 queues, as far as queue lengths are concerned (but not sojourn times, [5]), because of the memoryless property of the exponential service times.

In the present paper, the M/G/1 queue with FCFS queueing discipline for positive customers and a killing strategy which removes the last customer in the queue (RCE—Removal of Customer at the End) is considered. This is the most complex case which reduces to a Fredholm integral equation of the first kind to determine the generating function of the equilibrium queue length probability distribution, as in [6]. Here we focus instead on an algorithm which avoids the intractable numerical solution of this integral equation. The algorithm computes the equilibrium probability that there is one customer in the queue jointly with the density of the partial service it has received. The algorithm is complex, involving numerical Laplace transform inversion and numerical integrations over the positive reals. However, the approach is promising in view of the considerable recent research into numerical inversion

* Now at IRISA, Rennes, France

techniques. We use the method of Dubner and Abate, [1], but much more sophisticated methods have been developed since then.

Other combinations of queueing discipline for the positive customers and killing strategies for the negative are also of interest. A range of cases is investigated in [6]. In particular, when the killed customer is removed from the head of the queue (i.e. the one in service, if any), the problem can be approached in terms of the negative arrivals "helping the server" and so modifying the service time probability distribution in a standard M/G/1 queue. This approach also leads to some new results in the classical theory.

The paper is organised as follows. In the next section we define our terminology, describe the method of supplementary variables which we use and apply it to obtain the equations which define the required generating function. Our iterative algorithm is detailed in section 3. and we conclude in section 4..

2. Derivation of equations defining the generating function

We consider M/G/1 G-queues with Poisson arrivals with rates λ^+ for positive customers and λ^- for negative customers respectively and general service time distribution $B(t)$. We use the method of supplementary variables, including in the state of the queue the partial service time of any customer in service. This establishes the Markov property for the (queue length, partial service time) stochastic process, as in the classical case. Let

$N(t)$ be the number of customers in the system at time t,
$X(t)$ be the service already received (partial service time) by the customer in service at time t
$Q(z)$ be the generating function of the number of customers in the system in the steady state.

We define

$$\begin{aligned} P_k(t) &\triangleq P[N(t) = k] \\ P_k(t, t_1)\, dt_1 &\triangleq P[N(t) = k, t_1 < X(t) \leq t_1 + dt_1] \\ p_k &\triangleq \lim_{t \to \infty} P_k(t) \\ p_k(t_1) &\triangleq \lim_{t \to \infty} P_k(t, t_1) \end{aligned}$$

when the limits exist. The generating functions of $p_k(t)$ and p_k, $\forall k > 0$, $\forall t \geq 0$, $\forall z \in D(0,1)$ (the unit disk), are now defined by

$$R(z,t) \triangleq \sum_{k=1}^{\infty} p_k(t)\, z^k$$

$$R(z) \triangleq \int_0^\infty R(z,t)\,dt$$

so that

$$Q(z) \triangleq p_0 + R(z)$$

The hazard function, denoted $r(t)$, is the probability that a service completes in the interval $[t, t+h]$ given that completion has not occurred up to time t, i.e.

$$r(t) = \frac{b(t)}{1 - B(t)} = -\frac{d}{dt}\ln(1 - B(t))$$

We analyse the evolution of the state $Z(t) = (N(t), X_0(t))$ if $N(t) > 0$ or $Z(t) = 0$ if $N(t) = 0$ and consider an infinitesimal interval of time $[t, t+h]$ to derive $Q(z)$. At time $t+h$, the system may enter any of the following states $(k, t+h, t_1+h)$ for $k > 0$ or $(k, t+h, 0)$ for $k \geq 0$.

The state $(k, t+h, t_1+h)$, $\forall k > 0$ is reached either from the state

- $(k+1, t, t_1)$ with a negative arrival, i.e. w.p. $\lambda^- h + o(h)$, or
- $(k-1, t, t_1)$ if $k > 1$ with a positive arrival, i.e. w.p. $\lambda^+ h + o(h)$, or
- (k, t, t_1) with no positive or negative arrivals and no completion of service currently started, i.e w.p. $1 - \lambda^+ h - \lambda^- h - r(t_1)\,h + o(h)$.

This provides the following equation for $k > 0$

$$\begin{aligned} P_k(t+h, t_1+h) &= \lambda^+ h\, P_{k-1}(t, t_1)\, 1_{\{k>1\}} + \\ &\quad \lambda^- h\, P_{k+1}(t, t_1) + \\ &\quad (1 - (\lambda + r(t_1))h)\, P_k(t, t_1) + \\ &\quad o(h) \end{aligned}$$

Dividing the equation by h and taking the limits $t \to \infty$ and $h \to 0$, we obtain, $\forall k > 0$,

$$\begin{aligned} \frac{dp_k(t_1)}{dt_1} &= \lambda^+ p_{k-1}(t_1)\, 1_{\{k>1\}} + \\ &\qquad \lambda^- p_{k+1}(t_1) - (\lambda + r(t_1))\, p_k(t_1) \end{aligned}$$

Similarly, we obtain the following equations for $k \geq 0$:

$$\lambda^+ p_0 = \lambda^- p_1 + \int_0^\infty p_1(t_1)\, r(t_1)\, dt_1 \tag{2.1}$$

and, $\forall k > 0$,

$$p_k(0) = \int_0^\infty p_{k+1}(t_1)\, r(t_1)\, dt_1 + \lambda^+ p_0\, 1_{\{k=1\}} \tag{2.2}$$

We add to this set of equations the normalizing equation

$$p_0 + \sum_{k=1}^{\infty} \int_0^{\infty} p_k(t)\, dt = 1 \tag{2.3}$$

We can now obtain the following result:

Lemma 2.1.

$$\frac{\partial R(z,t)}{\partial t} = -(a(z) + r(t))\, R(z,t) - \lambda^- p_1(t) \tag{2.4}$$

$$\textit{with } a(z) \triangleq \lambda - \lambda^+ z - \frac{\lambda^-}{z} = (1-z)\,(\lambda^+ - \frac{\lambda^-}{z})$$

$$R(0,t) \triangleq 0$$

$$z\, R(z,0) = \int_0^{\infty} r(t)\, R(z,t)\, dt + \lambda^+ z(z-1)\, p_0 + \lambda^- z\, p_1 \tag{2.5}$$

We solve the linear first order differential equation (2.4) in t using the integrating factor method to obtain:

$$R(z,t) = \left[R(z,0) - \lambda^- \int_0^t \frac{p_1(u)}{1-B(u)}\, e^{a(z)\, u}\, du\right] \times (1 - B(t))\, e^{-a(z)\, t} \tag{2.6}$$

We now face the problem that we need to know more about $p_1(t)$ which turns out to be the key to the solution of our problem. Before pursuing this, we first obtain a relation for $R(z)$ by integrating term by term the relation (2.4) w.r.t. t from 0 to ∞, noting that $R(z,\infty) \triangleq 0$

$$-R(z,0) = -a(z)\, R(z) - \int_0^{\infty} r(t)\, R(z,t)\, dt - \lambda^- p_1$$

Then we use equation (2.5) to express $R(z)$ in terms of $R(z,0)$ only:

$$(1-z)\,(\lambda^+ - \frac{\lambda^-}{z})\, R(z) = (1-z)(R(z,0) - \lambda^+ z\, p_0 - \lambda^- p_1)$$

which yields the fraction

$$R(z) = z\, \frac{R(z,0) - \lambda^+ z\, p_0 - \lambda^- p_1}{\lambda^+ z - \lambda^-} \tag{2.7}$$

The next step is to determine $R(z,0)$ which we denote by $\Psi(z)$. When z is such that $\Re(a(z)) < 0$, let us define

$$V(z,t) \triangleq \frac{R(z,t)}{1-B(t)} \tag{2.8}$$

We then rewrite the differential equation (2.4) as follows:

$$\begin{aligned}\frac{\partial V}{\partial t} + a(z)\,V &= -\lambda^- \frac{p_1(t)}{1-B(t)}\\ V(0,t) &= 0\end{aligned}$$

(Notice that this is the *only* change of variable that gives a constant coefficient of V.) Taking the Laplace transform of V w.r.t. t in the differential equation of V, we obtain, when $\Re(s) > 0$

$$V^*(z,s) = \frac{\Psi(z) - \lambda^- \int_0^\infty \frac{p_1(t)}{1-B(t)}\, e^{-st}\, dt}{s + a(z)}$$

As $V^*(z,s)$ has to be defined whenever $\Re(s) > 0$, the denominator vanishes when $z = z_1(s) \triangleq \frac{s+\lambda-\sqrt{(s+\lambda)^2-4\lambda^+\lambda^-}}{2\lambda^+}$ which is inside the unit disk (i.e. $s = -a(z_1)$). This gives the condition, $\forall z$ s.t. $\Re(a(z)) < 0$,

$$\Psi(z) = \lambda^- \int_0^\infty \frac{p_1(t)}{1-B(t)}\, e^{a(z)t}\, dt \tag{2.9}$$

which simplifies equation (2.6) to

$$V(z,t) = \lambda^- e^{-a(z)\,t} \int_t^\infty \frac{p_1(u)}{1-B(u)}\, e^{a(z)\,u}\, du \tag{2.10}$$

This result, together with Lemma 2.1, leads to the following Fredholm integral equation of the first kind, in which z (of $a(z)$) is written $e^{i\theta}$.

Lemma 2.2. *Let ρ_{-1} be the smaller root of $\lambda^+ \cos(\theta)\rho^2 - \lambda\rho + \lambda^- \cos(\theta) = 0$. Then $\frac{p_1(t)}{p_0}$ is a solution of the Fredholm integral equation of the first kind defined by:*

$$\begin{aligned}\int_0^\infty K(z(s),t)\, p_1(t)\, dt &= \lambda^+ z(s)(1-z(s))p_0 \qquad \Re(s) > 0\\ \textit{where} \qquad K(z,t) &= \frac{\lambda^-}{1-B(t)} \left[z(1-B(t)) + b * e^{a(z)}(t) - z e^{a(z)\,t}\right]\\ \textit{and} \qquad z(s) &= \frac{s+\lambda-\sqrt{(s+\lambda)^2 - 4\lambda^+\lambda^-}}{2\lambda^+}\end{aligned}$$

$z(s)$ lies on a curve located inside $\Re_{\rho_{-1}}$, the region inside a curve ρ_{-1}, itself inside the unit disk. The notation $*$ is the usual one used for the convolution.

This equation is numerically intractable by all of the standard methods known to the authors; see [6]. Instead, we proceed to derive an iterative method for a numerical solution as follows.

3. An iterative algorithm

Equation (2.9) is the Laplace transform of $\frac{p_1(t)}{1-B(t)}$ and can be expressed as follows:

$$\int_0^\infty \frac{p_1(t)}{1-B(t)}\, e^{-st}\, dt = \frac{\Psi(z_1(s))}{\lambda^-}$$

$$= \frac{1}{\lambda^-}\Psi\left(\frac{s+\lambda-\sqrt{(s+\lambda)^2-4\lambda^+\lambda^-}}{2\lambda^+}\right)$$

This expression can be inverted numerically, when Ψ is known. Let us call the result of the inversion

$$\phi(t) =_{num} \frac{p_1(t)}{1-B(t)}$$

$V(z_1(s),t)$ can be computed by numerical integration using equations (2.8) and (2.6): $\forall s$ s.t. $\Re(s) > 0$

$$V(z_1(s),t) =_{num} \lambda^- e^{s\,t} \int_t^\infty \phi(u)\, e^{-s\,u}\, du$$

Finally we compute the r.h.s. of the 'initial' condition (2.5) with two more numerical integrations—of $b(t)V(z_1,t)$ and $p_1(t)$ (giving p_1) to derive the next iteration for Ψ. p_0 comes from either equation (2.1) (by another numerical integration) or equation (2.7) (observing that $R(1) = 1 - p_0$). If successive iterations match (according to some convergence criterion) at $z_1(s)$, $\forall s$, we can consider the solution to have been found. If not, we iterate with the newest value (or a new guess based upon it). Thus,

$$z_1\, \Psi_{k+1}(z_1) =_{num} \int_0^\infty b(t)\, V_k(z_1,t)\, dt \; +$$

$$\lambda^+ z_1(z_1-1)\, p_0 + \lambda^- z_1 \int_0^\infty p_{1k}(t)\, dt$$

where $\Psi_k(z)$ is the value of $\Psi(z)$ at the kth iteration, and V_k, p_{1k} similarly. For the first step of the iterative process, we choose the function $\Psi_0(z_1(s))$ derived (as an exact formula in [6]) for the FCFS-RCE M/M/1 case. This is equivalent to approximating the ratio $p_1(t)/p_0$ for the M/G/1 case by that for the M/M/1 case. Having converged on $p_1(t)$, we can then compute p_0, p_1, $Q(z)$ and the related quantities of interest.

4. Conclusion

Because of properties of the exponential distribution, it is a trivial problem to solve for the queue length probability distribution in an M/M/1 queue with negative customers—it is only necessary to modify the service time distribution which remains exponential. However, generalising the service time distribution causes surprising difficulties, particularly when customers are killed from the end of the queue (which is again immaterial in the M/M/1 case).

We have solved for the queue length probability distribution in the M/G/1 G-queue for the combination of FCFS queueing discipline with RCE killing strategy. We have proposed a numerical algorithm to compute $p_1(t)$ which has been at the centre of the analysis as it is required to obtain $Q(z)$. Our algorithm is essentially dependent on a reasonably accurate initial choice as it turns out to be intractable for more than a few iterations. This is partly because we chose to implement it with built-in functions of Mathematica [9]. A customised implementation could easily provide an order of magnitude improvement in performance. However, in [6] we show graphs obtained by the iteration for the functions $p_1(t)$ and $\Psi(z)$ for two simple non-exponential service time distributions: gamma and deterministic.

Further work could also lead to a proof that the algorithm is convergent under appropriate initial conditions. Indeed we have experienced that a bad starting point rapidly leads to divergence. Therefore our usage of the algorithm was more to validate a good guess in the initial iteration than to converge slowly to the right solution. Nevertheless, a considerable amount of work has been done on improving numerical inversion of Laplace transforms in recent years—in terms of range of applicability as well as accuracy and efficiency. Hence, appealing to this body of work holds the promise of providing a more reliable approach than seeking solutions to the "ill-posed" Fredholm integral equation of the first kind.

References

1. H. Dubner and J. Abate, "Numerical inversion of Laplace transforms by relating them to the finite Fourier Cosine transform", *JACM*, **15** 10, pp. 115–123, 1968.
2. E. Gelenbe, P. Glynn and K. Sigman, "Queues with negative arrivals", *J. Appl. Prob.*, **28**, pp. 245–250, 1991.
3. E. Gelenbe, "Product form networks with negative and positive customers", *J. Appl. Prob.*, **28**, pp. 656–663, 1991.
4. E. Gelenbe and R. Schassberger., "Stability of product form G-networks", *Probability in the Engineering and Informational Sciences*, **6**, pp. 271–276, 1992.
5. P.G. Harrison and E. Pitel, "Sojourn times in single server queues with negative customers", *Journal of Applied Probability*, **30**, pp. 943–963, 1993.
6. P.G. Harrison and E. Pitel, "The M/G/1 queue with negative customers", Accepted for publication in *Advances in Applied Probability*, **33**, June 1996.

7. W. Henderson, "Queueing networks with negative customers and negative queue length", *Journal of Applied Probability*, **30** 3, 1993.
8. E. Pitel, "Queues with negative customers", PhD Thesis, Dept. of Computing, Imperial College, London, 1994.
9. S. Wolfram, "Mathematica", Addison-Wesley, 1988.

Operational Analysis of Timed Petri Nets and Application to the Computation of Performance Bounds *

G. Chiola[1], C. Anglano[1], J. Campos[2], J. M. Colom[2], and M. Silva[2]

[1] Dipartimento di Informatica, Università di Torino, Italy
[2] Dpto. de Informática e Ing. de Sistemas, Universidad de Zaragoza, Spain

Summary. We use operational analysis techniques to partially characterize the behaviour of timed Petri nets under very weak assumptions on their timing semantics. New operational inequalities are derived that are typical of the presence of synchronization and that were therefore not considered in queueing network models. We show an interesting application of the operational laws to the statement and the efficient solution of problems related to the estimation of performance bounds insensitive to the timing probability distributions. The results obtained generalize and improve in a clear setting results that were derived in the last few years for several different subclasses of timed Petri nets. In particular the extension to Well-Formed Coloured nets appears straightforward and allows an efficient exploitation of models symmetries.

1. Introduction

Operational analysis is a conceptually very simple way of deriving mathematical equations relating observable quantities in queueing systems [12]. In [11] the reader can find some nice examples of how the application of operational analysis techniques can help in explaining and proving fundamental results in queueing network analysis. Here we apply operational analysis techniques to derive linear equations and inequalities relating interesting performance measures in timed Petri net models. The main conceptual difference between queueing and Petri net models is the presence of a synchronization primitive in the latter. Early works on extensions of operational analysis to Petri nets include [13], where however synchronization was neglected. New operational inequalities are derived here for synchronization elements that have no counterpart in operational laws for queueing networks.

Some classical results of queueing networks were already proven to hold in stochastic Petri net models. In this paper we derive, under much weaker conditions, a generalization of the classical *utilization law* for the case of multiply enabled transitions and several inequalities that relate throughput, average marking, and average transition firing time in case of synchronization transitions. All these results are derived for each possible observable sample

* This work was partially supported by the European ESPRIT BRA Project 7269 QMIPS, the Spanish PRONTIC's 354/91 and 242/94, and the Aragonese CONAI-DGA P-IT 6/91.

path. Therefore, in order to compare to classical queueing laws stated in a stochastic framework, the additional hypothesis of unique limit behaviour for each sample path must be assumed.

In addition to the mathematical interest of these derivations, we propose also an application of these results to the computation of performance bounds based on linear programming techniques. Such performance bounds are fairly inexpensive to compute compared to the cost of discrete event simulation or exact Markovian analysis, and moreover provide results that are insensitive of the probability distribution of the transition firing times. The linear programming problems (LPP's) presented in this paper represent also a generalization of some recent results published in [4, 5, 3] since they can be applied to arbitrary Petri net structures and reduce to the previous ones when the Petri net structure satisfies some particular constraints.

The paper is organized as follows. Section 2 presents the operational analysis of timed Petri nets and the derivation of the main equations. Section 3 shows the application of the operational laws, also considering the case of Well-Formed Coloured nets, to the statement of LPP's for the computation of performance bounds depending only on the average transition firing times, the structure, and the initial marking of the net. Section 4 provides an example of computation of such bounds in the case of a Coloured Well-Formed timed Petri net model. Finally, Section 5 contains some concluding remarks and ideas for future research on the topics.

The proofs of all the results presented here can be found in [2].

2. Observable quantities and operational laws

In this section we start by defining measurable quantities that characterize the state and the behaviour in time of a Petri net model. Then we derive and prove in a very simple and direct way some fundamental relations that hold true "operationally" among them, i.e. that are verified in any sample path that one can measure in an experiment.

We assume the reader to be familiar with the Petri net formalism and notation. We refer to [11] or [16] for an introduction to Petri nets and most of their behavioural properties and analysis techniques. We also refer to [1] for a detailed discussion of different timing semantics and related operation mechanisms. We just resume here the notation conventions that are used in the following of this paper.

$\mathcal{N} = (P, T, W, M_0)$ is a net system, where P is the set of places, T is the set of transitions, $W : P \times T \cup T \times P \rightarrow \mathbb{N}$ is the incidence function, and M_0 is the initial marking (in general, a marking is $M : P \rightarrow \mathbb{N}$, and $\forall p_i \in P$, $M[p_i]$ is the number of tokens in p_i). The input (output) set of $x \in P \cup T$ is ${}^\bullet x = \{y \in P \cup T \mid W(y, x) \geq 1\}$ ($x^\bullet = \{y \in P \cup T \mid W(x, y) \geq 1\}$).

2.1 Basic operational quantities

Assume that a generic timed Petri net is available for measurement, and that the following quantities can be collected during an experiment, starting at time $\tau = 0$ and ending at time $\tau = \theta > 0$, at which all transitions have been fired at least once. The total number of transitions firings during the experiment is assumed finite.

Instantaneous marking: $\forall p_k \in P, \forall \tau : 0 \leq \tau \leq \theta$, $M[p_k](\tau)$ represents the number of tokens in place p_k at time τ.

Average marking during the experiment interval:

$$\forall p_k \in P, \quad \bar{M}[p_k](\theta) = \frac{1}{\theta} \int_0^\theta M[p_k](\tau) d\tau$$

Instantaneous enabling degree: $\forall t_i \in T, \forall \tau : 0 \leq \tau \leq \theta$, $e_i(\tau)$ represents the internal concurrency of transition t_i at time τ, i.e.

$$e_i(\tau) = \max\{k \in \mathbb{N} : \forall p \in {}^\bullet t_i, \; M[p](\tau) \geq k \; W(p, t_i)\}$$

The following relation holds by definitions:

$$\forall t_i \in T, \quad \forall \tau, \quad e_i(\tau) = \min_{p \in {}^\bullet t_i} \left\lfloor \frac{M[p](\tau)}{W(p, t_i)} \right\rfloor \tag{2.1}$$

(where $\forall a \in \mathbb{R}$, $\lfloor a \rfloor$ denotes the largest integer not greater than a).

Average enabling degree: $\forall t_i \in T$, $\bar{e}_i(\theta) = \frac{1}{\theta} \int_0^\theta e_i(\tau) d\tau$ represents the average number of servers active in transition t_i during the experiment interval.

Since we use an "infinite-server" semantics for transition enabling, we need to consider the activities of the different servers in a given transition t_i independently. Without loss of generality we assume an ordering of the servers associated with transitions such that busy servers always come before idle servers, i.e., at any point in time τ the first $e_i(\tau)$ servers are active inside transition t_i, while the remaining ones are idle.

Under this assumption we can define the:

Number of firings completed by the j-th server in t_i from time 0 up to time θ, denoted $F_{i,j}(\theta)$.

Total number of firings of t_i during the experiment interval: $F_i(\theta) = \sum_{j=1}^{\infty} F_{i,j}(\theta)$ (by assumptions, $0 < F_i(\theta) < \infty$).

Throughput of t_i: $x_i(\theta) = \frac{F_i(\theta)}{\theta}$ that represents the average number of firings completed per time unit.

2.2 Conflict-free nets

In case of nets without conflicts one can easily define the average service time of transitions as a function of the busy times of all servers. In particular we define:

Instantaneous enabling of j-th server in t_i: $e_{i,j}(\tau) = $ if $e_i(\tau) \geq j$ then 1 else 0, characteristic function that evaluates to 1 if and only if the j-th server in transition t_i is busy at time τ.

Busy time for the j-th server of t_i: $\theta_{i,j}(\theta) = \int_0^\theta e_{i,j}(\tau)d\tau$

Service time for the j-th server of t_i: $S_{i,j}(\theta) = \frac{\theta_{i,j}(\theta)}{F_{i,j}(\theta)}$

Average service time for t_i: $\bar{S}_i(\theta) = \frac{\sum_{j=1}^{\infty} \theta_{i,j}(\theta)}{\sum_{j=1}^{\infty} F_{i,j}(\theta)}$

The following equation holds for any measurement experiment:

Enabling operational law:

$$\forall t_i \in T, \quad \bar{e}_i(\theta) = x_i(\theta)\bar{S}_i(\theta) \tag{2.2}$$

The above enabling law is the well-known "utilization law" derived in the framework of multiple server queues. From the enabling law it follows that if the average firing time of a transition is known, then its throughput is proportional to its average enabling degree. Of course in case of immediate transitions $\bar{S}_i(\theta) = 0$, so immediate transitions are never enabled for non-null intervals of time.

We are now in a position to state our *synchronization inequalities* that relate the throughput and the average marking of the input places for any transition.

Upper bound inequality: $\forall t_i \in T$,

$$x_i(\theta)\ \bar{S}_i(\theta)\ \leq \min_{p_k \in \bullet t_i} \left(\frac{\bar{M}[p_k](\theta)}{W(p_k, t_i)} \right) \tag{2.3}$$

The inequality becomes an equality whenever $\sum_{p \in \bullet t_i} W(p, t_i) = 1$.

This inequality establishes an upper bound for the average enabling (hence for the transition throughput once the service time is defined) in the case of transitions with more than one input place that model a synchronization. In the following we derive other inequalities that establish lower bounds as well. We shall see that in the particular case of transitions with a single input place the two inequalities reduce to a single equality.

Lower bound inequality for single input arc ($W(p, t_i) \geq 1$). $\forall t_i \in T$: $\bullet t_i = \{p\}$,

$$x_i(\theta)\ \bar{S}_i(\theta) \geq \frac{\bar{M}[p](\theta) - W(p, t_i) + 1}{W(p, t_i)} \tag{2.4}$$

Notice that in case $W(p,t_i)=1$ this reduces to $x_i(\theta)\ \bar{S}_i(\theta) \geq \bar{M}[p](\theta)$, that combined with the upper bound inequality (2.3) reduces to the equation $x_i(\theta)\ \bar{S}_i(\theta) = \bar{M}[p](\theta)$.

Observe that in the case that the right-hand expression in (2.4) is negative, a trivial inequality can be used: $x_i(\theta)\bar{S}_i(\theta) \geq 0$.

Improvement for bounded nets: $\forall t_i \in T\ :\ {}^\bullet t_i = \{p\}$, if $\forall \tau$, $M[p](\tau) \leq B_p$ and $w_{ip} = W(p,t_i)$ and $\exists k \in \mathbb{N}\ :\ w_{ip}k \leq B_p < (k+1)w_{ip}$

$$x_i(\theta)\ \bar{S}_i(\theta)\ \geq\ k\ \frac{\bar{M}[p](\theta) - w_{ip}k + 1}{B_p - w_{ip}k + 1} \tag{2.5}$$

Lower bound inequality for binary synchronization with ordinary arcs. $\forall t_i \in T\ :{}^\bullet t_i = \{p_1, p_2\}$ and $W(p_1,t_i) = W(p_2,t_i) = 1$, if $M[p_1](\tau) \leq B_1$ and $M[p_2](\tau) \leq B_2$ and $B_1 \leq B_2$ then

$$x_i(\theta)\ \bar{S}_i(\theta)\ \geq\ \bar{M}[p_1](\theta) + \frac{B_1}{B_2}\bar{M}[p_2](\theta) - B_1 \tag{2.6}$$

A general lower bound for bounded nets:
$\forall t_i \in T\ :\ {}^\bullet t_i = \{p_1, p_2, \ldots, p_n\}$, $\forall j \leq n$, $M[p_j](\tau) \leq B_j$ and $B_1 \leq B_j$

$$x_i(\theta)\ \bar{S}_i(\theta)\ \geq\ \frac{\bar{M}[p_1](\theta) - W(p_1,t_i) + 1 - B_1\ \max(f_j)}{W(p_1,t_i)} \tag{2.7}$$

where $\forall j\ :\ 2 \leq j \leq n$, $f_j = 1 - \frac{\bar{M}[p_j](\theta) - W(p_j,t_i)+1}{B_j - W(p_j,t_i)+1}$

2.3 General nets with conflicts

In the general case in which transitions may be enabled in conflict the definitions of service time and average enabling degree must be modified in order to take the possibility of preemption into account. In the literature two types of timed Petri net semantics have been proposed: *race* and *preselection* conflict resolution policies [1]. According to the race policy all enabled transitions start working, and the first one that completes its firing time seizes the tokens from the input places, thus possibly preempting other transitions. Instead, the preselection policy requires that conflicts be solved at the enabling time instant, so that only selected transitions put their servers to work and fire for sure after the elapsing of their firing time. In any case the same kind of results can be derived.

Conditional instantaneous enabling of j-th server in t_i:
$e'_{i,j}(\tau)$ = if "$e_i(\tau) \geq j$ and the enabling is not preempted" then 1 else 0, characteristic function that evaluates to 1 if and only if the j-th server in transition t_i is busy at time τ and its work will not be wasted due to the preemption from a conflicting transition. Of course $e'_{i,j}(\tau) \leq e_{i,j}(\tau)$ by definition.

Useful busy time for the j-th server of t_i: $\theta'_{i,j}(\theta) = \int_0^\theta e'_{i,j}(\tau)d\tau$

Useful service time for the j-th server of t_i: $S'_{i,j}(\theta) = \frac{\theta'_{i,j}(\theta)}{F_{i,j}(\theta)}$

Useful average service time for transition t_i: $\bar{S'}_i(\theta) = \frac{\sum_{j=1}^{\infty} \theta'_{i,j}(\theta)}{\sum_{j=1}^{\infty} F_{i,j}(\theta)}$

The enabling operational law is extended as:

$$\forall t_i \in T, \quad \bar{e'}_i(\theta) = x_i(\theta)\ \bar{S'}_i(\theta) \tag{2.8}$$

and the proof is similar to the one shown above. From the comparison with Equation 2.2 it also follows that $\bar{S'}_i(\theta) \leq \bar{S}_i(\theta)$ independently of the probability distribution of the firing time processes.

Equation (2.1) however becomes an inequality in case of nets with conflicting transitions:

$$\forall t_i \in T, \ \ \forall \tau, \quad e'_i(\tau) \leq \min_{p_k \in {}^\bullet t_i} \left(\frac{M[p_k](\tau)}{W(p_k, t_i)} \right) \tag{2.9}$$

The upper bound inequality (2.3) still holds in this more general setting by just substituting $S'_{i,j}(\theta)$ for $S_{i,j}(\theta)$.

2.3.1 Race versus preselection policy. The quantities $\bar{e'}_i(\theta)$ and $\bar{S'}_i(\theta)$ are in general measurable from an off-line processing of an experiment record without any further assumption.

Using the preselection policy, the useful service time of a transition is exactly the transition firing time. This allows one to derive an improved version of the upper bound inequality: $\forall p_k \in P$,

$$\sum_{t_i \in p_k^\bullet} \left(W(p_k, t_i)\ x_i(\theta)\ \bar{S}_i(\theta) \right) \ \leq\ \bar{M}[p_k](\theta) \tag{2.10}$$

In the case of race policy, instead, the useful average service time $\bar{S'}_i(\theta)$ might be strictly less than the nominal transition firing times due to the effect of preemption from conflicting transitions. Inequality (2.10) holds true in a race policy model only if all transitions that are output for place p_k are *behaviourally persistent* (i.e. their enabling is mutually exclusive). In other words, only the following modified version of inequality (2.3) holds true for behaviourally conflicting timed transitions with race policy:

$$\forall t_i \in T, \quad x_i(\theta)\ \bar{S'}_i(\theta) \ \leq\ \min_{p_k \in {}^\bullet t_i} \left(\frac{\bar{M}[p_k](\theta)}{W(p_k, t_i)} \right) \tag{2.11}$$

For what concerns the synchronization lower bounds, inequalities (2.4–2.7) in general apply only to persistent or immediate transitions (in the latter case $\bar{S}_i = \bar{S'}_i = 0$). The case of conflicting transitions with preselection policy may be treated by net transformation as follows, while for the case of conflicting timed transitions with race policy no synchronization lower bound inequality applies.

Consider transition t_i timed, potentially in conflict with other timed transitions and with preselection conflict resolution policy. Split t_i in two transitions t'_i and t''_i and add a new place p'_i such that $\forall p \in P\ W(p, t'_i) = W(p, t_i)$ and $\forall p \in P\ W(t''_i, p,) = W(t_i, p)$ and $W(t'_i, p'_i) = W(p'_i, t''_i) = 1$ and t'_i is immediate and $\bar{S}_{t''_i} = \bar{S}_i$. In the transformed net t''_i is persistent with single input arc (by construction), so that Inequality (2.4) applies. Transition t'_i is instead immediate, so that a subset of inequalities (2.4–2.7) applies even in presence of conflict.

3. Performance bounds based on operational laws

The inequalities that we derived in the previous section can be used to compute upper and lower bounds for the throughput of transitions or for the average marking of places for general timed Petri nets using linear programming techniques. The idea is to compute vectors $\bar{M}$ and $\vec{x}$ that maximize or minimize the throughput of a transition or the average marking of a place among those verifying the previous operational laws and other linear constraints that can be easily derived from the net structure.

A first set of linear equality constraints can be derived from the fact that the vector $\bar{M}$ is an average weight of reachable markings: $\bar{M} = \sum_{M_r \in RS(\vec{M}_0)} \beta_r M_r$. Since for each reachable marking $M_r = M_0 + C \cdot \vec{\sigma}_r$, we obtain that also the average marking must satisfy the same linear equation: $\bar{M} = M_0 + C \cdot \vec{\sigma}$, where $\vec{\sigma} = \sum_{M_r \in RS(\vec{M}_0)} \beta_r \vec{\sigma}_r$.

The following set of linear inequalities imposes that for each place the token flow out is less than or equal to the token flow in: $\forall p_k \in P$,

$$\sum_{t_i \in {}^\bullet p_k} x_i W(t_i, p_k) \geq \sum_{t_o \in p_k^\bullet} x_o W(p_k, t_o) \tag{3.1}$$

If place p_k is known to be bounded, then the above inequality becomes an equality which represents the classical *flow balance* equation: $C[p_k] \cdot \vec{x} = 0$.

On the other hand, for each pair of transitions t_i, t_j in (behavioural) free conflict (i.e., such that they are always simultaneously enabled or disabled) the following equation is verified: $\frac{x_i}{\alpha_i} = \frac{x_j}{\alpha_j}$, where α_i, α_j are the routing rates that define the resolution of the conflict between t_i and t_j.

Additionally, most of the operational inequality laws that were derived in the previous section linearly relate the average marking of places with the throughput of their output transitions. Hence they can be considered as constraints for an LPP.

3.1 Extension to TWN's

For timed Well-Formed Coloured nets (TWN's) [5] it is possible to derive, directly from the inequalities developed in the previous sections, operational relations allowing an efficient computation of performance bounds. Given a TWN, the basic idea is to consider the corresponding unfolded net and to apply the relations developed in the previous sections. The relations for the TWN are then obtained combining the partial results for the unfolded one.

A fundamental property that TWN's must have in order to be able to combine the results for the unfolded one is the *symmetry*, meaning that in the unfolded nets obtained from the Well-Formed ones all colour instances of a given place and of a given transition must be equivalent. To be more precise, if a transition t has average service time $\bar{S}_t$, then all of its instances have the same average service time. Moreover if a place p is bounded, then we assume that the maximum number of tokens that each of its instances can contain is the same.

In the rest of this section we show, as an example, the derivation of lower bound inequality for single input arc for TWN's. More details on the derivations can be found in [8].

3.1.1 Notation. In this section we give some notations used in the derivations of relations for TWN's ([5]).
Generic function: $f = \sum_{j=1}^{k} F_j$, where F_j is the jth tuple and its arity l is given by the number of colour classes composing the colour domain of the place. This definition of function is slightly different from the classical one, since here we allow linear combinations only outside the tuples (i.e. each tuple is composed only by elementary functions). For example the function $F =< S - x, y >$ is written as $F' =< S, y > - < x, y >$.
Cardinality of function: $|f| = \sum_{j=1}^{k} |F_j|$, where $|F_j| = \alpha_j \times \prod_{i=1}^{l} |(F_j)_i|$ is the cardinality of the jth tuple. The coefficient α_j denotes the product of the coefficients of the elementary functions composing the tuple and $(F_j)_i$ is the ith function of the jth tuple. For example if $F_j =< 3x, 2y >$, then $\alpha_j = 6$.
Family of arcs. Each tuple F_j of a function f identifies a set of arcs (with weight α_j), whose cardinality is $A(F_j) = \prod_{i=1}^{l} |(F_j)_h|$. The global number of arcs corresponding to function f is $A(f) = \sum_{j=1}^{k} A(F_j)$, where each $A(F_j)$ has the sign of the corresponding tuple F_j. When $A(f) = 1$, then we denote as α_f the weights associated to the unique family of arcs corresponding to f.
Input and Output relations. If t is an input transition of place p (with function f), then $IN(p,t) = \frac{|C(t)|}{|C(p)|} A(f)$ is the number of input instances of t for each instance of p. Similarly if t is an output transition of place p, then $OUT(p,t) = \frac{|C(t)|}{|C(p)|} A(f)$ is the number of output instances of t for each instance of p.

3.1.2 Lower bound inequality for single input arc. To apply this inequality to an unfolded net, the conditions for its applicability must be met

for all transition instances. This means that each instance t_i of a coloured transition t must have only one input place. This condition is met if the function f labelling the arc contains only *projection* and *successor* elementary functions (that is $A(f) = 1$).
Inequality for single input arc: $\forall t \in T : \ ^{\bullet}t = \{p\}, W^{-}(p,t) = f, \ \ A(f) = 1$

$$\alpha_f x_t \bar{S}_t \geq OUT(p,t)\bar{M}[p] - |C(t)| (\alpha_f - 1)$$

In a similar way it is possible to derive, for TWN's, the equivalent of relations devised for timed Petri nets.

3.2 LPP formulation

Performance bounds for TWN's can be computed solving the LPP of table 3.1 (whose constraints are the relations derived in previous sections) where f is a linear function of $\bar{M}$ and $\vec{x}$. The linear programming problem for bounds computation for non coloured timed Petri nets can be obtained from that of table 3.1 setting $OUT(p,t) = |C(p)| = |C(t)| = 1$, $\forall p \in P, t \in T$ and observing that condition $A(f) = 1$ always holds true. The average marking equation is written here in explicit form, but it could be written also in matricial form. Moreover relation (c_7) has been derived for TWN's under the hypothesis of strong symmetries. In particular we assumed that, for each input place of transition t in inequality (c_7), the weights of the arcs belonging to the families corresponding to the function labelling the arc are the same. Obviously the uncoloured version of (c_7) has no such restriction.

As we remarked in the case of timed Petri nets, also for TWN's constraint (c_2) becomes an equality for bounded places (c_2'). The equality sign also holds true in (c_4) if $\alpha_f = 1$ (i.e. the unique family of arcs corresponding to function f have weight 1) since in this case it may be combined with the opposite inequality (c_5). For the case of places with several output conflicting transitions, inequality (2.10) derived in previous section (or its coloured counterpart) can be added if preselection policy is assumed for the resolution of the conflict. The constraint labelled with (c_5) can be improved if the input place to t_i is bounded, by introducing the additional constraint (c_5').

The LPP of table 3.1 provides a general method to compute upper and lower bounds for arbitrary linear functions of average marking of places and throughput of transitions. For instance, if $f(\bar{M}, \boldsymbol{x}) = x_i$, then the problem can be used to compute an upper or a lower bound (depending on the selection of "max" or "min" optimization for the objective function) for the throughput of transition t_i. In an analogous way, upper or lower bounds for the average marking of a given place p_j can be derived by solving the LPP of table 3.1 for the objective function $f(\bar{M}, \boldsymbol{x}) = \bar{M}[p_j]$. The bounds are insensitive to the timing probability distributions since they are based only on the knowledge of the average service times.

Table 3.1. Linear programming problem.

	maximize [or minimize] $f(\bar{M}, \vec{x})$ subject to
(c_1)	$\bar{M}[p] = M_0[p] + \sum_{t_i \in {}^\bullet p} \mid f_i \mid \sigma_{t_i} - \sum_{k_j \in p^\bullet} \mid g_j \mid \sigma_{k_j}$; $\forall p \in P : W^+(p, t_i) = f_i,\ W^-(p, k_i) = g_j$;
(c_2)	$\sum_{t_i \in {}^\bullet p} \mid f_i \mid x_{t_i} \geq \sum_{k_j \in p^\bullet} \mid g_j \mid x_{k_j}$; $\forall p_k \in P : W^+(p, t_i) = f_i,\ W^-(p, k_i) = g_j$;
(c_2')	$\sum_{t_i \in {}^\bullet p} \mid f_i \mid x_{t_i} = \sum_{k_j \in p^\bullet} \mid g_j \mid x_{k_j}$; $\forall p_k \in P$ bounded ;
(c_3)	$\frac{x_i}{\alpha_i} = \frac{x_j}{\alpha_j}$; $\forall t_i, t_j \in T :$ behaviourally free choice;
(c_4)	$\mid f \mid \cdot x_t \bar{S}_t \leq OUT(p,t)\bar{M}[p]$; $\forall t \in T, \forall p \in {}^\bullet t : W^-(p,t) = f$;
(c_5)	$\alpha_f x_t \bar{S}_t \geq OUT(p,t)\bar{M}[p] - \mid C(t) \mid (\alpha_f - 1)$; $\forall t \in T$ persistent or immediate : ${}^\bullet t = \{p\}, W^-(p,t) = f,\ A(f) = 1$;
(c_5')	$x_t \bar{S}_t \geq k \frac{OUT(p,t)\bar{M}[p] + \mid C(t) \mid (1 - k\alpha_f)}{OUT(p,t) + \mid C(t) \mid (1 - k\alpha_f)}$; $\forall t \in T$ persistent or immediate : ${}^\bullet t = \{p\}$, $W^-(p,t) = f,\ A(f) = 1 \wedge k \in \mathbb{N} : k\alpha_f \leq B_p \leq (k+1)\alpha_f$;
(c_6)	$x_t \bar{S}_t \geq OUT(p,t)(\bar{M}[p] + \frac{B_p}{B_q}\bar{M}[q] - B_p)$; $\forall t \in T$ persistent or immediate: ${}^\bullet t = \{p, q\}$, $W(p,t) = f, W(q,t) = g, A(f) = A(g) = 1, \mid f \mid = \mid g \mid = 1$;
(c_6')	$\alpha_f x_t \bar{S}_t \geq OUT(p,t)\bar{M}[p] + \mid C(t) \mid (1 - \alpha_f) +$ $-OUT(p,t)B_p \cdot \left(\mid C(t) \mid - \frac{OUT(q,t)\bar{M}[q] + \mid C(t) \mid (1-\alpha_g)}{OUT(q,t)B_q + \mid C(t) \mid (1-\alpha_g)} \right)$; $\forall t \in T$ persistent or immediate : ${}^\bullet t = \{p, q\}$, $B_p \leq B_q,\ W(p,t) = f, W(q,t) = g, A(f) = A(g) = 1$;
(c_7)	$\alpha_1 x_t \bar{S}_t \geq OUT(p1,t)\bar{M}[p1] - \mid C(t) \mid (1 - \alpha_1) - OUT(p1,t)B_{p1} \max_{1 \leq j \leq n} fj$; with $fj = 1 - \frac{OUT(pj,t)\bar{M}[pj] + \mid C(pj) \mid (-\alpha_j + 1)}{B_{pj}/M_0[pj, \langle i \rangle] - \alpha_j + 1}$; $\forall t \in T$ persistent or immediate: ${}^\bullet t = \{p1, \ldots, pn\}$, $B_{p1} \leq B_{pj}, j \in \{2, \ldots, n\}, W(pi,t) = f_i,\ A(f_1) = 1$;
(c_8)	$\bar{M}, \vec{x}, \vec{\sigma} \geq 0$;

Notice also that most equalities and inequalities contain coefficients that depend only on the net structure and on the (known) average transition firing times (and probabilities in case of free choice immediate conflicts). The only coefficients that may be unknown at the time of the formulation of the model are the actual bounds for places B_i. If the modeller has no a-priori more precise knowledge of these bounds, notice that an upper bound for them that can be used in the LPP of table 3.1 may be computed from a simplified LPP that contains only constraint c_1 (structural marking bound).

An improvement of the proposed bounds can be obtained if additional constraints that improve the linear characterization of the average marking in terms of the equation $\bar{M} = M_0 + C \cdot \sigma$ are considered. For instance, if a *trap* P_T (i.e., $P_T \subseteq P, P_T^\bullet \subseteq {}^\bullet P_T$) is not a P-semiflow, the net is live, and we are interested only in the steady state performance, then we can add the constraint: $\sum_{p_k \in P_T} \bar{M}[p_k] \geq 1$.

Similarly, if a *siphon* P_S ($P_S \subseteq P$, $^\bullet P_S \subseteq P_S^\bullet$) is not a P-semiflow and the net is live, then we can add the constraint: $\sum_{p_k \in P_S} \bar{M}[p_k] \geq 1$.

The systematic method for the improvement of linear characterization of reachable markings based on the addition of *implicit places*, presented in [13], can be also applied as in [6].

We remark that linear programming problems can be solved in *polynomial time* [15], therefore the above presented method for the computation of (upper and lower) bounds for the throughput and for the average marking of general timed nets has a polynomial complexity on the number of nodes of the net. Moreover, the *simplex* method for the resolution of LPP's proceeds in linear time in most cases even if it has a theoretically exponential complexity.

Similar results, based on linear programming techniques, were presented in previous works [4, 5, 3] for the computation of throughput upper bounds for particular net subclasses, such as marked graphs or free choice nets. The new approach derived in this section generalizes those recent results in two ways: first, it can be applied to arbitrary Petri net structures; second, it allows one to compute upper and lower bounds for throughput and average marking in a simple and unified way. The proposed method produces the same results as previous ones [4, 5, 3] when the same net subclasses are considered.

4. An example of application

Let us present an example of application for the computation of bounds in the case of the TWN of figure 4.1. The architecture comprises a set of processing modules interconnected by a common bus called the "external bus". A processor can access its own memory module directly from its private bus through one port, or it can access non-local shared-memory modules by means of the external bus. In case of contention for the access to one shared-memory module, preemptive priority is given to external access through the external bus with respect to the accesses from the local processor. The experiments on the shared-memory model have been carried out assuming to have 4 processors and that the average service time of all the transitions are equal to 0.5. According to the arguments presented in the previous sections, bounds can be computed solving LPP's with constraints included in table 4.1, where the first letters of each transition name have been used for reasons of space. The solution for the LPP leads to upper and lower bounds, for the throughput of transitions, given by $\frac{8}{11} \leq x_{e\_e\_a} \leq 2$, while the "exact" solution with exponential distribution is $x_{e\_e\_a} = 1.71999$. An improvement in the lower bound can be obtained observing that when a token arrives in place Choice transition choose_m is enabled at least for one transition instance. This implies that the average marking of place Choice is equal to 0 (transition choose_m is immediate), so $\bar{M}[Choice] = 0$ and $B_{Choice} = 0$ (only tangible markings are

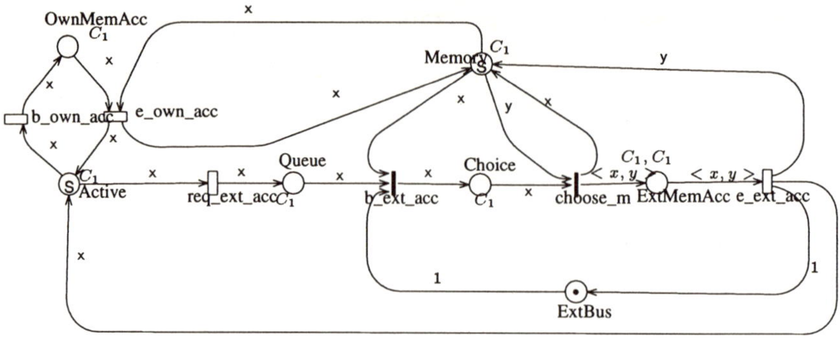

Fig. 4.1. TWN model of a shared-memory multiprocessor.

Table 4.1. Constraints for the model in figure 4.1.

(c_1)

$$\bar{M}[Active] = 4 + \sigma_{e\_e\_a} + \sigma_{e\_o\_a} - \sigma_{r\_e\_a} - \sigma_{b\_o\_a};$$
$$\bar{M}[Memory] = 4 + \sigma_{e\_e\_a} - \sigma_{b\_e\_a};$$
$$\bar{M}[OwnMemAcc] = \sigma_{b\_o\_a} - \sigma_{e\_o\_a};$$
$$\bar{M}[Queue] = \sigma_{r\_e\_a} - \sigma_{b\_e\_a};$$
$$\bar{M}[Choice] = \sigma_{b\_e\_a} - \sigma_{c\_m};$$
$$\bar{M}[ExtMemAcc] = \sigma_{c\_m} - \sigma_{e\_e\_a};$$
$$\bar{M}[ExtBus] = 1 + \sigma_{e\_e\_a} - \sigma_{b\_e\_a};$$

(c_2')

$$x_{e\_e\_a} + x_{e\_o\_a} = x_{r\_e\_a} + x_{b\_o\_a};$$
$$x_{b\_e\_a} = x_{c\_m} = x_{e\_e\_a} = x_{r\_e\_a};$$

(c_3)

$$x_{b\_o\_a} = x_{r\_e\_a};$$

$(c_4 \& c_5)$

$$x_{b\_o\_a}\bar{S}_{b\_o\_a} = \frac{\bar{M}[Active]}{2};$$
$$x_{r\_e\_a}\bar{S}_{r\_e\_a} = \frac{\bar{M}[Active]}{2};$$
$$x_{e\_e\_a}\bar{S}_{e\_e\_a} = \bar{M}[ExtMemAcc];$$

(c_4)

$$x_{e\_o\_a}\bar{S}_{e\_o\_a} \leq \bar{M}[OwnMemAcc];$$
$$x_{e\_o\_a}\bar{S}_{e\_o\_a} \leq \bar{M}[Memory];$$

(c_6)

$$x_{e\_o\_a}\bar{S}_{e\_o\_a} \geq \bar{M}[OwnMemAcc] + \frac{B_{OwnMemAcc}}{B_{Memory}}\bar{M}[Memory] - B_{Memory};$$

(c_7)

$$4(\bar{M}[ExtBus] - B_{ExtBus}(1 - \frac{\bar{M}[Memory]}{B_{Memory}})) \leq 0;$$
$$4(\bar{M}[ExtBus] - B_{ExtBus}(1 - \frac{\bar{M}[Queue]}{B_{Queue}})) \leq 0$$

considered) can be added to the set of constraints. Moreover place Memory is implicit w.r.t. the enabling of transition b_ext_acc, so we can consider this transition as having only two input places, so constraint (c_6) can be applied instead of constraint (c_7). Finally $B_{Queue} = 3$ can be added since the output transition of place Queue is immediate, and from the behaviour of the model it is clear that at most 3 processors can be waiting in the queue. The relations (c_7) in the above LPP can thus be replaced with the new constraint:

$$4(\bar{M}[ExtBus] + \frac{B_{ExtBus}}{B_{Queue}}\bar{M}[Queue] - B_{ExtBus}) \leq 0$$

where $B_{Queue} = 3$. Solving this reduced linear programming problem the values obtained for the upper and lower bounds are: $1 \leq x_{e\_e\_a} \leq 2$.

5. Conclusions

Operational analysis of timed Petri net models has been introduced. In particular, we have defined adequate observable quantities that allow the derivation of fundamental relations among them. These relations hold true "operationally," i.e., in each sample path that one can measure in an experiment. Among these relations the enabling operational law constitutes a restatement of the classical utilization law (derived in the framework of multiple server queues) for each timed transition of a general Petri net model with infinite server semantics. Bounding inequalities in both directions between throughput of a transition and average marking of its input places have also been derived. These results are typical on network models containing synchronization, and represent a novel result of operational analysis. Under the hypothesis of strong symmetries, analogous relations have been derived for Timed Well-Formed nets.

A direct and interesting application of the obtained operational laws is the computation of performance bounds insensitive to the timing probability distributions. Indeed the bounding technique proposed in this paper guarantees that the exact value of a given performance index falls in the computed interval, whatever its probability distributions is. In this sense this bound technique is substantially more robust with respect to practical application than any performance evaluation technique based on Markovian analysis or simulation (where in any case some hypothesis on the timing distribution must be introduced in order to produce sample execution traces).

Proper linear programming problems including the derived operational laws as constraints allow one to estimate upper and lower bounds for arbitrary linear functions of the throughput and the average marking (in particular, the throughput of a single transition or the average marking of a particular place). This approach constitutes a clear improvement and generalization of previous results valid only for particular net subclasses. An important characteristics of this new method is that it is "open" to the introduction of additional contraints besides the ones already described in this paper provided that they are expressed in linear algebraic form. The straightforward addition of some constraints deriving from a specific knowledge about some peculiar behavioural characteristics of a WN model may improve the quality of the bounds based on results developed for the analysis of the qualitative behaviour of untimed Petri net models.

The proposed method for bounds computation is cheap, since the solution of the LPPs is practically extremely fast in terms of CPU time compared to Markovian numerical analysis (not to mention simulation).

The size of the LPP depends only on the net structure (number of places, transitions and arcs); in particular it is also independent of the cardinality of the basic colour classes, thus adding a dimension on the parameterization of the results. If the computation of bounds for a 4 processor system takes less than 1 second of CPU time, it will take the same order of magnitude to compute bounds for a 1,000 processor system.

References

1. M. Ajmone Marsan, G. Balbo, A. Bobbio, G. Chiola, G. Conte, and A. Cumani, "The effect of execution policies on the semantics and analysis of stochastic Petri nets", *IEEE Trans. on Soft. Eng.*, **15** (7), pp. 832–846, July 1989.
2. G. Chiola, C. Anglano, J. Campos, J.M. Colom, and M. Silva, "Operational analysis of timed Petri nets and application to the computation of performance bounds", In *Proc. of the* 5th *Intern. Workshop on Petri Nets and Performance Models*, pp. 128–137, Toulouse, October 1993.
3. J. Campos, G. Chiola, J.M. Colom, and M. Silva, "Properties and performace bounds for timed marked graphs", *IEEE Trans. on Circ. and Syst. I: Fundamental Th. and App.*, **39** (5), pp. 386–401, May 1992.
4. J. Campos, G. Chiola, and M. Silva, "Ergodicity and throughput bounds for Petri nets with unique consistent firing count vector", *IEEE Trans. on Soft. Eng.*, **17** (2), pp. 117–125, Feb. 1991.
5. J. Campos, G. Chiola, and M. Silva, "Properties and performance bounds for closed free choice synchronized monoclass queueing networks", *IEEE Trans. on Aut. Cont.*, **36** (12), pp. 1368–1382, Dec. 1991.
6. J. Campos, J.M. Colom, and M. Silva, "Improving throughput upper bounds for net based models", In *Proc. of the IMACS-IFAC Symp. Modelling and Control of Tech. Syst.*, pp. 573–582, Lille, May 1991.
7. G. Chiola, "A graphical Petri net tool for performance analysis", In *Proc. of the* 3rd *Intern. Workshop on Modeling Techniques and Performance Evaluation*, Paris, March 1987.
8. G. Chiola and C. Anglano, "Linear programming performance bounds for symmetric coloured nets", *Tech. Rep.*, Dip. di Informatica, Univ. di Torino, Feb. 1993.
9. G. Chiola, C. Dutheillet, G. Franceschinis and S. Haddad, "Stochastic Well-Formed Coloured nets for symmetric modelling applications", *IEEE Trans. on Comp.*, 1993. Accepted for publication.
10. J.M. Colom and M. Silva, "Improving the linearly based characterization of P/T nets", In G. Rozenberg, ed. *Advances in Petri Nets 1990*, **483** of *LNCS*, pp. 113–145. Springer-Verlag, Berlin, 1991.
11. Y. Dallery and X.R. Cao, "Operational analysis of stochastic closed queueing networks", *Performance Evaluation*, **14**, pp. 43–61, 1992.
12. P.J. Denning and J.P. Buzen, "The operational analysis of queueing network models", *ACM Computing Surveys*, **10**, pp. 225–262, 1978.
13. E. Gelenbe, "Stationary deterministic flows in discrete systems: I", *Theoretical Computer Science*, **3** (2), pp. 107–127, April 1983.
14. T. Murata, "Petri nets: Properties, analysis, and applications", *Proceedings of the IEEE*, **77** (4), pp. 541–580, April 1989.
15. G.L. Nemhauser, A.H.G. Rinnooy Kan and M.J. Todd, eds. Optimization, **1** of *Handbooks in Operations Research and Management Science*. North-Holland, Amsterdam, 1989.
16. M. Silva, "Introducing Petri Nets", Chapter 1 of *Practice of Petri Nets in Manufacturing* (F. Dicesare et al.), Chapman & Hall, 1993.

Approximate Throughput Computation of Stochastic Marked Graphs *

J. Campos, J.M. Colom, H. Jungnitz, and M. Silva

Depto. de Informática e Ing. de Sistemas, Universidad de Zaragoza, Spain

Summary. A general iterative technique for approximate throughput computation of stochastic strongly connected marked graphs is presented. It generalizes a previous technique based on net decomposition through a single input-single output cut, allowing the split of the model through any cut. The approach has two basic foundations. First, a deep understanding of the qualitative behaviour of marked graphs leads to a general decomposition technique. Second, after the decomposition phase, an iterative response time approximation method is applied for the computation of the throughput. Experimental results on several examples generally have an error of less than 3 %. The state space is usually reduced by more than one order of magnitude; therefore the analysis of otherwise intractable systems is possible.

1. Introduction

Stochastic Marked Graphs (SMG's) are a well-known subclass of stochastic Petri net models. They allow concurrency and synchronization but not decisions. From a queueing network perspective, it can be seen [14] that, provided strong connectivity, they are isomorphic to *fork/join queueing networks with blocking* (FJQN/B).

In this paper we consider strongly connected SMG's with time and marking independent *exponentially distributed* service times associated with transitions. For this class of models, several computation techniques have been presented in the literature. Exact performance results can be obtained from the numerical solution of the underlying continuous time Markov chain (CTMC) [3], but the *state explosion problem* makes intractable the evaluation of large systems. The efficient computation of exact performance indices of SMG's cannot be done analytically because *local balance property* does not hold in general [16]. The alternative approach of *bounds computation* has been studied by several authors using different techniques (see, e.g., [5, 8]).

Concerning approximation techniques, several proposals have been done. In [4], a method is proposed for nets that admit a *time scale decomposition* based on *near-complete decomposability* of Markov chains. Near decomposability properties are also used in [11] for an iterative approximate solution of weakly connected nets. In [6], some particular queueing networks with subnetworks having *population constraints* are analyzed using *flow equivalent*

* This work was partially supported by the European ESPRIT BRA Project 7269 QMIPS, the Spanish PRONTIC's 354/91 and 242/94, and the Aragonese CONAI-DGA P-IT 6/91.

aggregation (i.e., a non-iterative technique) and Marie's method [21] (the idea is to replace a subsystem by an equivalent exponential service station with load-dependent service rates obtained by analyzing the subsystem in isolation under a load-dependent Poisson arrival process). An alternative approach is presented in [19] to compute approximate throughput for SMG's. In that work, the original system is also *split in subsystems* and a *delay equivalence* criterion is used for throughput approximation. The service rates for the aggregated subsystems are *marking dependent.* In [17], *response time approximation* is applied for an iterative computation of the throughput of SMG's. The main differences with respect to the work in [19] are two: first, the splitting of the MG is more firmly based on *qualitative theory* of MG's and second, the service rates for aggregated subsystems are *constant* (similar accuracy of the throughput is obtained with simpler and more robust algorithms).

A discussion of the above recalled techniques is presented in [18] for the throughput approximation of SMG's. We summarize now some of the conclusions. Flow equivalent aggregation is clearly the most efficient method (it is not an iterative method). In this method, the behaviour of the subsystem is assumed to be independent of the arrival process and depends only on the number of customers in the system. In many cases, this assumption is violated (see [17]), therefore the method cannot be applied.

Marie's method behaves correctly in many cases. As with many iterative methods, the uniqueness of the solution cannot be proven although numerical experience has shown that a unique point does indeed exist. The main drawback is that convergence sometimes presents a problem [7].

Concerning the delay equivalence technique presented in [19], its convergence may sometimes constitute a problem. The robustness of the method is improved in [20], where the service rates of the aggregated subsystems are made constant. Some problems of this approach have been reported in [17] where it is shown that the speed of convergence strongly depends on the initial values estimated for the service rates that represent the aggregated subsystem. Moreover, for several models the authors were not able to find initial values for which the method would converge.

Finally, the response time approximation method introduced in [17] shows similar accuracy as delay equivalence, but at a greatly reduced computational cost. The method seems to be insensitive with respect to the initial values of service rates and is the one which requires the least amount of iterations. The main drawback of this method is that the original MG must be decomposed into two subsystems each one with only one input place and only one output place (*single input-single output* or *SISO cut*), and such decomposition is not always possible. A generalization to *SIMO* (single input-multiple output), *MISO* (multiple input-single output), and *MIMO* (multiple input-multiple output) cuts has been proposed but it presents serious problems concerning the quality of the results [18]. These problems are due to the fact that the structure of the net must be modified, by adding a "dummy synchronization" transition, to get a SISO cut, and this transformation can lead to a system with a considerably different behaviour.

In this paper, we follow an *iterative response time approximation technique* that avoids the problems derived from the application of the method in [17] for the general cases (SIMO, MISO, or MIMO cuts). The approach is deeply based on *qualitative theory of MG's.* More precisely, given an arbitrary cut (subset of places producing a net partition), a *structural decomposition* technique is developed in this paper that allows us to split a strongly connected MG into two *aggregated subsystems* and a *basic skeleton system.* And what is more important, *the behaviours of the subsystems, including steps, language of firing sequences and reachable markings, are equivalent to the whole system behaviour* (projected on the corresponding subsets of nodes). The better the qualitative behaviour of the system is represented by the aggregated subsystems, the more accurate the quantitative approximation will be.

The paper is organized as follows. In Section 2, basic notation and fundamental properties on MG's and implicit places are presented. Section 3 includes the structural decomposition of MG's used in the rest of the paper. The iterative technique for approximate throughput computation is described in Section 4. Finally, concluding remarks are presented in Section 5.

The proofs of all the results presented here and some more numerical examples can be found in [9].

2. Basics on stochastic marked graphs

2.1 Basic notations

We assume that the reader is familiar with concepts of P/T nets. In this section we present notations used in later sections, for further extensions the reader is referred to [22, 23].

$\mathcal{N} = (P, T, F)$ is a net if P and T are disjoint sets of places and transitions, respectively and $F \subseteq (P \times T) \cup (T \times P)$. We shall only consider nets with finite and nonempty sets of places and transitions. A net is connected if and only if the least equivalence relation which includes F is $(P \cup T) \times (P \cup T)$.

Let $\mathcal{N} = (P, T, F)$ be a net. A path of $\mathcal{N}$ is a sequence $x_1 \ldots x_k$ of elements (places and transitions) of $\mathcal{N}$ satisfying $(x_1, x_2), \ldots, (x_{k-1}, x_k) \in F$. It is a circuit if $(x_k, x_1) \in F$. A path (circuit) is called simple if all elements in the sequence defining the path (circuit) are different. In this paper we only consider simple paths and circuits. We denote by $\mathcal{P}(x, y)$, $x, y \in P \cup T$, the set of simple paths from x to y. This notion is extended to sets of elements: $\mathcal{P}(X, Y)$ is the union of the $\mathcal{P}(x, y)$ for all $x \in X$ and for all $y \in Y$.

$\mathcal{N}$ is strongly connected if for every two elements x, y of $\mathcal{N}$ there exists a path $x \ldots y$. Pre- and Post-sets of elements are denoted by the dot-notation:

${}^{\bullet}x = \{y \,|\, (y,x) \in F\}$ and $x^{\bullet} = \{y \,|\, (x,y) \in F\}$. This notion is extended to sets of elements; ${}^{\bullet}X$ is the union of the pre-sets of elements of X, $X^{\bullet}$ is the union of the post-sets of elements of X.

A function $M : P \to \{0,1,\ldots\}$ (usually represented in vector form) is called a marking. A net system is a couple $\langle \mathcal{N}, M_0 \rangle$ of a net $\mathcal{N}$ and an initial marking M_0. A transition t is enabled at marking M if for all $p \in {}^{\bullet}t, M[p] > 0$. An enabled transition can be fired. The fact that M' is reached from M by firing t is represented by $M[t\rangle M'$. A sequence of transitions $\sigma = t_1 t_2 \ldots t_k$ is a firing sequence of $\langle \mathcal{N}, M_0 \rangle$ if there exist a sequence of markings such that $M_0[t_1\rangle M_1[t_2\rangle \cdots M_{k-1}[t_k\rangle M_k$, it can be written as $M_0[\sigma\rangle M_k$, and M_k is said to be reachable from M_0 by firing σ. A step at a marking M is a maximal set of transitions concurrently firable from M.

The reachability set $R(\mathcal{N}, M_0)$ is the set of all markings reachable from M_0. $L(\mathcal{N}, M_0)$ is the language of firing sequences of $\langle \mathcal{N}, M_0 \rangle$ ($L(\mathcal{N}, M_0) = \{\sigma \,|\, M_0[\sigma\rangle\}$).

A marked graph (MG) is a Petri net such that each place has exactly one input transition and exactly one output transition. MG's allow synchronization but no choice. MG's are a subclass of ordinary Petri nets for which a simple, powerful, and elegant theory allows very efficient analysis and synthesis algorithms. A summary of structure theory of MG's can be found in [22].

2.2 Implicit places and MG's

An *implicit place* never is the unique restricting the firing of its output transitions. Let $\mathcal{N}$ be any net and $\mathcal{N}^p$ be the net resulting from adding a place p to $\mathcal{N}$. If M_0 is an initial marking of $\mathcal{N}$, M_0^p denotes the initial marking of $\mathcal{N}^p$ and $m_0[p] = M_0^p[p]$. The incidence matrix of $\mathcal{N}$ is C and l_p is the incidence vector of place p.

Definition 2.1. [23] *Let $\langle \mathcal{N}, M_0 \rangle$ be a net system and $p \notin P$ be a place to be added. Then p is an implicit place (IP) with respect to $\langle \mathcal{N}, M_0 \rangle$ (or equivalently, it is an implicit place in $\langle \mathcal{N}^p, M_0^p \rangle$) iff the languages of firing sequences of $\langle \mathcal{N}, M_0 \rangle$ and $\langle \mathcal{N}^p, M_0^p \rangle$ coincide. That is, $L(\mathcal{N}, M_0) = L(\mathcal{N}^p, M_0^p)$.*

A place is an IP depending on the initial marking, M_0. Places which can be implicit for any M_0 are said to be *structurally implicit* (SIP). Inside the class of SIP's we are interested in the so called *marking structurally implicit places* (MSIP) whose structural characterization is given in the following result.

Theorem 2.1. [13] *Let $\mathcal{N}$ be a net and p be a place with incidence vector l_p. The place p is an MSIP in $\mathcal{N}^p$ iff there exists $Y \geq 0$ such that $Y^T \cdot C = l_p$.*

From this characterization of an MSIP, p, a method to compute an initial marking of p making it implicit with respect to $\langle \mathcal{N}, M_0 \rangle$ is presented in [13].

In the following, we characterize a special class of MSIP's with respect to strongly connected MG's called *TT-MSIP's*. These places have only one input arc and one output arc and therefore, $\mathcal{N}^p$ will be also an MG. The row of the incidence matrix corresponding to a TT-MSIP can be obtained from the summation of rows corresponding to the places in any path from the input transition to the output transition of the place. Moreover, we characterize the minimum initial marking making these places implicit with respect to $\langle \mathcal{N}, M_0 \rangle$ and preserving its steps.

Theorem 2.2. *Let $\mathcal{N} = (P, T, F)$ be a strongly connected MG and $p \notin P$ be a place to be added with one input transition $t_i \in T$ ($^\bullet p = \{t_i\}$) and one output transition $t_o \in T$ ($p^\bullet = \{t_o\}$). The place p is a TT-MSIP with respect to $\mathcal{N}$ and $\forall \pi \in \mathcal{P}(t_i, t_o)$, $l_p = \sum_{p_j \in \pi} l_{p_j}$.*

The following result characterizes the minimum initial marking of a TT-MSIP to be implicit *preserving all steps of the net system* $\langle \mathcal{N}, M_0 \rangle$. This marking is computed from the contents of tokens of the existing paths from the input transition of p to its output transition.

Theorem 2.3. *Let $\langle \mathcal{N}, M_0 \rangle$ be a strongly connected and live MG, and $p \notin P$ be a TT-MSIP to be added with $^\bullet p = \{t_i\}$ and $p^\bullet = \{t_o\}$. The minimum initial marking of p to be an IP in $\langle \mathcal{N}^p, M_0^p \rangle$ preserving all steps of $\langle \mathcal{N}, M_0 \rangle$ is*

$$m_0^{min}[p] = \min\{\sum_{p_j \in \pi} M_0[p_j] \mid \pi \in \mathcal{P}(t_i, t_o)\}.$$

Corollary 2.1. *Let $\langle \mathcal{N}, M_0 \rangle$ be a strongly connected and live MG, and $p \notin P$ be a TT-MSIP to be added with $^\bullet p = \{t_i\}$ and $p^\bullet = \{t_o\}$. The place p is an IP in $\langle \mathcal{N}^p, M_0^p \rangle$ preserving all steps of $\langle \mathcal{N}, M_0 \rangle$ for all initial marking $m_0[p] \geq m_0^{min}[p]$.*

The Theorem 2.3 characterizes the minimum initial marking of a TT-MSIP to be an IP with respect to $\langle \mathcal{N}, M_0 \rangle$ in terms of the contents of tokens of the paths $\mathcal{P}(t_i, t_o)$. The computation of this minimum initial marking can be done applying an algorithm from the graph theory to determine the cost of the shortest path from a source vertex to a sink vertex of a directed graph, $G = (V, E)$, obtained from the original MG (see [2] for implementations of these algorithms). In this graph, each vertex corresponds to a transition of the net. There exists a directed arc between two vertices if and only if there exists a place in the net connecting the two transitions that represent the two vertices. The sense of the arc is the sense of the tokens' flow between the transitions through the place. Each arc has a non-negative cost equal to the initial marking of the place that represents. Moreover, we add an arc $t \to t$ for each vertex t with a cost equal to ∞.

Therefore, if we apply the algorithm to solve the shortest path problem in the directed graph G, we obtain the smallest length of any path from t_i to t_o, denoted $length(t_i, t_o)$. Observe, that $length(t_i, t_o) = \min\{\sum_{p_j \in \pi} M_0[p_j] \mid \pi \in \mathcal{P}(t_i, t_o)\} = m_0^{min}[p]$.

3. Structural decomposition of MG's

The basic idea is the following: a strongly connected and live MG (see Fig. 3.1.a) is split into two subnets by a *cut* Q defined through some places ($Q = \{Z1, Z2, Z3\}$, in Fig. 3.1.a). From the cut we define three nets: two *aggregated subnets* ($\mathcal{AN}_1$ and $\mathcal{AN}_2$; see Figs. 3.1.b and 3.1.c) and a *basic skeleton* net ($\mathcal{BN}$; see Fig. 3.1.d). These nets will be obtained by substitution of the so called aggregable subnets, defined from the cut Q, by a set of places. We select an initial marking for each added place such that the behaviour of the aggregated subnet is the behaviour of the original MG hiding the behaviour of the aggregable subnet.

Fig. 3.1. An SMG (a), its decomposition in aggregated systems $\mathcal{AS}_1$ (b), $\mathcal{AS}_2$ (c), and the basic skeleton (d).

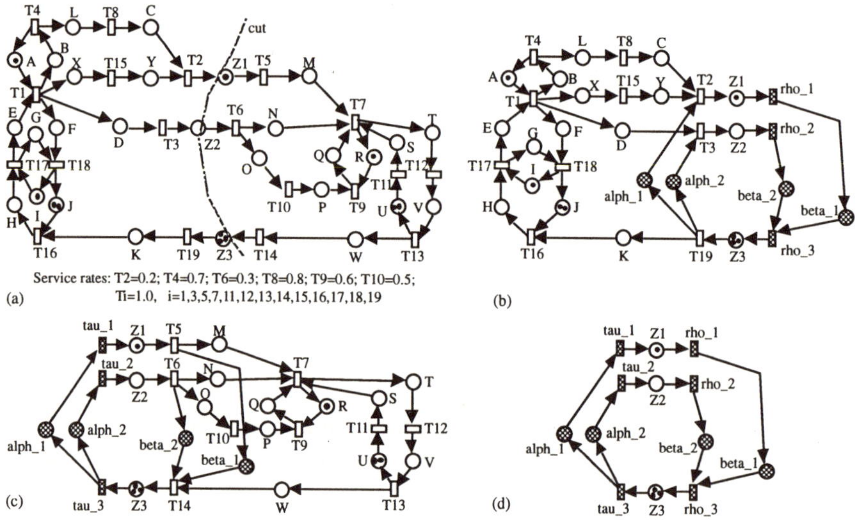

Definition 3.1. *Let $\mathcal{N} = (P, T, F)$ be a strongly connected MG. A subset of places, $Q \subseteq P$, is said to be a cut of $\mathcal{N}$ iff there exist two subnets, $\mathcal{N}_1 = (P_1, T_1, F_1)$ and $\mathcal{N}_2 = (P_2, T_2, F_2)$, of $\mathcal{N}$ verifying*

i) $T_1 \cup T_2 = T$, $T_1 \cap T_2 = \emptyset$
ii) $P_1 = T_1^\bullet \cup {}^\bullet T_1$, $P_2 = T_2^\bullet \cup {}^\bullet T_2$
iii) $P_1 \cup P_2 = P$, $P_1 \cap P_2 = Q$
iv) $F_i = F \cap ((P_i \times T_i) \cup (T_i \times P_i))$, $i \in \{1, 2\}$

Definition 3.2. *Let $\mathcal{N} = (P, T, F)$ be a strongly connected MG, $Q \subseteq P$ a cut of $\mathcal{N}$, and $\mathcal{N}_1 = (P_1, T_1, F_1)$, $\mathcal{N}_2 = (P_2, T_2, F_2)$ the two subnets associated with the cut (by Def. 3.1). The subnets $\mathcal{N}_{A_i} = (P_{A_i}, T_{A_i}, F_{A_i})$, $i \in \{1, 2\}$, are called the aggregable subnets of the cut Q, where*

i) $P_{A_i} = P_i \setminus Q$
ii) $T_{A_i} = T_i \setminus T_Q$, *where* $T_Q = {}^{\bullet}Q \cup Q^{\bullet}$
iii) $F_{A_i} = F_i \cap ((P_{A_i} \times T_{A_i}) \cup (T_{A_i} \times P_{A_i}))$

The places $p \in P_{A_i}$ *such that* ${}^{\bullet}p \cap T_{A_i} = \emptyset$ *(resp.,* $p^{\bullet} \cap T_{A_i} = \emptyset$*) are called source places (resp., sink places) of* $\mathcal{N}_{A_i}$*. The set of input transitions of the source places and output transitions of the sink places are called interface transitions of* $\mathcal{N}_{A_i}$*.*

We denote $\mathcal{P}_{A_i}$ the set of paths in the net $\mathcal{N}_{A_i}$ from a source place to a sink place. $\mathcal{IP}_{A_i}$ denotes the set of TT-MSIP's with respect to $\mathcal{N}$ obtained from each path of $\mathcal{P}_{A_i}$ by the linear combination of the rows in the incidence matrix corresponding to the path's places. In the sequel, we define the so called *aggregated subnets* of an MG $\langle \mathcal{N}, M_0 \rangle$ with respect to a cut Q. These subnets will be obtained by substituting in $\mathcal{N}$ of an aggregable subnet $\mathcal{N}_{A_i}$ by the set of places $\mathcal{IP}_{A_i}$. This substitution is an abstraction of the subnet $\mathcal{N}_{A_i}$. We select an initial marking for each place $p \in \mathcal{IP}_{A_i}$ (called *aggregation's initial marking*, $m_0^a[p]$) equal to $m_0^a[p] = \min\{\sum_{p_j \in \pi} M_0[p_j] \,|\, l_p = \sum_{p_j \in \pi} l_{p_j}$ and $\pi \in \mathcal{P}_{A_i}\}$. With this initial marking we prove that the behaviour of the aggregated subnet is the behaviour of the original MG by hiding the behaviour of $\mathcal{N}_{A_i}$.

Definition 3.3. *Let* $\langle \mathcal{N}, M_0 \rangle$ *be a strongly connected and live MG,* $Q \subseteq P$ *a cut of* $\mathcal{N}$*, and* $\mathcal{N}_{A_i}$*,* $i = 1, 2$*, be the aggregable subnets defined by the cut* Q*. The aggregated subsystem* $\mathcal{AS}_i = \langle \mathcal{AN}_i, M_0^{\mathcal{AN}_i} \rangle$ *is the net system obtained from* $\langle \mathcal{N}, M_0 \rangle$ *by substituting the subnet* $\mathcal{N}_{A_j}$ *by the set of places* $\mathcal{IP}_{A_j}$ *with* $m_0[p] = m_0^a[p]$*, for all* $p \in \mathcal{IP}_{A_j}$*,* $i = 1, 2$*;* $j = 1, 2$ *and* $j \neq i$*. The basic skeleton system,* $\mathcal{BS} = \langle \mathcal{BN}, M_0^{\mathcal{BN}} \rangle$*, is the system obtained from* $\langle \mathcal{N}, M_0 \rangle$ *by substituting the subnets* $\mathcal{N}_{A_1}$ *and* $\mathcal{N}_{A_2}$ *by the set of places* $\mathcal{IP}_{A_1}$ *and* $\mathcal{IP}_{A_2}$ *with* $m_0[p] = m_0^a[p] = \min\{\sum_{p_j \in \pi} M_0[p_j] \,|\, l_p = \sum_{p_j \in \pi} l_{p_j}$ *and* $\pi \in \mathcal{P}_{A_i}\}$*, for all* $p \in \mathcal{IP}_{A_1} \cup \mathcal{IP}_{A_2}$*.*

Theorem 3.1. *Let* $\langle \mathcal{N}, M_0 \rangle$ *be a strongly connected and live MG,* $Q \subseteq P$ *a cut of* $\mathcal{N}$ *and* $\mathcal{AS}_i$ *be the aggregated subsystem obtained from* $\langle \mathcal{N}, M_0 \rangle$ *by substituting the subnet* $\mathcal{N}_{A_j}$ *by the set of places* $\mathcal{IP}_{A_j}$ *with* $M_0^{\mathcal{AN}_i}[p] =$ **if** $p \in \mathcal{IP}_{A_j}$ **then** $m_0^a[p]$ **else** $M_0[p]$*,* $i = 1, 2$*;* $j = 1, 2$*, and* $j \neq i$*.*

i) $L(\mathcal{N}, M_0)|_{T \setminus T_{A_j}} = L(\mathcal{AN}_i, M_0^{\mathcal{AN}_i})$.
ii) $R(\mathcal{N}, M_0)|_{P \setminus P_{A_j}} = R(\mathcal{AN}_i, M_0^{\mathcal{AN}_i})|_{P_{\mathcal{AN}_i} \setminus \mathcal{IP}_{A_j}}$.

Corollary 3.1. *Let* $\langle \mathcal{N}, M_0 \rangle$ *be a strongly connected and live MG,* $Q \subseteq P$ *a cut of* $\mathcal{N}$*, and* $\mathcal{BS}$ *the basic skeleton system obtained from* $\langle \mathcal{N}, M_0 \rangle$ *by substituting the subnets* $\mathcal{N}_{A_1}$ *and* $\mathcal{N}_{A_2}$ *by the set of places* $\mathcal{IP}_{A_1}$ *and* $\mathcal{IP}_{A_2}$*, respectively, and* $M_0^{\mathcal{BN}}[p] =$ **if** $p \in \mathcal{IP}_{A_1} \cup \mathcal{IP}_{A_2}$ **then** $m_0^a[p]$ **else** $M_0[p]$*.*

i) $L(\mathcal{N}, M_0)|_{T \setminus (T_{A_1} \cup T_{A_2})} = L(\mathcal{BN}, M_0^{\mathcal{BN}})$.
ii) $R(\mathcal{N}, M_0)|_{P \setminus (P_{A_1} \cup P_{A_2})} = R(\mathcal{BN}, M_0^{\mathcal{BS}})|_{P_{\mathcal{BN}} \setminus (\mathcal{IP}_{A_1} \cup \mathcal{IP}_{A_2})}$.

The main drawback of the above theorems concerns the great number (exponential in the worst case) of places in $\mathcal{IP}_{A_i}$. In the following we present a method to reduce the number of places to add, characterizing a subset of $\mathcal{IP}_{A_i}$, denoted $\mathcal{BIP}_{A_i}$, with the property that all places of $\mathcal{IP}_{A_i} \setminus \mathcal{BIP}_{A_i}$ are implicit with respect to the places $\mathcal{BIP}_{A_i}$. Therefore, in order to build the aggregated subnet we only add the set of places $\mathcal{BIP}_{A_i}$ instead of $\mathcal{IP}_{A_i}$.

Let us consider the aggregable subnet $\mathcal{N}_{A_i}$ together with its interface transitions. We derive from this net a directed graph $G_{A_i} = (V, E)$ in the same way to that presented at the end of previous section.

If we apply the algorithm of R.W. Floyd to solve the *all-pairs shortest paths* problem (see [2] for implementations of this algorithm) to the directed graph G_{A_i}, we obtain for each ordered pair of vertices (i.e., transitions) (t, t') the smallest length of any path from t to t', denoted $length(t, t')$ (if this value is equal to ∞, there is no path from t to t'). Observe, that $length(t, t') = \min\{\sum_{p_j \in \pi} M_0[p_j] \mid \pi \text{ is a path from } t \text{ to } t'\}$. The computational complexity of this algorithm is $O(m^3)$, where m is the number of transitions of the considered net. From this values we define the set of places $\mathcal{BIP}_{A_i}$ as $\mathcal{BIP}_{A_i} = \{p \mid {}^\bullet p = \{t\}; p^\bullet = \{t'\}; t, t' \in T_Q; length(t, t') \neq \infty\}$.

For all $p \in \mathcal{BIP}_{A_i}$ we select an initial marking $m_0[p] = length(t, t')$. It is trivial to verify that this initial marking coincides with the previously defined *aggregation's initial marking*, $m_0^a[p]$. For instance, in the case of Fig. 3.1.b, $\mathcal{BIP}_{A_2} = \{$ *beta_1*, *beta_2* $\}$ and $m_0[beta\_1] = m_0[beta\_2] = 0$.

The following result states that all places of $\mathcal{IP}_{A_i} \setminus \mathcal{BIP}_{A_i}$ are implicit with respect to the places $\mathcal{BIP}_{A_i}$. Therefore, in order to build the aggregated subsystem we only add the set of places $\mathcal{BIP}_{A_i}$ instead of $\mathcal{IP}_{A_i}$.

Property 3.1. Each place $p \in \mathcal{IP}_{A_i} \setminus \mathcal{BIP}_{A_i}$ with an initial marking equal to $m_0^a[p]$ is implicit with respect to the set of places $\mathcal{BIP}_{A_i}$ each one with an initial marking equal to the aggregation's marking.

In many cases the set $\mathcal{BIP}_{A_i}$ is bigger than necessary because some places can be implicit in $\mathcal{AS}_i$. To remove one of these unnecessary places, p, we can apply the method described at the end of the previous section to compute the shortest path from ${}^\bullet p$ to $p^\bullet$. The place p can be removed if the output of this algorithm is less than or equal to the aggregation's marking of p.

4. Approximate throughput computation

In previous section, an algorithm to decompose an MG into two aggregated subsystems and a basic skeleton system (being also MG's) has been presented. In aggregated subsystem $\mathcal{AS}_i$ $(i = 1, 2)$, the subnet $\mathcal{N}_j$ $(j \neq i)$ is represented by the places in the cut Q, by the interface transitions of $\mathcal{N}_j$, $T_{I_j} = T_Q \cap T_j$, and by the new places that substitute the subnet $\mathcal{N}_{A_j}$.

The technique for an approximate computation of the throughput that we present now is, basically, a *response time approximation* method [1, 17, 18]. The interface transitions of $\mathcal{N}_j$ in $\mathcal{AS}_i$ approximate the response time of all the subsystem $\mathcal{N}_j$ ($i = 1,2; j \neq i$). A direct (non-iterative) method to compute the constant service rates of such interface transitions in order to represent the aggregation of the subnet gives, in general, low accuracy. Therefore, we are forced to define a *fixed-point search iterative process*, with the possible drawback of the presence of convergence and efficiency problems.

4.1 First approach: Ping-Pong algorithm

The first algorithm that we explored, called "Ping-Pong", follows.

```
select a cut Q;
derive aggregated subsystems AS_i, i = 1,2;
give value μ_t^0 for each t ∈ T_{I_1} in AS_2;
compute value of throughput χ_2^0 of AS_2;
k := 0;     {counter for iteration steps}
repeat
  k := k + 1;
  compute μ_t^k for each t ∈ T_{I_2} such that the
          throughput χ_1^k of AS_1 is close enough to χ_2^{k-1};
  compute μ_t^k for each t ∈ T_{I_1} such that the
          throughput χ_2^k of AS_2 is close enough to χ_1^k;
until convergence of χ_1^k and χ_2^k;
```

In the above procedure, once a cut has been selected and given some initial values for the service rates of interface transitions of $\mathcal{N}_1$ (which approximate the response time of all the subsystem $\mathcal{N}_1$), the underlying CTMC of aggregated subsystem $\mathcal{AS}_2$ is solved. From the solution of that CTMC, the first estimation χ_2^0 of the throughput of $\mathcal{AS}_2$ can be computed. Then, the initial estimated values of service rates of interface transitions that approximate the response time of subsystem $\mathcal{N}_2$ must be derived. This must be done in such a way that the throughput χ_1^1 of $\mathcal{AS}_1$ is "close enough" to χ_2^0. Then, a better estimation of rates μ_t^k for each $t \in T_{I_1}$ must be computed such that the throughput χ_2^1 of $\mathcal{AS}_2$ is close enough to χ_1^1. The process is iterated until χ_1^k and χ_2^k converge.

The first problem of the above sketch of approximation algorithm is that a *multidimensional search on the parameters* of a complex CTMC in order to get a given throughput cannot be done in an efficient way. A possible solution to this problem is the following. In the iterative process, each time that an aggregated subsystem $\mathcal{AS}_i, i = 1,2$, is solved, *the ratios* among the service rates μ_t^k of all the transitions in T_{I_i} are estimated. After that, when the other subsystem $\mathcal{AS}_j, j \neq i$, is solved, only a *scale factor* for these service rates must be computed. The goal is to find a scale factor of μ_t^k for all $t \in T_{I_j}$

(and fixed k) such that the throughput of $\mathcal{AS}_j$ and the throughput of $\mathcal{AS}_i$, computed before, are the same. And this can be achieved with a linear search of the scale factor in $\mathcal{AS}_j$.

At this point, the main technical problem is the following: How to estimate from the solution of $\mathcal{AS}_i$ the ratios among the service rates of all transitions in T_{I_i} that in the next step (solution of $\mathcal{AS}_j$) will be scaled to obtain an approximation of the response time of the subsystem $\mathcal{N}_i$?

We explain our answer to this question by means of the example depicted in Fig. 3.1. Figure 3.1.b represents the aggregated subsystem $\mathcal{AS}_1$ derived from the original MG. It is necessary to compute the ratio between the service rate of $T2$ and $T3$ to be used as input data for the linear search of the scale factor in $\mathcal{AS}_2$ (Fig. 3.1.c). In order to do that, the aggregated subsystem $\mathcal{AS}_1$ is transformed (as depicted in Fig. 3.1.b) with the addition of places $\mathcal{BIP}_{A_1} = \{alph\_1, alph\_2\}$. The obtained system is behaviourally equivalent to $\mathcal{AS}_1$ because the added places (which are those that will substitute $\mathcal{N}_{A_1}$), are implicit. These new places allow to estimate the ratio between the "aggregated service times" of transitions $T2$ and $T3$ (representing the response time approximation of $\mathcal{N}_1$), as the quotient of the mean marking of *alph_1* by the mean marking of *alph_2*, because the throughput of all transitions is the same.

Now, two problems arise. First, the linear search of the scale factor must be done in the aggregated subsystems, that can have a considerably large state space, thus the efficiency of the method falls down. Additionally, we have found convergence problems in many cases. A solution for both problems is proposed in the next subsection.

4.2 A solution: Pelota[1] algorithm

The more practical solution of the problem we found makes use of the third system (another MG) derived from the original one, in previous section: *the basic skeleton.* The basic skeleton contains the interface subsystem and a simplified view (using the places $\mathcal{BIP}_{A_i}, i = 1, 2$, computed by the algorithm in previous section) of subsystems $\mathcal{N}_{A_i}, i = 1, 2$.

The idea is to use the basic skeleton as an intermediate point (*fronton*) between the two aggregated subnets (rackets), as explained in this algorithm:

```
select a cut Q;
derive AS_i, i = 1,2 and BS;
give initial value μ_t^0 for each t ∈ T_{I_2};
k := 0;     {counter for iteration steps}
repeat
  k := k + 1;
```

[1] Game played by two players who use a basket strapped to their wrists or a wooden racket to propel a ball against a specially marked wall, called *fronton*.

Table 4.1. Iteration results for the SMG in Fig. 3.1.

$\mathcal{AS}_1$					$\mathcal{AS}_2$				
χ_1	tau_1	tau_2	tau_3	coeff	χ_2	rho_1	rho_2	rho_3	coeff
0.17352	0.05170	0.16810	0.88873	1.01167	0.12714	0.89026	0.21861	0.14354	0.98468
0.14093	0.06265	0.19707	0.91895	1.01318	0.13795	0.88267	0.21363	0.13509	0.98582
0.13856	0.06325	0.19821	0.92054	1.01306	0.13841	0.88239	0.21343	0.13467	0.98592
0.13844	0.06328	0.19827	0.92062	1.01306	0.13843	0.88237	0.21342	0.13465	0.98592
0.13843	0.06328	0.19827	0.92064	1.01307	0.13843	0.88238	0.21342	0.13465	0.98593

```
  solve aggregated subsystem AS_1 with
    input:  μ_t^{k-1} for each t ∈ T_{I_2},
    output: ratios among μ_t^k of t ∈ T_{I_1} and χ_1^k;
  solve basic skeleton system BS with
    input:  μ_t^{k-1} for each t ∈ T_{I_2},
            ratios among μ_t^k of t ∈ T_{I_1}, and χ_1^k,
    output: scale factor of μ_t^k of t ∈ T_{I_1};
  solve aggregated subsystem AS_2 with
    input:  μ_t^k for each t ∈ T_{I_1},
    output: ratios among μ_t^k of t ∈ T_{I_2} and χ_2^k;
  solve basic skeleton system BS with
    input:  μ_t^k for each t ∈ T_{I_1},
            ratios among μ_t^k of t ∈ T_{I_2}, and χ_2^k,
    output: scale factor of μ_t^k of t ∈ T_{I_2};
until convergence of χ_1^k and χ_2^k;
```

In this iterative process, each time that an aggregated subsystem $\mathcal{AS}_i, i = 1, 2$, is solved, only the throughput χ_i^k and the ratios among the service rates μ_t^k of all the transitions in T_{I_i} are estimated (with the method explained in previous subsection). After that, a scale factor for these service rates must be computed. This is achieved by using the basic skeleton system $\mathcal{BS}$. The goal is to find a scale factor of μ_t^k for all $t \in T_{I_i}$ such that the throughput of the basic skeleton and the throughput of $\mathcal{AS}_i$, computed before, are the same. A linear search of the scale factor must be implemented, but now in a net system with considerably fewer states (the basic skeleton). In each iteration of this linear search, the basic skeleton is solved by deriving the underlying CTMC.

Now, the existence and uniqueness of the solution, and the convergence of the method should be addressed. Although no formal proof gives positive answers so far to the above questions, extensive testing allows the conjecture that there exists one and only one solution, computable in a finite number of steps, typically between 2 and 5 if the convergence criterion is that the difference between the two last estimations of the throughput is less than 0.1 %.

Let us consider again the SMG depicted in Fig. 3.1.a. The exact value of the throughput is equal to 0.138341 (if single-server semantics is assumed).

The underlying CTMC has 89358 states. The aggregated systems $\mathcal{A}S_1$ and $\mathcal{A}S_2$ are depicted in Figs. 3.1.b and 3.1.c, respectively. The corresponding basic skeleton system is that in Fig. 3.1.d.

Table 4.1 shows the iterative results obtained for this example. The values in $\mathcal{A}S_1$ columns have been obtained from the solution of the aggregated system in Fig. 3.1.b: χ_1 is the throughput of $\mathcal{A}S_1$; columns *tau_1*, *tau_2*, and *tau_3* are the estimated values of the service rates of the aggregated transition tau_1, tau_2, and tau_3, computed in $\mathcal{A}S_1$; column *coeff* is the scale factor of previous estimated service rates, obtained by the linear search in the basic skeleton of Fig. 3.1.d. Columns related with $\mathcal{A}S_2$ represent the analogous values for the aggregated system in Fig. 3.1.c. Convergence of the method can be observed from the third iteration step. The error is -0.064333 %, after the fifth step. The following additional fact must be remarked: the underlying CTMC's of $\mathcal{A}S_1$, $\mathcal{A}S_2$, and the basic skeleton have 8288, 3440, and 231 states, respectively, while the original SMG has 89358 states.

5. Conclusions

In order to derive a general, efficient, and accurate technique for throughput approximation of stochastic marked graphs using the divide and conquer principle, qualitative theory ought to guide the decomposition phase (this principle underlies several previous works on the topic [6, 15, 17, 18, 19, 20]).

This was the first objective of the paper: the presentation of a general structural decomposition technique allowing to split a given marked graph through an arbitrary cut (subset of places) and to derive two aggregated subsystems whose qualitative behaviours are projections of the whole system qualitative behaviour. The technical tool to achieve this problem has been the use of implicit places: a subsystem of the original marked graph can be substituted by a minimal set of implicit places that represent an abstraction of the subsystem, leading to an aggregated subsystem. If the same process is applied to two complementary subsystems, two aggregated subsystems are derived, each one representing a portion of the behaviour of the whole system.

The second phase of the analysis problem is the selection of an approximate throughput computation algorithm. Iterative response time approximation technique was selected after a wide comparison with other approaches present in the literature. In order to assure the convergence of the method, a third subsystem was used for a correct tuning of parameters, the basic skeleton. It is obtained after the substitution of both subnets by the corresponding implicit places. Its behaviour is simple enough to allow a linear search of the correct value of a parameter in order to get a given throughput (the one obtained in previous iteration step).

Extensive numerical experiments using the method sketched in previous paragraphs showed very good results with respect to efficiency and accuracy. Convergence is generally observed after a couple of iteration steps and the approximate computation of throughput can be achieved with a considerable saving of time and memory (more than one order of magnitude in many cases) and with a very little error (less than 3 %).

Eventhough we have considered only strongly connected nets, the approach can be applied to non-strongly connected marked graphs: The iterative technique is used to compute the approximate throughput of each strongly connected component in isolation and, after that, [8, Theorem 5.1] applies.

An obvious generalization of the presented technique can be derived if the original system is partitioned into more than two subsystems, leading to the classical tradeoff between efficiency and accuracy. The extension to more general net subclasses, like macroplace-macrotransition nets proposed in [15], is being considered by the authors.

References

1. S. C. Agrawal, J. P. Buzen, and A. W. Shum, "Response time preservation: A general technique for developing approximate algorithms for queueing networks", In *Proc. of the 1984 ACM Sigmetrics Conf. on Measurement and Modeling of Computer Systems*, pp. 63–77, Cambridge, MA, Aug. 1984.
2. A. V. Aho, J. E. Hopcroft, and J. D. Ullman, *Data Structures and Algorithms*, Addison-Wesley, 1983.
3. M. Ajmone Marsan, G. Balbo, and G. Conte, *Performance Models of Multiprocessor Systems*. MIT Press, Cambridge, 1986.
4. H. H. Ammar and S. M. R. Islam, "Time scale decomposition of a class of generalized stochastic Petri net models", *IEEE Trans. Software Eng.*, **15** (6), pp. 809–820, June 1989.
5. F. Baccelli and Z. Liu, "Comparison properties of stochastic decision free Petri nets", *IEEE Trans. Automat. Contr.*, **37** (12), pp. 1905–1920, Dec. 1992.
6. B. Baynat and Y. Dallery, "Approximate techniques for general closed queueing networks with subnetworks having population constraints", *European Journal of Operational Research*, **69** pp. 250–263, 1993.
7. B. Baynat and Y. Dallery, "A unified view of product-form approximation techniques for general closed queueing networks", *Performance Evaluation*, **18** (3), pp. 205–224, Nov. 1993.
8. J. Campos, G. Chiola, J. M. Colom, and M. Silva, "Properties and performance bounds for timed marked graphs", *IEEE Trans. Circuits and Syst.—I: Fundamental Theory and Applications*, **39** (5), pp. 386–401, May 1992.
9. J. Campos, J. M. Colom, H. Jungnitz, and M. Silva, "Approximate throughput computation of stochastic marked graphs", *IEEE Trans. Software Eng.*, **20** (7), pp. 526–535, July 1994.
10. G. Chiola, "A graphical Petri net tool for performance analysis", In *Proc. of the* 3rd *Int. Workshop on Modeling Techniques and Performance Evaluation*, Paris, France, March 1987. AFCET.
11. G. Ciardo and K. Trivedi, "A decomposition approach for stochastic Petri nets models", In *Proc. of the 4th Int. Workshop on Petri Nets and Performance Models*, pp. 74–83, Melbourne, Australia, Dec. 1991. IEEE Comput. Soc. Press.

12. J. M. Colom, *Análisis Estructural de Redes de Petri, Programación Lineal y Geometría Convexa*, PhD thesis, Dpto. de Ingeniería Eléctrica e Informática, Univ. Zaragoza, Spain, June 1989.
13. J. M. Colom and M. Silva, "Improving the linearly based characterization of P/T nets", In G. Rozenberg (ed.), *Advances in Petri Nets 1990*, **483** of *LNCS*, pp. 113–145. Springer-Verlag, Berlin, 1991.
14. Y. Dallery, Z. Liu, and D. Towsley, "Equivalence, reversibility, symmetry, and concavity properties in fork-join queueing networks with blocking", *Journal of the ACM*, **41** (5), pp. 903–942, Sep. 1994.
15. A. Desrochers, H. Jungnitz, and M. Silva, "An approximation method for the performance analysis of manufacturing systems based on GSPN's", In *Proc. of the Rensselaer's Third Int. Conf. on Computer Integrated Manufacturing*, pp. 46–55, Troy, NY, May 1992, IEEE Comput. Soc. Press.
16. S. Donatelli and M. Sereno, "On the product form solution for stochastic Petri nets", In *Proc. of the 13th Int. Conf. on Applications and Theory of Petri Nets*, pp. 154–172, Sheffield, UK, June 1992.
17. H. Jungnitz, B. Sánchez, and M. Silva, "Approximate throughput computation of stochastic marked graphs", *Journal of Parallel and Distributed Computing*, **15**, pp. 282–295, 1992.
18. H. J. Jungnitz, *Approximation Methods for Stochastic Petri Nets*. PhD thesis, Dept. of Electrical, Computer and Systems Engineering, Rensselaer Polytechnic Institute, Troy, NY, May 1992.
19. Y. Li and C. M. Woodside, "Iterative decomposition and aggregation of stochastic marked graphs Petri nets", In *Proc. of the 12th Int. Conf. on Applications and Theory of Petri Nets*, pp. 257–275, Gjern, Denmark, June 1991.
20. Y. Li and C. M. Woodside, "Performance Petri net analysis of communications protocol software by delay-equivalent aggregation", In *Proc. of the 4th Int. Workshop on Petri Nets and Performance Models*, pp. 64–73, Melbourne, Australia, Dec. 1991, IEEE Comput. Soc. Press.
21. R. A. Marie, "An approximate analytical method for general queueing networks", *IEEE Trans. Software Eng.*, **5** (5), pp. 530–538, Sep. 1979.
22. T. Murata, "Petri nets: Properties, analysis, and applications", *Proceedings of the IEEE*, **77** (4), pp. 541–580, April 1989.
23. M. Silva, *Las Redes de Petri en la Automática y la Informática*. Editorial AC, Madrid, 1985.

Part III

Applications

Allocation of Customer Types to Servers: Clustering is Optimal

S.C. Borst

CWI, The Netherlands

Summary. The model under consideration consists of n customer types attended by m parallel non-identical servers. Customers are allocated to the servers in a probabilistic manner; upon arrival customers are sent to one of the servers according to an $m \times n$ matrix of routing probabilities. We consider the problem of finding an allocation that minimizes a weighted sum of the mean waiting times. We expose the structure of an optimal allocation and describe for some special cases in detail how the structure may be exploited in actually computing an optimal allocation.

1. Introduction

In this paper we consider a model consisting of several parallel servers which process jobs generated at several distinct sources. Such a model may arise quite naturally in a situation where a pool of resources is available for performing various kinds of activities, for example in distributed computer systems or in communication networks.

In such a situation, there is usually some freedom of decision as to which server is to process which job at what time. So there is typically a need for a scheduling strategy, i.e., a set of decision instructions for scheduling the jobs. At a global level, decisions need to be made about which server is to process which job. Subsequently, at a local level, decisions need to be made about the order of service. In this paper we mainly focus on the global scheduling problem; we hardly touch on the local scheduling problem. Locally, the order of service is assumed not to discriminate between the sources from which the jobs originated.

The main function of a global scheduling strategy is load sharing; a strategy should make the servers cooperate in sharing the load of the system so as to optimize the system performance. Load sharing is also frequently referred to as load balancing. The term load balancing arises from the intuition that to optimize the system performance, the load should be balanced among the servers. In the present paper we find however that the load, in the sense of traffic intensity, in general should *not* be completely balanced.

Wang & Morris [12] give a comprehensive survey of the overwhelming variety of approaches to load sharing in the literature. They identify some fundamentally distinguishing features of load sharing strategies. One important distinction refers to the side that takes the initiative in scheduling the jobs, either the sources, the servers, or both. Another distinction refers to the amount of information that is used in allocating the jobs. In purely static policies only information is used about the basic characteristics of the system, like the traffic intensities. In dynamic policies also information is used about the actual state of the system, like the queue lengths. Evidently, in principle the performance of the system may improve substantially by using such information in allocating the jobs. However, gathering such information and implementing a sophisticated dynamic allocation strategy may involve a considerable communication overhead and complicate the operation of the system significantly. Therefore, dynamic policies are not necessarily preferable to static policies.

In the present paper we assume that customers are allocated to the servers in a static probabilistic manner; upon arrival customers are sent to one of the servers according to a matrix of routing probabilities, independent of the state of the system. We are interested in the problem of finding an allocation matrix that minimizes a weighted sum of the mean waiting times.

The novelty of the model lies in the combination of heterogeneous servers (i.e. different processing rates), heterogeneous sources (i.e. different processing times), and a fairly general cost function. Buzacott & Shanthikumar [2] consider a version of the problem with homogeneous servers and the overall mean waiting time as performance measure, which we will discuss later on in greater technical detail. Buzen & Chen [3] consider a variant of the problem with a single source and the overall mean sojourn time as performance criterion. A natural approach to deal with heterogeneous servers and heterogeneous sources might be to aggregate the different sources into a single source, and then use the results of Buzen & Chen. Each server would thus handle a traffic mix of the same, heterogeneous, composition, but of possibly different intensity, depending on the processing rate of the servers. In the present paper we find however that *each server should handle a traffic mix as homogeneous as possible.*

Tantawi & Towsley [8], [9] and de Souza e Silva & Gerla [5] consider optimal load balancing models of distributed computer systems consisting of a number of heterogeneous host computers connected by a communication network. A job may be either processed at the host to which it arrives or transferred to another host. In the latter case, a transferred job incurs a communication delay in addition to the queueing delay at the host on which it is processed. The assumptions in [8], [9], and [5] on the service requirements of jobs are however somewhat restrictive.

The remainder of the paper is organized as follows. In section 2 we present a detailed model description. We expose the structure of an optimal allocation in section 3. In section 4 we describe for some special cases in detail how the structure may be exploited in actually computing an optimal allocation. In section 5 we conclude with some remarks and suggestions for further research.

2. Model description

The model under consideration consists of n customer types attended by m parallel non-identical servers. Customers arrive according to Poisson processes. The arrival rate of type-j customers is λ_j, $j = 1, \ldots, n$. The total arrival rate is $\lambda := \sum_{j=1}^{n} \lambda_j$. Upon arrival customers are routed to one of the servers. Type-j customers are routed to server i with probability x_{ij}, $i = 1, \ldots, m$, $j = 1, \ldots, n$. When processed at server i, type-j customers require service times having distribution $F_{ij}(t) = F_j(\mu_i t)$, i.e., type-j customers require amounts of service having distribution $F_j(t)$, while server i has processing rate μ_i. In other words, the servers may have different characteristics, the customer types may have different characteristics, but servers cannot 'specialize' in some of the customer types. Denote by β_j and $\beta_j^{(2)}$ the first and second moment of $F_j(t)$, $j = 1, \ldots, n$. We assume $F_j(0) < 1$, so $\beta_j > 0$, $\beta_j^{(2)} > 0$, $j = 1, \ldots, n$. Define the traffic intensity associated with type-j customers as $\rho_j := \lambda_j \beta_j$, $j = 1, \ldots, n$. The total traffic intensity is $\rho := \sum_{j=1}^{n} \rho_j$. The order of service is assumed not to discriminate between the various customer types. Further all arrival, service, and routing processes are assumed to be mutually independent.

The queues that form at the servers are ordinary $M/G/1$ queues. The arrival rate at server i is $\sum_{j=1}^{n} x_{ij}\lambda_j$. Customers that are routed to server i require service times having distribution $\sum_{j=1}^{n} x_{ij}\lambda_j F_j(\mu_i t) / \sum_{j=1}^{n} x_{ij}\lambda_j$ with first moment $[\sum_{j=1}^{n} x_{ij}\lambda_j\beta_j]/[\mu_i \sum_{j=1}^{n} x_{ij}\lambda_j]$ and second moment $[\sum_{j=1}^{n} x_{ij}\lambda_j\beta_j^{(2)}]/[\mu_i^2 \sum_{j=1}^{n} x_{ij}\lambda_j]$, $i = 1, \ldots, m$. Define the traffic intensity at server i as $\sum_{j=1}^{n} x_{ij}\lambda_j\beta_j$, $i = 1, \ldots, m$. Necessary and sufficient ergodicity conditions are

$$\sum_{j=1}^{n} x_{ij}\lambda_j\beta_j < \mu_i, \qquad i = 1, \ldots, m. \tag{2.1}$$

Denote by $\mu = \sum_{i=1}^{m} \mu_i$ the total processing rate of the servers. Summing (2.1) with respect to $i = 1, \ldots, m$ yields $\rho < \mu$, as $\sum_{i=1}^{m} x_{ij} = 1$, $j = 1, \ldots, n$. Throughout the paper $\rho < \mu$ is assumed to hold.

We are interested in the problem of finding an allocation that minimizes a weighted sum of the mean waiting times. Therefore we first derive a formula that describes the mean waiting times as function of the allocation matrix $x = (x_{ij})$. Denote by W_j the waiting time of an arbitrary type-j customer,

i.e., the time from its arrival to the start of its service. Denote by V_i the waiting time of an arbitrary customer that is routed to server i.
As the order of service is assumed not to discriminate between the various customer types,

$$EW_j = \sum_{i=1}^{m} x_{ij} EV_i, \qquad j = 1, \ldots, n. \tag{2.2}$$

As the queues that form at the servers are ordinary $M/G/1$ queues,

$$EV_i = \frac{\sum_{j=1}^{n} \lambda_j \beta_j^{(2)} x_{ij}}{2\mu_i \left(\mu_i - \sum_{j=1}^{n} \lambda_j \beta_j x_{ij} \right)}, \qquad i = 1, \ldots, m. \tag{2.3}$$

Let c_j represent the waiting cost per unit of time of a type-j customer, $j = 1, \ldots, n$. We assume $c_j > 0$, $j = 1, \ldots, n$. The mean total waiting cost per unit of time amounts to $\sum_{j=1}^{n} c_j \lambda_j EW_j$. Using (2.2) and (2.3),

$$\sum_{j=1}^{n} c_j \lambda_j EW_j = \sum_{i=1}^{m} \frac{\left(\sum_{j=1}^{n} \lambda_j c_j x_{ij} \right) \left(\sum_{j=1}^{n} \lambda_j \beta_j^{(2)} x_{ij} \right)}{2\mu_i \left(\mu_i - \sum_{j=1}^{n} \lambda_j \beta_j x_{ij} \right)}. \tag{2.4}$$

3. Finding an optimal allocation

In this section we consider the problem of finding an allocation that minimizes the mean total waiting cost per unit of time. Using (2.1) and (2.4), we formulate the problem as follows.

Problem (I).

$$\textit{min} \qquad f(x) = \sum_{i=1}^{m} \frac{\left(\sum_{j=1}^{n} \lambda_j c_j x_{ij} \right) \left(\sum_{j=1}^{n} \lambda_j \beta_j^{(2)} x_{ij} \right)}{\mu_i \left(\mu_i - \sum_{j=1}^{n} \lambda_j \beta_j x_{ij} \right)} \tag{3.1}$$

$$\textit{sub} \qquad \sum_{j=1}^{n} \lambda_j \beta_j x_{ij} < \mu_i, \qquad i = 1, \ldots, m; \tag{3.2}$$

$$\sum_{i=1}^{m} x_{ij} = 1, \qquad j = 1, \ldots, n; \tag{3.3}$$

$$x_{ij} \geq 0, \qquad i = 1, \ldots, m, \; j = 1, \ldots, n. \tag{3.4}$$

Problem (I) is a non-linear programming problem. It is easily verified that the objective function $f(\cdot)$ is not convex, so that it is not guaranteed that there exists a unique Kuhn-Tucker point. Moreover, finding a Kuhn-Tucker point is not quite straightforward.
All in all there is not an obvious way of solving problem (I). Nevertheless, if one were merely interested in computing an optimal allocation for some given parameters, then one could in principle proceed to solving problem (I) by standard non-convex programming techniques. That is however not what we are interested in here. What we are primarily interested in, is obtaining some insight into the structural properties of an optimal allocation. We will show that an optimal solution of problem (I) indeed exhibits a very characteristic structure. As secondary motivation, the structural properties do not only provide some insight, but are also very useful in calculating an optimal allocation. Specifically we will describe in section 4 how in cases with identical servers where all the customer types are in a sense ordered, the structure may be exploited in a very simple manner in actually computing an optimal solution of problem (I).

We now expose the structure of an optimal allocation x^*. We first introduce some notation. For a given allocation x, define $K_i(x) = \{j \mid x_{ij} > 0\}$ to be the index set of the customer types (partially) allocated to server i. Define $A_i(x) = \left\{ \left(\frac{c_j}{\beta_j}, \frac{\beta_j^{(2)}}{\beta_j} \right) \mid j \in K_i(x) \right\}$ to be the set of $\left(\frac{c_j}{\beta_j}, \frac{\beta_j^{(2)}}{\beta_j} \right)$-values corresponding to the customer types allocated to server i. Denote $P_i(x) = int(conv(A_i(x)))$, with int(conv($\cdot$)) denoting the interior of the convex hull. The set $P_i(x)$ may be interpreted as the global range of $\left(\frac{c_j}{\beta_j}, \frac{\beta_j^{(2)}}{\beta_j} \right)$-values corresponding to the customer types allocated to server i. Denote

$$B_i(x) = \left[\sum_{j=1}^{n} \lambda_j \beta_j^{(2)} x_{ij} \right] \Big/ \left[\mu_i \left(\mu_i - \sum_{j=1}^{n} \lambda_j \beta_j x_{ij} \right) \right],$$

$$C_i(x) = \left[\sum_{j=1}^{n} \lambda_j c_j x_{ij} \right] \Big/ \left[\mu_i \left(\mu_i - \sum_{j=1}^{n} \lambda_j \beta_j x_{ij} \right) \right].$$

The numbers $B_i(x)$ and $C_i(x)$ may be interpreted as measures for the '$\beta_j^{(2)}/\beta_j$-weight' and the 'c_j/β_j-weight' associated with the customer types allocated to server i.

We now expose the structure of an optimal allocation x^* in terms of the corresponding sets $P_i(x^*)$. Intuitively, it is to be expected that an optimal allocation will satisfy one of the following two (in general mutually exclusive) 'extremal' properties.

(i). Each server handles a traffic mix of the same composition (e.g. $x^*_{ij} = \mu_i/\mu$, $i = 1, \ldots, m$, $j = 1, \ldots, n$), so that the traffic mix at each server is completely heterogeneous;
(ii). Each server handles a traffic mix as homogeneous as possible, so that different servers deal with traffic mixes of a completely different composition. The next Lemma says that an optimal allocation in fact satisfies the second property (so the first property is *not* satisfied in general).

Lemma 3.1
$P_{i'}(x^*) \cap P_{i''}(x^*) = \emptyset$ for $i' \neq i''$.
In other words, if $\left(\frac{c_j}{\beta_j}, \frac{\beta_j^{(2)}}{\beta_j}\right) \in P_i(x^*)$, then $x^*_{ij} = 1$.

Proof
See appendix A.

□

Lemma 3.1 suggests that the customer types should be clustered according to the corresponding $\left(\frac{c_j}{\beta_j}, \frac{\beta_j^{(2)}}{\beta_j}\right)$-values. As a consequence, different servers will deal with different traffic mixes. The next Lemma says that different traffic mixes may however not involve an arbitrarily different '$\beta_j^{(2)}/\beta_j$-weight' and 'c_j/β_j-weight'.

Lemma 3.2
If $B_{i'}(x^*) \geq B_{i''}(x^*)$, $C_{i'}(x^*) \geq C_{i''}(x^*)$,
then $\mu_{i'} B_{i'}(x^*) C_{i'}(x^*) \leq \mu_{i''} B_{i''}(x^*) C_{i''}(x^*)$.

Proof
See appendix B.

□

Lemma 3.2 states that if one server carries both larger $B_i(x^*)$ and $C_i(x^*)$ than another, then it cannot carry larger $\mu_i B_i(x^*) C_i(x^*)$ as well.

In the remainder of the section, as well as in the next section, we consider the case of identical servers, i.e., $\mu_i = \mu/m$, $i = 1, \ldots, m$. Lemma 3.2 then states that it is no longer possible that one server carries both larger $B_i(x^*)$ and $C_i(x^*)$ than another.

Corollary 3.1
$B_{i'}(x^*) \geq B_{i''}(x^*) \Longleftrightarrow C_{i'}(x^*) \leq C_{i''}(x^*)$.

We now assume that the servers are indexed such that $B_{i'}(x^*) \geq B_{i''}(x^*)$, $C_{i'}(x^*) \leq C_{i''}(x^*)$ for $i' < i''$.

Lemma 3.3
Assume $x^*_{i'j'} > 0$, $x^*_{i''j''} > 0$.
If $\frac{c_{j'}}{\beta_{j'}} \leq \frac{c_{j''}}{\beta_{j''}}$, $\frac{\beta^{(2)}_{j'}}{\beta_{j'}} \geq \frac{\beta^{(2)}_{j''}}{\beta_{j''}}$, $\left(\frac{c_{j'}}{\beta_{j'}}, \frac{\beta^{(2)}_{j'}}{\beta_{j'}}\right) \neq \left(\frac{c_{j''}}{\beta_{j''}}, \frac{\beta^{(2)}_{j''}}{\beta_{j''}}\right)$, then $i' \leq i''$.

Proof
See appendix C.

□

Lemma 3.3 states that expensive, calm (cheap, wild) customer types with large (small) c_j/β_j and small (large) $\beta^{(2)}_j/\beta_j$ should be sent to servers with small (large) $B_i(x^*)$ and large (small) $C_i(x^*)$, thus experiencing a small (large) waiting time. Lemma 3.3 does however not indicate what should be done with expensive but wild (cheap but calm) customer types with large (small) c_j/β_j and large (small) $\beta^{(2)}_j/\beta_j$. Indeed, it depends not only on their own individual c_j/β_j and $\beta^{(2)}_j/\beta_j$, but also on some other more involved factors whether they should be sent to servers with small $B_i(x^*)$ and large $C_i(x^*)$ or with large $B_i(x^*)$ and small $C_i(x^*)$.
Lemma 3.3 allows us to strengthen the statements on the clustering of the customer types in Lemma 3.1. We first introduce some additional notation. Define

$$Q_i(x) = \bigcup_{j \in K_i(x)} \left\{ (y,z) : y \leq \frac{c_j}{\beta_j}, z \geq \frac{\beta^{(2)}_j}{\beta_j}, (y,z) \neq \left(\frac{c_j}{\beta_j}, \frac{\beta^{(2)}_j}{\beta_j}\right) \right\},$$

$$R_i(x) = \bigcup_{j \in K_i(x)} \left\{ (y,z) : y \geq \frac{c_j}{\beta_j}, z \leq \frac{\beta^{(2)}_j}{\beta_j}, (y,z) \neq \left(\frac{c_j}{\beta_j}, \frac{\beta^{(2)}_j}{\beta_j}\right) \right\}.$$

Denote $S_i(x) = Q_i(x) \cap R_i(x)$, $T_i(x) = P_i(x) \cup S_i(x)$. See Figure 3.1, where the bold dots constitute the set $A_i(x)$. The area inside the dotted lines corresponds to the set $P_i(x)$. The rectangular area represents the set $S_i(x)$.

Lemma 3.4
$T_{i'}(x^*) \cap T_{i''}(x^*) = \emptyset$ for $i' \neq i''$.
In other words, if $\left(\frac{c_j}{\beta_j}, \frac{\beta^{(2)}_j}{\beta_j}\right) \in T_i(x^*)$, then $x^*_{ij} = 1$.

Proof
See appendix D.

□

Lemma 3.4 suggests that in the case of identical servers, the customer types should be clustered according to the corresponding $\left(\frac{c_j}{\beta_j}, \frac{\beta_j^{(2)}}{\beta_j}\right)$-values in an even stronger sense than stated before in Lemma 3.1.
The optimality of clustering implies that the optimal routing probabilities are almost all equal to either 0 or 1. Although the settings are quite different, the latter observation strongly reminds of the vertex-allocation theorem for the optimal routing of single customer chains in closed product-form networks, saying that each customer should consistently select the same server for each request type rather than choose probabilistically, cf. Cheng & Muntz [4], Tripathi & Woodside [10], Woodside & Tripathi [11].

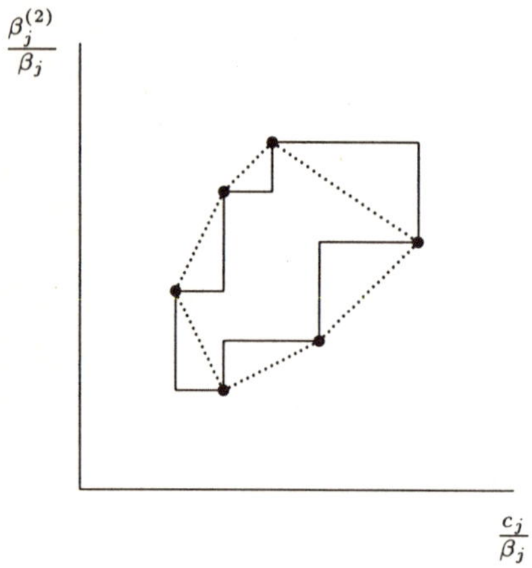

Figure 3.1 The sets $P_i(x)$ and $S_i(x)$.

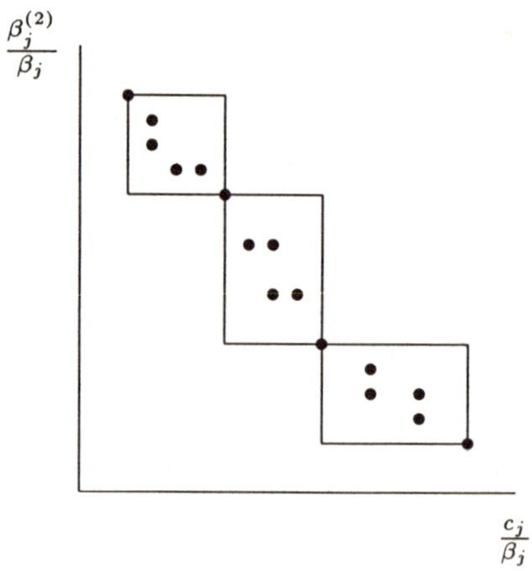

Figure 4.1 The case of ordered customer types.

4. The case of ordered customer types

In this section we show how the structure, as characterized in the Lemma's of the previous section, may be exploited in computing an optimal allocation. We make the following simplifying assumption.

Assumption 4.1 The customer types are ordered such that $\frac{c_{j'}}{\beta_{j'}} \leq \frac{c_{j''}}{\beta_{j''}}$, $\frac{\beta_{j'}^{(2)}}{\beta_{j'}} \geq \frac{\beta_{j''}^{(2)}}{\beta_{j''}}$, $\left(\frac{c_{j'}}{\beta_{j'}}, \frac{\beta_{j'}^{(2)}}{\beta_{j'}}\right) \neq \left(\frac{c_{j''}}{\beta_{j''}}, \frac{\beta_{j''}^{(2)}}{\beta_{j''}}\right)$ for $j' < j''$.

□

Note that if Assumption 4.1 is satisfied $P_i(x) \subseteq S_i(x)$ so that $T_i(x) = S_i(x)$. Lemma 3.4 then provides a very strong characterization of an optimal allocation. See Figure 4.1, where the rectangles represent the sets $T_i(x)$ for an instance with $m = 3$ servers and $n = 16$ customer types. The fact that the sets $T_i(x)$ do not intersect, completely determines their 'position', so that the only problem remaining is to determine their 'size'.
Theoretically speaking, Assumption 4.1 is somewhat restrictive. However, there are several cases of practical interest that satisfy Assumption 4.1.

Case i. $c_j/\beta_j = \gamma$, $j = 1, \ldots, n$.
In other words, the waiting costs per unit of time are proportional to the mean service times. This is the case when the goal is minimizing the mean amount of work or, when the customer types have the same mean service time, minimizing the overall mean waiting time.
For $c_j/\beta_j = \gamma$, $j = 1, \ldots, n$, the set $T_i(x)$ reduces to the line-segment

$$\left\{ (\gamma, z) \mid \min_{j \in K_i(x)} \frac{\beta_j^{(2)}}{\beta_j} < z < \max_{j \in K_i(x)} \frac{\beta_j^{(2)}}{\beta_j} \right\}.$$

Thus Lemma 3.4 says that the customer types should be clustered according to the corresponding $\beta_j^{(2)}/\beta_j$-values. As indicated in [1], this means that $\sum_{i=1}^{m} \rho_j x_{ij}^* = \rho/m$ for all $i = 1, \ldots, m$, will only hold when all the customer types not only have the same $c_j/\beta_j = \gamma$, but also happen to have the same $\beta_j^{(2)}/\beta_j$. So the total load should *not* be completely balanced in general.

Case ii. $\beta_j^{(2)}/\beta_j = \delta$, $j = 1, \ldots, n$.
In other words, the mean residual service times are constant. This is the case when the customer types have the same service time characteristics, but different priorities, reflected in different waiting costs per unit of time.
For $\beta_j^{(2)}/\beta_j = \delta$, $j = 1, \ldots, n$, the set $T_i(x)$ reduces to the line-segment

$$\left\{ (y, \delta) \mid \min_{j \in K_i(x)} \frac{c_j}{\beta_j} < y < \max_{j \in K_i(x)} \frac{c_j}{\beta_j} \right\}.$$

Thus Lemma 3.4 says that the customer types should be clustered according to the corresponding c_j/β_j-values (which strongly reminds of the $c\mu$-rule, cf. [7], although the $c\mu$-rule in fact refers to the order of service of customer types rather than the clustering of customer types). As derived in [1], this implies that $\sum_{i=1}^{m} \rho_j x_{ij}^* = \rho/m$ for all $i = 1, \ldots, m$, will only hold when all the customer types not only have the same $\beta_j^{(2)}/\beta_j = \delta$, but also happen to have the same c_j/β_j. So again we may conclude that the total load should *not* be completely balanced in general.

Case iii. $c_j = c$, $j = 1, \dots, n$, $\beta_{j'} \le \beta_{j''} \iff \beta_{j'}^{(2)}/\beta_{j'} \le \beta_{j''}^{(2)}/\beta_{j''}$.
In other words, the waiting costs per unit of time are constant. This is the case when the goal is minimizing the overall mean waiting time. Moreover, a larger mean service time corresponds to a larger mean residual service time. For the majority of service time distributions this is indeed the case.
Lemma 3.4 then says that the customer types should be clustered according to the corresponding β_j-values. Again it may verified that the total load should *not* be completely balanced, unless the values of λ_j, β_j, $\beta_j^{(2)}$ happen to satisfy some very specific relationships.

Remark 4.1 Buzacott & Shanthikumar [2] consider the problem of finding an optimal allocation in the case $c_j = c = 1$, $j = 1, \dots, n$, i.e., the goal is minimizing the mean overall waiting time. In addition they require that the total load be balanced. They show that if the agreeability condition $\beta_{j'} \le \beta_{j''} \iff \beta_{j'}^{(2)}/\beta_{j'} \le \beta_{j''}^{(2)}/\beta_{j''}$ is satisfied, then the customer types should be clustered according to the corresponding β_j-values, as we also concluded in Case iii. above, *without* requiring that the total load be balanced. In fact we concluded in Case iii. that the total load should *not* be completely balanced.

□

We now describe a method for determining an optimal allocation in cases that satisfy Assumption 4.1. Here we sketch the main idea of the method. In appendix E of [1] the method is described in greater detail.
Denote by $x_i = (x_{i1}, \dots, x_{in})$ the allocation to server i. From Lemma 3.4 we know that the structure of an optimal allocation is such that (i) $x_i^* = (0, \dots, 0, x_{ij_i'}^*, 1, \dots, 1, x_{ij_i''}^*, 0, \dots, 0)$ with $j_i'' = \max\{j : x_{ij}^* > 0\}$, $j_i'' = j_{i+1}'$. This knowledge, together with (ii) $\left\{\frac{\partial f(x)}{\partial x_{ij_i''}}\right\}_{|x=x^*} = \left\{\frac{\partial f(x)}{\partial x_{i+1 j_{i+1}'}}\right\}_{|x=x^*}$, allows us to essentially reduce the search for an optimal allocation in $m \times n$ dimensions to a binary search with regard to $s_1 = \sum_{j=1}^{n} x_{1j}$.
Step 1. Determine a lower and an upper bound for s_1^*.
Step 2. Make an estimate s_1 for s_1^*, somewhere in between lower and upper bound, which directly determines x_1.
Step 3. Given x_i, determine x_{i+1}, for $i = 1, 2, \dots, m-1$, from (i), (ii). In appendix E of [1] it is shown that through (i), (ii) x_i uniquely determines x_{i+1}, $i = 1, 2, \dots m-1$.
Step 4. Sooner or later one either runs out of servers or out of customer types. If one runs out of servers, then apparently $s_1 < s_1^*$, so then replace the old lower bound by s_1. If one runs out of customer types, then apparently $s_1 > s_1^*$, so then replace the old upper bound by s_1. Repeat the procedure until lower and upper bound are sufficiently close.

5. Concluding remarks and suggestions for further research

We considered the problem of finding an allocation that minimizes the mean total waiting cost per unit of time. We showed that the customer types should be clustered according to the corresponding $\left(\frac{c_j}{\beta_j}, \frac{\beta_j^{(2)}}{\beta_j}\right)$-values and we described for some special cases how that property may be exploited in computing an optimal allocation. In other cases (e.g. when the customer types are not ordered in the sense of Assumption 4.1), that property may still be exploited in calculating an optimal allocation, but not in a manner as simple. An interesting topic for further research might be to develop efficient (heuristic) methods for this.

In some situations it may be desirable that customer types are not split among different servers, in other words, that all the routing probabilities, the x_{ij}'s, are either 0 or 1. In that case, the problem of finding even a feasible solution is NP-hard, cf. [6], but in [1] it is indicated how the structure of an optimal non-integer allocation as exposed in the previous sections may still be used as a heuristic guideline in searching for an optimal integer allocation.

In the present paper we assumed that, in principle, any customer type could be allocated to any server. In some situations it may however occur that some customer types cannot be allocated to some servers, or that some customer types cannot be combined. Such restrictions may also be translated into additional constraints on the routing probabilities. It would be interesting to investigate how those restrictions on the x_{ij}'s affect the structure of an optimal allocation.

In the present paper we assumed the processing rates to be fixed. A natural extension to the model would be the simultaneous optimization of the processing rates, under the condition $\sum_{i=1}^{m} \mu_i = \mu$, the total processing rate μ being given. A further extension would be the simultaneous determination of the optimal number of servers, again with μ being given. The latter problem raises closely related issues, for example the question when resource sharing is preferable to complete partitioning.

Acknowledgement. The author is grateful to O.J. Boxma for several valuable discussions. Further the author is indebted to J. van den Berg for some useful suggestions concerning the proof of Lemma 3.3.

References

1. S.C. Borst, "Optimal probabilistic allocation of customer types to servers", CWI Report BS-R9415, 1994.

2. J.A. Buzacott and J.G. Shanthikumar, "Design of manufacturing systems using queueing models", *Queueing Systems* **12**, *Special Issue on Queueing Models of Manufacturing Systems*, pp. 135–213, 1992.
3. J.P. Buzen and P.P.-S. Chen, "Optimal load balancing in memory hierarchies", In: *Proc. IFIP 1974*, ed. J.L. Rosenfeld (North-Holland, Amsterdam), pp. 271–275, 1974.
4. W.C. Cheng and R.R. Muntz, "Optimal routing for closed queueing networks", In: *Perf. '90*, eds. P.J.B. King, I. Mitrani, R.J. Pooley (North-Holland, Amsterdam), pp. 3–17, 1990.
5. E. De Souza e Silva and M. Gerla, "Load balancing in distributed systems with multiple classes and site constraints", In: *Perf. '84*, ed. E. Gelenbe (North-Holland, Amsterdam), pp. 17–33, 1984.
6. M.R. Garey and D.S. Johnson, "Computers and Intractability: a Guide to the Theory of NP-Completeness", (Freeman, San Francisco), 1979.
7. I. Meilijson and U. Yechiali, "On optimal right-of-way policies at a single-server station when insertion of idle times is permitted", *Stoch. Proc. Appl.* **6**, pp. 25–32, 1977.
8. A.N. Tantawi and D. Towsley, "A general model for optimal static load balancing in star network configurations", In: *Perf. '84*, ed. E. Gelenbe (North-Holland, Amsterdam), pp. 277–291, 1984.
9. A.N. Tantawi and D. Towsley, "Optimal static load balancing in distributed computer systems", *J. ACM* **32**, pp. 445–465, 1985.
10. S.K. Tripathi and C.M. Woodside, "A vertex-allocation theorem for resources in queueing networks", *J. ACM* **35**, pp. 221–230, 1988.
11. C.M. Woodside and S.K. Tripathi, "Optimal allocation of file servers in a local network environment", IEEE *Trans. Softw. Eng.* **12**, pp. 844–848, 1986.
12. Y.-T. Wang and R.J.T. Morris, "Load sharing in distributed systems", IEEE *Trans. Comp.* **34**, pp. 204–217, 1985.

Appendices

A. Proof of Lemma 3.1

Lemma 3.1
$P_{i'}(x^*) \cap P_{i''}(x^*) = \emptyset$ for $i' \neq i''$.
In other words, if $\left(\frac{c_j}{\beta_j}, \frac{\beta_j^{(2)}}{\beta_j}\right) \in P_i(x^*)$, then $x_{ij}^* = 1$.

Proof
Suppose not. So, by definition of $P_i(x^*)$, there exist k_0, i', i'', $i' \neq i''$, such that

$$\left(\frac{c_{k_0}}{\beta_{k_0}}, \frac{\beta_{k_0}^{(2)}}{\beta_{k_0}}\right) = \sum_{k \in K_{i''}(x^*)} \alpha_k \left(\frac{c_k}{\beta_k}, \frac{\beta_k^{(2)}}{\beta_k}\right), \tag{A.1}$$

with $x_{i'k_0}^* > 0$, $x_{i''k}^* > 0$, $\alpha_k \geq 0$, $k \in K_{i''}(x^*)$, $\sum_{k \in K_{i''}(x^*)} \alpha_k = 1$. Moreover, not all the points $\left(\frac{c_k}{\beta_k}, \frac{\beta_k^{(2)}}{\beta_k}\right)$ with $\alpha_k > 0$ lie on a line, i.e., there is no linear equality that is satisfied by all the points $\left(\frac{c_k}{\beta_k}, \frac{\beta_k^{(2)}}{\beta_k}\right)$ with $\alpha_k > 0$.

Since x^* is an optimal solution of problem (I), the first-order effect on $f(x)$ around x^* of transferring a customer type from one server to another cannot be negative, i.e., $\left\{\frac{\partial f(x)}{\partial x_{i''k_0}} - \frac{\partial f(x)}{\partial x_{i'k_0}}\right\}_{|x=x^*} \geq 0$, $\left\{\frac{\partial f(x)}{\partial x_{i'k}} - \frac{\partial f(x)}{\partial x_{i''k}}\right\}_{|x=x^*} \geq 0$, $k \in K_{i''}(x^*)$, which may also be formally verified from the Kuhn-Tucker conditions.

Differentiating $f(\cdot)$ once,

$$\frac{\partial f(x)}{\partial x_{ij}} = \lambda_j c_j B_i(x) + \lambda_j \beta_j^{(2)} C_i(x) + \lambda_j \beta_j \mu_i B_i(x) C_i(x). \tag{A.2}$$

From (A.1),

$$\lambda_{k_0}(c_{k_0}, \beta_{k_0}^{(2)}, \beta_{k_0}) = \sum_{k \in K_{i''}(x^*)} \alpha_k \frac{\lambda_{k_0}\beta_{k_0}}{\lambda_k \beta_k} \lambda_k(c_k, \beta_k^{(2)}, \beta_k).$$

So

$$\left\{\frac{\partial f(x)}{\partial x_{i''k_0}} - \frac{\partial f(x)}{\partial x_{i'k_0}}\right\}_{|x=x^*} = --- \sum_{k \in K_{i''}(x^*)} \alpha_k \frac{\lambda_{k_0}\beta_{k_0}}{\lambda_k \beta_k} \left\{\frac{\partial f(x)}{\partial x_{i'k}} - \frac{\partial f(x)}{\partial x_{i''k}}\right\}_{|x=x^*}$$

As $\left\{\frac{\partial f(x)}{\partial x_{i''k_0}} - \frac{\partial f(x)}{\partial x_{i'k_0}}\right\}_{|x=x^*} \geq 0$, $\alpha_k \left\{\frac{\partial f(x)}{\partial x_{i'k}} - \frac{\partial f(x)}{\partial x_{i''k}}\right\}_{|x=x^*} \geq 0$, $k \in K_{i''}(x^*)$, we conclude that $\alpha_k \left\{\frac{\partial f(x)}{\partial x_{i'k}} - \frac{\partial f(x)}{\partial x_{i''k}}\right\}_{|x=x^*} = 0$, $k \in K_{i''}(x^*)$. So

$$\frac{c_k}{\beta_k}(B_{i'}(x^*) - B_{i''}(x^*)) + \frac{\beta_k^{(2)}}{\beta_k}(C_{i'}(x^*) - C_{i''}(x^*)) =$$

$$\mu_{i''} B_{i''}(x^*) C_{i''}(x^*) - \mu_{i'} B_{i'}(x^*) C_{i'}(x^*)$$

for all the points $\left(\frac{c_k}{\beta_k}, \frac{\beta_k^{(2)}}{\beta_k}\right)$ with $\alpha_k > 0$, i.e., there *is* a linear equality that is satisfied by all the points $\left(\frac{c_k}{\beta_k}, \frac{\beta_k^{(2)}}{\beta_k}\right)$ with $\alpha_k > 0$. Contradiction.

□

B. Proof of Lemma 3.2

Lemma 3.2
If $B_{i'}(x^*) \geq B_{i''}(x^*)$, $C_{i'}(x^*) \geq C_{i''}(x^*)$,
then $\mu_{i'} B_{i'}(x^*) C_{i'}(x^*) \leq \mu_{i''} B_{i''}(x^*) C_{i''}(x^*)$.

Proof
Suppose not, i.e.,

$$B_{i'}(x^*) \geq B_{i''}(x^*), C_{i'}(x^*) \geq C_{i''}(x^*), \tag{B.1}$$

$$\mu_{i'} B_{i'}(x^*) C_{i'}(x^*) > \mu_{i''} B_{i''}(x^*) C_{i''}(x^*).$$

Take k_0 such that $x^*_{i'k_0} > 0$.
As x^* is an optimal solution of problem (I), $\left\{ \frac{\partial f(x)}{\partial x_{i''k_0}} - \frac{\partial f(x)}{\partial x_{i'k_0}} \right\}_{|x=x^*} \geq 0$.
From (A.2), if (B.1) were to hold, $\left\{ \frac{\partial f(x)}{\partial x_{i''k_0}} - \frac{\partial f(x)}{\partial x_{i'k_0}} \right\}_{|x=x^*} < 0$. Contradiction.

□

C. Proof of Lemma 3.3

Lemma 3.3
Assume $x^*_{i'j'} > 0$, $x^*_{i''j''} > 0$.
If $\frac{c_{j'}}{\beta_{j'}} \leq \frac{c_{j''}}{\beta_{j''}}$, $\frac{\beta^{(2)}_{j'}}{\beta_{j'}} \geq \frac{\beta^{(2)}_{j''}}{\beta_{j''}}$, $\left(\frac{c_{j'}}{\beta_{j'}}, \frac{\beta^{(2)}_{j'}}{\beta_{j'}} \right) \neq \left(\frac{c_{j''}}{\beta_{j''}}, \frac{\beta^{(2)}_{j''}}{\beta_{j''}} \right)$, then $i' \leq i''$.

Proof
Suppose not, i.e., $x^*_{i'j'} > 0$, $x^*_{i''j''} > 0$, $i' \neq i''$,

$$\frac{c_{j'}}{\beta_{j'}} \leq \frac{c_{j''}}{\beta_{j''}}, \frac{\beta^{(2)}_{j'}}{\beta_{j'}} \geq \frac{\beta^{(2)}_{j''}}{\beta_{j''}}, \left(\frac{c_{j'}}{\beta_{j'}}, \frac{\beta^{(2)}_{j'}}{\beta_{j'}} \right) \neq \left(\frac{c_{j''}}{\beta_{j''}}, \frac{\beta^{(2)}_{j''}}{\beta_{j''}} \right), \tag{C.1}$$

$$B_{i'}(x^*) \leq B_{i''}(x^*), \;\; C_{i'}(x^*) \geq C_{i''}(x^*).$$

As x^* is an optimal solution of problem (I), $\left\{ \frac{\partial f(x)}{\partial x_{i''j'}} - \frac{\partial f(x)}{\partial x_{i'j'}} \right\}_{|x=x^*} \geq 0$,
$\left\{ \frac{\partial f(x)}{\partial x_{i'j''}} - \frac{\partial f(x)}{\partial x_{i''j''}} \right\}_{|x=x^*} \geq 0$.
From (A.2),

$$\frac{1}{\lambda_{j'}\beta_{j'}}\left\{\frac{\partial f(x)}{\partial x_{i''j'}}-\frac{\partial f(x)}{\partial x_{i'j'}}\right\}+\frac{1}{\lambda_{j''}\beta_{j''}}\left\{\frac{\partial f(x)}{\partial x_{i'j''}}-\frac{\partial f(x)}{\partial x_{i''j''}}\right\}=$$

$$\left(\frac{c_{j'}}{\beta_{j'}}-\frac{c_{j''}}{\beta_{j''}}\right)(B_{i''}(x)-B_{i'}(x))+\left(\frac{\beta^{(2)}_{j'}}{\beta_{j'}}-\frac{\beta^{(2)}_{j''}}{\beta_{j''}}\right)(C_{i''}(x)-C_{i'}(x)).$$

So, if (C.1) were to hold, then

$$\lambda_{j''}\beta_{j''}\left\{\frac{\partial f(x)}{\partial x_{i''j'}}-\frac{\partial f(x)}{\partial x_{i'j'}}\right\}_{|x=x^*}+\lambda_{j'}\beta_{j'}\left\{\frac{\partial f(x)}{\partial x_{i'j''}}-\frac{\partial f(x)}{\partial x_{i''j''}}\right\}_{|x=x^*}\leq 0.$$

Contradiction, unless $\left\{\frac{\partial f(x)}{\partial x_{i''j'}}-\frac{\partial f(x)}{\partial x_{i'j'}}\right\}_{|x=x^*}=0,\left\{\frac{\partial f(x)}{\partial x_{i'j''}}-\frac{\partial f(x)}{\partial x_{i''j''}}\right\}_{|x=x^*}=0.$
In that case the second-order effect on $f(x)$ around x^* of transferring customer types from one server to another cannot be negative, after which differentiating $f(\cdot)$ twice completes the proof, cf. [1].

□

D. Proof of Lemma 3.4

Lemma 3.4
$T_{i'}(x^*)\cap T_{i''}(x^*)=\emptyset$ for $i'\neq i''$.
In other words, if $\left(\frac{c_j}{\beta_j},\frac{\beta^{(2)}_j}{\beta_j}\right)\in T_i(x^*)$, then $x^*_{ij}=1$.

Proof
Suppose not. From Lemma 3.1 $P_{i'}(x^*)\cap P_{i''}(x^*)=\emptyset$. So, by definition of $P_i(x^*)$, $S_i(x^*)$, $T_i(x^*)$, there exist i', i'', $i'\neq i''$, $j'_{i'},j''_{i'}\in K_{i'}(x^*)$, $j'_{i''},j''_{i''}\in K_{i''}(x^*)$ (possibly either $j'_{i'}=j''_{i'}$ or $j'_{i''}=j''_{i''}$), such that

$$\frac{c_{j'_{i'}}}{\beta_{j'_{i'}}}\leq\frac{c_{j''_{i''}}}{\beta_{j''_{i''}}},\ \frac{\beta^{(2)}_{j'_{i'}}}{\beta_{j'_{i'}}}\geq\frac{\beta^{(2)}_{j''_{i''}}}{\beta_{j''_{i''}}},\ \left(\frac{c_{j'_{i'}}}{\beta_{j'_{i'}}},\frac{\beta^{(2)}_{j'_{i'}}}{\beta_{j'_{i'}}}\right)\neq\left(\frac{c_{j''_{i''}}}{\beta_{j''_{i''}}},\frac{\beta^{(2)}_{j''_{i''}}}{\beta_{j''_{i''}}}\right),$$

$$\frac{c_{j''_{i'}}}{\beta_{j''_{i'}}}\geq\frac{c_{j'_{i''}}}{\beta_{j'_{i''}}},\ \frac{\beta^{(2)}_{j''_{i'}}}{\beta_{j''_{i'}}}\leq\frac{\beta^{(2)}_{j'_{i''}}}{\beta_{j'_{i''}}},\ \left(\frac{c_{j''_{i'}}}{\beta_{j''_{i'}}},\frac{\beta^{(2)}_{j''_{i'}}}{\beta_{j''_{i'}}}\right)\neq\left(\frac{c_{j'_{i''}}}{\beta_{j'_{i''}}},\frac{\beta^{(2)}_{j'_{i''}}}{\beta_{j'_{i''}}}\right).$$

According to Lemma 3.3, on the one hand, $i'\leq i''$, as $x^*_{i'j'_{i'}}>0$, $x^*_{i''j''_{i''}}>0$; on the other hand, $i'\geq i''$, as $x^*_{i'j''_{i'}}>0$, $x^*_{i''j'_{i''}}>0$, So $i'=i''$. Contradiction.

□

Majorization and Stochastic Comparison Techniques for Scheduling of Parallel Systems

Z. Liu

INRIA Sophia Antipolis, France

Summary. Stochastic scheduling of parallel systems is a recent research area in computer science as well as in operations research. The problem under consideration in this chapter is the scheduling of parallel computations which are modeled by task graphs in multiprocessor systems. The particularity of this study is that task running times are assumed to be random variables, instead of known constants as in the literature of deterministic scheduling. Our goal here is to illustrate one of the most successful approaches, based on sample path analysis and stochastic comparison techniques, for solving such scheduling problems. Both monoprogrammed and multiprogrammed parallel systems are analyzed. New results are presented for these models.

Keywords. Stochastic Scheduling, Parallel Computation, Precedence Constraint, Makespan, Lateness, Stochastic Ordering, Majorization, Sample Path Analysis.

1. Introduction

Parallel programs are usually modeled by *task graphs* which are directed acyclic graphs. Their vertices represent *tasks* and arcs represent *precedence relations* between tasks. These tasks are to be executed on parallel processors subject to precedence constraints: a task can start execution only when all its predecessor tasks have completed execution. A parallel program, or simply a *job*, is said to finish its execution if all its tasks complete executions. This completion time is referred to the *job completion time*. In a *monoprogrammed system*, at any time instant only tasks belong to the same job can run simultaneously on different processors, whereas in a *multiprogrammed system*, a sequence of jobs arrive in the system and tasks belong to different jobs can run simultaneously.

For any given set of tasks, the scheduling problem consists in assigning tasks to available processors and schedule their executions in such a way that a task is assigned to only one processor, a processor executes at most one task at any time, and the precedence constraints are satisfied. In a monoprogrammed system, the goal of scheduling is to minimize the *makespan* (or *schedule length*), i.e. the job completion time. In a multiprogrammed system, however, the objective function becomes the job *response time*, defined as the difference between the job completion time and its arrival time. When a due date, or (soft) deadline, is associated with the jobs, the objective function can be the *lateness*, defined as the difference between the job completion time and its due date.

Due to the partial order relation defined on the set of tasks, such a scheduling problem is NP-hard in general (see [26]), even when the task running times are equal. The reader is referred to [14] for a survey of complexity results and optimal polynomial algorithms for special cases.

Most scheduling literature is concerned with the deterministic scheduling problem, where task running times are assumed to be known constants. However, in practice, task running times are difficult to obtain in advance. For example, when a task contains loops, the number of iterations can depend on the input data. Even if a task contains a fixed number of executions of several instructions, the number of memory cycles per instruction can depend on the contentions on shared memory.

In this chapter, we consider the scheduling problem where task running times are random variables. Our goal here is to illustrate one of the most successful approaches, the one based on sample path analysis and stochastic comparison techniques, for solving such scheduling problems. We will consider both monoprogrammed and multiprogrammed systems. We shall first review the related literature, and then derive some new results on these problems.

This chapter is organized as follows. In the next section, we define notions of majorization and stochastic ordering, and present their properties which are useful in stochastic scheduling. In Sections 3. and 4., we consider the scheduling problems in monoprogrammed systems and multiprogrammed systems, respectively. We use the sample path analysis combined with the stochastic comparison techniques to derive optimal scheduling policies in some particular cases. Concluding remarks are provided in Section 5..

2. Majorization and Stochastic Orders

In scheduling of parallel systems, due to precedence relations arising in task graphs, and due also to multidimensional performance measures in multiprogrammed systems, it is necessary to compare (deterministic or random) graphs and (real or random) vectors. In this section we introduce useful notions for such comparisons.

2.1 Comparison of Real Vectors

Define first notions used in the comparison of real vectors. Let $\boldsymbol{x} = (x_1, x_2, \cdots, x_n)$, $\boldsymbol{y} = (y_1, y_2, \cdots, y_n) \in I\!R^n$ be two real vectors. The usual comparison is the *component-wise inequality* $\leq$: $\boldsymbol{x}$ is said to be smaller than $\boldsymbol{y}$, denoted $\boldsymbol{x} \leq \boldsymbol{y}$, if $x_k \leq y_k$ $\forall k \in \{1, 2, \ldots, n\}$.

This inequality is quite strong and are not fulfilled by many pairs of vectors. Instead, the *partial-sum inequality* $\prec_p$ can be used: $\boldsymbol{x}$ is said to be smaller than $\boldsymbol{y}$ in the partial-sum sense, denoted $\boldsymbol{x} \prec_p \boldsymbol{y}$, if $\sum_{i=1}^{k} x_i \leq \sum_{i=1}^{k} y_i$, $\forall k \in \{1, 2, \ldots, n\}$.

An ordered partial-sum inequality results in the *weak majorization* $\prec_w$: $\boldsymbol{x}$ is said to be weakly majorized by $\boldsymbol{y}$, denoted $\boldsymbol{x} \prec_w \boldsymbol{y}$, if $\sum_{i=1}^k x_{[i]} \leq \sum_{i=1}^k y_{[i]}$, $\forall k \in \{1, 2, \ldots, n\}$, where $x_{[i]}$ (resp. $y_{[i]}$) is the i-th largest component of x (resp. y).

The weak majorization becomes *Schur majorization* when the two vectors have the same total sum: $\boldsymbol{x} \prec \boldsymbol{y}$ if $\boldsymbol{x} \prec_w \boldsymbol{y}$ and $\sum_{i=1}^n x_{[i]} \leq \sum_{i=1}^n y_{[i]}$. As an example, $(2,3,1) \prec (0,5,1)$.

A function $f : I\!R^n \to I\!R$ is called *Schur convex function* if $\boldsymbol{x} \prec \boldsymbol{y}$ implies $f(\boldsymbol{x}) \leq f(\boldsymbol{y})$. A function $f : I\!R^n \to I\!R$ is called *increasing Schur convex function* if $\boldsymbol{x} \prec_w \boldsymbol{y}$ implies $f(\boldsymbol{x}) \leq f(\boldsymbol{y})$. It can be shown that f is an increasing Schur convex function iff f is increasing and Schur convex.

It is clear that $\leq$ implies $\prec_p$ and $\prec_w$, and $\prec$ implies $\prec_w$. There are various properties established for weak majorization and Schur majorization. The interested reader is referred to [18]. We present here some of them which are frequently used in scheduling problems.

Proposition 2.1. *Let $\boldsymbol{x}, \boldsymbol{y}, \boldsymbol{z}, \in I\!R^n$, $\boldsymbol{w}_1, \boldsymbol{w}_2 \in I\!R^m$.*

- *Concatenation: if $\boldsymbol{x} \prec \boldsymbol{y}$ and $\boldsymbol{w}_1 \prec \boldsymbol{w}_2$ then $(\boldsymbol{x}, \boldsymbol{w}_1) \prec (\boldsymbol{y}, \boldsymbol{w}_2)$;* *if $\boldsymbol{x} \prec_w \boldsymbol{y}$ and $\boldsymbol{w}_1 \prec_w \boldsymbol{w}_2$ then $(\boldsymbol{x}, \boldsymbol{w}_1) \prec_w (\boldsymbol{y}, \boldsymbol{w}_2)$.*
- *Characterization: let $f : I\!R \to I\!R$.* *$\boldsymbol{x} \prec \boldsymbol{y}$ iff $\sum_{i=1}^n f(x_i) \leq \sum_{i=1}^n f(y_i)$ for all convex f;* *$\boldsymbol{x} \prec_w \boldsymbol{y}$ iff $\sum_{i=1}^n f(x_i) \leq \sum_{i=1}^n f(y_i)$ for all increasing and convex f.*

2.2 Comparison of Random Vectors

Many orderings between random vectors can be defined by integral inequalities. They are thus called *integral stochastic orderings*. Let $\boldsymbol{X} = (X_1, X_2, \cdots, X_n)$ and $\boldsymbol{Y} = (Y_1, Y_2, \cdots, Y_n)$ be two random vectors in $I\!R^n$, where n is an arbitrary strictly positive integer.

Let C_L be a class of functions from $I\!R^n$ to $I\!R$. The random vector $\boldsymbol{X}$ is said to be smaller than the random vector $\boldsymbol{Y}$ in the sense of $\leq_{\mathcal{L}}$, noted $X \leq_{\mathcal{L}} Y$, if $\forall f \in C_L$, $E[f(X)] \leq E[f(Y)]$, provided that the expectations exist. The binary relation $\leq_{\mathcal{L}}$ is called the integral stochastic ordering, or simply the *stochastic ordering*, generated by the class of functions C_L.

A binary relation $\leq_{\mathcal{L}}$ thus defined is known to realize a partial preordering on the space of real distribution functions (or random variables) on $I\!R^n$. We shall often use "ordering" instead of "preordering".

Various integral stochastic orderings are thus defined:

- *(strong) stochastic ordering*: $\boldsymbol{X} \leq_{st} \boldsymbol{Y}$ if $C_L = \{$increasing functions$\}$;
- *convex ordering*: $\boldsymbol{X} \leq_{cx} \boldsymbol{Y}$ if $C_L = \{$convex functions$\}$;
- *increasing convex ordering*: $\boldsymbol{X} \leq_{icx} \boldsymbol{Y}$ if $C_L = \{$ increasing and convex functions $\}$;
- *concave ordering*: $\boldsymbol{X} \leq_{cv} \boldsymbol{Y}$ if $C_L = \{$concave functions$\}$;

- *increasing concave ordering*: $\boldsymbol{X} \leq_{icv} \boldsymbol{Y}$ if $\mathcal{C}_L = \{$ increasing and concave functions $\}$;

These five relations are actually partial orders. Other examples include the class "increasing product" functions, that is: $f(x_1, \ldots, x_n) = \prod_1^n f_i(x_i)$, where for all i, $f_i : \mathbb{R} \to \mathbb{R}$ is increasing. When $f_i(x_i)$ is a polynomial with positive coefficients, this class is called the class of "moment functions", noted $\mathcal{C}_m^n$. One may also consider the class of linear functions $\mathcal{C}_l^n$, for which the relation $X \leq_l Y$ reduces to $EX \leq EY$.

The following simple properties are very useful:

$$\begin{aligned}
\boldsymbol{X} \leq_{st} \boldsymbol{Y} &\Rightarrow P(\boldsymbol{X} > \boldsymbol{x}) \leq P(\boldsymbol{Y} > \boldsymbol{x}) \\
\boldsymbol{X} \leq_{cx} \boldsymbol{Y} &\Rightarrow \mathrm{Var}(\boldsymbol{X}) \leq \mathrm{Var}(\boldsymbol{Y}) \\
\boldsymbol{X} \leq_{icx} \boldsymbol{Y} &\Rightarrow E[\boldsymbol{X}^m] \leq E[\boldsymbol{Y}^m], \quad m = 1, 2, \ldots
\end{aligned}$$

In the one-dimensional case, $X \leq_{st} Y$ iff $P(X > x) \leq P(Y > x)$ for all $x \in \mathbb{R}$. Two random variables $\boldsymbol{X}, \boldsymbol{Y} \in \mathbb{R}$ satisfy $\boldsymbol{X} \leq_{cx} \boldsymbol{Y}$ (resp. $\boldsymbol{X} \leq_{cv} \boldsymbol{Y}$) if and only if $\boldsymbol{X} \leq_{icx} \boldsymbol{Y}$ (resp. $\boldsymbol{X} \leq_{icv} \boldsymbol{Y}$) and $E\boldsymbol{X} = E\boldsymbol{Y}$. It is also easily seen from the definition that

$$\boldsymbol{X} \geq_{cv} \boldsymbol{Y} \iff \boldsymbol{X} \leq_{cx} \boldsymbol{Y} \iff -\boldsymbol{X} \leq_{cx} -\boldsymbol{Y}$$

$$-\boldsymbol{X} \geq_{st} -\boldsymbol{Y} \iff \boldsymbol{X} \leq_{st} \boldsymbol{Y} \Rightarrow \boldsymbol{X} \leq_{icx} \boldsymbol{Y} \iff -\boldsymbol{X} \geq_{icv} -\boldsymbol{Y}.$$

We can also define orderings induced by the class of Schur convex functions and its subclasses.

- $\mathcal{C}_1$ ($\mathcal{C}_1^{\uparrow}$) - the class of (increasing) Schur-convex functions,
- $\mathcal{C}_2$ ($\mathcal{C}_2^{\uparrow}$) - the class of (increasing) symmetric and convex functions,
- $\mathcal{C}_3$ ($\mathcal{C}_3^{\uparrow}$) - the class of functions of the form $f(\boldsymbol{X}) = \sum_{i=1}^n f(x_i)$ where f is (increasing) convex.

These classes define the *(increasing) Schur-convex ordering* $\leq_{E_1}$ ($\leq_{E_1^{\uparrow}}$), *(increasing) convex-symmetric ordering* $\leq_{E_2}$ ($\leq_{E_2^{\uparrow}}$), and *(increasing) separate-convex ordering* $\leq_{E_3}$ ($\leq_{E_3^{\uparrow}}$).

Any function $f : \mathbb{R}^n \to \mathbb{R}$ is Schur-convex if it is symmetric and convex. Therefore, $\leq_{E_1}$ (resp. $\leq_{E_1^{\uparrow}}$) $\Rightarrow \leq_{E_2}$ (resp. $\leq_{E_2^{\uparrow}}$) $\Rightarrow \leq_{E_3}$ (resp. $\leq_{E_3^{\uparrow}}$).

2.3 Relations Between Majorization and Stochastic Orderings

A fundamental theorem in stochastic comparison is Strassen's theorem which establishes a close relation between stochastic orderings and usual inequalities and majorizations. In what follows, $=_d$ denotes equality in distribution.

Theorem 2.1. *Two random vectors $\boldsymbol{X}, \boldsymbol{Y} \in \mathbb{R}^n$ satisfy $\boldsymbol{X} \leq_{st} \boldsymbol{Y}$ (resp. $\boldsymbol{X} \leq_{cx} \boldsymbol{Y}$, $\boldsymbol{X} \leq_{icx} \boldsymbol{Y}$, $X \leq_{E_1} Y$, $X \leq_{E_1^{\uparrow}} Y$) if and only if there exist two random vectors $\boldsymbol{X}'$ and $\boldsymbol{Y}'$ defined on a common probability space, such that $\boldsymbol{X} =_d \boldsymbol{X}'$, $\boldsymbol{Y} =_d \boldsymbol{Y}'$, and $\boldsymbol{X}' \leq \boldsymbol{Y}'$ (resp. $\boldsymbol{X}' = E[\boldsymbol{Y}'|\boldsymbol{X}']$, $\boldsymbol{X}' \leq E[\boldsymbol{Y}'|\boldsymbol{X}']$, $\boldsymbol{X}' \prec \boldsymbol{Y}'$, $\boldsymbol{X}' \prec_w \boldsymbol{Y}'$) almost surely (a.s.).*

2.4 Other stochastic orderings

Let $X, Y \in I\!R$ be two random variables with density functions f_X and f_Y respectively, and distribution functions F_X and F_Y respectively. The random variable X is smaller than Y in the *likelihood ratio ordering* (resp. *hazard rate ordering*), denoted by $X \leq_{lr} Y$ (resp. $X \leq_{hr} Y$), if for any x and any $a > 0$, $f_X(x)/f_X(x+a) \geq f_Y(x)/f_Y(x+a)$ (resp. for any x, $f_X(x)/[1 - F_X(x)] \geq f_Y(x)/[1 - F_Y(x)]$).

When X and Y are discrete random variables, the orderings $\leq_{lr}$ and $\leq_{hr}$ are similarly defined with density functions replaced by the probability distributions.

It is known that the likelihood ratio ordering implies the hazard rate ordering, which in turn implies the stochastic ordering, i.e., $X \leq_{lr} Y \Rightarrow X \leq_{hr} Y \Rightarrow X \leq_{st} Y$, where the symbol $\Rightarrow$ stands for the implication. Note that two constants are comparable in the sense of $\leq_{lr}$ ordering.

The random variable $X \in I\!R^+$ is said to be *increasing in likelihood ratio* (ILR) (resp. to have *increasing failure rate* (IFR)) if for all $0 \leq s \leq t$, $X_s \geq_{lr} X_t$ (resp. $X_s \geq_{st} X_t$) where X_t is the remaining lifetime of X from t on, given that it exceeds t. A random variable is ILR iff its density function is log-concave (or, Polya frequency of order 2). Examples of random variables that are ILR include those with the densities Gamma: $f(x) = \lambda e^{-\lambda x}(\lambda x)^{\alpha-1}/\Gamma(\alpha)$ with $\alpha > 1$, and densities Weibull: $f(x) = \alpha\lambda(\lambda x)^{\alpha-1}e^{-(\lambda x)^\alpha}$ with $\alpha \geq 1$.

3. Scheduling of Monoprogrammed Systems

3.1 Introduction and Notation

Consider now the scheduling in a monoprogrammed parallel system executing a single job represented by a task graph $G = (V, E)$. We shall assume that task running times are independent and identically distributed (i.i.d.) random variables with a common exponential distribution. The goal of scheduling is to find optimal preemptive schedule that stochastically minimizes the makespan.

Denote by $p(i)$ and $s(i)$ the sets of immediate *predecessors* and *successors* of $i \in V$. Graph G is an *in-forest*, illustrated in Figure 3.1(a) (resp. *out-forest*, illustrated in Figure 3.1(b)) if $|s(i)| \leq 1$ (resp. $|p(i)| \leq 1$) for all $i \in G$. Let $S(i)$ be the set of (not necessarily immediate) successors of $i \in V$. The set of successors $S(i)$ and the vertex i form a subgraph of G denoted by $S_i(G)$.

All vertices $i \in V$ that have no predecessor (resp. successor) are *initial* (resp. *final*) vertices. The level of the final vertices is zero by convention. The level of a vertex $i \in V$, denoted by $L(i)$, is the length of the longest path from it to final vertices. The level of graph G, denoted by $L(G)$, is the maximum level of its vertices. Let $N_k(G)$ be the number of tasks of G at level k, $k \geq 0$. Clearly $N_k(G) = 0$ for all $k > L(G)$.

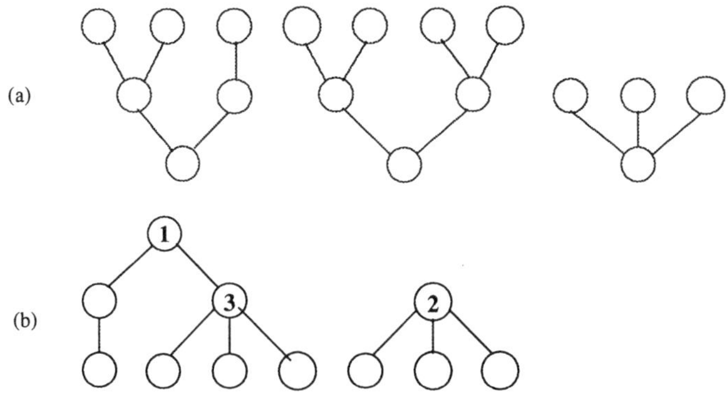

Fig. 3.1. (a) An example of in-forest. (b) An example of uniform out-forest

For any task graph $G = (V, E)$ and a level l, let $T_l(G) = (V(T_l(G)), E(T_l(G))$ and $D_l(G) = (V(D_l(G)), E(D_l(G)))$ be two subgraphs of G consisting of top and down vertices separated by level l. More precisely,

$$V(T_l(G)) = \{v | v \in V,\ L(v) \geq l\}, \quad V(D_l(G)) = \{v | v \in V,\ L(v) \leq l\},$$

and $E(T_l(G))$ and $E(D_l(G))$ are restrictions of E on $V(T_l(G))$ and $V(D_l(G))$.

Let G_1, G_2 be two out-trees. Out-tree G_1 is said to *embed* out-tree G_2, or G_2 is *embedded* in G_1, denoted by $G_1 \succ_e G_2$ or $G_2 \prec_e G_1$, if G_2 is isomorphic to a subgraph of G_1. Formally, G_1 embeds G_2 if there exists an injective function f from G_2 into G_1 such that $\forall u, v \in G_2$, $v \in s(u)$ implies $f(v) \in s(f(u))$. Function f is called an embedding function. An out-forest G is said to be *uniform* if all its subtrees $\{S_v(G),\ v \in G\}$ can be ordered by the embedding relation. For example, the out-forest in Figure 3.1(b) is a uniform out-forest.

3.2 Previous Results

When the task graph is an in-forest, and there are two (parallel and identical) processors, Chandy and Reynolds [3] proved that the Highest Level first (HL) policy minimizes the expected makespan. Bruno [2] subsequently showed that HL stochastically minimizes the makespan when the system has two identical parallel processors. Pinedo and Weiss [23] extended this last result to the case where tasks at different levels may have different expected task running times. Frostig [10] further generalized the result of Pinedo and Weiss to include increasing likelihood ratio distributions for the task running times. When the number of identical parallel processors in the system is arbitrarily fixed, and the task running times have a common exponential distribution, Papadimitriou and Tsitsiklis [22] proved that HL is asymptotically optimal as the number of tasks tends to infinity.

Coffman and Liu [5] investigated the stochastic scheduling of out-forest with exponential task running times. For the uniform out-forests where all the subtrees are ordered by an embedding relation, they showed that an intuitive priority scheduling policy induced by the embedding relation stochastically minimizes the makespan when there are two processors. For a more restrictive graph, the *r-uniform out-forests*, they showed the optimality of the greedy policy for arbitrary number of processors.

Liu and Sanlaville [13] proved the optimality of Most Successor (MS) policy when the task graph is an *interval-order* graph and when the task running times have a common exponential distribution. MS stochastically minimizes the makespan on any fixed number of processors.

Recently, Finta and Liu [9] extended the results on in-forest and out-forest to a class of fork-join graphs, referred to as *forest-cut* graphs, obtained from combination of in-forests and out-forests. They showed that when there are two processors, the policy Highest Level Most Successors (HLMS) stochastically minimizes the makespan on two processors.

In this section, we shall present the proof techniques used in [9] which are based on majorization relations (for comparing task graphs) and coupling arguments (for sample path analysis). We shall use a different scheme of proof than that of [9] in order to (slightly) generalize the result of [9] to the case of heterogeneous processors and variable profile, i.e. a system consisting of two processors with possibly different speeds, the subset of processors available to the task graph varies in time.

3.3 Forest-Cut Graphs

Several majorization notions will be useful for comparing graphs. Two graphs F and G are identical, $F = G$, if they have the same sets of vertices and arcs. We say that F is *flatter than* G, denoted by $F \prec_f G$, if

$$\forall i \geq 0: \qquad \sum_{k \geq i} N_k(F) \leq \sum_{k \geq i} N_k(G).$$

The embedding relation is extended to uniform out-forests: Let $G_1 = (V_1, E_1)$ and $G_2 = (V_2, E_2)$ be two uniform out-forests. Assume that the vertices of G_1 and G_2 are indexed in such a way that $S_1(G_j) \succ_e S_2(G_j) \succ_e \cdots \succ_e S_{|V_1|}(G_j)$, $j = 1, 2$. Out-forest G_1 is embedded in G_2, referred to as $G_1 \prec^e G_2$, if and only if

$$|V_1| \leq |V_2|, \quad \text{and} \quad \forall i,\ 1 \leq i \leq |V_1|: \quad S_i(G_1) \prec_e S_i(G_2).$$

We shall study a class $\mathcal{G}$ of task graphs, referred to as *forest-cut* graphs, which can be cut into an in-forest and a uniform out-forest. More precisely, $\mathcal{G}$ is the class of graphs satisfying the following conditions.

Definition 3.1. *For any graph $G = (V, E) \in \mathcal{G}$, there exists a level l such that*

1. *$D_l(G)$ is an in-forest;*
2. *$T_l(G)$ is a uniform out-forest, whose vertices can be labeled in such a way that $S_1(T_l(G)) \succ_e S_2(T_l(G)) \succ_e \cdots \succ_e S_{|V(T_l(G))|}(T_l(G))$,*
3. *and that the subgraphs are in the flatness relation $S_1(G) \succ_f S_2(G) \succ_f \cdots \succ_f S_{|V(T_l(G))|}(G)$.*

The level l will be called the cut level.

As an example, by combining the in-forest and out-forest of Figure 3.1, we obtain the forest-cut graph in Figure 3.2. Other examples of forest-cut graphs are fork-join task graphs, see e.g. [9].

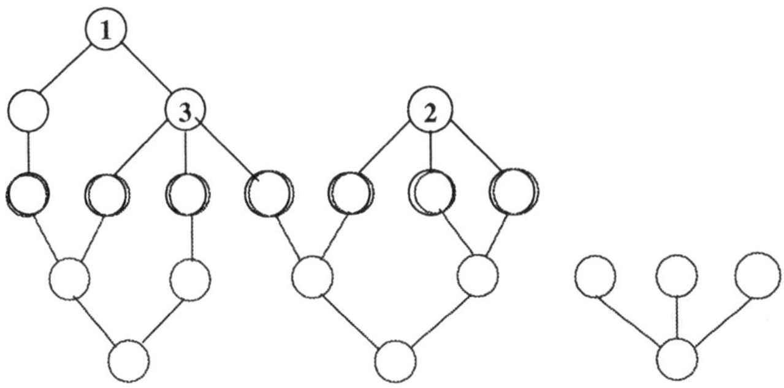

Fig. 3.2. An example of forest-cut graph

Note that the cut level of a graph is not unique. Note also that this class of graphs has the following closure property: if $G = (V, E) \in \mathcal{G}$ then $G - \{v\} \in \mathcal{G}$ for all $v \in V$ such that $p(v) = \emptyset$, where $G - \{v\}$ is the graph obtained by deleting vertex v and its adjacent edges. Such a closure property (by deletion) will be used in establishing our results.

We extend the notion of flatness as follows. Let $F, G \in \mathcal{G}$ be two forest-cut graphs with the same cut level l, the relation of *extended flatness*, denoted by $F \prec^f G$, means that

$$|V(T_l(F))| \leq |V(T_l(G))|, \quad \text{and} \quad \forall i,\ 1 \leq i \leq |V(T_l(F))| : \ S_i(F) \prec_f S_i(G).$$

We are now in a position to define the notion of *smaller* for comparison of forest-cut graphs.

Definition 3.2. *Two forest-cut graphs $F, G \in \mathcal{G}$ with the same cut level l are in the relation $F \prec_s G$ if and only if they satisfy*

$$F \prec_f G, \qquad T(F) \prec^e T(G), \qquad F \prec^f G.$$

Note that if F and G are two in-forests, then $F \prec_f G$ implies $F \prec_s G$. If F and G are two uniform out-forests, then $F \prec^e G$ implies $F \prec_s G$.

3.4 Stochastic Minimization of Makespan

In the system, there are two processors with speeds α_1 and α_2, where $\alpha_1 \geq \alpha_2$. Task processing requirements are i.i.d. random variables with a common distribution of parameter, say 1. Tasks assigned to processor 1 (resp. 2) have thus running times exponentially distributed with parameter α_1 (resp. α_2).

The set of processors available to these tasks varies in time, due to, e.g., failures of the processors or executions of higher-priority tasks. The availability of the processors is referred to as the *profile*, and is specified by the sequence $\{a_n, M_n\}_{n=1}^{\infty}$, where the random variables $0 = a_1 < a_2, < \cdots < a_n < \cdots$ are the time epochs where the profile is changed, and $M_n \subseteq \{1, 2\}$ is a random set whose elements are the indices of the processors available during the time interval $[a_n, a_{n+1})$. The profile $\{a_n, M_n\}_{n=1}^{\infty}$ is assumed to be independent of the running times of the tasks.

We define the Highest Level Most Successors (HLMS) policy as follows. The tasks of $G \in \mathcal{G}$ are labeled by $1, 2, \cdots, |V|$ in such a way that for any $1 \leq i \leq |V| - 1$, $L(i) \geq L(i+1)$, and if $L(i) = L(i+1)$ then $|S(i)| \geq |S(i+1)|$. At any time, only the *enabled tasks* (those without any unfinished predecessors, i.e. the initial vertices in the remaining task graph) with the smallest labels are executed on the available processors with the highest speeds. In other words, HLMS assigns the tasks at the highest level among the enabled tasks to available processors. If several enabled tasks are at the same level, the priority is given to the task with most successors. We will consider *preemptive* policies where executions of tasks can be preempted and resumed without penalty.

Let Ψ denote the class of preemptive policies which use no information on task running times. Due to the memorylessness property of exponential distributions, we can make some restrictions on the class of policies Ψ. Observe first that the distribution of the remaining running time of a task running on a processor is still exponential with the same parameter. Therefore, we can, without loss of generality, confine ourselves to the class of policies where preemptions and new task assignments occur only at the instants of task completions or profile changes. These instants are referred to as the *decision epochs.* A second consequence is that any idling scheduling policy is never optimal. Therefore, we assume that Ψ contains only nonidling preemptive policies. The last constraint on Ψ is that whenever there are two available processors, the faster processor (i.e. processor 1) is used in priority. It can be shown that optimal policies behave in this way (see [13]).

For any policy π, let $\pi(G)$ denote the makespan of G, i.e. the completion time of all tasks of G under policy π. Let γ denote policy HLMS.

Theorem 3.1. *For any graph $G \in \mathcal{G}$, any profile $\{a_n, M_n\}_{n=1}^{\infty}$, and any $\pi \in \Psi$,*

$$\gamma(G) \leq_{st} \pi(G). \tag{3.1}$$

Moreover, HLMS is the only policy that satisfies relation (3.1).

The proof of Theorem 3.1 makes use of the following lemmas.

Lemma 3.1. *Let $F = (V(F), E(F))$ and $G = (V(G), E(G))$ be two subgraphs of $H \in \mathcal{G}$ obtained by successively deleting initial vertices of H or of previously obtained subgraphs. If $F \prec_s G$, then*

$$\gamma(F) \leq_{st} \gamma(G) \tag{3.2}$$

Lemma 3.2. *Let $H \in \mathcal{G}$ be a task graph. Let $\pi \in \Psi$ be a policy which follows the HLMS rule all the time except at the first decision epoch. Then*

$$\gamma(H) \leq_{st} \pi(H).$$

The proof of Lemma 3.1 consists in analyzing a coupled processing model where both processors 1, 2 are continuously executing tasks. When a task is assigned to a processor, it is assigned a running time equal to the remainder of the running time already underway at that processor. Thus, if tasks $u \in F$ and $v \in G$ are assigned to the same processor at the same time, they have the same (remaining) running time. Let $F_n^\gamma = (V(F_n^\gamma), E(F_n^\gamma))$ and $G_n^\gamma = (V(G_n^\gamma), E(G_n^\gamma))$ be the remaining graphs of F, respectively G, at the n-th decision epoch of F and G under the HLMS policy in the coupled model. As in [9], we can show by induction that for all $n \geq 0$, $F_n^\gamma \prec G_n^\gamma$, which immediately implies $\gamma(F) \leq \gamma(G)$ a.s., so that (3.2) holds due to Strassen's theorem.

The proof of Lemma 3.2 also uses the coupled model and it is analogous to Lemma 6 of [9].

Using the above lemmas, the proof of Theorem 3.1 goes straightforward by an induction on n that for any $G = (V, E) \in \mathcal{G}$ such that $|V| \leq n$, the relation $\gamma(G) \leq_{st} \pi(G)$ holds for any profile. The reader is referred to the proof of Theorem 3.1 in [13] for details.

Notice that the optimality result of HLMS policy does not hold when there are at least three processors. In fact, even in the special cases of in-forests and out-forests, counterexamples have been provided in the literature for the minimization of the average makespan, see [3] for in-forests and [5] for out-forests.

4. Scheduling of Multiprogrammed Systems

4.1 Introduction

We consider now the problem of scheduling an arrival stream of parallel programs on a multiprocessor system. There are few results in the literature. Typically the effectiveness of policies is established through performance studies of simple models, either through analysis (e.g. first come first serve [19, 20], processor sharing [25], priority scheduling [21]) or through simulation (e.g., priority scheduling [17, 5].

In [1], extremal scheduling policies were established for a general model of multiprogrammed system. A sequence of jobs which are represented by the same task graph arrive in the system in an arbitrary way. Tasks have dedicated processors, i.e. tasks are preallocated to processors. Several tasks belonging to the same job can however be assigned to the same processor. Extremal properties of simple scheduling policies were obtained using stochastic comparison techniques for the performance measures such as throughput (in terms of number of jobs completed each unit of time), job response times and latenesses.

In [16], a dynamic processor allocation problem was considered. Jobs consist of a sequence of phases, each consisting of a number of (statistically identical) tasks that can be simultaneously executed. The number of phases are assumed to be i.i.d. geometric random variables, the number of tasks in phases are i.i.d. random variables, and task running times are i.i.d. exponential random variables. They showed that the Smallest Phase policy, the policy that schedules the current job with the smallest number of tasks, stochastically minimizes, within the class of preemptive policies, number of jobs in the multiprocessor system at all times.

In this section, we analyze a scheduling problem with static fixed task allocations. The problem is similar to that of [1], with the particularities that a processor executes at most one task from a job. The purpose of this study is again to illustrate the use of stochastic comparison techniques for solving such stochastic scheduling problems. The results are established using those of [1, 4, 15].

4.2 Problem Description

There are N jobs waiting in the system at time 0, where N is an arbitrary number. Job n has task graph $G_n = (V_n, E_n)$, $1 \leq n \leq N$. Assume that these graphs are ordered by the subgraph relation: $G_1 \subseteq G_2 \subseteq \cdots \subseteq G_N$. Denote by $T_{n,i}$, $i \in V_n$, task i of job n. Job n has due date d_n. All task running times are mutually independent random variables. These task running times are ordered by $\leq_{lr}$: for all $1 \leq n \leq N-1$ and $i \in V_n$, $T_{n,i} \leq_{lr} T_{n+1,i}$. There are $|V_N|$ processors. Tasks $T_{n,i}$, $1 \leq n \leq N$, are assigned to processor i.

The scheduling problem consists in schedule the executions of tasks $T_{n,i}$, $i \in V_n$, $n = 1, 2, \ldots, N$, at processor P_i subject to the precedence constraints in each job. Let Ψ denote the class of policies which use no information on task running times. Among other policies, we shall be concerned with order-preserving policies which are defined to schedule the tasks on all the processors using the same order of jobs. Two particular policies are *Smallest Job* and *Largest Job* policies which are defined to schedule the tasks on all the processors according to the increasing (decreasing) order of job indices. These two policies will be denoted by $\mathcal{S}$ and $\mathcal{L}$ respectively.

Denote by $C_n(\pi)$ the completion time of job n under scheduling policy π, and C_n^π the time of n-th job completion under π. The performance measures of interest are completion times: $\boldsymbol{C}^\pi = (C_1^\pi, \cdots, C_N^\pi)$, and lateness $L_n(\pi) = C_n(\pi) - d_n$, $\boldsymbol{L}(\pi) = (L_1(\pi), \cdots, L_N(\pi))$.

4.3 Extremal Policies

We first establish the following result

Theorem 4.1. *For any policy $\pi \in \Psi$ and any order-preserving policy $\phi \in \Psi$,*

$$\boldsymbol{C}^{\mathcal{S}} \leq_{st} \boldsymbol{C}^\pi, \qquad \boldsymbol{C}^\phi \leq_{st} \boldsymbol{C}^{\mathcal{L}}. \tag{4.1}$$

The assertion of the theorem follows from the lemma below. Let $a_{n,i}(\pi)$ and $c_{n,i}(\pi)$ be the time epochs when task $T_{n,i}$ is enabled and completed, respectively. Note that $a_{n,i}(\pi) = 0$ if $T_{n,i}$ is an initial task. Let $\boldsymbol{A}_i^\pi$ (resp. $\boldsymbol{C}_i^\pi$) be the vector with increasingly ordered components of $(a_{n,i}(\pi),\ i \in V_n)_n$ (resp. $(c_{n,i}(\pi),\ i \in V_n)_n$).

Lemma 4.1. *For any policy $\pi \in \Psi$, and for all $i \in V_N$,*

$$\boldsymbol{A}_i^{\mathcal{S}} \leq_{st} \boldsymbol{A}_i^\pi, \qquad \boldsymbol{C}_i^{\mathcal{S}} \leq_{st} \boldsymbol{C}_i^\pi. \tag{4.2}$$

For any order-preserving policy $\phi \in \Psi$, and for all $i \in V_N$,

$$\boldsymbol{A}_i^\phi \leq_{st} \boldsymbol{A}_i^{\mathcal{L}}, \qquad \boldsymbol{C}_i^\phi \leq_{st} \boldsymbol{C}_i^{\mathcal{L}}. \tag{4.3}$$

Sketch of the proof. The assertions are shown by induction on i. We shall only consider (4.2), relation (4.3) is similar.

Consider first the initial vertices of G_N, which are, by assumption, either initial vertices of G_n, or nonexisting in G_n, $1 \leq n < N$. For such i, applying a result of [4] implies that (4.2) holds.

Assume there is $k \geq 1$ such that (4.2) holds for all $i < k$. Let $P(k)$ be the set of predecessors of k in G_N Then, for all h, the h-th component of $\boldsymbol{A}_k^{\mathcal{S}}$ is equal to the maximum of the h-th components of $\boldsymbol{C}_j^{\mathcal{S}}$ for $j \in P(k)$, whereas the h-th component of $\boldsymbol{A}_k^\pi$ is, due to the precedence constraints for each job, larger than the maximum of the h-th components of $\boldsymbol{C}_j^\pi$ for $j \in P(k)$. Thus, $\boldsymbol{A}_k^{\mathcal{S}} \leq_{st} \boldsymbol{A}_k^\pi$. Using now again the result of [4] allows us to conclude $\boldsymbol{C}_k^{\mathcal{S}} \leq_{st} \boldsymbol{C}_k^\pi$. ∎

Consider now the minimization of lateness. The key issue is the use *partial orderings on permutations* which was first introduced in [1] and later generalized in [16]. We only present one of them here.

Denote by Γ the set of permutations on $\{1, 2, \cdots, n\}$, and $\boldsymbol{X}, \boldsymbol{Y} \in \mathbb{R}^n$ two random vectors. We define a binary relation $\mathcal{B}_{\boldsymbol{X}}^{st}$ on the symmetric group Γ: $\gamma' \mathcal{B}_{\boldsymbol{X}}^{st} \gamma$ if $\gamma' = \gamma$, or if $\exists j, k$, such that

$$X_j \leq_{st} X_k,$$
$$\gamma(j) > \gamma(k), \qquad \gamma'(j) = \gamma(k),\ \gamma'(k) = \gamma(j),\ \gamma'(i) = \gamma(i),\ i \neq j,\ i \neq k.$$

The partial order $\prec_{\boldsymbol{X}}^{st}$ on Γ is defined as the transitive closure of $\mathcal{B}_{\boldsymbol{X}}^{st}$. One of the important properties of such orderings is:

Proposition 4.1. *Assume that* $\boldsymbol{X}$ *is independent of* $\boldsymbol{Y}$ *and* $Y_1 \leq Y_2 \leq \cdots \leq Y_n$, *a.s. Denote by* $\boldsymbol{Y}_\gamma = (Y_{\gamma(1)}, \cdots, Y_{\gamma(n)})$. *If* $\gamma' \prec_{\boldsymbol{X}}^{st} \gamma$, *then* $(\boldsymbol{Y}_{\gamma'} - \boldsymbol{X}) \leq_{E_3} (\boldsymbol{Y}_\gamma - \boldsymbol{X})$.

As a consequence of Theorem 4.1 and Proposition 4.1, we obtain, by noticing that $\boldsymbol{C}^{\mathcal{S}} = \boldsymbol{C}(\mathcal{S})$ and $\boldsymbol{C}^{\mathcal{L}} = \boldsymbol{C}(\mathcal{L})$.

Theorem 4.2. *Assume that the due dates satisfy* $d_1 \leq_{st} d_2 \leq_{st} \cdots \leq_{st} d_N$. *Then, for any policy* $\pi \in \Psi$ *and any order-preserving policy* $\phi \in \Psi$,

$$\boldsymbol{L}(\mathcal{S}) \leq_{E_3^\uparrow} \boldsymbol{L}(\pi), \qquad \boldsymbol{L}(\phi) \leq_{E_3^\uparrow} \boldsymbol{L}(\mathcal{L}). \tag{4.4}$$

Orderings stronger than $\leq_{E_3^\uparrow}$ can be obtained when due dates are ordered by $\leq_{lr}$ and $\leq_{hr}$, see [15] for detailed. Results presented in this section still hold when all the jobs are not available at time 0, and arrive at times $a_1 \leq a_2 \leq \cdots \leq a_N$.

5. Concluding Remarks

We have presented and illustrated the use of sample path analysis and stochastic comparison techniques by analyzing two stochastic scheduling problems in parallel systems. These techniques turn out to be very useful to tackle complex scheduling problems like those considered in the chapter. It is worthwhile noticing that the assumption of independence between task times is not unreasonable when tasks are coarse grained. Variations in task times are due to inherent randomness as well as from queueing delays that result when tasks compete for shared resources. Although the the statistical assumptions made in our analysis may not hold in some applications, our optimality results can be used to suggest practical heuristics.

References

1. F. Baccelli, Z. Liu and D. Towsley, "Extremal Scheduling of Parallel Processing Systems with and without Real-Time Constraints." *Journal of the ACM*, **40**, pp. 1209–1237, 1993.
2. J. Bruno, "On Scheduling Tasks with Exponential Service Times and In-Tree Precedence Constraints", *Acta Informatica*, **22**, pp. 139–148, 1985.
3. K. M. Chandy and P. F. Reynolds, "Scheduling Partially Ordered Tasks with Probabilistic Execution Times", *Operating System Review*, **9**, pp. 169–177, 1975.
4. C.S. Chang and D.D. Yao, "Rearrangement, Majorization and Stochastic Scheduling", *Mathematics of Operations Research*, to appear.
5. E.G. Coffman and Z. Liu, "On the Optimal Stochastic Scheduling of Out-Forests", *Operations Research*, **40**, pp. S67–S75, 1992.

6. D. Dolev and M.K. Warmuth, "Scheduling Precedence Graphs of Bounded Height", *J. of Algorithms*, **5**, pp. 48–59, 1984.
7. D. Dolev and M.K. Warmuth, "Scheduling Flat Graphs", *SIAM J. on Comput.*, **14**, pp. 638–657, 1985.
8. D. Dolev and M.K. Warmuth, "Profile Scheduling of Opposing Forests and Level Orders", *SIAM J. Alg. Disc. Meth.*, **6**, pp. 665–687, 1985.
9. L. Finta and Z. Liu, "Makespan Minimization of Task Graphs with Random Task Running Times", In *Interconnection Networks and Mapping and Scheduling Parallel Computations*, D.F. Hsu et al. (Eds.), AMS, DIMACS series, to appear, 1995.
10. E. Frostig, "A Stochastic Scheduling Problem with Intree Precedence Constraints", *Operations Research*, **36**, pp. 937–943, 1988.
11. M.R. Garey, D.S. Johnson, R.E. Tarjan and M. Yanakakis, "Scheduling Opposite Forests", *SIAM J. Alg. Disc. Meth.*, **4**, pp. 72–93, 1983.
12. S. Leutenegger and M. Vernon, "The performance of multiprogrammed multiprocessor scheduling algorithms", *Proc. SIGMETRICS 1990.*, pp. 226–236, May 1990.
13. Z. Liu and E. Sanlaville, "Stochastic Scheduling with Variable Profile and Precedence Constraints", To appear in *SIAM J. on Computing.*
14. Z. Liu and E. Sanlaville, "Profile Scheduling by List Algorithms", In *Scheduling Theory and Its Applications*, P. Chretienne et al. (Eds.), J. Wiley, 1995.
15. Z. Liu and D. Towsley, "Stochastic Scheduling in In-Forest Networks". *Advances in Applied Probabilities*, **26**, pp. 222–241, 1994.
16. Z. Liu and D. Towsley, "Scheduling a Sequence of Parallel Programs Containing Loops within a Centralized Parallel Processing System". COINS Technical Report, TR 92-34, 1992.
17. S. Majumdar, D.L. Eager and R.B. Bunt, "Scheduling in multiprogrammed parallel systems", *Proc. SIGMETRICS 1988*, pp. 104–113, May 1988.
18. A.W. Marshall and I. Olkin, *Inequalities: Theory of Majorization and Its Applications*, Academic Press, 1979.
19. R. Nelson, D. Towsley and A.N. Tantawi, "Performance Analysis of Parallel Processing Systems", *IEEE Trans. on Software Engineering*, **14** (4), pp. 532–540, April 1988.
20. R. Nelson, "A Performance Evaluation of a General Parallel Processing Model," *Performance Evaluation Review*, **18** (1), pp. 13–26, 1990.
21. R. Nelson and D. Towsley, "A Performance Evaluation of Several Priority Policies for Parallel Processing Systems," *J. ACM*, **40**, pp. 714-740, 1993.
22. C.H. Papadimitriou and J.N. Tsitsiklis, "On Stochastic Scheduling with In-Tree Precedence Constraints", *SIAM J. Comput.*, **16**, pp. 1–6, 1987.
23. M. Pinedo and G. Weiss, "Scheduling Jobs with Exponentially Distributed Processing Times and Intree Precedence Constraints on Two Parallel Machines", *Operations Research*, **33**, pp. 1381–1388, 1985.
24. V. Strassen, "The Existence of Probability Measures with Given Marginals", *Ann. Math. Sta.*, **36**, pp. 423–439, 1965.
25. D. Towsley, G. Rommel and J.A. Stankovic, "Analysis of Fork-Join Program Response Times on Multiprocessors," *IEEE Transactions on Parallel and Distributed Systems*, **1** (3), pp. 286–303, July 1990.
26. J. D. Ullman, "NP-Complete Scheduling Problems", *J. Comput. System Sci.*, **10**, pp. 384–393, 1975.

Dependability of Distributed Programs: Algorithms and Performance

S. Chabridon[1] and E. Gelenbe[2]

[1] EHEI, Université René Descartes, France
[2] Department of Electrical Engineering, Duke University, USA

Summary. In this paper, we use task graph models to represent the behaviour of parallel programs. These models are characterized by execution times of the tasks, and by the precedence relation between the tasks. The latter can be represented by a probabilistic ordering, or can be provided with a specific known ordering for a given application. When failures occur in the processing system, we consider a recovery mechanism based on failure detection, and subsequent task restart. Both of these operations take additional processing times which are explicitly represented in the task graph characterization. Failures themselves are represented in the model by variable failure rates. We report on the design, analysis and simulation of novel algorithms which will ensure that application software runs correctly on an MIMD system in which processing units (PU) may fail. These algorithms are based on certain existing tasks which are selected within the program, which we call *agents*. Their role is to carry out failure detection and if necessary restart of other tasks, as soon as they have completed their own specific assigned work. The effect of these algorithms is evaluated using analytical approximations and simulation as a function of failure rates, and other system parameters. The comparison of the simulation results with the approximate analytical results, shows a very good level of accuracy for this degree of complexity, which indicates that simple analytical formulae can be used to obtain robust first-order estimates of program execution times with and without failures. We also provide specific examples of task graphs for two well known computations (matrix multiplication and the Fast Fourier Transform) and their parallel implementation. Finally we provide simulation results which evaluate the proposed failure detection and recovery algorithms for the specific case of the FFT algorithm.

1. Introduction

Fault-tolerance and reliability have always been of essential importance to designers and users of computers. With the increasing variety of parallel systems, from tightly coupled shared/distributed memory SIMD and MIMD architectures to loosely coupled *farms* of workstations, these concerns assume even greater significance.

Parallel and distributed systems, because of their size and complexity, are more prone than sequential machines to incidents which impair program execution. In addition to conventional failures which can occur in such systems, specific events may occur which can cause a particular application program's execution to fail. For instance: certain processing units (PU's) may be preempted unexpectedly by other programs, certain processing units may be turned off by users who are unaware of the ongoing application, and workload surges from higher priority applications may slow down a particular application's work on certain PUs, creating excessive delay for some tasks, which can then be interpreted as a failure. In some cases, such surges are known to eliminate certain processes from memory.

Task graphs are convenient models of the execution of parallel programs [6, 8, 11] and have been used widely to estimate the performance of parallel architectures and systems. They will be used in this paper as the basic tool for modeling the workload in a parallel system with failures. As such, we can view this paper as a continuation of our previous work based on task graph characterization, in the direction of systems with failures.

For sequential processing, a variety of techniques such as log-based recovery and recovery block mechanisms, have been suggested and analyzed [5, 7, 9, 10]. In recent research [12, 13, 14, 15, 16, 17] new techniques have been developed which guarantee that a parallel program of the fork-join or threads and barriers type can be modified so that processor failures can be detected, and processing rescheduled when processor failures occur.

In order to illustrate the need for the failure detection and recovery algorithms in distributed programs, we first present simulations of parallel programs running on a MIMD architecture with failures [3]. We assume that the machine running the program has more processors than are needed at any time by the program, so that failures are the only limiting factor on performance. The program is composed of a set of interdependent tasks, and when a PU on which a task is running fails, then the corresponding task is disabled. When a PU fails it remains unavailable for some time F, after which it becomes operational again (it is "repaired"). We consider two alternatives concerning task restart after the PU is again operational:

- (1) In the case with automatic restart, the task which was running on the failed PU is automatically restarted when the PU becomes operational again. Consequently, even without failure detection, tasks are restarted and the program as a whole has a chance to complete. The program's time to completion will depend on the failure rate and on the down time F.
- (2) If there is no automatic restart then – since we do not have failure detection – the program as a whole will have failed when any processor fails.

On Figure 1 we plot results from simulations we have carried out; we will not discuss the simulation model used in detail, since our purpose here is merely to motivate the results presented in the following Sections. These simulations deal with the percentage of programs which complete successfully, against the failure rate γ, for 1000 simulated programs selected at random. In order to normalize the time units involved, each individual task of a program has a unit (1) average execution time. The failure rate γ ranges from 0.0001 to 0.1 in logarithmic scale. Each simulated program contains $K = 50$ tasks. In order to concentrate the analysis on the reliability issues, these simulations assume that the number of PUs is unlimited and that communications times between tasks are small enough to be neglected. A program is stopped if

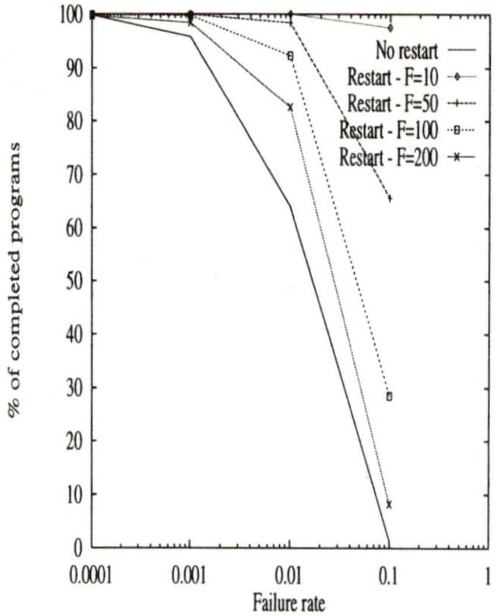

Figure 1. Effects of failures without detection

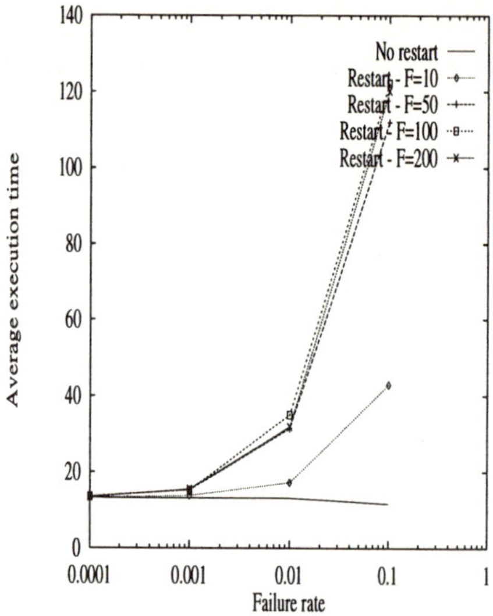

Figure 2. Average execution time of completed programs

it does not complete after a time $T_{max} = 200$. The results shown concern the case when there is no restart, and with automatic restart for four values of F: $10, 50, 100, 200$. In the case with restart, the percentage of completed programs decreases significantly when $F = 200$; for $\gamma = 0.1$, less than 10 % of the programs complete. When tasks are not restarted automatically, the percentage of completed programs decreases quickly as the failure rate increases, and almost no programs complete when $\gamma = 0.1$. Figure 2 shows the average execution time of the *successfully completed programs*, in the presence of failures and without the benefit of detection algorithms. Without restart, programs which complete in the presence of failures are simply those for which no PUs fail during their execution. Shorter programs are more likely to avoid failures: average execution time of completed programs decreases from 13.17 when $\gamma = 0.0001$ to 11.6 when $\gamma = 0.1$. With automatic restart the programs' average execution time increases rapidly as a function of the failure rate, attaining more than 10 times their original value when $\gamma = 0.1$. These simulations strongly motivate the need for better methods for handling failures, which will detect failures and reschedule tasks rapidly.

2. Detection and Recovery Algorithms

A distributed application is composed of many interdependent tasks, and each task is a granule of sequential code which is executed on a single PU. Tasks are related to each other by precedence constraints, by the exchange of data, or of messages, and by the transfer of control. Whenever a task successfully completes, it sends a message to its successor tasks, which requires a *perfectly reliable communication medium.* Another alternative, is that the task places information in shared memory, to indicate that it has completed and that it thus enables other tasks' execution; this assumes that there is a *small failsafe shared memory* which any task can interrogate. Throughout this study, we will assume that either one of these two options is available for tasks to communicate reliably.

We propose to select a subset of the tasks in the program, and make them responsible for executing the monitoring – i.e. failure detection and task reallocation – algorithm. These selected tasks will complete the computation they would carry out normally, and then actively detect failures, and assist the rest of the program's recovery from failures. We will call these selected tasks *agents.* Clearly, an agent can only examine its "sibling or successor tasks" for failure, i.e. those for which it is not a successor. The schemes we propose will guarantee full dependability only if at least one of the In particular we will consider the following alternatives for chosing the agents:

- **Alternative 1** – Here only tasks which have no successor (i.e. the "leaves" of the task graph) are agents. Each task which has finished execution and which has no successor in the task graph will first examine the other leaves of the task graph. An agent will not examine a task which has been – or is being – examined by another agent. If one of the leaves of a task is shown not to have completed, the agent will "investigate" it by examining its predecessors until all tasks are accounted for either as "not yet started", "running but unfinished" or "failed". The agent will then reassign the failed task which it has detected (if it finds one) to a PU which is up, and then the task will be restarted.
  This will work very well when failures are infrequent, since it introduces little overhead. When failures are more frequent, this approach may delay detection for too long; in fact, it may delay it "for ever" since none of the leaves may be reached.
- **Alternative 2** – Here we choose a certain number of intermediate tasks also to be agents, in addition to the leaves. The purpose is to detect failures soon enough to avoid that the distributed application fails completely before the leaves are reached. In most cases, any failure will be detected by the intermediate tasks without having to wait for leaves to be activated.
  Let the "rank" of a task be the longest path from itself back to a source task (a source being a task without predecessors). We may select some ranks, and assign the role of agent to some tasks in each rank. An agent will examine other tasks having its own rank, and then those of lesser rank, in order to detect failures. We call this "look-back detection".
- **Alternative 3** – This is an extension of Alternative 2. Here, agents will carry out "look-ahead" for failures, in addition to the "look-back" of Alternative 2. When an agent finds a task of the same rank which has completed its execution, it will test its successors. The purpose is to detect failures as

soon as possible and to favor the rapid successful completion of the whole program.

Three options can be combined with Alternatives 1,2 and 3.

- **Active Wait Option (W)** – Detection can be improved by charging the leaf task which completes earliest, with carrying out failure detection periodically until the whole program completes. In fact, this can be extended to all completed leaf tasks.
- **Restart Option (R)** – The purpose here is to protect from complete program failure. Thus if a program does not complete execution by some predetermined date T_{max}, it is restarted from scratch. Clearly a small value of T_{max} will lead to "false alarms", while a very large value will lead to excessive waits when the program has failed.
- **W+R Option** – Combining the two previous options, we obtain a scheme in which some or all leaf tasks are kept alive as failure detectors, and in addition the program as a whole is restarted after a time T_{max}.

The assumptions concerning the manner in which failures may occur, as well as their nature (intermittent or permanent) are important. We consider the following relevant failure assumptions:

- *Failure Assumption A (FAA)* – Tasks cannot autonomously restart. Any task whose processor *has not failed* by the end of its computational step will not subsequently fail until all of the program terminates. Thus any task which carries out the role of "agent" is preserved from failures. This is clearly a "best case" assumption, and would be valid if the agents' detection and restart functions were carried out on highly reliable special PUs.
- *Failure Assumption B (FAB)* – Tasks cannot autonomously restart. Agents which have terminated their normal work, and which are now carrying out failure detection and restart for other tasks, can fail as well. This assumption is more realistic.
- *Failure Assumption C (FAC)* – Under failure assumption C, tasks which fail can restart autonomously without the help of agents, simply because when the corresponding PU is repaired the failed task immediately restarts autonomously. Note that restarts can also be caused by agents and agents themselves be restarted after a failure. This is the most complex scenario.

Failure Assumption A is overly optimistic with respect to the fact that agents are protected from failure, while Assumption C is perhaps too complex to be implemented. Failure Assumption B, where agents can also fail, and tasks cannot restart autonomously, describes a realistic operating condition.

3. Approximate Analysis and Simulations

We simulate the following model of a set of parallel programs running on a distributed architecture. Each program is represented by a *Task-graph*; these models have been successfully used to represent parallel programs and to study their performance [6, 11, 18, 19]. In the task-graph model, a program is represented by a set of K tasks numbered $\{1, \ldots, \mathrm{K}\}$: each task is an indivisible unit of code and data which has to be executed sequentially. An acyclic graph G with K nodes represents the precedence relations between the tasks. The graph is acyclic because we are dealing with a computation which must eventually terminate. Each task i has an execution time t_i on a PU, and it may be executed on any one of the PUs in the same amount of time. When a task finishes its execution it informs all of its successors in the precedence graph, either by sending a message or through a shared memory. A task can begin execution when it is informed that all of its predecessors have terminated their execution.

In the simulations, each task graph representing a program, is generated at random. A probability p will be selected, and used to determine whether some task j, with $j > i$ is a successor of task i. By not allowing a task j to be a successor of some task $k < j$, we will guarantee that the graph is acyclic. By choosing a small value of p, we will simulate programs which are very "parallel" since any task will have few successors, while a larger value of p will limit the amount of parallelism in the program. For the sake of simplicity, the failure process is assumed to be Poisson, and all and durations are exponentially distributed unless otherwise stated.

The simulations have to account for the time spent by an agent both in detection, and in failure recovery: each time a task is tested by an agent, a constant time w is added to the execution time of the agent. When a task is restarted after a failure is detected, it takes an additional constant time C for the agent to do so.

3.1 Approximate Analytical Results

Let us present a simple analysis of the main trade-offs of "agent based" recovery, using the task-graph model of parallel programs. As before, the average task execution time is normalized to be 1. The analysis will be based on results reported in [6, 11].

The smallest or best possible execution time of a parallel program E is obtained when the program has access to an unlimited number of processing units, assuming that communication times can be neglected. It has been shown [11] that the smallest possible execution time of a parallel program represented by a task graph is given approximately by the following expression:

$$E = \frac{2Kp}{p+1}. \tag{3.1}$$

Extrapolating from this formula, the average execution time of a program with failure detection, but without any failures, is approximately:

$$E_d = \frac{2Kp(1+\pi D)}{p+1}, \tag{3.2}$$

where π is the probability that a particular task is an agent, and D is the time that each agent spends doing failure detection. Since all tasks, including agents, will have to be tested and because there are πK agents, each agent spends on the average a time:

$$D = \frac{wK}{\pi K} = \frac{w}{\pi} \tag{3.3}$$

so that the average program execution time without failures but with failure detections is obtained as:

$$E_d = \frac{2Kp(1+w)}{p+1}. \tag{3.4}$$

This is identical to the formula we would have obtained if we had added the time spent in failure detection to each task's execution time.

Let us now consider the possibility of failures, and let f be the probability that a failure occurs during a tasks execution. Then the total average task execution time X becomes:

$$X = 1 + D + Xf + Rf, \qquad or \qquad X = \frac{1 + D + Rf}{1 - f} \tag{3.5}$$

where D is the failure detection time, and R is the time it takes the agent which detects the failure to reschedule the task. This is because with probability $(1-f)$, $X = 1+D$, while with probability f we have $X = 1+D+X+R$, since failures can repeat in the future even after a task has been rescheduled. Assuming agents also can fail, detection and restart can only be accomplished by non-failed agents, so:

$$D = \frac{w}{\pi(1-f)}, \qquad and \qquad R = \frac{C}{\pi(1-f)} \tag{3.6}$$

Thus the total average program execution time in the presence of failures E_F is estimated as:

$$E_F = \frac{2Kp[1 + \frac{w}{\pi(1-f)} + \frac{C}{\pi(1-f)}]}{(1-f)(p+1)}. \tag{3.7}$$

We compare these approximate formulae with simulation results on Figure 3 for values of K in the range 10 to 300, p = 0.1, π=1 and f = 10^{-3}. the detection cost w is taken equal to 0.1 and the restart cost C is 1. The analytical results presented here are simple but they provide a useful bounds for the cost of the detection algorithm and of the failures. They can be therefore be used as "fast" estimators of performance under failure detection and recovery, to complement the simulation results.

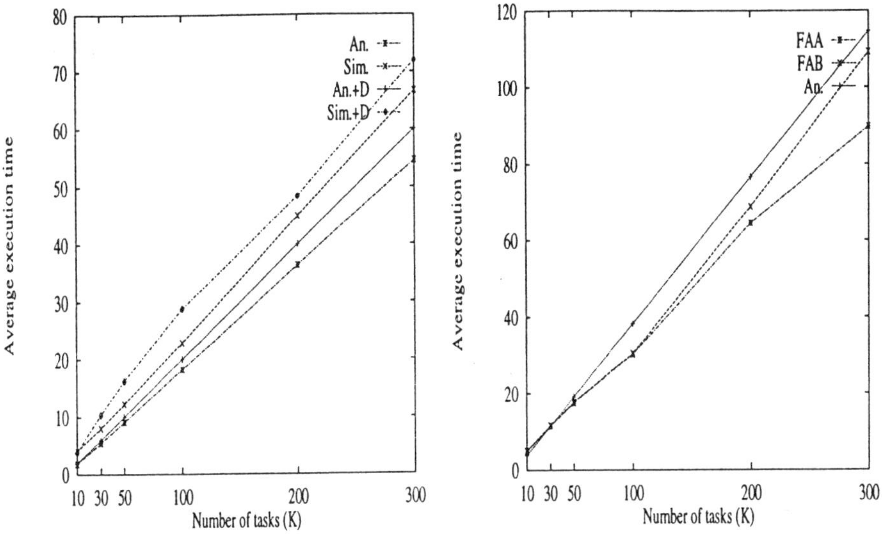

Figure 3. Comparison of analytical and simulation results

3.2 Comparing Detection Algorithms

Let us now evaluate and compare the failure detection Algorithms 1, 2 and 3. We evaluate the overhead due to each detection algorithm when there is no failure. Figure 4 presents simulation measurements for the average execution time of 10 different programs as a function of the program's size in number of tasks K. The detection and restart durations are respectively $w = 0.1$ and $C = 1$. When there is no failure, Algorithm 1 is the one which has smallest overhead. Algorithm 3 has more overhead than Algorithm 2. For $K = 200$, the average execution time obtained with algorithm 3 and $\pi = 1$ is 180 when it is only 40 without detection. Thus, Algorithm 3 increases the average execution time by 140, i.e. more than five times the cost of 28 of Algorithm 2 with $\pi = 1$.

Figures 5 and 6 present the average execution times over 10 programs as a function of the failure rate γ under failure assumptions FAA and FAB respectively. The average down period F is taken equal to 100. The figures show only one curve for algorithms 2 and 3 corresponding to the value of π which gave the lowest execution time. Under FAA, algorithm 2 gives the best result with $\pi = 0.25$ for $\gamma = 0.0001$ and $\gamma = 0.001$, and with $\pi = 1$ for $\gamma = 0.01$ and $\gamma = 0.1$. Still under FAA, algorithm 3 is plotted with $\pi = 0.25$ for $\gamma = 0.0001, 0.001$ and 0.01 and with $\pi = 1$ for $\gamma = 0.1$.

For failure assumption FAB, algorithm 2 gives the best result with $\pi = 0.25$ for $\gamma = 0.0001$ and $\gamma = 0.001$, with $\pi = 1$ for $\gamma = 0.01$ and with $\pi = 0.75$ for $\gamma = 0.1$; algorithm 3 is plotted with $\pi = 0.25$ for each value of γ.

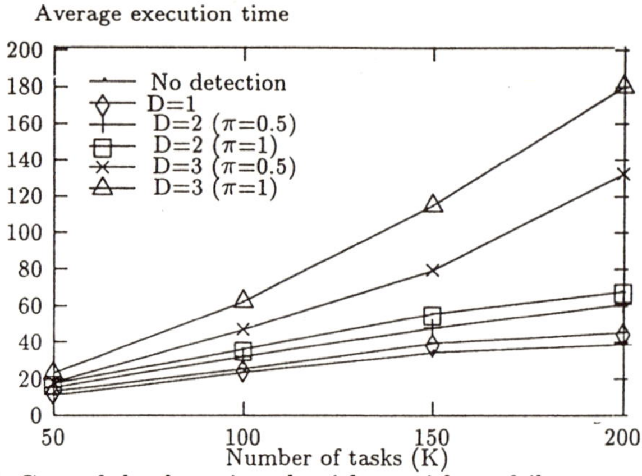

Figure 4. Cost of the detection algorithms without failures.

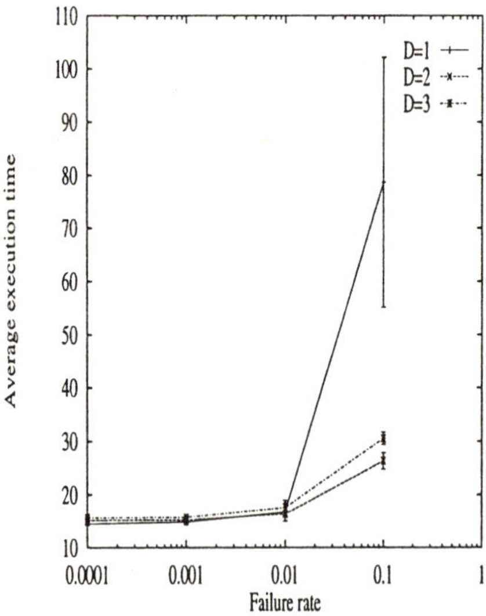

Figure 5. Average execution time under Failure Assumption A

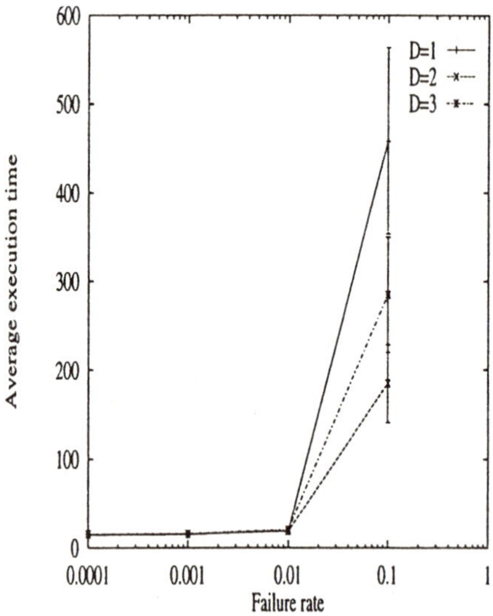

Figure 6. Average execution time under Failure Assumption B

4. An Example: A Task-Graph for Matrix Multiplication

As an example of the construction of task graphs corresponding to a parallel computation we will consider matrix multiplication. Parallel matrix multiplication is very broadly used and easily implemented on a MIMD machine. Consider the matrix product: $C = A \text{ x } B$, where A, B and C are square matrices of size n by n. The n^2 terms c_{ij} of C are computed using the formula:

$$c_{ij} = \sum_{k=0}^{n-1} a_{ik} * b_{kj}$$

Clearly the total number of operations necessary to compute the matrix C is given by $n^2(2n-1)$. At this point, we construct the task graph corresponding to this computation. For the sake of illustration, we present two different graphs on Figure 1 for $n = 4$. In Graph 1, the computation of one term c_{ij} requires only one task which performs n multiplications and $(n-1)$ additions. If each operation has an execution time of t, each task will then require $(2n-1)t$ time units.

In Graph 2, c_{ij} is computed in two parts. First the n products $a_{ik} * b_{kj}$ are computed for $k = 1, \ldots, n$. Then, the n terms previously obtained are added in a tree fashion requiring $\log_2 n$ steps. This means that one term c_{ij} is obtained using $2n-1$ tasks. In this case, to compute all the n^2 terms of the matrix C, $n^2(2n-1)$ tasks are necessary. In the first part, each task performs one multiplication; this gives an execution time of t. In the second part, each task performs one addition and has also an execution time of t.

Consequently Graph 2 will result in lower execution times than Graph 1 if a large number of processors is available. To quantify the number of processors necessary, we need to evaluate the degree of parallelism of each task graph, which is the maximum number of tasks present in the same generation of the graph. For Graph 1, there are n^2 tasks that can be computed in parallel using n^2 processors in only $(2n-1)*t$ time units. For Graph 2, the first generation is the one with the largest number of tasks which is n^3. If n^3 processors are available, then the total execution time of the second graph is $(\log_2 n + 1) * t$ time units. So the first graph has an execution time of $O(n)$ and needs no more than n^2 processors while the second has an execution time in $O(log_2 n)$ if n^3 processors are available. However, since both task graphs involve the same number $n^2(2n-1)$ of operations, if only n^2 processors are available the second task graph will have the same execution time of $(2n-1)*t$ units as the first graph.

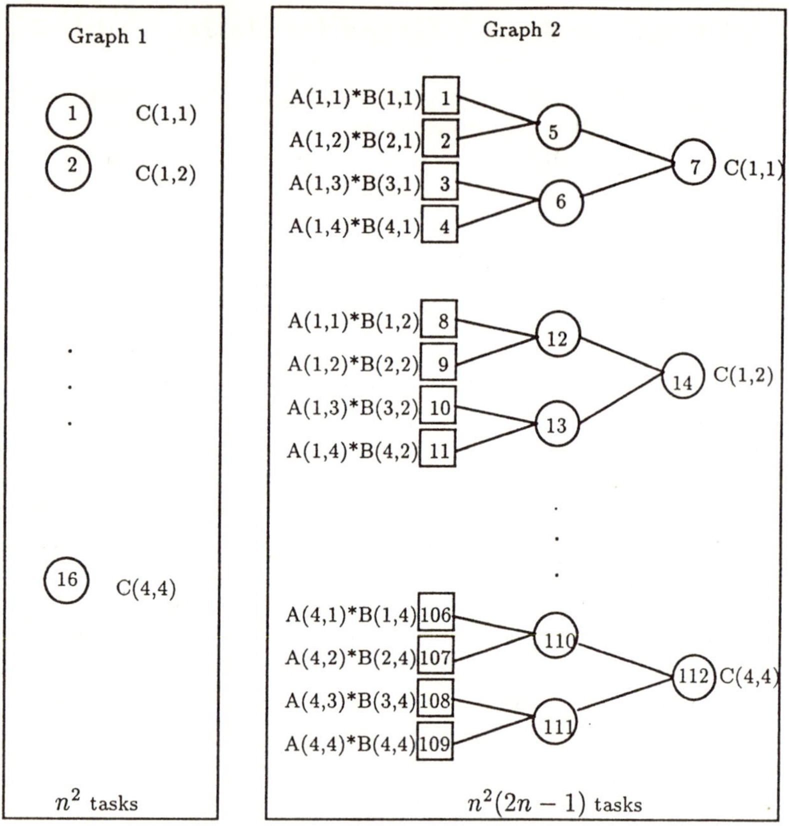

Figure 7. Two different task graphs for parallel matrix multiplication with $n = 4$.

5. An Example: Dependable Execution of the Parallel FFT Algorithm

In order to proceed further in the understanding of how our proposed failure detection and recovery algorithms work, and the manner in which they affect a practical parallel application, we will consider the discrete Fourier transform which is widely used in a variety of application areas, ranging from statistics to signal processing. Much effort has been spent by researchers to find efficient implementations of this algorithm, especially on parallel machines. In particular, the Fast Fourier Transform algorithm [4] is an efficient version which we consider in parallel form in this section.

We first describe the FFT algorithm, its parallelization as well as the corresponding task graph structure. Then we conduct simulations of the execution of the FFT task graph on a set of failing parallel processors with our failure detection and recovery algorithms.

For a given complex vector X, its discrete Fourier transform is given on a finite number of input samples by:

$$y(k) = \sum_{i=0}^{N-1} x(i)\omega_N^{ik}, \qquad k = 0, 1, ..., N-1$$

where $\omega_N = e^{j(2\Pi/N)}$ is the Nth of unity. Clearly the computation of all the components of the complex vector Y requires N^2 complex multiplications and additions. It is possible to rewrite the above equation as:

$$y(k) = y_{even}(k) + \omega^k * y_{odd}(k), \qquad 0 \leq k \leq N/2 - 1$$

$$y(k + N/2) = y_{even}(k) - \omega^k * y_{odd}(k), \qquad 0 \leq k \leq N/2 - 1$$

where Y_{even} is the Fourier transform of the even points of X, and Y_{odd} is the Fourier transform of the odd points of X.

The Fast Fourier Transform (FFT) [4] uses the two previous recursive equations. It computes the discrete Fourier transform of a vector using $1/2N \log_2 N$ instead of N^2 operations. We show on Figure 2 an example of a task graph for the FFT algorithm for $N = 16$ with $Nlog_2N = 64$ tasks. The connections between the tasks represent the flow of data during the computation. Initially, a source task receives the component of X whose index is the bit-reversal-permutation of the task number decremented by 1. For example, the task 2 ($2 - 1 = 1$ being coded 0001 on $log_2N = 4$ bits) will receive the component $x(8)$. Then each task performs one complex multiplication and one complex addition. If each task has an execution time t, the total execution time of the parallel FFT algorithm is $log_2N * t$ time units with at least N processors.

Before we go into the simulation results, let us discuss the algorithmic specifics.

5.1 Detailed Algorithmics of Failure Detection and Recovery

We will discuss several failure detection and recovery algorithms in this section. A first algorithm will be presented (Algorithm 1), and then several other algorithms which are essentially refinements of the basic scheme will be discussed.

The basic idea in all of these algorithms is that some – or all – of the tasks in the application are empowered with the failure detection and recovery procedure. Any task which is allowed to play this additional role (i.e. additional in the sense that this failure detection and recovery is carried out in addition to the ordinary computational function of the task) is said to be an **agent**.

Algorithm 1 – In this basic algorithm the tasks which have no successor (i.e. the "leaves" of the task graph) are allowed to carry out failure detection and recovery – they are the only agents in the application. This activity will be carried out in the following manner. After the leaf task i sets $V(i)$ to FINISHED, it will first examine the other leaves of the task graph. For each leaf seen not to be in the BLOCKED state, the agent will examine its predecessors until all tasks are accounted for as BLOCKED, READY, FINISHED, or ACTIVE but unfinished. This last case covers tasks which may have been stopped due to processor failure. The agent will examine the corresponding processors and reinitialize all such tasks by stopping their current execution and rescheduling them on another processor.

This algorithm is efficient when failures are rare but it will delay the detection of failures till at least one leaf completes execution. Indeed, it may happen that no leaf will ever be executed due to preceding failures and the application may be stopped as a whole. To remedy this deficiency, it is necessary to select intermediate tasks that will run the detection algorithm in addition to the leaves. The following algorithms differ in the way the selection of agents is performed and in the manner in which they follow the edges of the task graph.

Algorithm 2 – Here, we select agents from a certain number of "ranks", where the rank of a task is the longest path from itself back to a source task (one without predecessors). Each task having those selected ranks is an agent. An agent then begins examining its sibling tasks for failure, i.e. those for which it is neither a predecessor nor a successor, and then proceeds to smaller ranks as the need arises.

Algorithm 3 – When an agent finds a task of the same rank which has completed its execution, it will proceed to test in turn the successors of this completed task. The intention is to detect failures as soon as possible and to favor the rapid and successful completion of the whole program. Agents are still selected by choosing some of the ranks. Thus while Algorithms 1 and 2 carry out *look back* recovery, Algorithm 3 does look back followed by *look-forward*.

Algorithm 4 – Algorithm 4 first selects the leaves to be agents. Then it selects other tasks to be agents at random with probability π. Note that when $\pi = 1$, all the tasks are agents. Algorithm 4 only uses look-back for detection and recovery.

Algorithm 5 – This algorithm acts in the same way as Algorithm 3 (it uses look-back and look-forward) but in addition to the leaves, it selects agent tasks at random with probability π.

Several variants of these algorithms can also be considered. For instance detection can be improved by forcing the leaf task which is first to complete the detection algorithm, to perform the detection again after some delay. This leaf task can be kept alive as long as the program is not completed as a whole. Furthermore, if a program is not completed after some time-out t_{max} it may be restarted as a whole; this may be necessary when failure rates are very high.

5.2 Simulations for the Dependable Parallel FFT Algorithm

We have run simulations for the case where $N = 256$ generating a graph with 2048 tasks and we have used $M = 256$ processors. Each task has an execution time t corresponding to one complex multiplication and one complex addition; we have taken $3.24E-04$ for the average duration of a complex multiplication and $1.04E-04$ for the average duration of a complex addition (in seconds); these are realistic figures related to current workstation technology. The detection step duration w is taken equal to $6.5E-05$ which corresponds to the average time necessary to test the state of a task. The restarting step duration C is taken equal to $10E-05$; this is a relatively small value which implies that a processor's registers can be very rapidly loaded with the status of a task.

For all the simulations presented, we have computed confidence intervals with the probability of 95 %. The intervals we have thus obtained range from 0 % to 10 % of the average program execution times for all the simulations. They are not directly shown on the figures in order not to clutter the information which is being presented.

We easily see that when no detection algorithm is running, and when failures cannot occur, the total execution time of the graph with $N = 256$ is $(\log_2 N) * t = (\log_2 256) * (3.24E-04 + 1.04E-04) = 3.424E-03$ time units. However when there are no failures but a detection algorithm *is* running, this will generate obvious overhead.

In all the subsequent figures, the symbol D is used to denote the Detection algorithm concerned by a particular curve. Note that this is a change from the notation used in Section 3.

For Algorithms 2, 3, 4 and 5, in addition to the leaves, tasks are selected to be agents using a probabilistic assignment. Therefore we have run simulations with four values of the probability π that an arbitrary task is an agent: 0.25, 0.5, 0.75 and 1. Without failures, the smallest execution time (1.99E-02) is obtained with Algorithm 1 since it has only $N = 256$ tasks (the leaves) running the detection, while the other algorithms also have intermediate tasks running the detection algorithm. The largest execution time (3.78E-01) is encountered when we use Algorithm 5 for $\pi = 0.25$ giving an average detection overhead of $4.096E-02$.

In order to analyze the behavior of the detection algorithms, we have evaluated the FFT execution time with each detection algorithm for three values of the failure rate γ: 0.001, 0.005 and 0.01. We first consider the failure

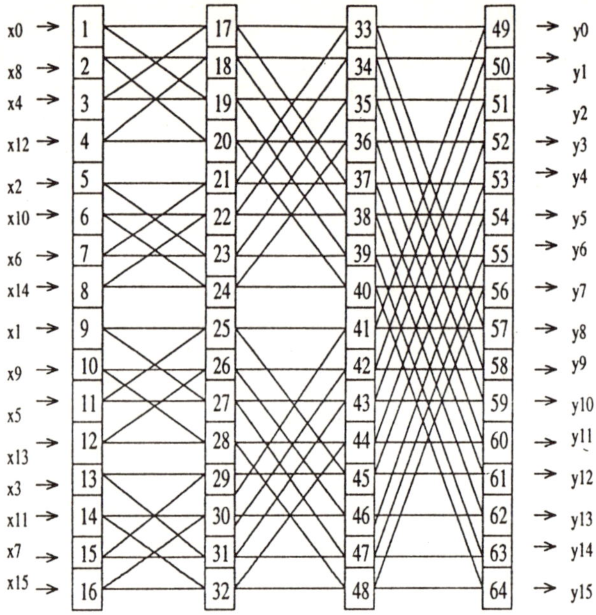

Figure 8. Task graph for the FFT computation

assumption A (FAA) where a task running the detection algorithm is supposed not to fail until it has completed the detection. We have taken for the maximum program duration allowed t_{max} the value 0.5 for $\gamma = 0.001$, 1 for $\gamma = 0.001$ and 1.5 for $\gamma = 0.001$.

We show on Figure 9 the average execution times for the parallel FFT algorithm for each of the failure detection and recovery techniques which we consider, as a function of the failure rate. For Algorithms 2 to 5 only the value of π which gave the shortest execution time is shown for each value of failure rate. For Algorithms 2, 3 and 4, $\pi = 0.25$ always provided the smallest execution time for any value of γ. For Algorithm 5, $\pi = 0.75$ appeared to be the best choice for any value of γ.

Algorithm 2 gives the smallest execution times for any value of γ, even though we observe that it results in average job execution times which are very close to Algorithm 3 for low values of γ (e.g. $\gamma = 0.001$). Algorithm 5 gives the largest execution times.

Finally, Figure 10 presents the effect of communication overhead, quantified by the parameter Z representing the time taken to exchange a message from a task to its successor task.

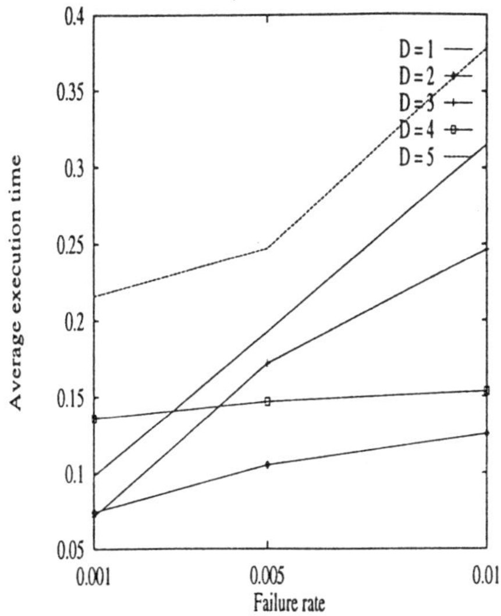

Figure 9. Comparison of the detection algorithms

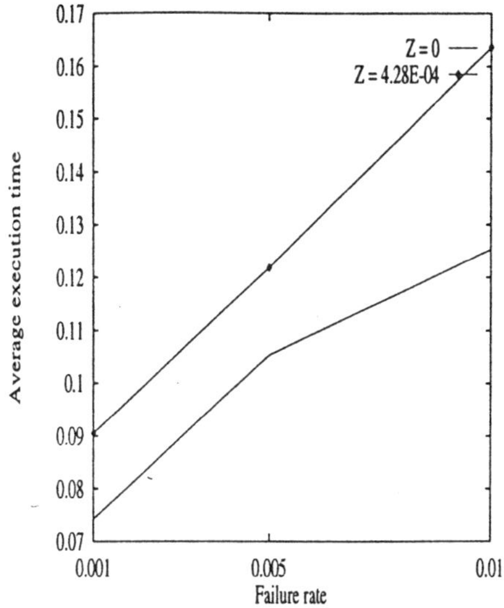

Figure 10. Execution times with and without communication

References

1. B. Bhargava and S.-R. Lian, "Independent Checkpointing and Concurrent Rollback for Recovery in Distributed Systems - An Optimistic Approach", Proc. 7th IEEE Symposium on Reliable Distributed Systems, 1988.
2. P. Bernstein, V. Hadzilacos and N. Goodman, "Concurrency Control and Recovery in Database Systems", Addison-Wesley, 1987.
3. S. Chabridon and E. Gelenbe, "Dependable execution of distributed programs", Proc. Massively Parallel Processing Conference '94, (North-Holland Elsevier), Delft, June 21-23, 1994.
4. J.M. Cooley and J.W. Tukey, "An algorithm for the machine calculation of complex Fourier series", Mathematics of Computation, **19**, pp. 297–301, 1965.
5. E. Gelenbe, "A model of roll-back recovery with multiple checkpoints", Proc. ACM-IEEE 2nd International Symposium on Software Engineering, October 1976, pp. 251–255.
6. E. Gelenbe, "Multiprocessor performance", John Wiley & Sons, New York, 1989.
7. E. Gelenbe, "On the Optimum Check-Point Interval", Journal of the ACM, **26**, pp. 259–270, 1979.
8. E. Gelenbe, "Temps d'exécution asymptotique d'un programme parallèle", Comptes-Rendus Acad. Sci. Paris (Proc. French National Academy of Science), **309** (I), pp. 399–402, 1989.
9. E. Gelenbe and D. Derochette, "Performance of roll-back recovery systems under intermittent failures", Comm. ACM, **21** (6), June 1978, pp. 493–499.
10. E. Gelenbe and I. Mitrani, "Modeling the Execution of Block Structured Processes with Hardware and Software Failures", in G. Iazeolla, P. Courtois, and A. Hordijk (eds.), Mathematical Computer Performance and Reliability, North Holland Pub. Co., 1983.

11. E. Gelenbe, R. Nelson, T. Philips and A. Tantawi, "Asymptotic processing time of a model of parallel computation", Proc. National Computer Conference (U.S.A.), pp. 127–138, 1986.
12. P.C. Kanellakis and A.A. Shvartsman, "Efficient parallel algorithms can be made robust", Distributed Computing, pp. 201–217, 1992.
13. P.C. Kanellakis, A.A. Shvartsman, J.F. Buss and P.L. Radge, "Parallel algorithms with processor failures and delays", Brown University Tech. Rep. No. CS-91-54.
14. Z. Kedem and K. Palem, "Transformations for the Automatic Derivation of Resilient Parallel Programs", Proc. 1992 IEEE Workshop on Fault-Tolerant Parallel and Distributed Systems, pp. 16–25, 1992.
15. Z. Kedem, K. Palem, M. Rabin, and A. Raghunathan, "Efficient Program Transformations for Resilient Parallel Computation via Randomization", Proc. 24th ACM Symp. on Theory of Computing, pp. 306–317, 1992.
16. Z. Kedem, K. Palem, A. Raghunathan, and P. Spirakis, "Resilient Parallel Computing on Unreliable Parallel Machines", Lectures on Parallel Computation, Eds. A. Gibbons and P. Spirakis, Cambridge University Press, pp. 145–172, 1993.
17. Z. Kedem, K. Palem, and P. Spirakis, "Efficient Robust Parallel Computations", Proc. 22nd ACM Symp. on Theory of Computing, pp. 138–148, 1990.
18. N. Pekergin and J. Vincent, "Stochastic bounds on parallel program execution times", IEEE Trans. on Software Engineering, **17** (10), pp. 105–113, 1991.
19. R.A. Sahner and K.S. Trivedi, "Performance and reliability using directed acyclic graphs", IEEE Trans. on Software Engineering, **13** (10), pp. 1105–1114, 1987.

A Fixed-Point Model of a Distributed Memory Consistency Protocol

A.J. Field and P.G. Harrison

Department of Computing, Imperial College, UK

Summary. We present a new analytical performance model of the IEEE P1596 Standard Coherent Interface operating on the default unidirectional ring architecture. The performance metrics are derived from the equilibrium probability of a cache line being in a given state; these are found by solving a set of fixed point equations. From this we derive expressions for the message traffic emanating from each node and over the ring taking into account the relevant traffic priorities in SCI. Further analysis then yields the mean memory access time and processor utilisation. We demonstrate the application of the model by comparing the performance of two different node configurations.

1. Introduction

In this paper we present an analytical model of a ring-based shared-memory multiprocessor operating the IEEE P1596 Standard Coherent Interface (SCI) [3] and we assume an implementation of the protocol on the default unidirectional ring network. Full details of the protocol may be found in [2, 3], for example, but we note the key point which is that, in the absence of a shared bus for broadcasting coherency information, the sharers of a cache line are represented explicitly in the form of a *sharing list.* We demonstrate the use of this model by comparing the performance of two internal node architectures when the protocol is being used as an interconnect medium for multiple bus-based multiprocessors.

To date, the only analytical model relevant to SCI that we are aware of is that of [5] which uses an M/G/1 model for analysing slotted ring networks, suitably adapted for a subset of the SCI traffic. The paper does not address SCI cache coherency, however, and so does not model the message traffic generated by each node to maintain a coherent global memory. Our approach is based on that of [4] for modelling bus-based coherency protocols; it differs in its characterisation of memory usage and in the way it models ring traffic and queueing for the cache and memory.

1.1 Workload Assumptions

We assume that memory accesses are either to *private* or *shareable* memory and that shareable memory is further classified into *control variables* and *shared areas.* Control variables comprise synchronisation variables like semaphores and locks for controlling access to shared structures; these variables are typically relatively small in number but addressed with relatively high frequency. The shared areas contain larger data structures, typically with access priveliges governed by control variables, that are relatively infrequently accessed. It is assumed that the control variables are memory mapped in such a way that they may *all* reside in the SCI cache at the same time so that there are no conflicts in the cache between accesses to these variables. The cache thus contains disjoint sets of lines: those which may contain both control variables and shared area data (we call this "Region I" of the cahe) and those which may contain only shared area data ("Region II"). Within the control variables and shared areas, memory accesses are assumed to be uniformly distributed; within each region, the cache lines are then statistically identical.

2. A New Model for SCI

The approach we have taken uses the basic method in [4] to obtain the equilibrium cache line state probabilities and uses them to determine the message arrival rates for a separate model of the ring.

We assume the following parameters:

α – the probability of a read
β – the probability of a hit in the SCI cache
γ_1 – the probability that a memory access is to a control structure
γ_2 – the probability that a memory access is to the shared areas
γ_3 – the probability that a memory accesses is to private data
σ – the probability that an access to private data, which is mapped into the global address space, is held locally
K – The number of nodes
N – The total number of shareable memory blocks
m – The number of (shareable) lines containing control variables
n – The capacity (in blocks) of each SCI cache
τ – The rate at which a busy processor leaves the "think" state (note that $1/\tau$ is the mean think period)

Note that $\gamma_1 + \gamma_2 + \gamma_3 = 1$. We aim to determine the probability, π, that a processor is busy doing useful work and also the mean time to service a memory request.

Cache Line States

A memory block is either **Home** (uncached) or **Cached** and cached copies may either be *clean* or *dirty.* There are eleven basic line states although eight of them we will subdivide further in accordance with the type of data they contain (control variables or shared area data). The states are: **1 Private Clean**–The location contains a clean copy of private (non-shareable) data; **2**

Private Dirty; **3 Only Clean**–The location contains the only cached copy of a memory block and is clean; **4 Only Dirty**; **5 Head Clean**–As 3 but it is at the head of a list containing at least two members; **6 Head Dirty**; **7 Mid Clean**–The location is in the middle of the list (i.e. at neither the head nor tail) and the cached copy is clean; **8 Mid Dirty**; **9 Tail Clean**–As 5 but the location is at the tail of the sharing list; **10 Tail Dirty**; **11 Invalid**. For Region I of the cache we annotate states 3–10 with the subscript 'a' if the (shared) block contains control information and 'b' if it contains shared region data. We make the assumption that different types of data do not co-exist on the same cache line which is easily ensured by a suitable allocation of global memory addresses. The cache lines in Region I therefore have nineteen possible states, and those of Region II eleven.

2.1 Actions generated by a processor

A given processor emerges from the think state at rate τ, and according to the state of the cache location it is accessing will generate one of the following processor *actions* (the distinguishing subscripts 'a' and 'b' are omitted as the actions are the same for each): **Creation (CR)**–A read or write miss on a location in state 11 not cached by other processors; **Addition (AD)**–As above but already cached. **Deletion-Creation (DC)**–A read or write miss on a *home* block mapping to a cache location previously in state 3–10; **Deletion-Addition (DA)**–A read miss on an already *cached* block mapping to a location in state 3–10; **Deletion-Reduction (DR)**–A write miss on a *cached* block mapping to a location in state 3–10; **Take-Reduction (TR)**–A write hit on a block mapping to a location in state 7–10; **Head-Reduction (HR)**–A write hit on a location in the processor's cache but in state 3,4; **Invalid-Reduction (IR)**–A write miss on a *cached* block mapping to a location in state 11.

To add to a sharing list a processor sends a short message to the memory, which sends another short message to the current head, which in turn sends a long message containing the up-to-date copy of the block to the processor. Deleting from a list requires either one or two short messages depending on whether the cache line is at the head/tail or middle of its sharing list. Note that for each Deletion operation in state 2 then a *writeback* of the line will also be performed, requiring one additional long message to the memory.

2.2 The analytical model

We assume that the evolution of the state of a given location in a cache follows a Markov process, independent of the states of other locations. This process is irreducible, aperiodic and has a finite state space and thus has a steady-state. A separate Markov process is established for each cache region for the reasons already stated.

Let q_j be the steady state probability that a given cache location in Region I is in state j for $j = 1, 2, 3_a, 3_b, ..., 10_b, 11$. It is also the average proportion of cache locations in state j in equilibrium. Let q'_j be the same for Region II, $j = 1, ..., 11$.

State Transitions

The state transitions occur as a result of read and write operations to the cache. We imagine we are looking at a particular "observed" line of a cache and consider the various read/write operations which can change the state of that line. We omit much of the detail but note that the length of the mid portion of a sharing list is assumed to be geometrically distributed. With this assumption we can easily find the mean sharing list length (L_a, L_b for Region I and L' for Region II).

An alternative and apparently more accurate representation of the line states would store the length of each sharing list explicitly with the state in order to avoid assumptions about the distribution of the sharing list length. However, this requires the state of *every* line in the cache system to be considered in order that the correct transitions can be determined. For example, in the event of a read miss the new state of the observed line would be determined by the state (i.e. current length) of the new sharing list to which the line must be added. This cannot be determined by considering the cache line in isolation.

Transition Rates

The processors leave the think state at rate $\pi\tau$ and we consider those memory accesses which cause a change in line state. Note that the transition rates do not cover transitions from a state to itself, for example as a result of a read hit in states 1–10. Consider Region I first and define η_r to be the probability that, given a cache miss on a type r memory block, the block is cached elsewhere and ϵ_r to be the probability that a cached copy of a type r line is clean (r is either a or b). We define:

$$\begin{aligned}
s &\equiv \text{state variable} \\
a &= \{3a, ..., 10a\} \\
b &= \{3b, ..., 10b\} \\
\overline{a} &= \{1, 2, 11\} \cup b \\
\eta_a &= 1 - (1 - \sum_{i \in a} q_{i_a} + q_{i_b})^{K-1} \\
\eta_b &= \frac{q_{3_b} + q_{4_b} + q_{5_b} + q_{6_b})\, n\, (K-1)}{(N-m)} \\
\epsilon_r &= \frac{q_{3_r} + q_{5_r}}{q_{3_r} + q_{4_r} + q_{5_r} + q_{6_r}}
\end{aligned}$$

whereupon the transition rates may be written:

$$\begin{aligned}
\{b, 11\} &\to 1 && \frac{\alpha\gamma_3}{n} \\
\{1, 2\} &\to 1 && \frac{\alpha(1-\beta)\gamma_3}{n} \\
s &\to 2 && \frac{(1-\alpha)\gamma_3}{n} \\
\bar{a} &\to 3a && \frac{\alpha\gamma_1(1-\eta_a)}{m} \\
\{5a, 9a\} &\to 3a && \frac{p_{3_a}(1-\gamma_1)(1-\beta)}{n} \\
\{1, 2, a\} &\to 3b && \frac{\alpha\gamma_2(1-\eta_b)}{n} \\
\{b, 11\} &\to 3b, s \neq 5b, 9b && \frac{\alpha(1-\beta)\gamma_2(1-\eta_b)}{n} \\
\{5b, 9b\} &\to 3b && \frac{\alpha(1-\beta)\gamma_2(1-\eta_b)}{n} + \frac{p_{3_b}(1-\beta)}{n} \\
s &\to 4a, s \neq 6a, 10a && \frac{(1-\alpha)\gamma_1}{m} \\
\{6a, 10a\} &\to 4a && \frac{(1-\alpha)\gamma_1}{m} + \frac{p_{3_a}(1-\gamma_1)(1-\beta)}{n} \\
s &\to 4b, s \neq 6b, 10b && \frac{(1-\alpha)\gamma_2}{n} \\
\{6b, 10b\} &\to 4b && \frac{(1-\alpha)\gamma_2}{n} + \frac{p_{3_b}(1-\beta)}{n} \\
\bar{a} &\to 5a && \frac{\alpha\gamma_1\eta_a\epsilon_a}{m} \\
7a &\to 5a && \frac{p_{1_a}(1-\gamma_1)(1-\beta)}{n} \\
\{1, 2, a\} &\to 5b && \frac{\alpha\gamma_2\eta_b\epsilon_b}{n} \\
\{b, 11\} &\to 5b, s \neq 7b && \frac{\alpha(1-\beta)\gamma_2\eta_b\epsilon_b}{n} \\
7b &\to 5b && \frac{\alpha(1-\beta)\gamma_2\eta_b\epsilon_b}{n} + \frac{p_{1_b}(1-\beta)}{n} \\
\bar{a} &\to 6a && \frac{\alpha\gamma_1\eta_a(1-\epsilon_a)}{m} \\
8a &\to 6a && \frac{p_{1_a}(1-\gamma_1)(1-\beta)}{n} \\
\{1, 2, a\} &\to 6b && \frac{\alpha\gamma_2\eta_b(1-\epsilon_b)}{n} \\
\{b, 11\} &\to 6b, s \neq 8b && \frac{\alpha(1-\beta)\gamma_2\eta_b(1-\epsilon_b)}{n}
\end{aligned}$$

$$8b \rightarrow 6b \qquad \frac{\alpha(1-\beta)\gamma_2\eta_b(1-\epsilon_b)}{n} + \frac{p_{1_b}(1-\beta)}{n}$$

$$5a \rightarrow 7a, 6a \rightarrow 8a \qquad \frac{(K-L_a)\alpha\gamma_1}{m}$$

$$5b \rightarrow 7b, 6b \rightarrow 8b \qquad \frac{(K-L_b)\alpha(1-\beta)\gamma_2}{N-m}$$

$$3a \rightarrow 9a, 4a \rightarrow 10a \qquad \frac{(K-1)\alpha\gamma_1}{m}$$

$$3b \rightarrow 9b, 4b \rightarrow 10b \qquad \frac{(K-1)\alpha(1-\beta)\gamma_2}{N-m}$$

$$7a \rightarrow 9a, 8a \rightarrow 10a \qquad \frac{p_{2_a}(1-\gamma_1)(1-\beta)}{n}$$

$$7b \rightarrow 9b, 8b \rightarrow 10b \qquad \frac{p_{2_b}(1-\beta)}{n}$$

$$a \rightarrow 11 \qquad \frac{(K-1)(1-\alpha)\gamma_1}{m}$$

$$b \rightarrow 11 \qquad \frac{(K-1)(1-\alpha)\gamma_2}{N-m}$$

To clarify these equations we consider some specific examples:

$s \rightarrow 2$, i.e. a transition from any state to the state "Private Dirty". This happens when private data (held in the global address space), whose address maps to the observed cache line, is written to. The associated transition rate is thus $\pi\tau\frac{(1-\alpha)\gamma_3}{n}$.

$\{1, 2, 3a, ..., 10a\} \rightarrow 6b$. A cache line holding private data or control variables will transit to "head dirty" if a read to a dirty, and already cached, copy of a shared area variable maps to the observed line address. The transition rate is thus $\pi\tau\frac{\alpha\gamma_2\eta_b(1-\epsilon_b)}{n}$.

$5a \rightarrow 7a, 6a \rightarrow 8a$. This happens on a remote read miss from one of the (average $K - L_a$) processors who do not currently have a cached copy of the control variable in the observed line. A new entry will be added to the sharing list making the observed line state transit from "head" to "mid". The associated rate is $\frac{(K-L_a)\alpha\gamma_1}{m}$.

The transitions for Region II involve only eleven states since they may. In the following equations η and ϵ are the Region II equivalents of η_r and ϵ_r, for $r = a, b$ for Region I:

$$s \rightarrow 1 \qquad \frac{\alpha(1-\beta)\gamma_3}{n}$$

$$s \rightarrow 2 \qquad \frac{(1-\alpha)\gamma_3}{n}$$

$$s \rightarrow 3, s \neq 9, 5 \qquad \frac{\alpha(1-\beta)(1-\eta)\gamma_2}{n}$$

$$5 \to 3, 9 \to 3 \qquad \frac{\alpha(1-\beta)(1-\eta)\gamma_2}{n} + \frac{p_3'(1-\beta)}{n}$$

$$s \to 4, s \neq 6, 10 \qquad \frac{(1-\alpha)\gamma_2}{n}$$

$$6 \to 4, 10 \to 4 \qquad \frac{(1-\alpha)\gamma_2}{n} + \frac{p_3'(1-\beta)}{n}$$

$$s \to 5, s \neq 7 \qquad \frac{\alpha(1-\beta)\eta\epsilon\gamma_2}{n}$$

$$7 \to 5 \qquad \frac{\alpha(1-\beta)\eta\epsilon\gamma_2}{n} + \frac{p_1'(1-\beta)}{n}$$

$$s \to 6, s \neq 8 \qquad \frac{\alpha(1-\beta)\eta(1-\epsilon)\gamma_2}{n}$$

$$8 \to 6 \qquad \frac{\alpha(1-\beta)\eta(1-\epsilon)\gamma_2}{n} + \frac{p_1'(1-\beta)}{n}$$

$$5 \to 7, 6 \to 8 \qquad \frac{(K-L')\alpha(1-\beta)\gamma_2}{N-m}$$

$$3 \to 9, 4 \to 10 \qquad \frac{(K-1)\alpha(1-\beta)\gamma_2}{N-m}$$

$$7 \to 9, 8 \to 10 \qquad \frac{p_2'(1-\beta)\gamma_2}{n}$$

$$b \to 11 \qquad \frac{(K-1)(1-\alpha)\gamma_2}{N-m}$$

The balance equations can be derived from the transition rates; these are not linear, but define a *fixed point* on the vector of steady-state probabilities for each region and so in practice are solved iteratively.

The probability that a processor emerging from a think state generates each action may be conveniently expressed by a table δ indexed by state and action. This is shown in Table 2.1. For example Pr{CR in state $11a$} $= \delta_{11a,CR} = 1 - \eta_a$, Pr{ DA in state $7a$} $= \delta_{7a,DA} = \alpha\eta_a(1-\beta)$ and so on.

State	*Actions*							
	CR	AD	DC	DA	DR	TR	HR	IR
1,2	0	0	$\overline{\eta}\overline{\beta}$	$\alpha\eta\overline{\beta}$	$\overline{\alpha}\eta$	0	0	0
3,4	0	0	$\overline{\eta}\overline{\beta}$	$\alpha\eta\overline{\beta}$	$\overline{\alpha}\eta$	0	0	0
5,6	0	0	$\overline{\eta}\overline{\beta}$	$\alpha\eta\overline{\beta}$	$\overline{\alpha}\eta$	0	$\overline{\alpha}\beta$	0
7,8	0	0	$\overline{\eta}\overline{\beta}$	$\alpha\eta\overline{\beta}$	$\overline{\alpha}\eta$	$\overline{\alpha}\beta$	0	0
9,10	0	0	$\overline{\eta}\overline{\beta}$	$\alpha\eta\overline{\beta}$	$\overline{\alpha}\eta$	$\overline{\alpha}\beta$	0	0
11	$\overline{\eta}$	$\alpha\eta$	0	0	0	0	0	$\overline{\alpha}\eta$

Table 2.1. State transitions from remote operations

Message Streams

Each action makes the processor send and receive a certain number of long or short messages through the ring. In order to calculate the time these messages take to be transmitted we need to calculate the rate at which they are produced. The next step requires us to define six new tables S, S', L, C, C' and M representing the number of short messages (Region I and Region II respectively), long messages, cache accesses (Region I and Region II respectively) and memory accesses, indexed by the line state and the action initiated. For example, an AD action first experiences a cache miss and then takes a copy of the required block, adding it to the head of the current sharing list. It thus issues one short message to memory requesting the head of the sharing list (involving a memory access); this in turn sends a short message to the head of the list (involving a cache access), which in turn sends a long message containing the latest copy of the line to the originating processor (this must be written to the processor's cache and therefore involves one further cache access). Note that some messages may be destined for the local memory block of the processor and so will create no ring traffic. These are explicitly annotated with an * in the table. Thus, for the example above we have, $S_{11,AD} = 1^* + 1, S'_{11,AD} = 1^* + 1, L_{11,AD} = 1^*, C_{11,AD} = 3, C'_{11,AD} = 3$ and $M_{11,AD} = 1$. Similarly for the other actions/states. We do not list the table here, referring the interested reader to [1] for the full details.

2.3 Mean transmission Time

Given the above tables we can now determine the mean transmission time of a message around the ring. All messages issued by a transmitting node will perform one full circuit of the ring (i.e. through $K-1$ ring buffers). The receiving node will extract the incoming packet and, at the same time, pass it on as an echo packet which we will assume is the same length as a short packet.

In SCI messages originating from the ring have priority over messages in the transmit queue originating from the node and so we appeal to Cobham's formulae to determine the mean transmission time of short and long messages around the ring, T_s and T_l respectively, on the assumption that the messages arriving at a processor are Poisson. This analysis assumes that the length of a long message is a fixed multiple M of the length of a short message. The various transmission times and utilisations can then be expressed in terms of the transmission time of a short message, t_{short} which is determined by the SCI link speed.

2.4 Cache/Memory Access Delay

We model the cache/memory controller as a first-come-first-served queue and appeal to a separate M/G/1 model of the queue in which the service time distribution is a probabilistic mixture of the (constant) cache and memory access times, t_{cache} and t_{mem} respectively. We will use the model to compare two alternative node architectures: the first is that of the conventional SCI model and the second a similar design in which the node memory is decoupled from the node cache and relocated on the main system bus, to which the processors are also attached. The latter model is thus of a collection of conventional bus-based multiprocessors interconnected using SCI and is interesting as it presents the simplest method for constructing a scalable parallel machine from existing shared-memory multiprocessors.

We first define the probabilities P_I and P_{II} that a memory reference addresses the cache in Regions I and II respectively:

$$\begin{aligned} P_I &= \gamma_1 + (\gamma_2 + \gamma_3(1-\sigma))\frac{m}{n} \\ P_{II} &= (\gamma_2 + \gamma_3(1-\sigma))\frac{n-m}{n} \end{aligned}$$

Note that $P_I + P_{II} = 1 - \gamma_3\sigma$ which we denote by P_s and we write $\overline{P_I} = P_I/P_s, \overline{P_{II}} = P_{II}/P_s$.

Case 1: Standard Memory Model The mean number of cache and memory accesses (n_c and n_m respectively) for each action can be found from P_I and P_{II}, the equilibrium line state probabilities and the various tables defined earlier. ¿From these we can find the rate at which cache (λ_c) and memory (λ_m) accesses are produced by a processor:

$$\begin{aligned} \lambda_c &= \tau P_s + \lambda_t \frac{n_c}{n_c + n_m} \\ \lambda_m &= \tau\gamma_3\sigma + \frac{\tau(\gamma_1+\gamma_2)(1-\beta)}{K} + \lambda_t \frac{n_m}{n_c + n_m} \end{aligned}$$

$\lambda_t = \lambda_s + \lambda_l$ is the rate at which messages are produce by a node. Short messages are produced at the rates:

$$\begin{aligned} \lambda_s &= \tau P_I \sum_{s,a} q_s \, \delta_{s,a} \, S_{s,a} \\ &+ \tau P_{II} \sum_{s',a} q'_{s'} \, \delta'_{s',a} \, S'_{s',a} \end{aligned}$$

The equation for λ_l is identical except that L and L' replace S and S' respectively. Since the total arrival rate of cache and memory accesses is $\lambda_{cm} = \lambda_c + \lambda_m$ we can obtain the mean queuing time at the cache/memory controller from the Pollaczek-Khinchine formula:

$$Q_{cm} = \frac{\lambda_c t_{cache}^2 + \lambda_m t_{mem}^2}{2(1-\rho_{cm})}$$

where ρ_{cm} is the cache/memory controller utilisation given by: $\rho_{cm} = \lambda_c t_{cache} + \lambda_m t_{mem}$ The mean time to service a memory request is then

$$
\begin{aligned}
T &= P_s[\frac{\lambda_s T_s + \lambda_l T_l}{\tau P_s} \\
&+ n_c(Q_{cm} + t_{cache}) + n_m(Q_{cm} + t_{mem}) \\
&+ p_{hit}\ (Q_{cm} + t_{cache})] \\
&+ \sigma\gamma_3(Q_{cm} + t_{mem})
\end{aligned}
$$

where

$$p_{hit} = \overline{P_I}\left(1 - \sum_{s,a}\delta_{s,a}\right) + \overline{P_{II}}\left(1 - \sum_{s',a}\delta_{s',a}\right)$$

The processor utilisation is then:

$$\pi = \frac{\frac{1}{\tau}}{\frac{1}{\tau} + T} = \frac{1}{1 + \tau T}$$

Case 2: Revised Memory Model We now consider the revised memory model. The operation of this design is similar to that of the original except that requests to the memory from the SCI ring may now have to compete with other requests on the local system bus. Equally, however, some accesses to memory, specifically private accesses which require no intervention from the SCI cache, can proceed independently of the SCI node controller. Thus the relative performance of the two designs is determined by the nature of the workload.

Requests from the SCI ring will be diverted to the system bus if the request is a read to a home block which has been cached and dirtied by a local processor, or if the request is an invalidation (i.e. part of a list reduction). In order to estimate the memory access time, and also the load on the system bus, we need an additional workload parameter in this case, which is the system bus load due to local (i.e. snoopy protocol) coherency traffic among the processor/cache units. We shall refer to this as τ'.

The traffic on the bus comes from either the processors attached to it, or from the ring. The total arrival rate to the bus is therefore:

$$\lambda'_{bus} = \tau + \tau' + \lambda_t \frac{n_m}{n_c + n_m}$$

The queueing time is then given by:

$$Q'_{bus} = \frac{\lambda'_{bus}\ M_{2_{bus}}}{2(1 - \rho'_{bus})}$$

The rate at which the cache/memory directory supplies data to the system bus, τ_{cm} say, is given by

$$\tau_{cm} = \tau(1 - \gamma_3\sigma - \frac{\gamma_1 + \gamma_2}{K}(1 - \beta))$$

so that:

$$\begin{aligned} \rho'_{bus} &= \tau_{cm} t_{cache} + (\lambda'_{bus} - \tau_{cm}) t_{mem} \\ M_{2_{bus}} &= \frac{\tau_{cm}}{\lambda'_{bus}} t^2_{cache} + (1 - \frac{\tau_{cm}}{\lambda'_{bus}}) t^2_{mem} \end{aligned}$$

The same quantities for the cache-memory controller bus are thus:

$$\begin{aligned} \lambda'_{cm} &= \tau(1 - \gamma_3 \sigma) + \lambda_t \\ Q'_{cm} &= \frac{\lambda'_{cm} t^2_{cache}}{2(1 - \rho'_{cm})} \\ \rho'_{cm} &= \lambda'_{cm} t_{cache} \end{aligned}$$

3. Results and Validation

Some sample numerical results may be found in [1]. We are currently validating the model with respect to an execution-driven simulation of the SCI protocol running codes from the SLASH suite. SPLASH programs are executed in order to measure not only performance metrics like processor utilisation and memory access time, but also the parameters used in the model. By running the model with these parameters we can then compare the model output with that of the original executing SPLASH code. Preliminary results show a promising match for MP3D at least but this exercise is, as yet, incomplete.

References

1. A.J. Field and P.G. Harrison. "An Analytical Model of the Standard Coherent Interface 'SCI"', Internal Report, Department of Computing, Imperial College, 1995.
2. S. Gjessing, D.B. Gustavson, J.R. Goodman, D.V. James and E.H Kristiansen. "The SCI Cache Coherence Protocol". In Scalable Shared Memory Multiprocessors, M. Dubois and S. Thakkar, eds., Kluwer academic Publishers, Norwell, Mass. 1992.
3. The IEEE. "IEEE P1596 Standard Specification". IEEE Publication, 1989.
4. A.G. Greenberg and I.Mitrani "Analysis of Snooping Caches", Proc. of Performance 87, 12th Int. Symp. on Computer Performance, Brussels, December 1987.
5. S.L. Scott, J.R. Goodman and M.K. Vernon. "Performance of the SCI ring", In Proc. of the 19th Annual Int. Sym. on Computer Architecture, May 1992.

Routing Among Different Nodes Where Servers Break Down Without Losing Jobs

N. Thomas and I. Mitrani

Computing Science Department, University of Newcastle, UK

Summary. Jobs generated by a single Poisson source can be routed through N alternative gateways, modelled as parallel $M/M/1$ queues. The servers are subject to random breakdowns which leave their corresponding queues intact, but may affect the routing of jobs during the subsequent repair periods.

The marginal equilibrium queue size distributions are determined by spectral expansion. This can be done, at least in principle, for any number of queues. Several routing strategies are evaluated and compared empirically. In the special case $N = 2$, it may also be possible to find the joint distribution of the numbers of jobs in the two queues.

1. Introduction

The modelling literature contains many studies dealing with the performance and availability of systems subject to breakdowns and repairs. Problems of this type arise in areas as diverse as computing, communications, manufacturing and transport. However, most of the work has concentrated on models involving a single job queue served by one or more processors (e.g., see [1, 8, 13, 14]). Very few results are available for systems with more than one queue. An approximate solution for a general Jackson network of unreliable nodes was suggested in [7]. Mikou [5] analysed a tightly coupled two-node network with simultaneous breakdowns and repairs, by a far from trivial reduction to a boundary value problem. More recently, Mitrani and Wright [11] examined a system with N parallel queues where the consequences of a breakdown are (a) the loss of all jobs in the corresponding queue and (b) the re-direction or loss of all arrivals to that queue during the subsequent repair period. Those assumptions imply that the queue of a broken server is necessarily empty. Idrissi-Kacemi et al. [6] have studied the case of two queues, only one of which is subject to breakdowns; all jobs present are transfered, and new jobs are redirected, to the other queue after a breakdown.

Of the above citations, only [11] obtains exact performance measures for a model with more than two queues.

Here we consider a system where jobs from a common incoming stream may be directed to one of N alternative nodes, each of which consists of a single server and an unbounded queue. The service, breakdown and repair processes at the different nodes are independent of each other and have different parameters, in general. The consequences of a breakdown at a server are not too catastrophic: service stops and the existing jobs remain in place; new arrivals during the subsequent repair period may or may not be re-directed to other nodes, depending on the routing policy. There are no job losses.

The routing policies that are examined are *almost static*. That is, the choice of where to send an incoming job is Bernoulli, independent of past history and of the current queue sizes. However, the probability of selecting a given node may depend on the current server configuration, i.e. on which servers are operative and which are not.

Our motivation for studying this system comes from the field of networking: the jobs are messages generated by some source, and the servers are alternative gateways through which those messages may be routed. Gateways are subject to failures that interrupt service for random periods of time. The source finds out about such failures and may redirect traffic. This naturally raises the question of how to set the routing probabilities. The main purpose of the analysis, therefore, is to determine performance measures so that different routing policies can be evaluated and compared.

The model and its parameters are specified in section 2. Ideally, one would like to find the joint stationary distribution of the set of operative servers and the numbers of jobs in the corresponding queues. To determine that distribution, it is necessary to solve a non-separable multidimensional Markov process, which is an intractable problem in the general case. The only case for which the joint distribution is attainable is $N = 2$. An outline of that analysis is presented in section 6.

On the other hand, the performance measures of practical interest are mainly concerned with local or global averages, e.g. the average number of jobs present at a given node or the overall average response time. To calculate such performance measures, it is enough to determine the marginal queue size distributions. This last problem can be solved, at least in principle, for arbitrary N (section 3). Problems of comparison and optimization of routing policies can thus be tackled numerically. Several such numerical evaluations are reported in section 4. Various generalisations of the model, where the same solution methodology applies, are mentioned in section 5.

2. The model

Jobs arrive into the system in a Poisson stream with rate λ. There are N servers, each with an associated unbounded queue, to which incoming jobs may be directed. Server k goes through alternating independent operative and inoperative periods, distributed exponentially with means $1/\xi_k$ and $1/\eta_k$, respectively. While it is operative, the jobs in its queue receive exponentially distributed services with mean $1/\mu_k$, and depart upon completion. When a server becomes inoperative (breaks down), the corresponding queue, including the job in service (if any), remains in place. Services that are interrupted in this way are eventually resumed from the point of interruption. The system model is illustrated in figure 1.

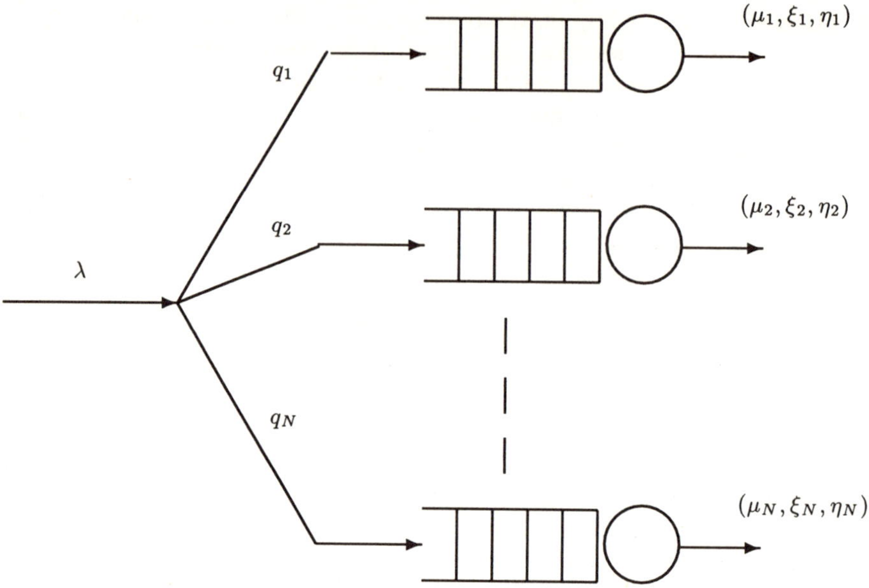

Fig. 2.1. A single source split among N unreliable nodes

The *system configuration* at any moment is specified by the subset, σ, of servers that are currently operative (that subset may be empty, or it may be the set of all servers): $\sigma \subset \{1, 2, \ldots, N\}$. There are of course 2^N possible system configurations. The steady-state marginal probability, p_σ, of configuration σ is given by

$$p_\sigma = \prod_{k \in \sigma} \frac{\eta_k}{\xi_k + \eta_k} \prod_{k \in \overline{\sigma}} \frac{\xi_k}{\xi_k + \eta_k} \quad , \quad \sigma \subset \{1, 2, \ldots, N\} \; , \tag{2.1}$$

where $\overline{\sigma}$ is the complement of σ with respect to $\{1, 2, \ldots, N\}$ and an empty product is by definition equal to 1. These expressions follow from the fact that servers break down and are repaired independently of each other.

If, at the time of arrival, a new job finds the system in configuration σ, then it is directed to node k with probability $q_k(\sigma)$. These decisions are independent of each other, of past history and of the sizes of the various queues. Thus, a routing policy is defined by specifying 2^N vectors,

$$q(\sigma) = [q_1(\sigma), q_2(\sigma), \ldots, q_N(\sigma)] \quad , \quad \sigma \subset \{1, 2, \ldots, N\} \; , \tag{2.2}$$

such that for every σ,

$$\sum_{k=1}^{N} q_k(\sigma) = 1 \; .$$

The system state at time t is specified by the pair $[I(t), J(t)]$, where $I(t)$ indicates the current configuration (the configurations can be numbered, so that $I(t)$ is an integer in the range $0, 1, \ldots, 2^N - 1$), and $J(t)$ is an integer vector whose k'th element, $J_k(t)$, is the number of jobs in queue k ($k = 1, 2, \ldots, N$). Under the assumptions that have been made, $X = \{[I(t), J(t)] \ , \ t \geq 0\}$ is an irreducible Markov process. The condition for ergodicity of X is that, for every queue, the overall arrival rate is lower than the overall service capacity:

$$\lambda \sum_{\sigma \subset \{1,2,\ldots,N\}} p_\sigma q_k(\sigma) < \mu_k \frac{\eta_k}{\xi_k + \eta_k} \quad , \quad k = 1, 2, \ldots, N \ . \tag{2.3}$$

When the routing probabilities depend on the system configuration, the process X is not separable (i.e., it does not have a product-form solution). Consequently, the problem of determining its equilibrium distribution is intractable for $N > 2$. In the case $N = 2$, a solution is possible but is rather complex (see section 5). However, the quantities of principal interest are the steady-state average queue sizes, L_k, and the the overall average response time, W, given by

$$W = \frac{1}{\lambda} \sum_{k=1}^{N} L_k \ . \tag{2.4}$$

To determine those performance measures, it suffices to study the stochastic processes $Y_k = \{[I(t), J_k(t)] \ , \ t \geq 0\}$ ($k = 1, 2, \ldots, N$), modelling the behaviour of the system configuration and the size of an individual queue. The state space of Y_k is infinite in one dimension only, which simplifies the solution considerably and makes it tractable for reasonably large values of N. The important observation here is that Y_k is also an irreducible Markov process, for every k. This is because the arrivals into, and departures from queue k during a small interval $(t, t + \Delta t)$ depend only on the system configuration and the size of queue k at time t, and not on the sizes of the other queues.

The next task, therefore, is to find the equilibrium distribution of Y_k :

$$p_k(i,j) = \lim_{t \to \infty} P[I(t) = i \ , \ J_k(t) = j] \quad , \quad i = 0, 1, \ldots, 2^N - 1 \ , \ j \geq 0 \ . \tag{2.5}$$

Given the probabilities $p_k(i,j)$, the average size of queue k is obtained from

$$L_k = \sum_{j=1}^{\infty} j \sum_{i=0}^{2^N - 1} p_k(i,j) \ . \tag{2.6}$$

3. Queue size distributions

The process Y_k is of the *block tri-diagonal*, or *Quasi-Birth-and-Death* type. Its possible transitions are:

(a) from state (i,j) to state (i',j), where i' is a configuration with either one more, or one fewer operative server;
(b) from state (i,j) to state $(i,j+1)$, if the routing probability to queue k in configuration i, $q_k(i)$, is non-zero;
(c) from state (i,j) to state $(i,j-1)$, if $j>0$ and server k is operative in configuration i.

The balance equations for Y_k are best written in vector and matrix form. Define the (row) vector of equilibrium probabilities of all states with j jobs in queue k:

$$v_k(j) = [p_k(0,j), p_k(1,j), \ldots, p_k(2^N-1,j)] \ , \ j \geq 0 \, . \tag{3.1}$$

Let $A = (a_{i,i'})$ $(i,i' = 0,1,\ldots,2^N-1)$ be the matrix of instantaneous transition rates corresponding to transitions (a). If in configuration i the subset of operative servers is σ, and in i' it is $\sigma+\{\ell\}$, for some server ℓ, then $a_{i,i'} = \eta_\ell$; similarly, if in i' the configuration is $\sigma-\{\ell\}$, for some server ℓ, then $a_{i,i'} = \xi_\ell$. It is also useful to introduce the diagonal matrix, D_A, whose i'th diagonal element is the i'th row sum of A $(i = 0,1,\ldots,2^N-1)$.

Let B_k be the diagonal matrix whose i'th diagonal element is equal to $\lambda q_k(i)$; these elements are the instantaneous transition rates corresponding to transitions (b). Also, let C_k be the diagonal matrix whose i'th diagonal element is equal to μ_k if server k is operative in configuration i, and 0 otherwise; these are the instantaneous transition rates corresponding to transitions (c).

When $j>0$, the vectors (3.1) satisfy the balance equations

$$v_k(j)(D_A+B_k+C_k) = v_k(j)A + v_k(j-1)B_k + v_k(j+1)C_k \ , \ j \geq 1 \, . \tag{3.2}$$

For $j=0$, the equation is slightly different:

$$v_k(0)(D_A+B_k) = v_k(0)A + v_k(1)C_k \ . \tag{3.3}$$

In addition, all probabilities must sum up to 1:

$$\sum_{j=0}^{\infty} v_k(j)e = 1 \ , \tag{3.4}$$

where e is a column vector with 2^N elements, all of which are equal to 1.

The above equations can be solved by several methods. Perhaps the best approach is to use *spectral expansion* (see [9, 10]). Rewrite (3.2) in the form

$$v_k(j)Q_{k,0} + v_k(j+1)Q_{k,1} + v_k(j+2)Q_{k,2} = 0 \ , \ j = 0,1,\ldots \ , \tag{3.5}$$

where $Q_{k,0} = B_k$, $Q_{k,1} = A - D_A - B_k - C_k$ and $Q_{k,2} = C_k$. This is a homogeneous vector difference equation of order 2, with constant coefficients. Associated with it is the characteristic matrix polynomial, $Q_k(z)$, defined as

$$Q_k(z) = Q_{k,0} + Q_{k,1}z + Q_{k,2}z^2 \quad . \tag{3.6}$$

Denote by $z_{k,\ell}$ and $\psi_{k,\ell}$ the *generalized eigenvalues and left eigenvectors* of $Q_k(z)$. These quantities satisfy

$$\psi_{k,\ell}Q_k(z_{k,\ell}) = 0 \quad , \quad \ell = 1, 2, \ldots, d \quad , \tag{3.7}$$

where $d = degree\{det[Q_k(z)]\}$.

The eigenvalues do not have to be simple, but it is assumed that if $z_{k,\ell}$ has multiplicity r, then it has r linearly independent left eigenvectors. This is invariably observed to be the case in practice. Under that assumption, any solution of (3.5) is of the form

$$v_k(j) = \sum_{\ell=1}^{d} x_{k,\ell}\psi_{k,\ell}z_{k,\ell}^j \quad , \quad j \geq 0 \, , \tag{3.8}$$

where $x_{k,\ell}$ ($\ell = 1, 2, \ldots, d$), are arbitrary (complex) constants.

Moreover, since only normalizeable solutions are acceptable, if $|z_{k,\ell}| \geq 1$ for some ℓ, then the corresponding coefficient $x_{k,\ell}$ must be set to 0. Numbering the eigenvalues of $Q_k(z)$ in increasing order of modulus, the spectral expansion solution of equation (3.5) can be written as

$$v_k(j) = \sum_{\ell=1}^{c} x_{k,\ell}\psi_{k,\ell}z_{k,\ell}^j \quad , \quad j = 0, 1, \ldots \quad , \tag{3.9}$$

where c is the number of eigenvalues strictly inside the unit disk (each counted according to its multiplicity).

In the numerical experiments carried out with this model, the eigenvalues and eigenvectors of $Q_k(z)$ have always been observed to be simple, real and positive.

Substituting (3.9), for $j = 0$ and $j = 1$, into (3.3), yields a set of homogeneous linear equations for the unknown coefficients $x_{k,\ell}$. There are $2^N - 1$ independent equations in this set (rather than 2^N) because the generator matrix of the Markov process is singular. A further, non-homogeneous equation is provided by (3.4), which now becomes

$$\sum_{\ell=1}^{2^N} \frac{x_{k,\ell}\psi_{k,\ell}e}{1 - z_{k,\ell}} = 1 \quad .$$

These equations can be solved uniquely for the coefficients $x_{k,\ell}$, if $c = 2^N$. This turns out to be the case when (2.3) is satisfied. Indeed, the ergodicity condition is equivalent to the requirement that $Q_k(z)$ has exactly 2^N eigenvalues strictly inside the unit disk.

Having determined the coefficients $x_{k,\ell}$, the average number of jobs in queue k is obtained by substituting (3.9) into (2.6):

$$L_k = \sum_{\ell=1}^{2^N} \frac{x_{k,\ell}z_{k,\ell}\psi k, \ell e}{(1 - z_{k,\ell})^2} \quad . \tag{3.10}$$

4. Evaluation of scheduling strategies

In order to reduce the number of parameters that have to be given values when defining the routing strategy, we shall evaluate and compare several strategies based on a single routing vector, $q = (q_1, q_2, \ldots, q_N)$. In each case, the optimization problem is to chose the elements of that vector so as to minimize the average response time, given by (2.4).

1 *The fixed strategy.*

The most straightforward way of splitting the incoming stream is to send each job to node k with probability q_k, regardless of the system configuration. Then the N nodes are independent of each other; node k can be considered in complete isolation, as an M/M/1 queue with breakdowns and repairs. In this simple case, there is a well known explicit formula for the average queue size (see [1, 8, 14]):

$$L_k = \frac{\lambda q_k[(\xi_k + \eta_k)^2 + \xi_k \mu_k]}{(\xi_k + \eta_k)[\eta_k \mu_k - \lambda q_k(\xi_k + \eta_k)]} \ . \tag{4.1}$$

2 *The selective strategy.*

Intuitively, it seems better not to send jobs to nodes where the server is inoperative, unless that is unavoidable. This suggests the following strategy: If the subset of operative servers in the current system configuration is σ, and that subset is non-empty, send jobs to node k only if $k \in \sigma$, with probability proportional to q_k :

$$q_k(\sigma) = \frac{q_k}{\sum_{\ell \in \sigma} q_\ell} \ , \quad k \in \sigma \ .$$

If σ is empty (i.e. all servers are broken), send jobs to node k with probability q_k $(k = 1, 2, \ldots, N)$.

3 *The fixed(m) strategy.*

It is possible that some nodes are unable, under any circumstances, to receive jobs when broken. Suppose that the last $N - m$ nodes are of this type $(m > 0)$, and that jobs are sent to the first m nodes regardless of their state. Thus, when the system configuration is σ, an incoming job can be directed to any node k for which $k \leq m$ or $k \in \sigma$, or both, with probability

$$q_k(\sigma) = \frac{q_k}{\sum_{\ell \in \{1,2,\ldots,m\} \cup \sigma} q_\ell} \ , \quad (k \leq m) \vee (k \in \sigma) \ .$$

4 *The selective(m) strategy.*

This strategy, like the selective one, does not send jobs to broken nodes unless that is unavoidable. In addition, the last $N - m$ nodes are completely unable to receive jobs when broken $(m > 0)$. In other words, if the system configuration is σ, and $\sigma \neq \emptyset$, an incoming job is directed to node k, only if $k \in \sigma$, with probability proportional to q_k :

$$q_k(\sigma) = \frac{q_k}{\sum_{\ell \in \sigma} q_\ell} \ , \quad k \in \sigma \ .$$

If σ is empty, the job is sent to one of the first m nodes, with probability

$$q_k(\sigma) = \frac{q_k}{\sum_{\ell=1}^{m} q_\ell} \quad , \quad k = 1, 2, \ldots, m \ .$$

Clearly, the fixed strategy is a special case of the fixed(m) one, when $m = N$. Similarly, the selective strategy is a special case of the selective(m) one, when $m = N$. All strategies except the fixed are evaluated by the spectral expansion method.

Intuitively it would seem that, for a given routing vector, the selective strategy should perform better than the others, since it appears to make the best use of all servers. The fixed strategies may be expected to perform poorly, since they largely or completely disregard the current availability of servers. When the majority of the servers are quite reliable, the performance of a selective(m) strategy should not depend much on m and should resemble that of the selective strategy (since the only differences arise when all servers are broken).

This intuition is confirmed by experimental results. In general, every selective strategy out-performs every fixed one. The different selective strategies tend to have quite similar behaviour. Within the fixed strategies, it is worth noting that fixed(1) and fixed(2) may start off better than fixed, but become worse when the load increases. This is because the prohibition on sending jobs to some servers when they are broken helps to balance the load at low arrival rates, but saturates the other servers when the load is high. Experiments indicate that if, instead of keeping the routing vector constant, it is optimized for each value of λ, then fixed(1) becomes uniformly better than fixed(2), which in turn becomes better than fixed.

Despite their plausibility, the above remarks are not universally valid. In particular, it is possible to construct examples where the fixed strategy performs better than the selective (e.g. $N = 2$, $\lambda = 10$, $\mu_1 = 30$, $\mu_2 = 10, \xi_1 = 100$, $\xi_2 = 1$, $\eta_1 = 100$, $\eta_2 = 100000$; admittedly, that example is rather contrived, with one fast and fairly unreliable server, while the other is slower and extremely reliable).

To study the effect of the routing policy in more detail, a 2-node system was evaluated for different routing vectors, $(q, 1-q)$, on the range $0 \leq q \leq 1$ (remember that that vector is used in making routing decisions only when both servers are operative or, in the case of the selective strategy, when both are broken). The system parameters are such that each server is operatove approximately 90% of the time, while server 1 is 50% faster than server 2. The results for the fixed, fixed(1) and selective strategies are illustrated in figure 4.1.

An obvious remark is that when $q = 1$, the fixed and fixed(1) strategies are identical. This follows from the definitions. The selective(1) strategy is not plotted because its performance is very close to the selective one. In fact, selective(1) is identical to fixed(1) at $q = 0$ and to selective at $q = 1$.

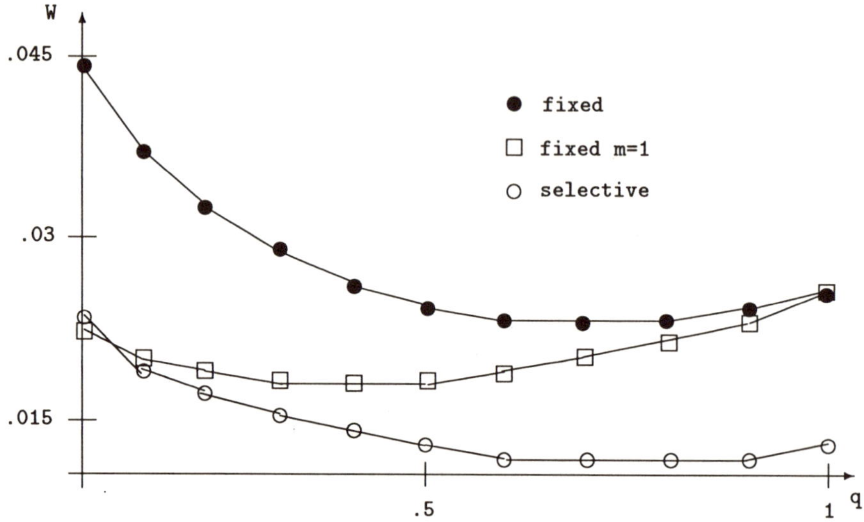

Fig. 4.1. Average response time in a 2-node system, as a function of the routing vector $(q, 1-q)$. $\lambda = 50$, $\mu_1 = 150$, $\mu_2 = 100$, $\xi_1 = \xi_2 = 1$, $\eta_1 = \eta_2 = 10$

Two further observations are worth making, of which the first is quite intuitive, and the second is somewhat counter-intuitive:

(a) For the fixed and selective strategies, the best routing vector sends the majority of the jobs (70% - 80%) to the faster server.
(b) For the fixed(1) strategy, it is best to send fewer jobs (40%) to the faster server than to the slower one.

To explanain (b), note that under the fixed(1) strategy, node 1 is obliged to receive all jobs whenever server 2 is broken, regardless of its own state. This load should be compensated by sending it fewer jobs when there is a choice, i.e. when both servers are operative.

A numerical search for the optimal routing vector is expensive, and rapidly becomes more so when the number of nodes increases. It is desirable, therefore, to find a good heuristic that avoids the search and yet produces a nearly optimal performance. One candidate for such a heuristic is the following: Assign to node i a weight, w_i, given by

$$w_i = \frac{\mu_i \eta_i}{\xi_i + \eta_i} \; , \quad i = 1, 2, \ldots, N \; .$$

This is the available service capacity of server i (the average amount of service it can provide per unit time). Let the ith element of the routing vector be

$$q_i = \frac{w_i}{\sum_{j=1}^{N} w_j} \quad , \quad i = 1, 2, \ldots, N \; .$$

Thus the suggestion is to ignore the job arrival rate and simply split the input stream in proportion to the available service capacities.

In figure 4.2, the performance of the above heuristic is compared to that of the optimal routing vector (which does depend on λ), and also to the 'dumb' splitting based on the vector $(\frac{1}{N}, \frac{1}{N}, \ldots, \frac{1}{N})$. It can be seen that, while the heuristic is very close to the optimal performance throughout the range of arrival rates, the equal splitting clearly fails to balance the loads at the different servers. The penalty of not using a good routing vector can be very large.

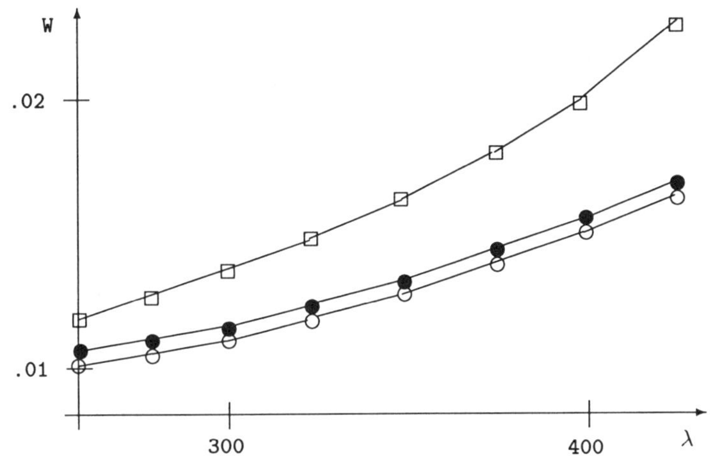

Fig. 4.2. Optimal average response time as a function of the job arrival rate. $N = 5$, $\mu_1 = 150$, $\mu_2 = 100$, $\xi_1 = \xi_2 = 1$, $\eta_1 = \eta_2 = 10$

5. Generalizations

The solution methodology described in section 3 can be applied to more general models involving routing and breakdowns. For example, a breakdown may be accompanied by the loss of the job in service (if any), with a given probability. The only effect of that assumption is to complicate slightly the *Death* transitions of the process Y_k : these can now be from state (i, j) to state $(i', j-1)$ ($i' = i$ if the departure is due to a service completion and $i' \neq i$

if to a breakdown). The matrix C_k is no longer diagonal but the solution procedure remains unchanged.

Similarly, a breakdown may be *caused*, with a certain probability, by the arrival of a job into a node. That complicates the *Birth* transitions of Y_k, making them from state (i, j) to state $(i', j+1)$. The matrix B_k is then no longer diagonal. Both the above effects may be present in the same model.

It would be easy to modify the selective and selective-m strategies by making them lose incoming jobs when all servers are broken. In all these models where losses are possible, the average number of jobs lost per unit time is an important performance measure. That quantity is obtained directly from the probabilities (2.1) and from the distributions of the processes Y_k.

Another possible generalization concerns the introduction of more operative states. For instance, instead of being just operative or broken, a server may be *fully operative*, *partially operative* and *broken*. Perhaps when fully operative the server can both accept and serve jobs, when partially operative it can accept but not serve, and when broken it can neither accept nor serve. In general, a server could be in one of n possible opperative states, with different arrival and service characteristics in different states, and with transitions between states governed by an arbitrary Markov chain.

Of course, the price paid for such an increase in generality is a corresponding increase in complexity. Changing the composition of the matrices A_k, B_k and C_k does not alter signifficantly the computational complexity of the solution, but changing their size does. That size is determined by the number of system configurations. If, instead of the 2 possible operative states for each server there are n states, the total number of system configurations grows from 2^N to n^N. This imposes obvious limitations on the size of problems that can be solved numerically.

6. Joint distribution for $N = 2$

It has already been pointed out that the problem of determining the steady-state joint distribution of the numbers of jobs at two nodes is of mainly theoretical interest. Moreover, the methods for solving two-dimensional Markov processes by reduction to boundary value problems are quite well known (see [3, 2]). We shall therefore present the analysis of the case $N = 2$ only in outline, omitting many of the details. On the other hand, this model has some unusual features which justify the inclusion of such an outline.

A two-node system has four possible configurations: both servers broken, server 2 operative and server 1 broken, server 1 operative and server 2 broken, both servers operative. These configurations will be numbered 0, 1, 2 and 3, respectively. To simplify the notation, assume that the selective routing policy with routing vector (q_1, q_2) is employed (other strategies are treated similarly). Thus, in configuratiobs 0 and 3, jobs are directed to node k with probability q_k ($k = 1, 2$), while in configurations 1 and 2 they go to the only operative server with probability 1.

Denote by $p_i(j_1, j_2)$ the steady-state probability that the configuration is i, and there are j_1 jobs in queue 1 and j_2 jobs in queue 2. Introduce the generating functions

$$g_i(x,y) = \sum_{j_1=0}^{\infty} \sum_{j_2=0}^{\infty} p_i(j_1,j_2) x^{j_1} y^{j_2} \quad , \quad i = 0,1,2,3 \ . \tag{6.1}$$

It is a simple matter to transform the balance equations of the Markov process into four equations involving these generating functions:

$$\alpha(x,y) g_0(x,y) = \xi_2 g_1(x,y) + \xi_1 g_2(x,y) \ , \tag{6.2}$$

$$\beta(y) g_1(x,y) = \eta_2 y g_0(x,y) + \xi_1 y g_3(x,y) - \mu_2(1-y) g_1(x,0) \ , \tag{6.3}$$

$$\gamma(x) g_2(x,y) = \eta_1 x g_0(x,y) + \xi_2 x g_3(x,y) - \mu_1(1-x) g_2(0,y) \ , \tag{6.4}$$

and

$$\begin{aligned} R(x,y) g_3(x,y) = & -\mu_1 y(1-x) g_3(0,y) - \mu_2 x(1-y) g_3(x,0) \\ & + \eta_1 xy g_1(x,y) + \eta_2 xy g_2(x,y) \ , \end{aligned} \tag{6.5}$$

where

$$\alpha(x,y) = \lambda q_1(1-x) + \lambda q_2(1-y) + \eta_1 + \eta_2 \ ,$$

$$\beta(y) = \lambda y(1-y) - \mu_2(1-y) + \xi_2 y + \eta_1 y \ ,$$

$$\gamma(x) = \lambda x(1-x) - \mu_1(1-x) + \xi_1 x + \eta_2 x \ ,$$

$$\begin{aligned} R(x,y) = & \lambda q_1 xy(1-x) + \lambda q_2 xy(1-y) - \mu_1 y(1-x) - \mu_2 x(1-y) \\ & + (\xi_1 + \xi_2) xy \ . \end{aligned}$$

The first step of the solution is to use (6.2), (6.3) and (6.4) in order to eliminate $g_0(x,y)$, and express $g_1(x,y)$ and $g_2(x,y)$ in terms of $g_3(x,y)$ and the two 'boundary' functions $g_1(x,0)$ and $g_2(0,y)$. This yields two relations of the form

$$D(x,y) g_k(x,y) = a_k(x,y) g_1(x,0) + b_k(x,y) g_2(0,y) + c_k(x,y) g_3(x,y) \ , \tag{6.6}$$

for $k = 1, 2$, where $D(x,y)$, $a_k(x,y)$, $b_k(x,y)$ and $c_k(x,y)$ are known.

Now consider (6.5), and suppose for the moment that $g_1(x,y)$ and $g_2(x,y)$ are known. Then in the right-hand side of that equation there are two unknown boundary functions, $g_3(x,0)$ and $g_3(0,y)$. These can be obtained by exploiting the fact that whenever $R(x,y) = 0$ and $g_3(x,y)$ is finite, the r.h.s. of (6.5) must vanish (for a similar development see [11]). There is an algebraic curve $y = \varphi_1(x)$, which satisfies $R(x, \varphi_1(x)) = 0$, such that when x is on a certain closed contour (in this case the circle $|x| = \sqrt{\mu_1/(\lambda q_1)}$), $\varphi_1(x)$ is real. Using that curve, the problem of determining $g_3(x,0)$ is reduced to one of finding a function which is analytic in the interior of a closed contour and satisfying on that contour a specific boundary condition. That is a boundary value problem, whose solution is given in an integral form.

In the same way, by using an algebraic curve $x = \varphi_2(y)$, with $R(\varphi_2(y), y) = 0$, y on a closed contour and $\varphi_2(y)$ real, the determination of $g_3(0, y)$ is reduced to the solution of another boundary value problem.

Thus, if $g_1(x, y)$ and $g_2(x, y)$ are known on the two curves $y = \varphi_1(x)$ and $x = \varphi_2(y)$, the function $g_3(x, y)$ can be determined for all x and y. There are also a couple of unknown constants that appear in the solution (e.g., $g_3(1, 0)$ and $g_3(0, 1)$). These are obtained from the known marginal probabilities.

A similar approach applies to the solution of (6.6). If $g_3(x, y)$ is known on two curves, $y = \psi_1(x)$ and $x = \psi_2(y)$, which satisfy $D(x, \psi_1(x)) = 0$ and $D(\psi_2(y), y) = 0$ respectively, then $g_1(x, y)$ and $g_2(x, y)$ can be determined for all x and y by solving two (different) boundary value problems.

The above discussion suggests an iterative procedure for finding all unknown functions:

1. Make an initial guess for the values of $g_3(x, y)$ on the curves $y = \psi_1(x)$ and $x = \psi_2(y)$;
2. Compute $g_1(x, y)$ and $g_2(x, y)$ on the curves $y = \varphi_1(x)$ and $x = \varphi_2(y)$;
3. Compute $g_3(x, y)$ on the curves $y = \psi_1(x)$ and $x = \psi_2(y)$;
4. Repeat steps 2 and 3 untill the differences between two consecutive iterates for $g_1(x, y)$, $g_2(x, y)$ and $g_3(x, y)$ becomes sufficiently small.

Thus the solution of the model is reduced, via the boundary value problems, to determining the fixed point of three functional equations. If the ergodicity condition is satisfied and the iterative procedure converges to valid generating functions, then it must provide the unique solution of the Markov process. We do not have a proof of convergence. As is often the case with fixed-point solution methods, the only way of assessing the feasibility and efficiency of the approach is by numerical experimentation. That is outside the scope of this paper.

7. Conclusions

The system considered here has a property which may loosely be described as *quasi-separability*. An individual node can be analysed in isolation of the others, provided that the full server configuration is included as a state variable. Because of that property, one can determine exactly the performance measures in models with more than two nodes. It is also possible to optimize the splitting of the input stream among the nodes, under different routing policies. However, such an optimizations involves a search in a multidimensional space, together with the solution of many instances of the model. Computationally, this can be very expensive. A simple heuristic has been proposed, that appears to work well for selective routing policies. Further progress can be made either by discovering more accurate heuristics, or by developing fast approximate solutions whose complexity does not grow exponentially with N. Both these avenues of further research are worth pursuing.

Acknowledgement. This work was carried out in connection with the Basic Research projects QMIPS (Quantitative Methods In Parallel Systems), and PDCS 2 (Predictably Dependable Computer Systems), funded by the European Union. The first author is supported by a CASE scholarship and is sponsored by British Telecom.

References

1. B. Avi-Itzhak and P. Naor, "Some Queueing Problems with the Service Station Subject to Breakdowns", *Operations Research*, **11**, pp. 303–320, 1963.
2. J.W.Cohen and O.J. Boxma, "Boundary Value Problems in Queueing System Analysis", North-Holland (Elsevier), 1983.
3. G. Fayolle and R. Iasnogorodski, "Two Coupled Processors: The reduction to a Riemann-Hilbert Problem Z", *Wahrsheinlichkeitstheorie*, **47**, pp. 325–351, 1979.
4. F.D. Gakhov, "Boundary Value Problems", Addison Wesley, 1966.
5. N. Mikou. "A Two-Node Jackson Network Subject to Breakdowns", *Stochastic Models*, **4**, pp. 523–552, 1988.
6. O. Idrissi-Kacemi, N. Mikou and S. Saadi, "Two Processors Only Interacting During Breakdown: The Case Where the Load is Not Lost", submitted for publication.
7. I. Mitrani, "Networks of Unreliable Computers", in *Computer Architectures and Networks* (ed. E. Gelenbe and R. Mahl), North-Holland, 1974.
8. I. Mitrani and B. Avi-Itzhak, "A Many-Server Queue with Service Interruptions", *Operations Research*, **16** (3), pp. 628–638, 1968.
9. I. Mitrani and R. Chakka, "Spectral Expansion Solution for a Class of Markov Models: Application and Comparison with the Matrix-Geometric Method", *Performance Evaluation*, **23**, 1995.
10. I. Mitrani and D. Mitra, "A Spectral Expansion Method for Random Walks on Semi-Infinite Strips", in *Iterative Methods in Linear Algebra* (ed. R. Beauwens and P. de Groen), North-Holland, 1992.
11. I. Mitrani and P.E. Wright, "Routing in the Presence of Breakdowns", *Performance Evaluation*, **20**, pp. 151–164, 1994.
12. N.I. Muskhelishvili, "Singular Integral Equations", P. Noordhoff, 1953.
13. B. Sengupta, "A Queue with Service Interruptions in an Alternating Markovian Environment", *Operations Research*, **38**, pp. 308–318, 1990.
14. H.C. White and L.S. Christie, "Queueing with Preemptive Priorities or with Breakdown", *Operations Research*, **6**, pp. 79–95, 1958.

Modeling Symmetric Computer Architectures by SWNs *

G. Chiola[1], G. Franceschinis[2], and R. Gaeta[2]

[1] DISI, Università di Genova, Italy
[2] Dipartimento di Informatica, Università di Torino, Italy

Summary. Stochastic Well-formed nets (SWNs) have been introduced as a good modeling tool for complex systems with inherently high degree of symmetry. Analysis and simulation algorithms allow the automatic exploitation of model symmetries to improve their efficiency. Fairly strong constraints are posed over the color definition syntax in order to support such automatic symmetry exploitation as compared to other high level Petri net formalisms. In this paper we derive several models of parallel computer architectures in order to show not only that the formalism is adequate for this class of applications, but also how the different types of symmetries can be mapped into the allowed specification formalism. From this set of case studies we conclude that SWNs are an "intermediate level" formalism, closer to the application domain than P/T nets, yet requiring some ingenuity and experience from the modeler in order to exploit their (high) potential.

1. Introduction

An ideal modeling tool for the study of complex systems such as parallel computer architectures has at least three main requirements that partially contradict one the other: (1) it should be based on a very simple and intuitive formalism, so that it can be used by people that are not expert modelers; a graphic representation is usually preferred by users if the formalism has the capability of conveying the main ideas in a few small pictures; (2) it should be powerful enough so that all basic problems and mechanisms in the selected application domain may be represented in a concise and efficient way; (3) it should be amenable to efficient analysis or (at least) simulation.

High level Petri nets have been pushed by several academic researchers as well as profit organizations as a good trade-off among these main requirements. In particular, the idea of folding the behavior representation expressed in net form by identifying several token types in the places is most effectively exploited for the representation of symmetric systems.

Although the proposed formalisms (Pr/T, CPN, etc.) have the power to handle the folding of inhomogeneous process behavior, up to the extreme case in which the complete system state is encoded in the data structure associated with a single token in a single place (manipulated by a single transition) [1], this power is never fully exploited in practice. The practical reason for stopping the folding process at a given point is that this folding in general

* This work was supported by the ESPRIT–BRA project No.7269 "QMIPS" and the Italian MURST 40% project.

shifts the complexity from the graphic structure to the textual description. Usually the only practical case in which the modeler feels him/herself confident to be able to master the complexity of color inscriptions in high level Petri net model is when a substantial amount of symmetry is inherent to the color definition part [2, 3]. Hence, well-formed colored nets (WNs) [4, 5] where only two basic forms of symmetries give the basis of color structures are not usually perceived as a severely restricted formalism for practical applications. On the contrary, the simplicity of their basic constructs might be seen as an advantage from the point of view of understanding the model specification by non experts. On the other hand, the syntactic restrictions of the formalism provide the condition for efficient analysis as well as simulation algorithms [6, 7] to deal with models of large systems.

Stochastic WNs (SWNs) appear then as a very good modeling formalism for highly symmetric systems: their graphic representation can be kept small and easy to understand, their color structures do not "hide" complexity of the model behavior, the actual size of the system in terms of number of similarly behaving module components may be parameterized in the color class cardinality and may (in several cases) affect only marginally the complexity of the model analysis and/or simulation.

Most parallel computer architectures, on the other hand, tend to be extremely regular interconnections of (small or large quantities of) uniformly behaving components. The design and implementation is heavily based on such symmetry properties, so that it appears quite natural to base also the modeling techniques used for their behavioral and/or quantitative evaluation on the same symmetry properties for better efficiency.

The purpose of this work is to assess the adequacy of the SWN formalism for behavioral and performance modeling of typical problems and mechanisms found in parallel architectures. We carry out this assessment by developing and studying two models of classical problems in this domain. The rest of the paper is organized as a set of independent sections, each one devoted to the development of efficient SWN models for the study of different aspects and mechanism related to parallel processing. Each considered example is characterized by some intrinsic symmetry that is exploited using the SWN formalism in order to simplify both the model structure and its analysis/simulation. The last section resumes the main results obtained on these case studies and contains an organic discussion of the practical modeling power of the formalism for the particular application domain. For the sake of brevity we decided to sacrifice the self-containment of the paper by not including a definition of the WN/SWN formalism. The reader is referred to [4, 5] for such a definition.

2. Multilevel Fat Trees

The first model that we consider, represents an interconnection network similar to that used in the Connection Machine CM-5. This interconnection network, introduced by Leiserson in [8], is called *fat-tree*. The net structure is a k-ary tree, whose leaves are the processors while the internal nodes are switching elements. The tree structure is called *fat* because the branches of the tree closer to the root are "thicker" (i.e., they may support a larger number of communications in parallel).

The CM-5 data network is implemented with a 4-ary fat tree; each internal node is made up of several router chips; when a process mapped on processor i wants to communicate with a process mapped on processor j, the message climbs up towards the root of the tree until the closest common ancestor is found, then it descends towards the destination processor leaf.

The hierarchical structure of the network naturally suggests a hierarchical naming schema for the tree nodes: each node is uniquely identified by a pathname. Since we are dealing with a 4–ary tree, we can label all the nodes with common father with four different labels, e.g., a, b, c, and d, and then identify a generic node "n" with the sequence of labels associated with the nodes on the path from the root to "n". Consider the three-levels tree in Figure 2.1, the pathname for processor j is $\langle a, a, d\rangle$, while the pathname for processor i is $\langle a, b, c\rangle$. Their closest common ancestor is identified by the pathname $\langle a\rangle$. Notice that the pathname of the closest common ancestor of two nodes corresponds to the longest common prefix in their pathnames. This encoding of the net nodes easily translates in a specification for the color structure of the SWN model of the interconnection network: k-ary trees of depth D require a single (non ordered) color class C of cardinality k, and a token representing a node at depth level[1] j $(1 \leq j \leq D)$ is a tuple of arity j.

The SWN in Figure 2.2 represents a 4–ary fat tree of depth three. The model includes a very simple specification of the messages workload: each processor "p" runs one process that performs local computation for an average time of $1/\lambda$ (transition *start* represents the end of a local computation), then it sends a message to a randomly chosen destination (the firing of immediate transition *choose* represents the choice of a destination); the probability of chosing a given destination is uniformly distributed among all remaining processors in the system.

The presence of a 6-tuple $\langle s_3, s_2, s_1, r_3, r_2, r_1\rangle$ in place *level*3 means that a message is being sent from processor $\langle s_3, s_2, s_1\rangle$ to processor $\langle r_3, r_2, r_1\rangle$. The routing of a message is modeled by a three-level subnet. The level i subnet contains two places "level$_i$" and "comm$_i$", and two transitions "sc$_i$" and "ec$_i$". Transitions "climb$_j$" represent the search for the sender-receiver common ancestor (predicates are associated with these transitions that compare the prefixes of the two nodes up to the considered level). Places "rootlink", "link32", "link21" and "leaves" represent the resources needed to set up the communication between the sender and receiver processors: the initial marking of these places is set to the maximum number of concurrent communications that can pass through a switch at a given level. For example the initial

[1] The depth level of the root is 0, while for the leaves it is D.

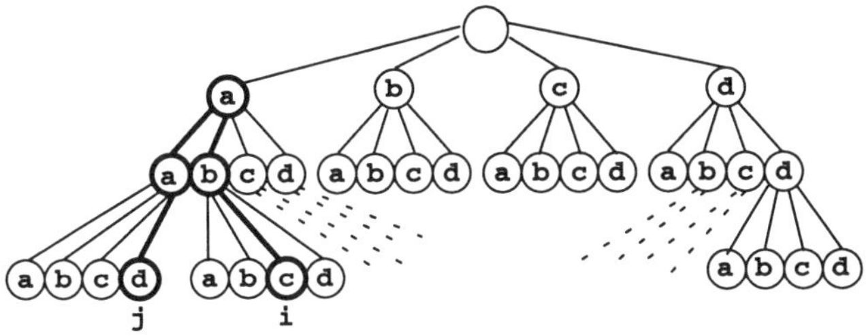

Fig. 2.1. Naming nodes through pathnames in a 3 level 4-ary tree.

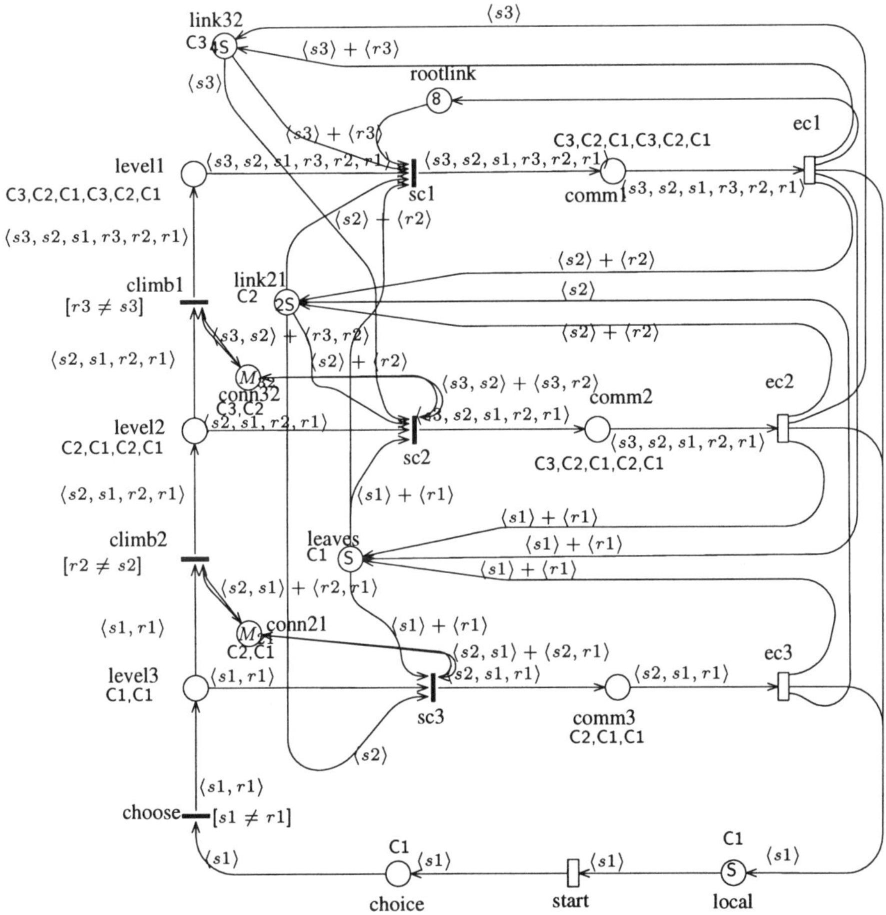

Fig. 2.2. First SWN model of the messages routing in a 3 level 4-ary fat-tree.

marking of place "rootlink" is 8, hence at most 8 communications that need to be routed through the root may be concurrently served. Place "link21" initially contains two copies of each identifier $\langle s_3, s_2 \rangle$ representing a switch at level two meaning that at most two communications can be concurrently routed through the switch $\langle s_3, s_2 \rangle$. Finally, place "link32" initially contains four copies of each identifier $\langle s_3 \rangle$ representing a switch at level one meaning that at most four communications can be concurrently routed through the switch $\langle s_3 \rangle$.

Observe that any k-ary fat tree with three levels can be modeled by the same net structure, changing only the definition of the basic color class C, so that $|C| = k$. On the contrary, k-ary fat trees with $d \neq 3$ levels require that the place and transition color domains and the arc functions are changed to reflect the fact that processor pathnames have length d; moreover the routing subnet should comprise d submodels, each representing the climbing of one tree level, to model the fact that messages may need to climb up to d levels towards the root.

The model is thus fully parametrized with respect to the arity k of the tree, while its structure changes when the number of levels d changes. Notice that the net structure is highly regular with respect to parameter d as well, and a folding of the subnets representing the tree climbing could be obtained at the price of using much more complex arc functions (guarded functions are needed to model the fact that a different number of resources —i.e., switches— have to be acquired depending on the number of climbed levels). In the SWN in Figure 2.2 there are actually three color classes of cardinality four: $C1 = \{a, b, c, d\}$, $C2 = \{a, b, c, d\}$, $C3 = \{a, b, c, d\}$. Class Ci is used to represent labels of nodes at level $d - i + 1$. This is to stress the fact that the algorithm has to consider the colors used to identify objects at different levels of the tree as independent. If the three color components were not considered as independent by the SRG construction algorithm, the degree of aggregation achieved would be substantially decreased. A discussion on the concept of independent color components can be found in [9].

We first ran our prototype SRG computation program on a model representing a 2-level binary tree, obtaining a SRG with 184 tangible and 731 vanishing symbolic markings. The size of the ordinary RG for this model was 505 tangible and 2020 vanishing markings (thus obtaining an average compaction factor of about 3 by using the SRG instead of the RG technique in this case).

By analyzing the symbolic markings we observed that the degree of reduction achieved was lower than expected. This was due to the fact that the specified color structure introduces an unnecessary dependence between nodes that have different fathers but same associated color characterizing the postfix of the pathname. Let us explain the problem on the following example. Consider the three states depicted in Figure 2.3: all of them represent a situation in which two concurrent communications are in progress,

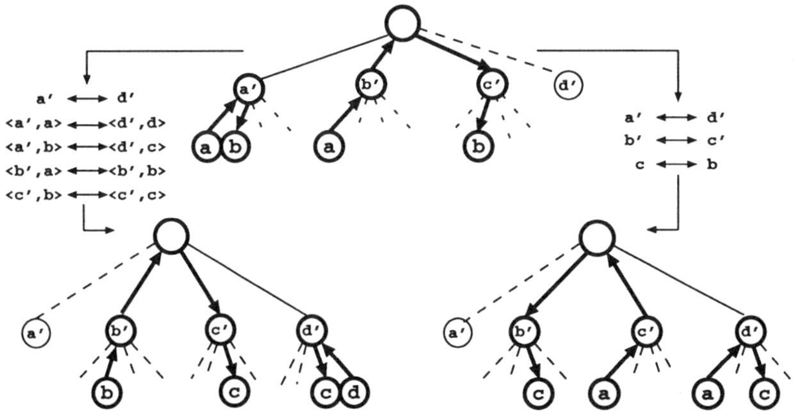

Fig. 2.3. Equivalent markings.

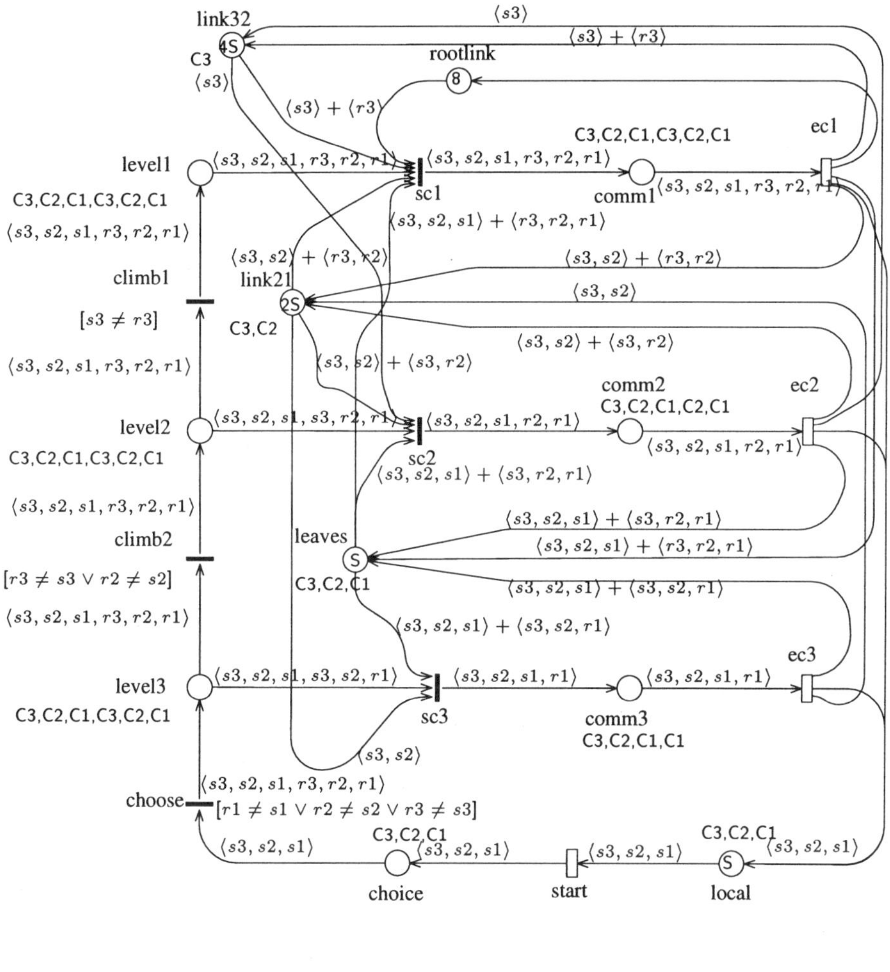

Fig. 2.4. SWN model of 3 level 4-ary "fat tree" interconnection capturing all permutation symmetries

the former involves two leaves l_1 and l_2 with a common father f_1, while the latter traverses two levels and involves two leaves with father different from f_1. Intuitively we would like to consider these markings as equivalent. Instead the SRG keeps two of them in the same symbolic marking (the one at the top of the figure and that on the lower-right corner) while it associates the third with a different symbolic marking. The equivalence relation that we have in mind relates any two states that can be obtained one from the other by permutation of the nodes at the same level with the only constraint of preserving the father-children connection. The equivalence relation used by the SRG generation algorithm, instead, adds a further constraint due to the fact that the permutations used to define the symbolic markings operate at the basic color class level. Since leaves with different fathers are associated with labels from the same class $C1$ in the model, an example of allowed permutation is the exchange of objects a and c in class $C1$, that has the effect of simultaneously permuting nodes $\langle x, y, a\rangle$ and $\langle x, y, c\rangle$ for all $\langle x, y\rangle \in C3, C2$, thus preventing the possibility of exchanging at the same time $\langle x', y', a\rangle$ and $\langle x', y', b\rangle$ for some $\langle x', y'\rangle$ in $C3, C2$.

An easy solution to this problem is obtained as follows. Define class Ci (representing the nodes at level $d-i+1$) as a color set of cardinality k^{d-i+1}, and then represent the father-children relation of the tree structure in the initial (symbolic) marking. For example in the SWN model of a 3 level 4-ary tree depicted in Figure 2.4, color classes are defined as follows:
$C1 = \{aaa, aab, \cdots, ddc, ddd\}; C2 = \{aa, ab, \cdots, dc, dd\}; C3 = \{a, b, c, d\}$, $|C1| = 64$, $|C2| = 16$, $|C3| = 4$. Moreover place "conn21" represents the father-children relation at the leaves level (i.e., a pair $\langle x, y\rangle, x \in C2, y \in C1$ is in this place iff x is father of y) while place *conn*32 represents the father-children relation one level above. The initial marking of these places is defined in a symbolic form: class $C1$ is partitioned into 16 *dynamic subclasses* $(Z_1^i, i = 1, \ldots, 16)$ of cardinality four[2] (objects in the same dynamic subclass represent siblings); 16 dynamic subclasses $(Z_2^i, i = 1, \ldots, 16)$ of cardinality one are defined for class $C2$; 4 dynamic subclasses $(Z_3^i, i = 1, \ldots, 4)$ of cardinality one are defined for class $C3$. The initial marking of place "conn21" and "conn23" are then defined as follows:

$$\mathcal{M}_0(conn21) = \sum_{i=1}^{16} \langle Z_2^i, Z_1^i\rangle; \quad \mathcal{M}_0(conn32) = \sum_{i=1}^{4} \sum_{j=1}^{4} \langle Z_3^i, Z_2^{4(i-1)+j}\rangle$$

meaning that the object represented by subclass Z_2^i is father of the four objects in subclass Z_1^i, and that the object represented by subclass Z_3^1 is father of the four objects represented by subclasses $\{Z_2^1, \ldots Z_2^4\}$, etc.

The initial symbolic marking represents several initial ordinary markings corresponding to all the possible ways of connecting labeled nodes in

[2] The cardinality completely characterizes a dynamic subclass; a partition of a class in dynamic subclasses denotes *any* partition satisfying the given subclass cardinality constraints.

a father-children relation consistently with the desired tree structure. As a consequence, the SRG represents $|\mathcal{M}_0|$ ordinary reachability graphs (the different RGs are not connected with each other).

This new representation allows us to achieve the goal of allowing independent permutations within sets of siblings associated with different fathers. Applying the SRG computation algorithm to an SWN model of a 2-level binary tree represented in the new proposed form, 113 tangible and 301 vanishing symbolic markings are generated. The model can be further refined to reduce the number of vanishing markings by "fusing" immediate transitions "choose", "climb2" and "climb1" into timed transition "start" using the transformations described in [10]. The reduced model of the two-level binary tree has 113 tangible and 73 vanishing symbolic states, thus yielding a compaction factor of about 4.5 on tangible markings.

The solution of a 2-level ternary tree was already beyond the possibilities of our SRG construction program prototype (the current implementation is rather inefficient). Even if the SRG generation did not complete for time and space limits, we could analyze the SRG portion generated (that included 9232 tangible and 5447 vanishing symbolic states) to evaluate the level of aggregation achieved. The initial symbolic marking represents 1680 ordinary markings, while the symbolic markings average cardinality is in the order of one million of states. Hence the average compaction factor (i.e., the ratio between number of states in the ordinary RG and number of symbolic states in the SRG), obtained by dividing the average symbolic marking cardinality by $|\mathcal{M}_0|$ gives about 700 (please compare with the compaction factor of about 4.5 for the 2-level binary tree). Similar levels of improvement can be obtained in simulation by using the symbolic simulation technique instead of the usual event-driven simulation for colored Petri nets.

Discussion. In this section we have developed a modeling exercise with the aim of highlighting an aspect of SWN color structure definition that may influence the degree of state space reduction achieved using the SRG construction algorithm. The equivalence relation that defines symbolic markings is given in terms of permutation of objects within the same color class, as a consequence the reduction factor is proportional to the product over the set of color classes of the number of possible permutations in each class. Hence it is important to distinguish classes used to denote different objects even if they have the same cardinality. Since it is possible to automatically check on the model structure for the color classes independence, it would be helpful to implement this feature in the SRG generator to overcome a source of incomplete reduction.

It is also important to avoid creating unnecessary dependence among objects belonging to the same set. In the model of a k-ary tree with d levels described in this section, the first encoding chosen for describing nodes used classes of cardinality k for each level. As a consequence only a maximal potential reduction proportional to $(k!)^d$ is achievable. Indeed, this encoding introduced an artificial dependence between nodes at the same level. By defining a cardinality k^i class to describe the set of nodes at level i, a much higher potential reduction degree can be achieved. In our example, the degree of reduction achieved on a ternary tree with two levels was about 36 using the first model and 700 using the second model. For larger tree configurations (4-ary trees of depth ≥ 2) the compaction factor becomes enormous, so that its exploitation becomes the only hope to attack the analysis of such models, not only in the case of state space enumeration but also in the case of discrete event simulation.

3. Multidimensional Mesh interconnection

Let us consider MIMD distributed-memory architectures with n-dimensional mesh interconnection structure, possibly having a different number of processors in each dimension. Despite its regularity this interconnection topology it is not fully symmetric. Internal nodes in the structure show indeed the same interconnection pattern with their nearest neighbor nodes. However part of the regularity is lost when we consider the "boundary" nodes, which show a reduced number of connections compared to the internal nodes.

A "slight" modification of this interconnection schema is the folding obtained by addition of one link connecting the last node to the first one in each dimension. In this way we obtain an interconnection schema called (n-dimensional) torus, which is instead completely symmetric.

For the sake of simplicity let us first consider the case of 1-dimensional torus, i.e., a set of m processing units connected in a ring. Let us consider a very simple WN model that represent the choice of one neighbor from a node that wants to communicate. This (trivial) WN model is depicted in Figure 3.1. Each processing node is uniquely associated with one element

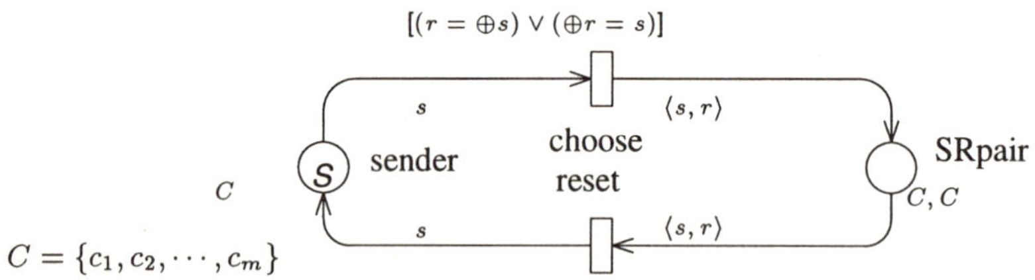

Fig. 3.1. Basic color definitions for nearest neighbor identification in 1-dimensional torus (ring).

of the ordered basic class C. The predicate associated with the enabling of transition "choose" restricts the identity of the receiver to be either the previous or the next element with respect to the sender.

The symmetry of the structure is captured by the WN model that allows a reduction of $1/|C|$ in the number of symbolic markings with respect to the number of ordinary markings. The use of SWN models for n-dimensional torus topologies (composed as explained later on by Cartesian product of the color class C) yields a compaction factor of $1/\prod_1^n |C_i|$, and can thus be considered natural and efficient at the same time; indeed it results in models that are parametric on the number of nodes, whose color structure is very easy to understand, and that are efficient to analyze using either the SRG or the symbolic simulation technique.

The correct treatment of boundary conditions for mesh interconnections requires the introduction of predicates that distinguish inner node identities from boundary node identities. A careless and direct introduction of such predicates completely destroys all symmetry properties of the WN model, thus giving rise to models that are still easy to draw and describe, somewhat cumbersome to understand for what concerns the treatment of boundary conditions, and impossible to analyze efficiently. Of course, one might "approximate" the behavior of a mesh interconnection by ignoring the anomalies due to the boundary nodes and using the torus model instead of the mesh model. In this example, however, we are interested in representing such boundary anomalies in an accurate way in order to compare the performance of mesh versus torus interconnection. We first introduce a direct representation of the structure in terms of color structure that has all the problems just mentioned, and then refine the model in order to be able to capture and exploit those symmetries that are anyhow present in the system.

The case of 1-dimensional mesh can be obtained by refining the predicate associated with transition "choose" in order to distinguish the two boundary nodes from the others. The new predicate definition requires that the ordered class C be partitioned in three subsets (F, M and L), so that it is possible to identify the first (the only element of subclass F) and the last (the only element of subclass L) elements (of course all other elements belong to subclass M). The predicate associated with the enabling of transition "choose" is now defined as:

$$(s \notin L) \wedge (r = \oplus s) \vee (s \notin F) \wedge (\oplus r = s)$$

it restricts the identity of the receiver to be either the previous or the next element with respect to the sender identity for internal nodes. Boundary nodes have only one neighbor (the next for node c_1 and the previous for node c_m).

The extension to higher dimension levels is trivial both from a conceptual and a practical point of view. For example, let us consider the 3-dimensional case. We need to define three basic color classes:

$$C1 = F1 \cup M1 \cup L1;\ F1 = \{a_1\};\ M1 = \{a_2, \cdots, a_{m_a-1}\};\ L1 = \{a_{m_a}\}$$
$$C2 = F2 \cup M2 \cup L2;\ F2 = \{b_1\};\ M2 = \{b_2, \cdots, b_{m_b-1}\};\ L2 = \{b_{m_b}\}$$
$$C3 = F3 \cup M3 \cup L3;\ F3 = \{c_1\};\ M3 = \{c_2, \cdots, c_{m_c-1}\};\ L3 = \{c_{m_c}\}$$

The color domain of place "sender" is now defined as $C1, C2, C3$, while that of place "SRpair" is $C1, C2, C3, C1, C2, C3$. The functions associated with the input and output arcs of place "sender" are both defined as $< s1, s2, s3 >$, while those associated with the input and output arcs of place "SRpair" are both defined as $< s1, s2, s3, r1, r2, r3 >$. The new predicate associated with transition "choose" is:

$$[((s1 \notin L1) \wedge (r1 = \oplus s1) \vee (s1 \notin F1) \wedge (\oplus r1 = s1)) \wedge (s2 = r2) \wedge (s3 = r3) \vee \\ ((s2 \notin L2) \wedge (r2 = \oplus s2) \vee (s2 \notin F2) \wedge (\oplus r2 = s2)) \wedge (s1 = r1) \wedge (s3 = r3) \vee \\ ((s3 \notin L3) \wedge (r3 = \oplus s3) \vee (s3 \notin F3) \wedge (\oplus r3 = s3)) \wedge (s1 = r1) \wedge (s2 = r2)]$$

Observe that it has increased in complexity to handle the boundary condition in each dimension. The mapping of the interconnection structure into color structures remains however straightforward to understand.

Unfortunately, the partitioning of the ordered color classes (that is necessary to distinguish boundary conditions by means of predicates) destroys all useful model symmetries: symbolic marking representations collapse to ordinary marking representation, thus making the complexity of the model analysis to increase dramatically with both the number of dimensions and the size in each dimension. On the other hand, some kind of symmetries are still enjoyed by our interconnection schema, even if they are not directly captured by the the last two WN models described. The kind of symmetry that we should model is, in each dimension, the symmetry with respect to the central point of a segment.

The "mirror" symmetry that we need in order to efficiently handle this case is not directly supported by the WN formalism, but it can be "simulated" as a special case of "rotation". Two ordered basic classes are used to this purpose: $D = F \cup M \cup L$; $F = \{d_1\}$; $M = \{d_2, \cdots, d_{m-1}\}$; $L = \{d_m\}$; and $R = \{l, r\}$. The "coordinate" of each processing node is encoded using a pair in $D \times R$. The first component in the pair represents the distance from the center of the segment, and the second one the direction (left or right) with respect to the center. The class representing the distance is still partitioned in subclasses to identify the first and last elements. The class representing the direction is instead not partitioned, thus inducing actual symmetric folding of the symbolic marking representation.

The color domains of places "sender" and "SRpair" are defined as D, R and D, R, D, R respectively. The predicate associated with transition "choose" is defined as:

$$[(sd \notin L) \wedge (rd = \oplus sd) \wedge (rr = sr) \vee (sd \notin F) \wedge (\oplus rd = sd) \wedge (rr = sr) \vee \\ (sd \in F) \wedge (rd = sd) \wedge (rr = \oplus sr)] \ .$$

The functions associated with the input and output arcs of place "sender" are both defined as $\langle sd, sr \rangle$, while those associated with the input and output arcs of place "SRpair" are defined as $\langle sd, sr, rd, rr \rangle$.

The extension from 1-dimensional to n-dimensional mesh interconnections may be as straightforward in principle as in the first model in which symmetries were not captured: one may just replicate the pair of basic classes as many times as the number of dimensions (thus also expanding the complexity of the predicate associated with transition "choose").

The degree of compaction of the symbolic marking representation is only a factor of 2 in the case of 1-dimensional mesh. It increases however exponentially with the dimension, thus providing a factor 2^n of compaction in the case of n-dimensional mesh. Notice that the case of "n-dimensional hypercube" in which the number of nodes per dimension is fixed to 2 is particularly advantageous from the symmetric folding point of view: the color class D can be omitted and the coordinate of a node reduces to a set of n colors of type R for which complete symmetry is available.

Notice also that, even in the case of completely homogeneous local computation workload, the compaction factor 2^n is the best result that we may obtain. Indeed, processing nodes at different distances from the center (or, equivalently, from the nearest boundary) are subject to different communication loads (due to the different number of neighbors on the boundary), thus making the exact aggregation of nodes at different distances impossible from a performance evaluation point of view.

In the case of equal number of components in two or more dimensions, however, another form of permutation symmetry with respect to the ordering of dimensions may be observed. In other words, if we focus on a 2-dimensional case with $2m$ homogeneous nodes in each dimension, we can observe a new form of symmetry corresponding to a flip of the structure with respect to either main diagonal. This additional symmetry can be properly taken into account at the price of some additional complication in the encoding of the coordinates of each node and in the predicate that establishes the nearest neighbor connection. In particular, the identity of a node may be encoded by means of a 5-tuple of type R, R, R, D, D of the two following basic color classes:

$$D = F \cup M \cup L; \quad F = \{d_1\}; \quad M = \{d_2, \cdots, d_{m-1}\} \quad L = \{d_m\};$$
$$R = Z \cup NZ; \quad Z = \{0\}; \quad NZ = \{-1, 1\};$$

the first one ordered (with a successor function defined among elements), and the second one not ordered. The first two elements in the encoding identify one among four "quadrants" in the mesh. The third element is zero for the nodes laying on the main diagonals, and either 1 or -1 for the other nodes (see Fig. 3.2). Hence the three components of type R are used to encode one out of eight "sectors". The last two elements of type D identify a specific node in a sector, by encoding its "latitude" and "longitude"; for instance in Fig. 3.2 the encoding of node **a1** is $\langle 1, 0, 0, 3, 1 \rangle$, that of node **f2** is $\langle 0, 1, 1, 2, 2 \rangle$, and finally that of node **b6** is $\langle 0, -1, -1, 3, 2 \rangle$.

A valid identification of a node is subject to the following restrictions: call $\langle dx, dy, dd, r, l \rangle$ a color instantiation corresponding to a node,

$$dx \neq 0 \text{ iff } dy = 0 \quad \wedge \text{ if } dd = 0 \text{ then } l = d_1 \quad \wedge$$
$$l \leq r \text{ (i.e. if } r = d_i \text{ then } l = d_j \ \wedge \ j \leq i \text{)}$$

The resulting model is cumbersome to draw and to explain, so that it is not reported here. The compaction factor in this case of 2-dimensional mesh

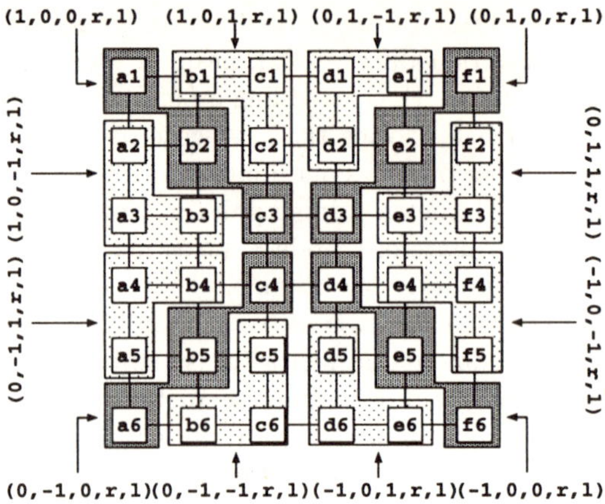

Fig. 3.2. Encoding of nodes of a 2-dimensional structure.

varies with number of nodes per dimension from a minimum of 4 in the case of $m = 1$ (i.e., a 2-dimensional hypercube) to a limiting value of 8 in the case $m \to \infty$ (which corresponds to the number of symmetric sectors defined in the color encoding).

Discussion. The formalism provides a direct mapping of the interconnection structure into the model color structure. In case of torus and hypercube topologies the direct mapping into the color structures and functions captures all the symmetries of the model, while in the case of mesh interconnection it does not. Less trivial WN representations may be found that capture system symmetries of mesh interconnection at different levels at the expense of an increasing model complexity. Some conceptually simple extensions of the formalism such as the direct support of the "mirror" type symmetry or the "flip" across color components (permutation of elements in a tuple) would allow the treatment of such more difficult cases in a natural way.

4. Conclusions

We have developed a set of examples of use of the SWN formalism for the description of problems arising in the study of parallel computer architectures. The common denominator of these cases that makes the use of SWNs practically advantageous is their intrinsic high degree of symmetry. In some cases the system symmetry directly matches the basic ones provided by the formalism, while in other cases the basic color and function definitions must be composed in a non trivial way in order to capture the desired system symmetries.

In this sense, the WN formalism can be seen as an intermediate level of abstraction in which some more complex symmetric structures can be reproduced only at the cost of some model complexity. From a practical point of view, it would be better to have the possibility of adding (possibly problem or domain specific) color structures and associated manipulation functions in order to match more closely the modeling needs.

On the other hand, the basic principle of restricting the color complexity so that it is mainly related to the symmetry of the system to be modeled seems to be the key for the success of this modeling approach. Future works on the subject should include the development of a clean method to define a library of ready-to-use symmetry structures together with their appropriate manipulation functions that allow efficient implementation of the symbolic firing technique.

References

1. H.J. Genrich, "Equivalence transformations of Pr/T nets", In Proc. 9th Europ. Workshop on Application and Theory of Petri Nets, Venezia, Italy, June 1988.
2. C. Lin and D-C. Marinescu, "Stochastic high level Petri nets and applications", *IEEE Transactions on Computers*, **37** (7), pp. 815–825, July 1988.
3. J.A. Carrasco, "Automated construction of compound Markov chains from generalized stochastic high-level Petri nets", In Proc. 3rd Intern. Workshop on Petri Nets and Performance Models, pp. 93–102, Kyoto, Japan, December 1989. IEEE-CS Press.
4. G. Chiola, C. Dutheillet, G. Franceschinis, and S. Haddad, "On well-formed coloured nets and their symbolic reachability graph", In Proc. 11th International Conference on Application and Theory of Petri Nets, Paris, France, June 1990. Reprinted in High-Level Petri Nets. Theory and Application, K. Jensen and G. Rozenberg (editors), Springer Verlag, 1991.
5. G. Chiola, C. Dutheillet, G. Franceschinis, and S. Haddad, "Stochastic well-formed coloured nets for symmetric modelling applications", *IEEE Transactions on Computers*, **42** (11), November 1993.
6. G. Chiola, G. Franceschinis, and R. Gaeta, "A symbolic simulation mechanism for well-formed coloured Petri nets", In Proc. 25th SCS Annual Simulation Symposium, Orlando, Florida, April 1992.
7. G. Chiola, R. Gaeta, and M. Ribaudo, "Designing an efficient tool for Stochastic Well-Formed Coloured Petri Nets", In R. Pooley and J. Hillston, editors, Proc. 6th Int. Conference on Modelling Techniques and Tools for Computer Performance Evaluation, pp. 391–395, Edinburg, UK, September 1992, Antony Rowe Ltd.
8. C.E. Leiserson, "Fat-trees: Universal networks for hardware efficient supercomputing", *IEEE Transactions on Computers*, **C-34** (10), October 1985.
9. G. Chiola and G. Franceschinis, "A structural colour simplification in Well-Formed coloured nets", In Proc. 4th Intern. Workshop on Petri Nets and Performance Models, pp. 144–153, Melbourne, Australia, December 1991. IEEE-CS Press.
10. G. Chiola, S. Donatelli, and G. Franceschinis, "GSPN versus SPN: what is the actual role of immediate transitions?", In Proc. 4th Intern. Workshop on Petri Nets and Performance Models, pp. 20–31, Melbourne, Australia, December 1991. IEEE-CS Press.

Arrival Theorems for Product-Form Stochastic Petri Nets*

G. Balbo[1], S.C. Bruell[2], and M. Sereno[1]

[1] Dipartimento di Informatica, Università di Torino, Italy
[2] Computer Science Department, University of Iowa, Iowa City, USA

Summary. We consider a particular class of Stochastic Petri Nets whose stationary probabilities at arbitrary instants exhibit a product form. We study these nets at specific instants in the steady state that occur directly after the firing of a transition. We focus our attention on the instant *after* tokens are removed from the places specified by a transition's input bag and just *before* tokens are entered into the places specified by the same transition's output bag. We show that the stationary probabilities at "arrival instants" are related to corresponding stationary probabilities at arbitrary instants in net(s) with lower load. We then show how one of the "arrival" theorems can be applied to the derivation of a formula for the mean sojourn time of a token in a place at steady state.

1. Introduction

Stochastic Petri Nets (SPNs) are a powerful tool for modeling and evaluating the performance of systems involving concurrency, nondeterminism, and synchronization. They are equivalent to continuous-time Markov chains and their steady-state analysis can thus be expressed as the solution of a system of equilibrium equations, one for each possible marking in the corresponding state space. The major problem in the computation of performance measures for SPNs is that the size of their reachability set increases exponentially both with the number of tokens in the initial marking and with the number of places in the net. As a consequence, except for special classes of nets, the size of the reachability set and the time complexity of the solution procedure preclude the exact numerical evaluation of many interesting models.

Recently, a class of SPNs has been discovered [6, 7] that is characterized by the fact that the stationary probability distribution of any net in this class can be factored into a product of terms, one term per place in the net. Nets possessing this property are called *Product-Form Stochastic Petri Nets* (PF-SPNs) and are easily identified by the structural criteria proposed by Coleman, Henderson, Lucic and Taylor [3, 6, 7]. Moreover, the product-form solution for this class of nets closely resembles that of a class of Queueing Networks (QN) [1, 5, 8] for which efficient computational algorithms have

* This work has been supported in part by the Italian National Research Council "Progetto Finalizzato Sistemi Informatici e Calcolo Parallelo (Grant N. 92.01563.PF69)," by the ESPRIT–BRA project No.7269 "QMIPS," and by a grant from 3M.

Reprinted by permission from the ACM SIGMETRICS '94 Conference proceedings..

been derived. This similarity has led to the development of analogous algorithms for this class of SPNs as well [3, 12, 13].

In this paper we describe[1] a set of "arrival" theorems similar in spirit to those discovered for queueing networks [10, 15]; the first two theorems concern the states of the whole net that are seen by an arriving token. We show that these arrival theorems, just as with their queueing network counterparts, can be used as the theoretical underpinnings for the development of a "mean value analysis" algorithm for the computation of performance indices in PF-SPNs. In particular, we will show how to apply one of the arrival theorems to the derivation of a formula for the mean sojourn time of a token in a place at steady state. This result resembles that for the mean waiting time that a customer experiences at a station in a load-independent product-form queueing network. For the sake of simplicity our theorems are presently derived for ordinary PF-SPNs (i.e., PF-SPNs in which all the arcs have multiplicity one [11]).

The balance of this paper is outlined as follows. Section 2. defines what a product-form Stochastic Petri Net is. Section 3. describes our "arrival" theorems for these nets, as well as presenting an example PF-SPN to aid in the understanding of the theorems. Section 4. is devoted to the computation of the mean sojourn time of a token in a place and explains the relationship between the expression developed, its QN counterpart, and its application to obtain an alternative proof of the basic equation of a mean-value analysis algorithm for PF-SPNs [13]. Finally, Section 5. provides some concluding remarks.

2. Product-Form Stochastic Petri Nets: Basic Definitions

The purpose of this section is first to introduce the notation relating to Stochastic Petri Nets and then to describe the salient features of the class of PF-SPNs that are the main focus of this paper.

2.1 Definition of Stochastic Petri Nets

What follows is a quick review of the notation and of the definitions used to describe Stochastic Petri Nets.

Definition 2.1 (*Stochastic Petri Net*). *A continuous-time Stochastic Petri Net is defined as a six-tuple:* $(\mathcal{P}, \mathcal{T}, I, O, \mathcal{Q}, \boldsymbol{m_0})$, *where:* $\mathcal{P} = \{p_1, p_2, \dots, p_P\}$ *is a set of places;* $\mathcal{T}=\{t_1, t_2, \dots, t_T\}$ *is a set of transitions;* $\mathcal{P} \cap \mathcal{T} = \emptyset \wedge \mathcal{P} \cup \mathcal{T} \neq \emptyset$; $I, O : \mathcal{T} \times \mathcal{P} \rightarrow \mathbb{N}$ *are the input and output functions, identifying the arcs that connect places to transitions and transitions to places;*

[1] The complete derivations and proofs for all the arrival theorems can be found in [14].

$\mathcal{Q} = \{\mu(t_1), \mu(t_2), \ldots, \mu(t_T)\}$ *is a set of firing rates for the exponentially distributed transition firing times;* $\boldsymbol{m_0}$ *is a vector of P non-negative integers (also referred to as a P-vector) that is called the initial marking.*

From the functions $I(.,.)$ and $O(.,.)$ we derive the vectors $\boldsymbol{I}(t) = [I_1(t), I_2(t), \ldots, I_P(t)]^T$ and $\boldsymbol{O}(t) = [O_1(t), O_2(t), \ldots, O_P(t)]^T$, $\forall\, t \in \mathcal{T}$, where $I_i(t) = I(t, p_i)$ and $O_j(t) = O(t, p_j)$, $\forall\, p_i, p_j \in \mathcal{P}$. Unless otherwise stated all vectors are assumed to be column vectors. The vectors $\boldsymbol{I}(t)$ and $\boldsymbol{O}(t)$, $\forall\, t \in \mathcal{T}$, are called the *input* and *output bags* of transition t, respectively. The input bag $\boldsymbol{I}(t)$ of transition t provides the enabling condition for t, i.e., transition t is enabled in a given marking $\boldsymbol{m}$ if and only if $\boldsymbol{m} \geq \boldsymbol{I}(t)$ (where we are using component-wise inequality so that $m(p_i) \geq I_i(t), \forall i$). Let $m(p_i)$ denote the number of tokens in place p_i. Any transition t that is enabled in a marking $\boldsymbol{m}$ can fire producing a new marking $\boldsymbol{m'} = [m'(p_1), \ldots, m'(p_P)]^T$ where $m'(p_i) = m(p_i) - I_i(t) + O_i(t)$, with $1 \leq i \leq P$. Symbolically we write this as $\boldsymbol{m}[t > \boldsymbol{m'}$. **[Pre-set and Post-set]** The *pre-set* and *post-set* of a place are denoted by $^\bullet p =$ the set of input transitions of place p; and $p^\bullet =$ the set of output transitions of place p.

Given an SPN $(\mathcal{P}, \mathcal{T}, I, O, \mathcal{Q}, \boldsymbol{m_0})$, the *reachability set*, $R(\boldsymbol{m_0})$, is defined as follows: $\boldsymbol{m_0} \in R(\boldsymbol{m_0})$; if $\boldsymbol{m_i} \in R(\boldsymbol{m_0})$ and $\exists\, t \in \mathcal{T}$ such that $\boldsymbol{m_i}[t > \boldsymbol{m_{i+1}}$, then $\boldsymbol{m_{i+1}} \in R(\boldsymbol{m_0})$.

The *incidence matrix* $\boldsymbol{A}$ is a $T \times P$ matrix of integers. The entries $A[t,p] = O(t,p) - I(t,p)$, with $t \in \mathcal{T}$ and $p \in \mathcal{P}$, represent the change in the number of tokens at place p when transition t fires. A P-vector $\boldsymbol{s}$ of positive integers is called an *S-semiflow* if $\boldsymbol{A} \cdot \boldsymbol{s} = \boldsymbol{0}$. A semiflow $\boldsymbol{s}$ is called *minimal* if there is no other semiflow $\boldsymbol{s'}$ such that $\boldsymbol{s'} \leq \boldsymbol{s}$ (component-wise inequality). $\boldsymbol{S}$ is the matrix whose rows are the minimal S-semiflows. A T-vector $\boldsymbol{x}$ of positive integers is called a *T-semiflow* if $\boldsymbol{A}^T \cdot \boldsymbol{x} = \boldsymbol{0}$. A semiflow $\boldsymbol{x}$ is called *minimal* if there is no other semiflow $\boldsymbol{x'}$ such that $\boldsymbol{x'} \leq \boldsymbol{x}$. Note that S- and T- semiflows are computed from the incidence matrix, and are thus independent of any notion of initial marking. Semiflows characterize the structural properties of an SPN. An S-semiflow identifies a set of places such that the weighted sum of the number of tokens distributed over them remains constant (invariant) for all markings in the reachability set (see Section 3.2 for an example); this weighted sum is called an S-invariant. If all places of an SPN are in at least one of the S-semiflows, then the SPN is bounded (i.e., the maximum number of tokens in the places of the net in any reachable marking is finite). The T-semiflows represent sequences of transitions whose firing may bring the net back to its initial state. There are results showing that any *live* and *bounded* SPN is covered by both S and T-semiflows [11]. In the following we only consider nets that are live, bounded, and ordinary.

Definition 2.2 (*Reachability Condition*). *Given an SPN with initial marking* $\boldsymbol{m_0}$ *and the matrix* $\boldsymbol{S}$ *whose rows are the minimal S-semiflows, a necessary and sufficient condition for the reachability of any marking* $\boldsymbol{m}$ *is*

$$\boldsymbol{S} \cdot \boldsymbol{m_0} \quad = \quad \boldsymbol{S} \cdot \boldsymbol{m}. \tag{2.1}$$

The term $\boldsymbol{S} \cdot \boldsymbol{m_0}$ provides the initial token distribution of each S-semiflow and thus identifies the S-invariants of the SPN. In the following the vector $\boldsymbol{k_0}$, such that $\boldsymbol{k_0} = \boldsymbol{S} \cdot \boldsymbol{m_0}$, is called the *load vector*, while SPNs satisfying Equation (2.1) are called *S-invariant reachable*.
Given an S-invariant reachable SPN $(\mathcal{P}, \mathcal{T}, I, O, \mathcal{Q}, \boldsymbol{m_0})$ with load vector $\boldsymbol{k_0} = \boldsymbol{S} \cdot \boldsymbol{m_0}$, the following notation represents an alternative way of denoting the reachability set:

$$E(\boldsymbol{k_0}) = \{\boldsymbol{m} | \boldsymbol{S} \cdot \boldsymbol{m} = \boldsymbol{k_0}\}. \tag{2.2}$$

Note that Equation (2.1) is always necessary for the reachability of a certain marking $\boldsymbol{m}$; for our arrival theorems to hold we are also requiring that the condition be sufficient. We will use Condition (2.1) in the derivations that follow to ensure that any marking $\boldsymbol{m'}$ that we obtain by removing tokens from the net (in an appropriate manner) is a legal (reachable) marking for the same net with a reduced initial marking characterized by the new load vector $\boldsymbol{k_0}' = \boldsymbol{S} \cdot \boldsymbol{m}'$. In general in Petri nets we may have that $R(\boldsymbol{m_0}) \subseteq E(\boldsymbol{k_0})$ (i.e., it is possible to find markings that satisfy Condition (2.1), but that are not reachable from $\boldsymbol{m_0}$). There are many interesting practical SPNs for which $R(\boldsymbol{m_0}) = E(\boldsymbol{k_0})$. Live and bounded free choice nets are S-invariant reachable in some cases [4], as are the simpler marked graphs and state machines [11]; another large class of nets that are S-invariant reachable are the so called Macroplace-Macrotransition nets [9].

2.2 Definition of Product-Form Stochastic Petri Nets

In the following we are concerned with any ordinary SPN that has a product-form equilibrium distribution. The PFS for SPN criterion considered here is that proposed by Coleman, Henderson, Lucic and Taylor [3, 6]. The authors of this PFS proposal showed that for an SPN to possess a PFS it has to satisfy the structural constraints specified by the following definition:

Definition 2.3 (*Structural Conditions*). *1. For each transition $t \in \mathcal{T}$, $\boldsymbol{O}(t) = \boldsymbol{I}(s)$ for some $s \in \mathcal{T}$.*
2. For each transition $s \in \mathcal{T}$, $\boldsymbol{I}(s) = \boldsymbol{O}(t)$ for some $t \in \mathcal{T}$.

In [3, 6] it was shown that Definition 2.3 provides necessary conditions for an SPN to have a product-form equilibrium distribution that contains as many factors as there are places in the net; this equilibrium distribution is shown in Equation 2.3.
[Product-Form Solution]

$$\pi(\boldsymbol{m}; \boldsymbol{k_0}) \quad = \quad \frac{1}{G(\boldsymbol{k_0}, \mathcal{P})} \prod_{i=1}^{P} y_i^{m(p_i)} \tag{2.3}$$

$$\text{with} \quad \boldsymbol{m} \in E(\boldsymbol{k_0}) \text{ and } \boldsymbol{k_0} = \boldsymbol{S} \cdot \boldsymbol{m_0},$$

where $G(\boldsymbol{k_0}, \mathcal{P})$ is a normalization constant, $\mathcal{P}$ denotes the finite set of places, P is the number of places in the net, the y_i are functions of the utilization of the transitions connected to place p_i,$m(p_i)$ is the i-th term in the marking vector $\boldsymbol{m}$, $\boldsymbol{S}$ is the matrix of minimal S-semiflows, and $\boldsymbol{k_0}$ is a load vector.

3. Arrival Theorems for PF-SPNs

The purpose of this section is to first describe what an "intermediate marking" is. All of our arrival theorems relate the probability that a PF-SPN with load vector $\boldsymbol{k_0}$ "sees" a particular intermediate marking to the steady-state probability of that intermediate marking in a related PF-SPN with a "lower" load vector. After the first arrival theorem is stated we immediately follow it by an example that illustrates the salient features of the theorem. After that we show how the theorem can be generalized when the "direction" that a transition fires in is considered. The last subsection describes further refinements of the arrival theorems that are "direction" independent, but that characterize the view that arriving tokens in a given place have of the portion of the state of the net represented by the marking of that place only.

3.1 What is an Intermediate Marking

Consider what happens when a net moves from one marking to another. This occurs whenever an enabled transition fires. If in marking $\boldsymbol{m}'$ transition t fires, the new marking $\boldsymbol{m}''$ is obtained by removing tokens from the places specified by the input bag of t and depositing tokens in the places specified by the output bag of the same transition. If we let $\boldsymbol{m}' = \tilde{\boldsymbol{m}} + \boldsymbol{I}(t)$, then the new marking is $\boldsymbol{m}'' = \tilde{\boldsymbol{m}} + \boldsymbol{O}(t)$. The "marking" $\tilde{\boldsymbol{m}}$ is not actually a feasible marking in the net (i.e., $\tilde{\boldsymbol{m}} \notin E(\boldsymbol{k_0})$). One may, though, view it as an *intermediate* marking in going from marking $\boldsymbol{m}'$ to $\boldsymbol{m}''$. In fact, it is the "marking" obtained right *after* transition t removes tokens from the places specified by its input bag, but right *before* it deposits tokens in the places specified by its output bag.

3.2 Example: Illustration of Intermediate Markings

Figure 3.1 depicts a simple four place, four transition PF-SPN, covered by two non-disjoint S-semiflows. The first semiflow covers places p_1, p_3, and p_4 and the second covers places p_2 and p_4 (cf. the $\boldsymbol{S}$-matrix in the caption of the figure). With an initial marking of three tokens in place p_1 and two tokens in place p_2, the load vector $\boldsymbol{k_0}$ is $\boldsymbol{S} \cdot \boldsymbol{m_0} = [3, 2]^T$. From this load vector and the two semiflows, we know that three tokens will forever be circulating among the places p_1, p_3, and p_4 and two tokens will forever be circulating among the places p_2 and p_4. The reader is urged to fire any enabled transition and verify that these conditions always hold.

Now consider transition t_2. Its input bag is $\boldsymbol{I}(t_2) = [1,1,0,0]^T$ and its output bag is $\boldsymbol{O}(t_2) = [0,0,0,1]^T$. If transition t_2 fires with $\boldsymbol{m}' = \boldsymbol{m_0} = [3,2,0,0]^T$, then one token is removed from each of the places p_1 and p_2 and one token is added to place p_4. Hence, $\boldsymbol{m}'' = [2,1,0,1]^T$. The intermediate marking that is "seen" in going from marking $\boldsymbol{m}'$ to $\boldsymbol{m}''$ is $[2,1,0,0]^T$ ($= \boldsymbol{m}' - \boldsymbol{I}(t_2) = \boldsymbol{m}'' - \boldsymbol{O}(t_2)$).

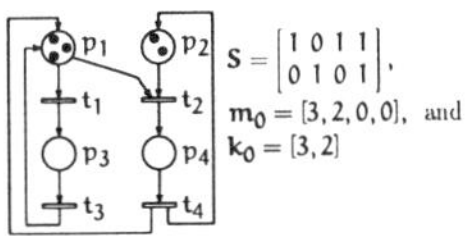

Fig. 3.1. Example PF-SPN

Figure 3.2 contains the reachability graph for the original net with initial marking $\boldsymbol{m_0} = [3,2,0,0]^T$. We have identified two different sets of "intermediate markings" corresponding to the firing of transition t_3 (the markings surrounded by dotted circles) and to the firing of transition t_4 (the markings surrounded by dotted boxes). Consider the feasible marking $[1,1,1,1]^T$, in which both transitions t_3 and t_4 are enabled. If transition t_3 fires first, one token is removed from place p_3 and one token is put in place p_1. On its arrival to place p_1 via the firing of transition t_3, this new token "sees" the net in "intermediate marking" $[1,1,0,1]^T$. If on the other hand transition t_4 fires first, one token is removed from place p_4 and one token is put in each of the places p_1 and p_2, respectively. The token added to place p_1 via the firing of transition t_4 "sees" the net in "intermediate marking" $[1,1,1,0]^T$. In either case a token arrives to place p_1. The intermediate marking "seen" by the arriving token depends on which of the two transitions fire. It is for this reason that the token arrival probability (that is about to be defined) is a function of both a place and a transition.

3.3 Global Arrival Theorem by Transition for a PF-SPN

We are now in a position to state our first result. Let $\pi^a_{jt}(\tilde{\boldsymbol{m}}; \boldsymbol{k_0})$ denote the probability that a token arriving in place p_j due to the firing of transition $t \in {}^\bullet p_j$ sees the net in the intermediate marking $\tilde{\boldsymbol{m}}$.

Theorem 3.1. *[Global Arrival Theorem] Given an S-invariant reachable PF-SPN with load vector $\boldsymbol{k_0}$, the probability of finding marking $\tilde{\boldsymbol{m}}$ on arrival to place p_j when transition t fires is given by*

$$\pi^a_{jt}(\tilde{\boldsymbol{m}}; \boldsymbol{k_0}) = \pi(\tilde{\boldsymbol{m}}; \boldsymbol{k_0} - \boldsymbol{S} \cdot \boldsymbol{I}(t)), \tag{3.1}$$

where $\pi(\tilde{\boldsymbol{m}}; \boldsymbol{k_0} - \boldsymbol{S} \cdot \boldsymbol{I}(t))$ is the steady-state probability of marking $\tilde{\boldsymbol{m}}$ in a PF-SPN with load vector $\boldsymbol{k_0} - \boldsymbol{S} \cdot \boldsymbol{I}(t)$.

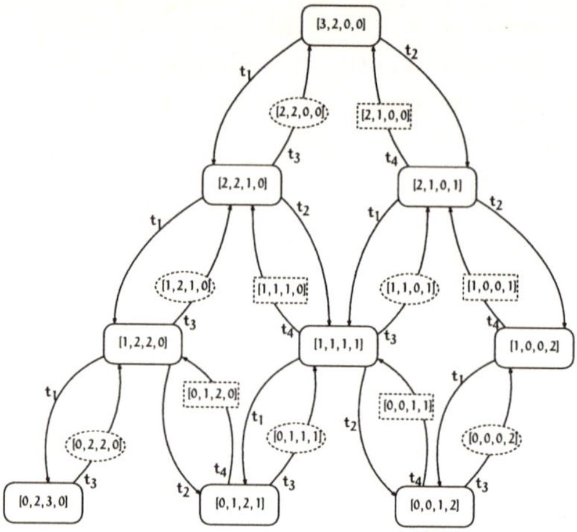

Fig. 3.2. Reachability Graph of Example PF-SPN

In words what Theorem 3.1 states is that the probability that a token arriving to place p_j via a firing of transition t sees intermediate marking $\tilde{m}$ is equal to the probability of being in marking $\tilde{m}$ in a PF-SPN with load vector $\boldsymbol{k_0} - \boldsymbol{S} \cdot \boldsymbol{I}(t)$. At this point an example is helpful to gain a better understanding of this theorem.

3.4 Example: Illustration of Theorem

Consider a token arriving to a specific place, say p_1, of Figure 3.1. A token arrives to place p_1 as the result of the firing of a transition in the pre-set of p_1 (i.e., ${}^\bullet p_1 = \{t_3, t_4\}$). Figure 3.3 isolates this place and these transitions. Let us assume that the initial marking is, as before, $[3,2,0,0]^T$ so that $\boldsymbol{k_0} = \boldsymbol{S} \cdot \boldsymbol{m} = [3,2]^T$.

Consider the situation when enabled transition t_3 fires. A token is then removed from place p_3 and a token is deposited in place p_1. At the instant the token is removed (but before it is deposited), we have that $m(p_1) + m(p_3) + m(p_4) = 2$ and $m(p_2) + m(p_4) = 2$. This implies that the token arriving to place p_1 (the token that will be deposited in place p_1) will always find one less token in the set of places p_1, p_3, p_4, but the same number of tokens (=2) in the set of places p_2, p_4. So what the token arriving to place p_1 "sees" as the set of intermediate markings can be obtained by removing this token from the net. The set of intermediate markings is obtained from the same net with a load vector of $\boldsymbol{k_1} = [2,2]^T$.

Next consider the situation when enabled transition t_4 fires. At the instant a token is removed from place p_4 (but before tokens are deposited in places p_1 and p_2), we have that $m(p_1) + m(p_3) + m(p_4) = 2$ and $m(p_2) + m(p_4) = 1$. So what the token arriving to place p_1 upon firing t_4 "sees" as the set of intermediate markings can also be obtained by removing this token from the net. But removing this token affects *both* place semiflows, since place p_4 participates in both semiflows. The set of intermediate markings is obtained from the same net with a load vector of $\boldsymbol{k}_2 = [2,1]^T$.

It should be carefully noted that the token arriving to place p_1 as the result of firing transition t_3 "sees" a different set of intermediate markings than the token arriving to place p_1 as the result of firing transition t_4. In fact, the two sets of intermediate markings have no members in common (cf. Figure 3.2). From the theorem if transition t_3 fires, the set of intermediate markings seen by the "arriving token" is obtained from a net with load vector $\boldsymbol{k_0} - \boldsymbol{S} \cdot \boldsymbol{I}(t_3) = [3,2]^T - [1,0]^T = [2,2]^T = \boldsymbol{k}_1$, and if t_4 fires, $\boldsymbol{k_0} - \boldsymbol{S} \cdot \boldsymbol{I}(t_4) = [3,2]^T - [1,1]^T = [2,1]^T = \boldsymbol{k}_2$.

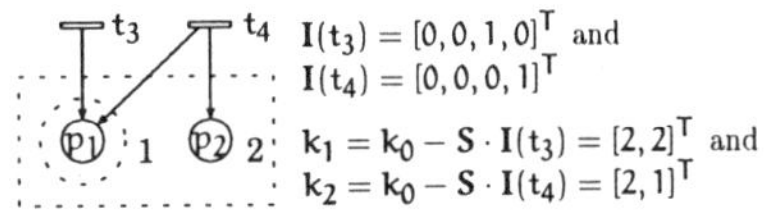

Fig. 3.3. Isolation of place p_1 in Example PF-SPN

The set of intermediate markings seen by firing transition t_3 corresponds to the reachability set of the net with initial marking $[2,2,0,0]^T$. To see this consider the firing of transition t_3 from the feasible marking $[2,2,1,0]^T$. In this case the token arriving in place p_1 sees the net with marking $[2,2,0,0]^T$ and we can interpret this as if the token on its way to place p_1 observes the stationary situation of the net with such a smaller initial marking. Similarly the set of intermediate markings seen by firing transition t_4 corresponds to the initial marking $[2,1,0,0]^T$ that can be seen from the token arriving in place p_1 when transition t_4 fires from marking $[2,1,0,1]^T$.

$\boldsymbol{k}_1 = \boldsymbol{k_0} - \boldsymbol{S} \cdot \boldsymbol{I}(t_3)$ $[2,2]^T$			$\boldsymbol{k}_2 = \boldsymbol{k_0} - \boldsymbol{S} \cdot \boldsymbol{I}(t_4)$ $[2,1]^T$		
$\tilde{\boldsymbol{m}}$	$\pi^a_{1,3}(\tilde{\boldsymbol{m}};\boldsymbol{k_0})$ $\pi(\tilde{\boldsymbol{m}};\boldsymbol{k}_1)$	$\pi^a_{1,3}(\tilde{\boldsymbol{m}};\boldsymbol{k_0})$ simulation	$\tilde{\boldsymbol{m}}$	$\pi^a_{1,4}(\tilde{\boldsymbol{m}};\boldsymbol{k_0})$ $\pi(\tilde{\boldsymbol{m}};\boldsymbol{k}_2)$	$\pi^a_{1,4}(\tilde{\boldsymbol{m}};\boldsymbol{k_0})$ simulation
$[2,2,0,0]$	0.2652	0.2659	$[2,1,0,0]$	0.3294	0.3286
$[1,2,1,0]$	0.1326	0.1327	$[1,1,1,0]$	0.1647	0.1654
$[1,1,0,1]$	0.2273	0.2281	$[1,0,0,1]$	0.2824	0.2820
$[0,2,2,0]$	0.0662	0.0658	$[0,1,2,0]$	0.0824	0.0821
$[0,1,1,1]$	0.1137	0.1133	$[0,0,1,1]$	0.1412	0.1418
$[0,0,0,2]$	0.1949	0.1943			

Table 3.1. Arrival Probabilities to Place p_1 for Example PF-SPN

Assuming that the firing rates of transitions t_1, t_2, t_3, and t_4 have values 1, 3, 2, and 3.5, respectively, we obtain the numerical results exhibited in Table

1. The (exact) stationary state probabilities were computed using GreatSPN [2] and the arrival probabilities were confirmed by a simulation of a sequence of almost 400000 transitions firings of the example PF-SPN.

3.5 The Notion of Direction

The set of transitions $^\bullet p_j$ can be partitioned into equivalence classes according to the following equivalence relation:

$$\forall\ t_r, t_s \in\ ^\bullet p_j\ \ t_r \sim t_s \ \text{ iff }\ \boldsymbol{S}\cdot\boldsymbol{O}(t_r) = \boldsymbol{S}\cdot\boldsymbol{O}(t_s) \tag{3.2}$$

Let L_j denote the number of equivalence classes generated by this equivalence relation. We identify the classes with an index l such that $1 \leq l \leq L_j$. We can assume that a function $\mathcal{L}_j(t)$ exists that returns the index of the equivalence class to which transition t belongs. Moreover, let σ_l denote the set of transitions belonging to the *l-th* equivalence class. Finally, let us denote by $\boldsymbol{V}_l$ the vector $\boldsymbol{S} \cdot \boldsymbol{O}(t)$ $(t \in \sigma_l)$ that characterizes the *l-th* equivalence class.

Intuitively if we group together all the transitions of the same equivalence class (as in Figure 3.4), we can identify the different directions that arriving tokens take to place p_j. Each equivalence class identifies a possible direction

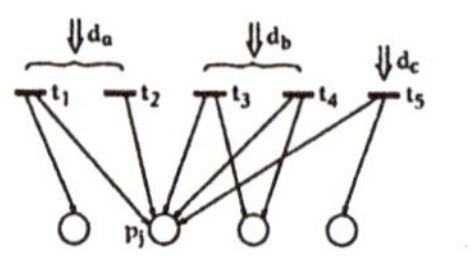

Fig. 3.4. Groupings of transitions that fire in the same "direction"

of arrival of tokens to place p_j. Tokens arriving in place p_j from direction l have the interesting property of seeing the *same* set of possible intermediate markings, independent of which transition of the equivalence class fires to put them there. Tokens entering a place from different directions (i.e., from the firing of transitions belonging to different equivalence classes) see, instead, different sets of possible intermediate markings. This follows by observing that

$$t_r, t_s \in \sigma_l \Rightarrow \boldsymbol{S} \cdot \boldsymbol{O}(t_r) = \boldsymbol{S} \cdot \boldsymbol{O}(t_s) = \boldsymbol{V}_l$$

and that when transitions t_r and t_s fire, the following facts hold true:

$$\begin{aligned}
&(\tilde{\boldsymbol{m}} + \boldsymbol{I}(t_r))\,[t_r > (\tilde{\boldsymbol{m}} + \boldsymbol{O}(t_r)) \ \Rightarrow \\
&\ \tilde{\boldsymbol{m}} \in E(\boldsymbol{k_0} - \boldsymbol{S}\cdot\boldsymbol{O}(t_r)) = \\
&\ \ E(\boldsymbol{k_0} - \boldsymbol{S}\cdot\boldsymbol{I}(t_r)) = E(\boldsymbol{k_0} - \boldsymbol{V}_l) = E(\boldsymbol{k}_l)
\end{aligned}$$

$$\begin{aligned}&(\tilde{\boldsymbol{m}} + \boldsymbol{I}(t_s))\,[t_s > (\tilde{\boldsymbol{m}} + \boldsymbol{O}(t_s)) \;\Rightarrow\\ &\quad \tilde{\boldsymbol{m}} \in E(\boldsymbol{k_0} - \boldsymbol{S} \cdot \boldsymbol{O}(t_s)) =\\ &\quad E(\boldsymbol{k_0} - \boldsymbol{S} \cdot \boldsymbol{I}(t_s)) = E(\boldsymbol{k_0} - \boldsymbol{V}_l) = E(\boldsymbol{k}_l)\end{aligned}$$

where $\boldsymbol{k}_l = \boldsymbol{k_0} - \boldsymbol{V}_l$ is the load vector of the net yielding the set of markings visible from direction l. From these relationships we can conclude that the same set of markings is visible from t_r and t_s. If instead $t_u \in \sigma_{l'}$ where $l' \neq l$, then

$$\begin{aligned}&t_u \in \sigma_{l'} \Rightarrow \boldsymbol{S} \cdot \boldsymbol{O}(t_u) = \boldsymbol{V}_{l'}\\ &(\tilde{\boldsymbol{m}} + \boldsymbol{I}(t_u))\,[t_u > (\tilde{\boldsymbol{m}} + \boldsymbol{O}(t_u)) \Rightarrow\\ &\quad \tilde{\boldsymbol{m}} \in E(\boldsymbol{k_0} - \boldsymbol{S} \cdot \boldsymbol{O}(t_u)) = E(\boldsymbol{k_0} - \boldsymbol{V}_{l'}) = E(\boldsymbol{k}_{l'})\end{aligned}$$

But $E(\boldsymbol{k_0} - \boldsymbol{V}_l) \neq E(\boldsymbol{k_0} - \boldsymbol{V}_{l'})$ so that the set of intermediate markings visible from t_u is different from that of t_r and t_s. The notion of direction thus implies that the distributions of markings seen at arrival by tokens coming from direction l are similar in the sense that they are defined on the same set of intermediate markings.

We can now restate the global arrival theorem with the notion of direction added.

Theorem 3.2. *[Global Arrival Theorem by Direction] Given an S-invariant reachable PF-SPN with load vector $\boldsymbol{k_0}$, the probability of finding marking $\tilde{\boldsymbol{m}}$ on arrival to place p_j when transition t fires is given by*

$$\pi^a_{jt}(\tilde{\boldsymbol{m}}; \boldsymbol{k_0}) = \pi(\tilde{\boldsymbol{m}}; \boldsymbol{k_0} - \boldsymbol{V}_l) \qquad \textit{where } l = \mathcal{L}_j(t) \tag{3.3}$$

The implication of this result is that tokens arriving to a place from the same direction not only see the same set of intermediate markings, but they also see them with the same probability distribution!

3.6 Local Arrival Theorems

The arrival theorems derived so far formalize the view that a token arriving to a particular place has of the whole net. An important characterization of Petri Nets is that of describing the global behavior of a system in terms of local contributions and thus of breaking down the description of a system state into a collection of local states. We can thus specialize the results developed in the previous sections by deriving some "local" arrival theorems, in which we capture the characteristics of the view that a token arriving to a given place has of the net by restricting its view to the (local) state of the place in which it is arriving.

To this end let $\pi^a_{jt}(h; \boldsymbol{k_0})$ denote the probability that a token arriving to place p_j after firing a transition $t \in {}^\bullet p_j$ sees h tokens in place p_j. The following theorem is an immediate consequence of Theorem 3.2 and is derived by forming a marginal distribution from $\pi^a_{jt}(\tilde{\boldsymbol{m}}; \boldsymbol{k_0})$ where we sum over all $\tilde{\boldsymbol{m}}$ such that $\tilde{m}_j = h$.

Theorem 3.3. *[Local Arrival Theorem by Direction] Given an S-invariant reachable PF-SPN with load vector $\boldsymbol{k_0}$, the probability of finding h tokens on arrival to place p_j when transition t fires is given by*

$$\pi^a_{jt}(h; \boldsymbol{k_0}) = \pi(h; \boldsymbol{k_0} - \boldsymbol{V}_l) \qquad \textit{where } l = \mathcal{L}_j(t) \tag{3.4}$$

Our aim is to derive a formula for the mean sojourn time of a token in place p_j. In order to obtain the expression for this quantity we need the next arrival theorem, that formalizes the view that a token arriving from any possible direction to a particular place has of the situation of this place. In this theorem we introduce the notion of departure rate of tokens from places. Let $P(\boldsymbol{m} \geq \boldsymbol{V}, \boldsymbol{k_0})$ represent a shorthand notation for the probability that a marking of the net does not fall below a certain threshold vector $\boldsymbol{V}$. From the steady-state probability distribution we have that

$$P(\boldsymbol{m} \geq \boldsymbol{V}; \boldsymbol{k_0}) = \sum_{\substack{\boldsymbol{m} \in E(\boldsymbol{k_0}) \\ \boldsymbol{m} \geq \boldsymbol{V}}} \pi(\boldsymbol{m}; \boldsymbol{k_0})$$

When h tokens are present in place p_j, the rate at which tokens are removed from that place is equal to the sum of the firing rates of the transitions that are enabled and that have place p_j among their input places. Since we are dealing with ordinary nets, a transition that has place p_j (with h tokens) in its input bag is enabled whenever the net is in a marking that contains at least one token in each of its other input places. The set of such markings can be obtained by "freezing" one token in place p_j and considering the reachability set that is derived from letting the other tokens move throughout the net. The probability of the markings that have $h-1$ tokens in place p_j in this "reduced" reachability set is $\pi_j(h-1, \boldsymbol{k_0} - \boldsymbol{S}_j)$ while $P(\boldsymbol{m} \geq \boldsymbol{I}(t) - \boldsymbol{e}_j, m_j = h-1; \boldsymbol{k_0} - \boldsymbol{S}_j)$ is the probability of the subset of markings that enable transition t. The ratio between these two quantities provides the conditional probability that transition t is enabled, given that $m(p_j) = h$; the rate at which tokens are removed from place p_j when there are h tokens in place p_j can be defined in the following manner

$$q_j(h; \boldsymbol{k_0}) = \sum_{t \in p_j^\bullet} \mu(t) \frac{P(\boldsymbol{m} \geq \boldsymbol{I}(t) - \boldsymbol{e}_j, m_j = h-1; \boldsymbol{k_0} - \boldsymbol{S}_j)}{\pi_j(h-1, \boldsymbol{k_0} - \boldsymbol{S}_j)} \tag{3.5}$$

Knowing these marking dependent rates, the overall rate at which tokens are removed from place p_j can be obtained in the following manner

$$\begin{aligned} q_j(\boldsymbol{k_0}) &= \sum_{i=1}^{\max} \pi_j(i; \boldsymbol{k_0}) q_j(h; \boldsymbol{k_0}) \\ &= \sum_{t \in p_j^\bullet} \mu(t) P(\boldsymbol{m} \geq \boldsymbol{I}(t) - \boldsymbol{e}_j; \boldsymbol{k_0} - \boldsymbol{S}_j) \end{aligned} \tag{3.6}$$

For the sake of brevity, we omit the details of the derivations of these equations as well as the proof of the following theorem; interested readers can find these details in reference [14].

Theorem 3.4. *[Local Arrival Theorem Independent of Direction] Given an S-invariant reachable PF-SPN with load vector $\boldsymbol{k_0}$, the probability of finding h tokens on arrival to place p_j is given by*

$$\pi_j^a(h; \boldsymbol{k_0}) = \pi_j(h; \boldsymbol{k_0} - \boldsymbol{S}_j) \cdot \frac{q_j(h+1; \boldsymbol{k_0})}{q_j(\boldsymbol{k_0})} \tag{3.7}$$

Observe that this theorem allows us to compute an arrival probability in a net with load vector $\boldsymbol{k_0}$ by computing a steady-state probability in a net with a lower load vector (i.e., $\boldsymbol{k_0} - \boldsymbol{S}_j$). We exploit this property in the derivation of the mean sojourn time.

Before starting the next section we briefly review the meaning of the arrival theorems obtained so far, in order to provide a better intuition about the goal that we are striving to obtain. Theorems 1 and 2 formalize the view that a token arriving to a particular place, when a given transition fires, has of the whole net. Theorems 3 and 4 instead describe the "local" view that an arriving token to a particular place has of the situation of that place. In Theorem 3 there is the notion of direction that is not present in Theorem 4. In fact, the last theorem describes the local situation "independent" of the arriving direction. This theorem will be used in the next section to obtain a formula that allows us to compute the mean sojourn time of a token in a given place.

4. Mean Sojourn Time

In this section we describe the expression of the mean sojourn time of a token in a place, which is a quantity similar to the mean waiting time of a customer in a queueing network. By exploiting our last arrival theorem, we show that the mean sojourn time of a token in a place of a net with the "current load vector" can be computed from PF-SPNs at "lower load vector(s)." An analogous result has been derived for product-form queueing networks, in which a recursive equation for the mean waiting time at the "current load" is derived from performance measures computed from the same queueing network at a "lower load" using the "arrival theorem" for PF-QNs.

The mean sojourn time of a token in a place is the average amount of time the token spends in the place before departing. Although the firing rates of transitions in PF-SPNs are marking independent, we have seen in the previous section that the departure rate of tokens from a place is not marking independent. In particular, the departure rate depends on the number of tokens that the place contains and on the fact that all the other places that are part of the input bags of the transitions belonging to $p_j^\bullet$ are marked. This is reflected in the expression for the rate $q_j(h; \boldsymbol{k_0})$ by the presence of a ratio among probability terms. Since the behavior of a place in front of a transition is similar to that of a queue in front of a server, we can compute the mean sojourn time of a token in place p_j using the following formula

$$sj_j(\boldsymbol{k_0}) = \sum_h h \cdot \frac{1}{q_j(h; \boldsymbol{k_0})} \cdot \pi_j^a(h-1; \boldsymbol{k_0}) \tag{4.1}$$

Using the result of Theorem 3.4 (Equation 3.7) we obtain that

$$sj_j(\boldsymbol{k_0}) = \frac{1 + np_j(\boldsymbol{k_0} - \boldsymbol{S}_j)}{\sum_{t \in p_j^\bullet} \mu(t) P(\boldsymbol{m} \geq \boldsymbol{I}(t) - \boldsymbol{e}_j; \boldsymbol{k_0} - \boldsymbol{S}_j)} \tag{4.2}$$

where $np_j(\boldsymbol{k_0} - \boldsymbol{S}_j)$ is the average number of tokens in place p_j in a net with load vector $\boldsymbol{k_0} - \boldsymbol{S}_j$. We observe that Equation (4.2) for the mean sojourn time is similar to the formula used to compute the mean waiting time of a customer at a station in a load-independent PF-QN. Furthermore, it is extremely interesting to note that the departure rate dependency on the number of tokens in a place does not appear in the computation of the mean sojourn time except for the particular expression of the denominator that globally accounts for the fact that the transitions withdrawing tokens from place p_j are not necessarily enabled in markings that contain at least one token in place p_j.

Equation (4.2) was first derived in [13] and was used together with applications of Little's formula to obtain a mean value analysis algorithm for PF-SPNs whose time complexity is polynomial in the number of tokens in the initial marking and the number of places in the net. Equation (4.2) also shows how the collection of arrival theorems presented in this paper represent the theoretical basis for the development of a Mean Value Analysis for PF-SPNs.

5. Conclusion

We have shown that the stationary probabilities at "arrival instants" are related to corresponding stationary probabilities at arbitrary instants in Product-Form SPNs with lower loads. We first showed that the probability that an arriving token "sees" a particular intermediate marking is equal to the probability of that marking in the same net with a lower load. We then introduced the notion of direction that takes into account the fact that a token may arrive in a place from different avenues. In particular, tokens arriving to a place from the same direction not only see the same set of intermediate markings, but they also see them with the same probability distribution. Using this basic result, we derived several additional arrival theorems. One of these was used as the basis for the derivation of the mean sojourn time that a token spends in a place (Equation (4.2)). This equation allows us to compute the mean sojourn time by using quantities previously computed in nets with lower load vectors. Equation (4.2) is the fundamental equation used in the development of a mean value analysis algorithm for the computation of performance indices in PF-SPNs. This MVA algorithm does not generate the reachability set and thereby avoids the exponential time complexity of the traditional solution algorithm. In fact, using this MVA algorithm product-form nets with many places and many tokens in their initial marking can now be solved efficiently.

References

1. F. Baskett, K.M. Chandy, R.R. Muntz, and F. Palacios, "Open, closed and mixed networks of queues with different classes of customers", *Journal of the ACM*, **22** (2), pp. 248–260, April 1975.
2. G. Chiola, "GreatSPN 1.5 software architecture", In Proc. 5th Intern. Conf. Modeling Techniques and Tools for Computer Performance Evaluation, Torino, Italy, February 1991.
3. J.L. Coleman, W. Henderson, and P.G. Taylor, "Product form equilibrium distributions and an algorithm for classes of batch movement queueing networks and stochastic Petri nets", Tech. rep., University of Adelaide, 1992.
4. J. Desel and J. Esparza. "Reachability in reversible free-choice systems", Technical Report TUM-I9023, Institute Fur Informatik, 1990.
5. W.J. Gordon and G.F. Newell, "Closed queueing systems with exponential servers" *Operations Research*, **15**, pp. 254–265, 1967.
6. W. Henderson, D. Lucic, and P.G. Taylor, "A net level performance analysis of stochastic Petri nets" *Journal of Austr. Math. Soc. Ser. B*, **31**, pp. 176–187, 1989.
7. W. Henderson and P.G. Taylor, "Embedded processes in stochastic Petri nets", *IEEE TSE*, **17** (2), February 1991.
8. J. R. Jackson, "Jobshop-like queueing systems", *Management Science*, **10** (1), pp. 131–142, October 1963.
9. H. Jungnitz, A. Desrochers, and M. Silva, "Approximation techniques for Stochastic Macroplace/Macrotransition nets", Technical report, University of Zaragoza, Spain, 1992.
10. S.S. Lavenberg and M. Reiser, "Stationary state probabilities at arrival instants for closed queueing networks with multiple types of customers", *Journal of Applied Probability*, **17**, pp. 1048–1061, 1980.
11. T. Murata, "Petri nets: properties, analysis, and applications", *Proceedings of the IEEE*, **77** (4), pp. 541–580, April 1989.
12. M. Sereno and G. Balbo, "Computational algorithms for product form solution stochastic Petri nets", In Proc. 5th Intern. Workshop on Petri Nets and Performance Models, Toulouse, France, October 1993. IEEE-CS Press.
13. M. Sereno and G. Balbo, "Mean value analysis of stochastic Petri nets", Technical report, University of Torino, 1993. Submitted for publication.
14. M. Sereno, G. Balbo, and S. Bruell, "Arrival theorems for product-form stochastic Petri nets", Technical report, University of Torino, 1993.
15. K.C. Sevcik and I. Mitrani. "The distribution of queueing network states at input and output instants", *Journal of the ACM*, **28** (2), pp. 358–371, April 1981.

Bibliography

Bibliography

1. J. Aguilar, "L'allocation des tâches, l'équilibrage de charge et l'optimisation combinatoire", Doctoral Thesis, Univ. Paris V, Jan. 1995.
2. J. Aguilar, "Combinatorial optimization methods. A study of the graph partitioning problem", Proc. Panamerican Workshop on Applied and Computational Mathematic, Caracas, Venezuela, 1993.
3. J. Aguilar, "Heuristic Algorithms for task assignment of parallel programs", Proc. Intl Conference on Massively Parallel Processing, Applications and Development, Delft, Elsevier Science Publishers, Jun. 1994.
4. J. Aguilar, "Comparison between the random neural network model and other optimization combinatorial methods for the large acyclic graph partitioning problem", Proc. 7th Intl Symposium on Computer & Information Sciences, Antalya, Turkey, Nov. 1992.
5. E. Altman and G. Koole, "Stochastic scheduling games with Markov decision arrival processes", *Computers and Mathematics with Applications*, **26**, pp. 141–148, 1993.
6. E. Altman and G. Koole, "On Submodular Value Functions of Dynamic Programming", in preparation.
7. A. Ametistova and I. Mitrani, "Modelling and Evaluation of Cache Coherence Protocols in Multiprocessor Systems", in Computer and Telecommunication Systems Performance Engineering, (eds. M.E. Woodward, S. Datta and S. Szumko), Pentech Press, London, 1994.
8. F. Baccelli and M. Canales, "Parallel Simulation of Stochastic Petri Nets using Recurrence Equations", ACM Tomacs, **1** (3), January 1993.
9. F. Baccelli, B. Gaujal and N. Furmento, "Parallel and Distributed Simulation of Free Choice Nets", *Ninth Workshop on Parallel and Distributed Simulation (PADS'95)*, Lake Placid, June 1995.
10. F. Baccelli and S. Foss, "On the Saturation Rule for the Stability of Queues", INRIA Report #2015, *Journal of Applied Probability*, June 1995.
11. F. Baccelli, S. Foss and B. Gaujal, "Structural, timed and stochastic properties of free choice Petri nets", INRIA Report #2411, *IEEE Trans. Automatic Control*, to appear, 1995.
12. F. Baccelli and J. Mairesse, "Ergodic Theory of Stochastic Operators and Discrete Event Networks", Idempotency, Cambridge Univ. Press, 1995, Submitted.
13. F. Baccelli and V. Schmidt, "Taylor Series Expansions for Poisson Driven (max,+)-Linear Systems", Rapport INRIA #2494, March 1995, Submitted to *Annals of Applied Probability*.
14. S.C. Borst, "Polling Systems", Ph.D. Thesis Tilburg University, CWI Press, November 1994.
15. S.C. Borst, "Optimal probabilistic allocation of customer types to servers", In: Proc. ACM Sigmetrics/Performance '95, Ottawa, pp. 116–125, 1995, an updated version appears in these proceedings.
16. S.C. Borst and O.J. Boxma, "Polling models with and without switchover times", CWI Report BS-R9421, to appear in Oper. Res.
17. S.C. Borst, O.J. Boxma, J.H.A. Harink and G.B. Huitema, "Optimization of fixed time polling schemes", *Telecommunication Systems*, **3**, pp. 31–59, 1994.
18. S.C. Borst, O.J. Boxma and H. Levy, "The use of service limits for efficient operation of multi-station single-medium communication systems", *IEEE Trans. Networking*, to appear in October, 1995.

19. R.J. Boucherie, "A characterization of independence for competing Markov chains with applications to stochastic Petri nets", *IEEE Transactions on Software Engineering*, **20**, pp. 536–544, 1994.
20. R.J. Boucherie and O.J. Boxma, "The workload in the M/G/1 queue with work removal", CWI Report BS-R9505, February 1995.
21. R.J. Boucherie and M. Sereno, "A structural characterisation of product form stochastic Petri nets", CWI Report BS-R9402, 1994.
22. O.J. Boxma, "Static optimization of queueing systems", In: R.P. Agarwal (ed.), Recent Trends in Optimization Theory and Applications, World Scientific Publ., Singapore, 1995.
23. O.J. Boxma and G.J. van Houtum, "The compensation approach applied to a 2×2 switch", *Probability in the Engineering and Informational Sciences*, **7**, pp. 471–493, 1993
24. O.J. Boxma and M. Kelbert, "Stochastic bounds for a polling system", *Annals of Oper. Res.*, **48**, pp. 295–310, 1994.
25. O.J. Boxma and G.M. Koole, "Performance Evaluation of Parallel and Distributed Systems", Proceedings 3rd QMIPS Workshop in Torino, CWI Tracts 105 and 106, 1994.
26. O.J. Boxma, G.M. Koole and Z. Liu, "Queueing-theoretic solution methods for models of parallel and distributed systems", In: Proc. 3rd QMIPS workshop: Performance Evaluation of Parallel and Distributed Systems, eds. O.J. Boxma and G.M. Koole, CWI Tract 105, pp. 1-24, 1994.
27. O.J. Boxma, G.M. Koole and I. Mitrani, "A two-queue polling model with a threshold service policy", Mascots'95, North Carolina, pp. 84-88, 1995.
28. O.J. Boxma and J.A.C. Resing, "Tandem queues with deterministic service times", *Annals of Operations Research*, **49**, pp. 221–239, 1994.
29. J.L. Briz, J.M. Colom and M. Silva, "Discrete event simulation based on timed Petri nets using linear enabling functions", In Proceedings of the IEEE International Conference on Systems, Man, and Cybernetics, pp. 1671–1676, San Antonio, Texas, October 1994.
30. J. Campos, J. M. Colom, H. Jungnitz and M. Silva, "Approximate throughput computation of stochastic marked graphs", *IEEE Transactions on Software Engineering*, **20** (7), pp. 526–535, July 1994.
31. J. Campos, B. F. Plo and M. San Miguel, "Boundedness on stochastic Petri nets", *Revista Matemática de la Universidad Complutense de Madrid*, **6** (1), pp. 123–136, 1993.
32. J. Campos and M. Silva, "Embedded product-form queueing networks and the improvement of performance bounds for Petri net systems", *Performance Evaluation*, **18** (1), pp. 3–19, July 1993.
33. M. Canales, "Simulation Parallèle de réseaux de Petri Stochastiques", PhD thesis, Univeristy of Nice, Februray 1994.
34. S. Chabridon, "Execution fiable de programmes répartis en environnement peu fiable", Doctoral Thesis, Univ. Paris V, 1995 (in preparation).
35. S. Chabridon and E. Gelenbe, "Dependable distributed computing with the help of agents", Proc. EUREMICRO'95, Sanremo, Jan. 1995.
36. R. Chakka, "Spectral Expansion Solution for Large Markov Processes with Finite State Space", 3rd Int. Workshop on Queueing Networks with Finite capacity, Bradford, 1995.
37. R. Chakka, "Performance and Reliability Modelling of Computer Systems Using Spectral Expansion", PhD Thesis, University of Newcastle, 1995.
38. R. Chakka and I. Mitrani, "A Numerical Solution Method for Multiprocessor Systems with General Breakdowns and Repairs", Procs. 6th Int. Conf. on Modelling Techniques, Edinburgh, 1992.

39. R. Chakka and I. Mitrani, "Heterogeneous Multiprocessor Systems with Breakdowns: Performance and Optimal Repair Strategies", *Theoretical Computer Science*, **125**, pp. 91–109, 1994.
40. G. Chiola, C. Anglano, J. Campos, J. M. Colom and M. Silva, "Operational analysis of timed Petri nets and application to the computation of performance bounds", In Proceedings of the 5th International Workshop on Petri Nets and Performance Models, pp. 128–137, Toulouse, France, October 1993. IEEE-Computer Society Press.
41. J.W. Cohen, "On a class of two-dimensional nearest-neighbour random walks", In: Studies in Applied Probability – Papers in honour of Lajos Takács, eds. J. Galambos and J. Gani, *J. Appl. Probab.*, **31A**, pp. 207–237, 1995.
42. J.W. Cohen, "Two-dimensional nearest-neighbour queueing models, a review and an example", In: these proceedings, 1995.
43. M.B. Combé and O.J. Boxma, "Optimization of static traffic allocation policies", *Theor. Comp. Sci.*, **125**, pp. 17–43, 1994.
44. S. Coury amd P.G. Harrison, "Asymptotic properties of queueing networks", in Proc 7th Int. Conf.on Modelling Techniques and Tools for Computer Performance Evaluation, Vienna, May 1994.
45. S. Coury and P.G. Harrison, "Waiting time distribution in a class of wireless multi-channel local area networks", in Proc. International Conference on Local and Metropolitan Communication Systems, Kyoto, Japan, December 1994.
46. M. Ettl and I. Mitrani, "Applying Spectral Expansion in Evaluating the Performance of Multiprocessor Systems", in Performance Evaluation of Parallel and Distributed Systems, CWI Tract (eds. O.J. Boxma and G.M. Koole), 1994.
47. A.J. Field and P.G. Harrison, "Transmission times in buffered full crossbar communication networks with cyclic arbitration", in proc Int. Conf. on Parallel Processing, St. Charles, Illinois, USA, 1993.
48. A.J. Field and P.G. Harrison, "An analytical model of the standard coherent interface 'SCI'", in proc Int. Conf. on Parallel Processing, Oconomowoc, Wisconsin, USA, 1995.
49. A.J. Field, P.G. Harrison and N. Lehovetski, "A Uniform-memory Access Model of a Distributed Coherent Cache System", in Proc. 10th UK Performance Engineering Workshop, Edinburgh, September, 1994.
50. L. Finta and Z. Liu, "Scheduling of Parallel Programs in Single-Bus Multiprocessor Systems", INRIA Report #2302, 1994.
51. L. Finta and Z. Liu, "Single Machine Scheduling Subject to Precedence Delays",INRIA Report #2198, 1994.
52. L. Finta, Z. Liu, I. Milis and E. Bampis, "Scheduling UET-UCT Series-Parallel Graphs on Two Processors", INRIA Report #2566, 1995.
53. J.M. Fourneau, E. Gelenbe and R. Suros "G-networks with multiple classes of positive and negative customers, *Theoretical Computer Science*, in press, 1995.
54. S. Gaubert and J. Mairesse, "Task Resource Models and (max,+) Automata", Idempotency, Cambridge University Press, 1995, Submitted.
55. B. Gaujal, "Parallélisme et simulation des systèmes à événements discrets", PhD thesis, University of Nice Sophia Antipolis, June 1994.
56. B. Gaujal, "Optimal allocation sequence of two processes sharing a resource", INRIA Report #2223, 1994.
57. B. Gaujal and A. Jean-Marie, "Computational Issues in Recursive Stochastic Systems", In Idempotency, J. Gunawardena (ed.), Cambridge Univ. Press, 1995. Submitted.

58. B. Gaujal, A. Jean-Marie and J. Mairesse, "Minimal Representation of Uniform Recurrence Equations". INRIA Report #2568, June 1995.
59. E. Gelenbe, "G-networks with instantaneous customer movement", *Journal of Applied Probability*, **30** (3), pp. 742–748, 1993.
60. E. Gelenbe, "G-Networks with signals and batch removal", *Probability in the Engineering and Informational Sciences*, **7**, pp 335–342, 1993.
61. E. Gelenbe, "G-networks: An unifying model for queueing networks and neural networks," *Annals of Operations Research*, **48** (1–4), pp 433–461, 1994.
62. E. Gelenbe, "G-networks and minimum cost functions", Invited Paper, Proc. MASCOTS'95, pp. 135–141, IEEE Computer Society Press, Los Alamitos, CA 1995.
63. E. Gelenbe, O. Boxma, J.M. Fourneau, M. Hernandez, P. Harrison and E. Pitel, 'G-networks", Hot-Topics Seccion, ACM-SIGMETRICS and IFIP WG 7.3 Sysmposium on System Performance Evaluation, Ottawa, May 1995.
64. E. Gelenbe and S. Chabridon, "Scheduling distributed tasks for survivability of the application", Proc. Parallel Computing Symposium, Delft, Elsevier Science Publishers, 1994.
65. E. Gelenbe and S. Chabridon, "Dependable execution of distributed programs", *Simulation Practice and Theory*, in Press, 1995.
66. E. Gelenbe and W. Jin, "Convergence of a numerical procedure for the stationary solution of G-networks", submitted to *Journal of Applied Probability.*
67. E. Gelenbe and R. Kushwaha, "Dynamic load balancing in distributed systems", Invited Paper, Proc. MASCOTS'94, pp 245–249, IEEE Computer Society Press, Los Alamitos, CA 1994.
68. E. Gelenbe and A. Labed, "Multiple class G-networks with trigerred customer movement", submitted for publication.
69. E. Gelenbe and M. Schassberger, "Stability of product form G-Networks", *Probability in the Engineering and Informational Sciences*, **6**, pp 271–276, 1992.
70. P.G. Harrison and J. Hillston, "Exploiting Quasi-reversible Structures to Find Product Form Solutions in Markovian Process Algebra Models", in Proc. PAPM, Edinburgh, Springer-Verlag Workshop Series, 1995.
71. P.G. Harrison and A. de C. Pinto, "An approximate analysis of asynchronous, packet-switched, buffered Banyan networks with blocking", Performance Evaluation, 1993.
72. P.G. Harrison and A. de C. Pinto, "Response time distributions in packet-switched banyan networks", in Proc. 2nd International Workshop on Performance Modelling and Evaluation of ATM Networks, Bradford, July 1994. Extended version in D. Kouvatsos, ed., Performance Modelling and Evaluation of ATM Networks, Chapman-Hall, 1995.
73. P.G. Harrison and E. Pitel, "Sojourn Times in Single Server Queues with Negative Customers", *Journal of Applied Probability*, 1993.
74. P.G. Harrison and E. Pitel, "Response time distributions in queueing network models", State-of-the-art Tutorial, Performance 93, Rome, Italy, 1993, Springer-Verlag, LNCS.
75. P.G. Harrison and E. Pitel, "Response time distributions in tandem G-networks", *Journal of Applied Probability*, 1995.
76. P.G. Harrison and E. Pitel, "M/G/1 Queues with Negative Arrivals: an iteration to solve a Fredholm integral equation of the first kind", in Proc. MASCOTS '95, North Carolina, 1995.
77. P.G. Harrison and E. Pitel, "The M/G/1 queue with negative customers", *Adv. Appl. Prob.*, June 1996.

78. A. Jean-Marie, "Analytical computation of Lyapunov exponents in stochastic event graphs", In O. Boxma and G. Koole, editors, Third QMIPS Workshop, CWI Tracts #106, 1994.
79. A. Jean-Marie and O.J. Olsder, "Analysis of Stochastic Min-Max Systems: Results and Conjectures", in preparation, September 1993.
80. A. Jean-Marie, "On Queueing Systems with Poisson Inputs and Known Services", in preparation, 1995.
81. G.M. Koole, "On the power series algorithm", In: Proc. 3rd QMIPS workshop: Performance Evaluation of Parallel and Distributed Systems, eds. O.J. Boxma and G.M. Koole, CWI Tract 105, pp. 139–155, 1994.
82. G.M. Koole, "Assigning a single server to inhomogeneous queues with switching costs", CWI Report BS-R9405, 1994.
83. Z. Liu, "Performance bounds of stochastic timed Petri nets by linear programming approach". In preparation.
84. Z. Liu and J. Resing, "Duality and Equivalencies in Closed Tandem Queueing Networks", INRIA Report #2115, 1994.
85. Z. Liu and D. Towsley, "Optimality of the Round Robin Routing Policy", *Journal of the Applied Probability*, **31**, pp. 466–575, June 1994.
86. J. Mairesse, "A graphical approach of the spectral theory in the (max,+) algebra", *IEEE Trans. Automatic Control*, September 1995. To appear.
87. J. Mairesse, "Products of irreducible random matrices in the (max,+) algebra", Technical Report #1939, INRIA, Sophia Antipolis, France, 1993. To appear in *JAP*.
88. J. Mairesse, "Stabilité des systèmes à événements discrets stochastiques", PhD thesis, Ecole Polytechnique, Paris, June 1995.
89. I. Mitrani, "Queues with Breakdowns", 2nd Int. Workshop on Performability Modelling of Comp. and Comm. Sys., Mont St Michel, 1993.
90. I. Mitrani, "The Spectral Expansion Solution for Markov Processes on Lattice Strips", in Advances in Queueing: Models, Methods & Problems, (ed. J.H. Dshalalow), CRC Press, 1995.
91. I. Mitrani and R. Chakka, "Spectral Expansion Solution for a Class of Markov Models: Application and Comparison with the Matrix-Geometric Solution", *Performance Evaluation*, **23**, 1995.
92. I. Mitrani and A. Puhalskii, "Limiting Results for Multiprocessor Systems with Breakdowns and Repairs", *Queueing Systems*, **14**, pp. 293–311, 1993.
93. I. Mitrani and P.E. Wright, "Routing in the Presence of Breakdowns", *Performance Evaluation*, **20**, pp. 151–164, 1994.
94. I. Mitrani and P.E. Wright, "On the Interaction of Unreliable Routes", Chapter 9 in Probability, Statistics and Optimization, (ed. F.P. Kelly), Wiley, 1994.
95. K. Onaga, M. Silva and T. Watanabe, "Qualitative analysis of periodic schedules for deterministically timed Petri net systems", *IEICE Transactions on Fundamentals of Electronics, Communications, and Computer Sciences*, **76** (4), pp. 580–592, April 1993.
96. C.J. Pérez-Jiménez, J. Campos and M. Silva, "On approximate throughput computation of deterministic systems of sequential processes", Research Report GISI-RR-95-03, Dept. de Informática e Ingeniería de Sistemas, Univ. Zaragoza, March 1993.
97. A. de C. Pinto and P.G. Harrison, "An approximation for end-to-end delay distributions in buffered multistage interconnection networks", in Proc. International Conference on Local and Metropolitan Communication Systems, Kyoto, Japan, December 1994.

98. L. Recalde, E. Teruel and M. Silva. "On well-formedness analysis: The case of deterministic systems of sequential processes", In J. Desel, editor, Proceedings of STRICT '95, Springer Verlag, 1995, (To appear).
99. M. Silva and J. Campos, "Performance models based on Petri nets", In Proceedings of the IMACS/IFAC Second International Symposium on Mathematical and Intelligent Models in System Simulation, pp. xiv–xxi, Brussels, Belgium, April 1993, Invited paper.
100. M. Silva and J. Campos, "Structural performance analysis of stochastic Petri nets", In Proceedings of the IEEE International Computer Performance and Dependability Symposium, pp. 61–70, Erlangen, Germany, April 1995. Invited paper.
101. M. Silva and J.M. Colom. "Petri nets applied to the modelling and analysis of computer architecture problems", *Microprocessing and Microprogramming*, **38** (1-5), pp. 1–11, 1993.
102. M. Silva and E. Teruel, "Analysis of autonomous Petri nets with bulk services and arrivals", In Cohen and Quadrat, eds., 11th Int. Conf. on Analysis and Optimization of Systems. Discrete Event Systems, *Lecture Notes in Control and Information Sciences*, **199**, pp. 131–143, Springer Verlag, 1994.
103. A. Stafylopatis and E. Gelenbe, "Resequencing under subset associations," *International Journal of Modelling and Simulation*, **14** (1), pp 18–21, 1994.
104. B. Strulo, D.M. Gabbay and P.G. Harrison, "Temporal logic in a stochastic environment", in L. Bolk and A. Szalas, eds., Time and Logic, Artificial Intelligence Series of UCL Press, 1994.
105. E. Teruel, J. M. Colom and M. Silva, "Linear analysis of deadlock-freeness of Petri net models", In Proceedings of the 2nd European Control Conference, **2**, pp. 513–518. North-Holland, 1993.
106. E. Teruel, J. M. Colom and M. Silva, "Deterministic concurrent systems with bulk services and arrivals", Research Report RR-95-04, DIIS. Univ. Zaragoza, 1995. Submitted paper. A short version appeared as "Modelling and Analysis of Deteministic Concurrent Systems with Bulk Services and Arrivals", in M. Cosnard and R. Puigjaner (eds.), Decentralized and Distributed Systems, IFIP Transactions A-39, Elsevier, pp. 213–224, 1994.
107. E. Teruel and M. Silva, "Liveness and home states in Equal Conflict systems", In Ajmone Marsan, ed., Application and Theory of Petri Nets 1993, *Lecture Notes in Computer Science*, **691**, pp. 415–432, Springer Verlag, 1993.
108. E. Teruel and M. Silva, "Structure theory of Equal Conflict systems", Research Report GISI-RR-93-22, DIEI. Univ. Zaragoza, November 1993. (Revised in Mar. 1994, 30 pages. To appear in *Theoretical Computer Science*).
109. E. Teruel and M. Silva, "Well-formedness of Equal Conflict systems", In Valette, ed., Application and Theory of Petri Nets 1994, *Lecture Notes in Computer Science*, **815**, pp. 491–510, Springer Verlag, 1994.
110. E. Teruel, M. Silva, J. M. Colom and J. Campos, "Functional and performance analysis of cooperating sequential processes", In G. Cohen and J.P. Quadrat, editors, Analysis and Optimization of Systems: Discrete Event Systems, *Lecture Notes in Control and Information Sciences*, **199**, pp. 169–175, Springer-Verlag, London, 1994. A revised version appears in this book.
111. M. Tilgner and M. Silva, "Approximate performance analysis on Petri net based models of manufacturing systems", In Proceedings of the 1994 IEEE International Conference on Robotics and Automation, San Diego, California, May 1994.

Esprit Basic Research Series

J. W. Lloyd (Ed.): **Computational Logic.** Symposium Proceedings, Brussels, November 1990. XI, 211 pages. 1990

E. Klein, F. Veltman (Eds.): **Natural Language and Speech.** Symposium Proceedings, Brussels, November 1991. VIII, 192 pages. 1991

G. Gambosi, M. Scholl, H.-W. Six (Eds.): **Geographic Database Management System.** Workshop Proceedings, Capri, May 1991. XII, 320 pages. 1992

R. Kassing (Ed.): **Scanning Microscopy.** Symposium Proceedings, Wetzlar, October 1990. X, 207 pages. 1992

G. A. Orban, H.-H. Nagel (Eds.): **Artificial and Biological Vision Systems.** XII, 389 pages. 1992

S. D. Smith, R. F. Neale (Eds.): **Optical Information Technology.** State-of-the-Art Report. XIV, 369 pages. 1993

Ph. Lalanne, P. Chavel (Eds.): **Perspectives for Parallel Optical Interconnects.** XIV, 417 pages. 1993

D. Vernon (Ed.): **Computer Vision: Craft, Engineering, and Science.** Workshop Proceedings, Killarney, September 1991. XIII, 96 pages. 1994

E. Montseny, J. Frau (Eds.): **Computer Vision: Specialized Processors for Real-Time Image Analysis.** Workshop Proceedings, Barcelona, September 1991. X, 216 pages. 1994

J. L. Crowley, H. I. Christensen (Eds.): **Vision as Process.** Basic Research on Computer Vision Systems. VIII, 432 pages. 1995

B. Randell, J.-C. Laprie, H. Kopetz, B. Littlewood (Eds.): **Predictably Dependable Computing Systems.** XIX, 588 pages. 1995

F. Baccelli, A. Jean-Marie, I. Mitrani (Eds.): **Quantitative Methods in Parallel Systems.** XVIII, 298 pages. 1995

J. F. McGilp, D. Weaire, C. H. Patterson (Eds.): **Epioptics.** Linear and Nonlinear Optical Spectroscopy of Surfaces and Interfaces. XII, 230 pages. 1995

Printing: Mercedesdruck, Berlin
Binding: Buchbinderei Lüderitz & Bauer, Berlin